# Ireland

For a '91 - '92
Rotary Scholar
- Scott Fehlan,
R.S. '90 - '91

# Fodor's 90

# Ireland

**FODOR'S TRAVEL PUBLICATIONS, INC.**
New York & London

### Fodor's Ireland

**Executive Editor:** Richard Moore
**Assistant Editors:** Caz Philcox, Barbara Vesey
**Area Editor:** Alannah Hopkin
**Editorial Contributors:** Stan Gebler Davies,
    Edward F. MacSweeney
**Drawings:** Lorraine Calaora
**Maps and Plans:** Swanston Graphics
**Cover Photograph:** David A. Burnett/Stock, Boston

**Cover Design:** Vignelli Associates

### Special Sales

Fodor's Travel Publications are available at special discounts for bulk purchases (100 copies or more) for sales promotions or premiums. Special editions, including personalized covers, excerpts of existing guides, and corporate imprints, can be created in large quantities for special needs. For more information, write to Special Marketing, Fodor's Travel Publications, 201 East 50th Street, New York, NY 10022. Enquiries from the United Kingdom should be sent to Fodor's Travel Publications, 30–32 Bedford Square, London WC1B 3SG.

MANUFACTURED IN THE UNITED STATES OF AMERICA
10 9 8 7 6 5 4 3 2 1

# CONTENTS

## NORTHERN IRELAND

**FACTS AT YOUR FINGERTIPS**

**Planning Your Trip:** National Tourist Office 261; Seasonal Events 261; Costs in Northern Ireland 262.

**Getting to Northern Ireland:** From North America by Air 262; From the U.K. by Air 262; From the U.K. by Train 262; From the U.K. by Bus 263; From the U.K. by Car 263; Customs on Arrival 263.

**Staying in Northern Ireland:** Changing Money 264; Hotels 264; Camping 264; Youth Hostels 265; Bed & Breakfast and Farmhouses 265; Restaurants 265; Tipping 265; Opening Times 265; Mail 266; Places of Interest 266; Sports 266.

**Getting Around Northern Ireland:** By Train 267; By Bus 267; By Car 267; By Bike 267; By Inland Waterway 268.

# FOREWORD

The Republic of Ireland is virtually free from the dilemmas of its neighbor to the north, and can provide a legion of opportunities for interesting and memorable holidays. Over the last few years, millions of pounds have been poured into developing tourist projects, with the result that the range of accommodations and the general quality of facilities have improved enormously. In every way, Southern Ireland is an easier place to travel around in than it used to be. There are better hotels, the countryside has been opened up by road systems and scenic drives, beaches have been cared for and monuments restored. In sum, a great deal of thought, imagination and hard cash has been lavished on showing to the best advantage the beauties that were always there, though not always accessible.

The amenities which are now available for sports or for quiet relaxation ensure that Ireland has something to offer everyone, whatever his or her tastes. Golf and fishing head the list, of course: with all those lovely lakes and streams, how could it be otherwise? But close behind come the beaches, with surfing or scuba-diving readily available. Then there is the chance of wandering down those gently winding lanes in a horse-drawn caravan, or cruising along the peaceful rivers (the Shannon alone has 140 navigable miles of enjoyment). High on the list of popular attractions are the stately homes and gardens which form so rich a part of Ireland's heritage.

\*\*\*

The task of creating this edition would not have been possible without the help of many friends both in Ireland and in tourist offices abroad. We would especially like to express our gratitude to Bord Fáilte, the Irish Tourist Board, in London and in Dublin, and to Swanston Graphics, who have provided the maps for this edition. Above all, we would like to thank Alannah Hopkin, without whose tireless efforts and expertise this volume would never have seen the light of day.

\*\*\*

While every care has been taken to assure the accuracy of the information in this guide, the passage of time will always bring change, and consequently the publisher cannot accept responsibility for errors that may occur.

All prices and opening times quoted in this guide are based on information available to us at press time. Hours and admission fees may change, however, and the prudent traveler will avoid inconvenience by calling ahead.

Fodor's wants to hear about your travel experiences, both pleasant and unpleasant. When a hotel or restaurant fails to live up to its billing, let us know and we will investigate the complaint and revise our entries where the facts warrant it.

Send your letters to the editors of Fodor's Travel Publications, 201 E. 50th Street, New York, NY 10022.

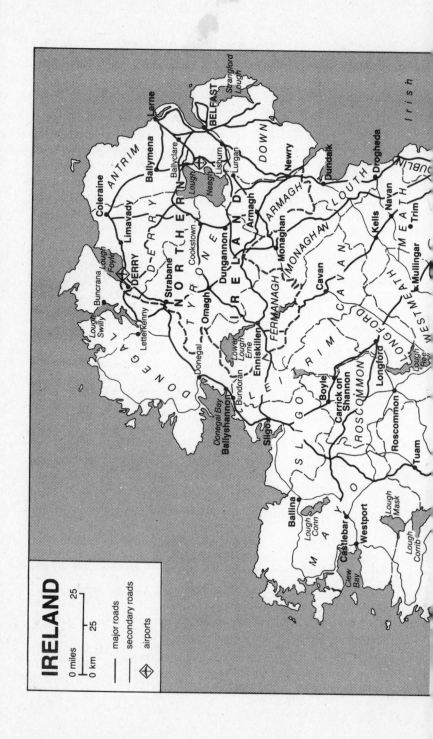

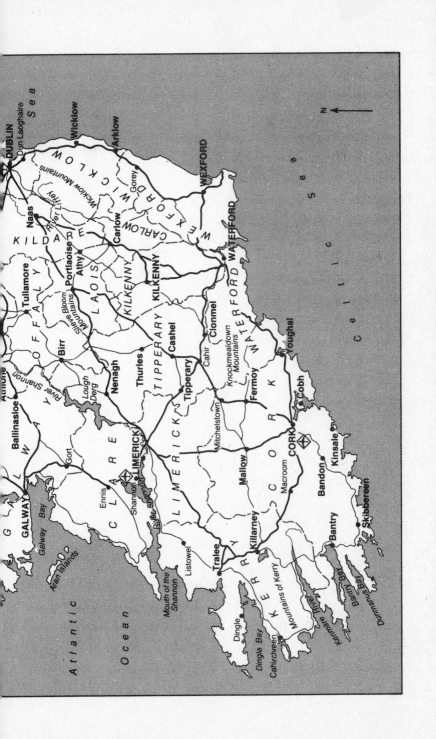

# FACTS AT YOUR FINGERTIPS

# FACTS AT YOUR FINGERTIPS

## *Planning Your Trip*

**NATIONAL TOURIST OFFICE.** The major source of information for anyone planning a trip to Ireland is the Irish Tourist Board. They can supply information on all aspects of travel to and around Ireland, from which type of vacation is best suited to your needs and purse to the best and most economical ways of getting there. They produce copious amounts of information, much of it free and all of it useful.

Their addresses are:

**In the U.S.:** 757 Third Ave., New York, NY 10017 (212–418–0800).
**In Canada:** 10 King St. East, Toronto, Ont. M5C 1C3 (416–364–1301).
**In the U.K.:** 150 New Bond St., London W1Y 0AQ (01–493 3201).

**TOURS.** The range of holidays to Ireland is immense, from fully-escorted bus tours of the entire island—or around Ireland and the U.K.—to self-drive vacations around just one small corner. Gourmet, art, architecture, music, antiques, gardens, crafts, history, staying in a castle or a cottage, plus a wide range of sports (though naturally with the emphasis on golf and fishing) are all catered for, and at prices to suit all pocket books.

Full details of all tour operators are available from the Irish Tourist Board and your travel agent, but we give a summary below of some of the more typical and a partial list of some of the better-known tour operators. (All details are for 1989, so check for up-to-the-minute information.)

### Tours From the U.S.

"The Best of Neighbours" is a 13-day tour offered by Lismore Tours for about $1,659 (land cost only) per person. Included are continental or full Irish breakfasts and most dinners. The tour begins with two nights in London, then proceeds to York, Edinburgh, the Lake District, and Wales, before reaching Ireland. After two nights in Dublin, the tour heads south to the horse-breeding region of Naas, the medieval city of Kilkenny, Blarney Castle, the Ring of Kerry, Killarney, and Adare, before ending in Shannon.

1

Several companies specializing in Irish tours offer self-drive schemes in which you can stay in Irish country homes and farmhouses. A typical low-season rate for lodging and breakfast in a farmhouse or cottage ranges from $35 to $75 per night; a first-class hotel runs from $52 to $98. All prices are per person for a party of two and include a self-drive car with unlimited mileage. Contact Celtic International Tours for details.

Ireland also has a unique "Rent-a-Cottage" program that invites you to "step back a century into an Irish village and live in a typical Irish thatched cottage, complete with half-door, open fireplace, traditional furnishings—but also endowed with all the modern conveniences that make life more liveable." Arrangements through several operators including Lismore Tours and Lynott Tours; cost from $250 to $840 per week.

For around $1,300 you can be guided for 10 days among the makers of traditional crafts (details from Lynott), while Maupintour offers two less specialist tours: eight days for $1,290 to $1,518 per person and 15 days for approximately $2,498 to $2,928.

If you'd like to take to the sea, Cunard's luxury trans-Atlantic liner *QE2* makes two calls annually to Cobh in Co. Cork. The inclusive price for flight and cruise starts at $1,785. If you are returning on the *QE2*, Aer Lingus will give you a free flight to Ireland provided you purchase one of their accommodations packages. Contact O'Connor's Fairways Travel for details.

**U.S. Tour Operators. Aer Lingus,** 122 East 42nd St., New York, NY 10168-0016 (212–557–1110).

**American Express Travel Related Services,** 822 Lexington Ave., New York, NY 10021 (800–241–1700).

**Arrangements Abroad,** 50 Broadway, New York, NY 10004 (212–514–8921).

**BMIT, Inc.,** Box 202317, Austin TX 78720 (512–250–1658; 800–922–9505; in Texas, 800–222–4967).

**Brendan Tours,** 15137 Califa St., Van Nuys, CA 91411 (818–785–9696).

**Brian Moore International Tours,** Box 144, 116 Main St., Medway, MA 02053 (508–533–6683).

**Brit-Rail Travel,** 630 Third Ave., New York, NY 10017 (212–599–5400).

**Caravan Tours,** 401 North Michigan Ave., Chicago IL 60611 (312–321–9800).

**Celtic International Tours,** 161 Central Ave., Albany, NY 12206 (518–463–5511).

**Certified Tours,** Box 1525, Ft. Lauderdale, FL 33302 (305–522–1440).

**CIE Tours International,** 122 East 42nd St., New York, NY 10168 (212–972–5600).

**Cultural Heritage Alliance,** Falcon Bldg., 107–115 S. Second St., Philadelphia, PA 19106 (215–923–7060).

**Grand European Tours,** Box 1889, Lake Oswego, OR 97035 (503–635–9627).

**International Weekends,** 300 First Ave., Needham Heights, MA 02194 (800–225–5498; 617–449–5460).

**Lismore Tours,** 106 East 31 St., New York, NY 10016 (212–685–0100).

**Lynott Tours, Inc.,** 350 Fifth Ave., New York, NY 10118 (212–760–0101).

**Maupintour,** Box 807, Lawrence, KS 66044 (800–255–4266).

**O'Connor's Fairways Travel,** 800 Second Ave., New York, NY 10017 (800–228–7609; 212–661–0550).

**Old Country Tours,** Box 307, Burtonsville, MD 20866 (301–622–1022; 800–368–2743).

**Tara Tours,** 500 NE Multnomah, Suite 1205, Portland, OR 97232 (503–231–1656).

**TWA Getaway Vacations,** 28 South Sixth St., Philadelphia, PA 19106 (215–925–7885).

### Tours from the U.K.

Aer Lingus offer a wide range of inclusive holidays in Ireland ranging from their "Golden Motoring Holiday"—seven nights from around £247, including round-trip airfare from London, staying in a variety of castles, country houses and luxury hotels, plus self-drive car hire—to their simpler, but no less delightful, "Shannon Cruise"—seven nights afloat from £180 per person, including round-trip airfare from London.

CIE Tours offer a choice of seven- and eight-day guided coach tours including sea-crossing, accommodations, breakfast and most dinners from £268. Sealink's self-catering holidays for motorists start at £115 per person for round-trip car ferry and six nights in a cottage. A week's holiday from Angler's World starts at £53 per person for a self-catering cottage, round-trip car ferry and information pack. A wide range of weekends and short breaks are available—an overnight break in Dublin starts at £59 with B & I, including ferry and bus transfers. Some of the best deals are fly-drive: Aer Lingus offer a "Gourmet Weekend" in Kinsale, Co. Cork, a picturesque, small port famed for its 10 gourmet restaurants, which includes two nights' top-grade accommodations, two gourmet dinners, self-drive car and round-trip air travel from £174 per person.

**U.K. Tour Operators. Aer Lingus Holidays,** Aer Lingus House, 83 Staines Rd., Hounslow, Middlesex TW3 3JD (01–569 4646 or 01–569 5555).

**Angler's World Holidays,** 25 Market Pl., Bolsover, Chesterfield, Derbyshire (0246–826350).

**Atlantic Golf,** 54A Richmond Rd., Twickenham, Middlesex (01–891 6451).

**B & I Line Tours,** Reliance House, Water St., Liverpool 2 (051–236–8325).

**CIE Tours International,** 150 New Bond St., London W1Y 0AQ (01–629 0564).

**PAB Travel,** 11 Dale End, Birmingham B4 7LN (021–233–1252).

**Ryan's Tourist Group,** 200 Earl's Court Rd., London SW5 9QX (01–244 6355).

**Sealink Travel,** Charter House, Park St., Ashford, Kent TN24 8EX (0233–47033).

**Thomson's Citybreaks,** 1st Floor, Greater London House, Hampstead Rd., London NW1 7SD (01–387 6534).

**Time Off,** Chester Close, Chester St., London S.W.1 (01–235 8070).

**WHEN TO GO.** The summer remains the most popular time to visit Ireland, and for good reasons. The weather is at its kindest, the summer days at their longest and the countryside at its most beautiful. Prices and crowds—in the cities and most popular spots at least—are at their peak, of course, though never prohibitively so. Fall and spring can also be delightful, though the weather, never too reliable at the best of times, can be unpredictable and some tourist facilities—smaller museums, stately homes, even some hotels—may be closed. St. Patrick's Week in March adds extra spice to a visit in the spring. Participation in the traditional St. Patrick's Day Parade in Dublin by Irish-American bands and groups has become de rigueur these days, though the fun isn't all for the Irish. There's a special spot on the reviewing stand for American visitors and to round off the day (and night) there's the Lord Mayor's Ball. Other cities and towns also have special events during the week.

The winter is generally gloomy: dank and overcast. You will also find many hotels and facilities closed. Nonetheless, lower prices (except at Christmas) and the almost complete absence of other visitors, coupled with cheerful open fires in almost all hotels, have all helped make the winter a little more popular lately.

Christmas itself is always a good time to visit: the Irish have a particular knack at maintaining the spirit of the season and a warm welcome is guaranteed. Many hotels arrange special entertainments and outdoor activities: horse races, hunting, following the beagles.

**Climate.** Ireland suffers no extremes of climate: the sweep of the warm Gulf Stream up the west coast helps ensure that. In winter, the temperature ranges around 40° to 42° Fahrenheit (5° to 7° Centigrade). In summer, the range is around 60° to 65° Fahrenheit (15° to 17° Centigrade), with a "hot" day going up to about 80° (25° Centigrade).

Ireland has a reputation—well deserved some would say—for rain. How else would you explain the lush green of the countryside? The familiar tag "The Emerald Isle" was coined by a Belfast man, one William Drennan, in the 18th century, and has stuck ever since. Still, even if it does rain a lot, the Irish term "a soft day" sums it up nicely. The rain is rarely hard and is usually short lived.

Average maximum afternoon temperatures:

| Dublin | Jan. | Feb. | Mar. | Apr. | May | June | July | Aug. | Sept. | Oct. | Nov. | Dec. |
|---|---|---|---|---|---|---|---|---|---|---|---|---|
| F° | 45 | 46 | 50 | 54 | 57 | 64 | 66 | 66 | 63 | 57 | 50 | 46 |
| C° | 7 | 8 | 10 | 12 | 14 | 18 | 19 | 19 | 17 | 14 | 10 | 8 |

**SEASONAL EVENTS. January.** At least six major race meetings are held at centers such as Thurles (Co. Tipperary), Naas (Co. Kildare), Leopardstown (Co. Dublin), and Gowran Park (Co. Kilkenny). The Point-to-Point season opens; small but exciting meetings are held every Sunday. The Aer Lingus Young Scientists' Exhibition takes place in Dublin.

**February.** At the beginning of February Dublin Airport hosts an International Arts Festival. On St. Valentine's Day, February 14, the saint is honored in the Carmelite Priory in Dublin, site of his tomb. Limerick holds its festival of Irish music and dancing, Feile Luimni. Important pure-bred cattle shows and sales take place in Dublin, Cork and Belfast;

the Punchestown Bloodstock Sales are also held, one of the most important race horse auctions. There's an international rugby match between
England and Ireland in the middle of the month.

**March.** St. Patrick's Day, March 17, is the focus of the month, with
parades in Dublin, guest bands from the U.S., and a festival of traditional
Irish music, the Dublin Feis Ceoil. In March, the World Irish Dancing
Championships take place (venue to be announced). Limerick hosts an
international marching band competition. Ireland play Scotland in a rugby
international in Dublin. Motoring enthusiasts take part in the Circuit of
Ireland rally.

**April.** Easter provides one of the biggest events of the racing calendar,
the two-day Irish Grand National meeting at Fairyhouse, Co. Meath,
about 12 miles from Dublin. Another of the big race meetings is held at
the famous Punchestown track in Co. Kildare, about 20 miles from Dublin. The leadership of the Gaelic Football League is decided in the capital,
at Croke Park. Cork City holds its International Choral and Folk Dance
Festival, and Dublin Opera holds its Spring Season.

**May.** This month sees the opening of Ireland's agricultural shop window, the Royal Dublin Society Spring Show and Industries Fair at Ballsbridge. As the holiday season gets underway, so do Ireland's festivals.
These range from the Festival of Irish Traditional Music, Song and Dance
in Ennis, Co. Clare, to a Maytime Festival at Dundalk and a Mussel Festival in Bantry. Pan Celtic Week brings together members of the Celtic
races—Irish, Scots, Manxmen, Cornishmen and Bretons—for a festival
of traditional music, song and dance in Killarney.

**June.** Listowel Writers' Week spreads farther than this Co. Kerry town
and embraces more than writers; scheduled to end on the first Sunday in
June. Among the month's fishing events is the Lough Swilly International
Tope Festival at Rathmullen, Co. Donegal. The town of Cahir in Tipperary brings its past alive with a Norman Festival. One of the richest and
most exciting horse races in the world, the Budweiser Irish Derby, is run
at the Curragh, headquarters of Irish racing, 30 miles from Dublin. The
Festival of Music in Great Irish Houses—a delightful and sophisticated
series—consists of classical music concerts given in different stately homes
within 20 miles of Dublin. Bloomsday, June 16, is celebrated in Dublin,
and Kinsale, Co. Cork, offers an Arts Week with a special emphasis on
readings by contemporary Irish writers. Youghal, Co. Cork, commemorates its connections with Sir Walter Raleigh by holding a Potato Festival.

**July.** Youghal Sea Anglers hold a deep-sea shark safari in Co. Cork;
Athlone has a freshwater angling festival on the Shannon. The Shannon
Boat Show Rally finishes with the sailing of an armada of small craft up
the Shannon from Athlone to Carrick-on-Shannon. Another of Ireland's
classic horse races, the Guinness Oaks, takes place at the Curragh. On
the last Sunday in July, many thousands of pilgrims, some in bare feet,
climb the stony slopes of Croagh Patrick (2,510 ft) in Co. Mayo to honor
Saint Patrick. University College, Dublin, holds its 41st International
Summer School for all aspects of Irish studies.

**August.** Dublin Horse Show attracts the best of Irish bloodstock and the crowds for the principal social-sporting event of the year, invariably in the second week of August. International jumping events every day for six days. The Royal Horticultural Society's Summer Show of flowers is held in conjunction with the Horse Show. Highly entertaining is Puck Fair in Killorglin, Co. Kerry, a mid-month event, while at the end of the month in the same county, the Rose of Tralee is selected. The Connemara Pony Show at Clifden, Co. Galway, invariably attracts a cosmopolitan crowd, and apart from the ponies there is an exhibition of arts and crafts in the Gaelic tradition. Kilkenny Arts Week gets going at the end of the month. Carroll's International Golf Championship takes place on the Royal Dublin Course.

**September.** In Galway, the oyster season opens with appropriate celebrations. The Hurling and Gaelic Football finals are played at Croke Park in Dublin, an occasion when excitement reaches fever pitch. Waterford's Light Opera season attracts internationally-known stars. The September Bloodstock Sales at Kill, Co. Kildare, attract those with an eye for a future winner. The Matchmaking Festival in Lisdoonvarna is the traditional place for bachelor farmers to seek a wife; its revival is proving popular with American husband-seekers. The Dublin Theater Festival starts in September, as do the Cork Film Festival, Sligo Arts Week, and the Waterford International Festival of Light Opera, all running on into early October.

**October.** The Ballinasloe October Fair in Co. Galway is one of the biggest, and oldest, horse and cattle fairs in Europe. The restaurants of Kinsale, Co. Cork, organize their Gourmet Festival on the first weekend of October. Wexford Opera Festival assembles international singers, directors and conductors who present unfamiliar operatic gems in a tiny restored Georgian theater, the Theater Royal. The festival also offers fringe events and much excellent hospitality. Cork holds its International Jazz Festival on the last weekend of October. The Dublin City Marathon on the last Monday of the month attracts thousands of runners and engenders a carnival spirit.

**November.** The hunting season starts and continues through until April. Racing, which never really ends in Ireland, continues at 11 different venues, and there are trotting races in the south. Famous bloodstock sales are held at Goff's Kildare Paddocks, Kill, Co. Kildare. The Irish Rugby Football season gets under way with hotly-contested games between the four provinces: Connacht, Leinster, Munster and Ulster.

**December.** The Dublin Grand Opera season gets under way at the start of the month. The personal feeling the Irish have for Christmas overcomes their commercial interests. Racing breaks off briefly in mid-month, but resumes on December 26 with traditional meetings at Leopardstown, outside Dublin, and Limerick.

**National Holidays 1990.** January 1; March 17 (St. Patrick's Day); April 13 (Good Friday); April 16 (Easter Monday); June 4; August 6; October 29; December 25, 28 (Christmas Day and St. Stephen's Day).

**WHAT TO PACK.** The golden rule is to travel light; generally, try not to take more than you can carry yourself. Not only are porters more or less wholly extinct in Europe these days (where you can find them they're very expensive anyway), the less luggage you take the easier checking in and out of hotels becomes, similarly airports (increasingly the number one nightmare of all modern travel) become much easier to get through, and if you only take one piece of luggage, the less risk there is of your luggage being lost en route, and, in theory anyway, the less time you need to wait for it to appear when you get off the plane. Remember also that there are strict regulations governing the amount of luggage you can take with you on the plane. Each passenger is allowed two pieces of luggage, neither of which must exceed 62″ (height + width + length) and which together do not exceed 106″. Penalties for excess baggage are high. Carry-on luggage must not exceed 45″ (length + width + height) and must fit under the seat or in the overhead compartment.

It's an excellent idea also to make sure that your luggage is sturdy; there's no worse way to start or finish your vacation than by discovering that your clothes are generously distributing themselves along a station platform or, even worse, have already scattered themselves around the hold of a 747.

Finally, remember to leave space for gifts. Most Irish shops will ship goods back to the States—essential for larger items and advisable for breakable items—but if you want to take gifts and souvenirs back with you, leave room for them!

**Clothes.** The Irish are generally very informal about clothes—it's the person that matters, not their clothes—and there are likely to be very few occasions when you'll need to dress up. Basically, take the same as you would if you were visiting Maine, say, plus the odd smarter outfit. But don't forget that Ireland, or parts of it anyway, is the wettest country in Europe, so bring your umbrella and raincoat. If you think you're likely to buy an Aran sweater or tweed jacket in Ireland, for example, then you might consider leaving a sweater or jacket at home.

If you wear contact lenses or glasses, take along your prescription. There are no problems about getting medicines. There are plenty of pharmacies, called variously "Chemists" or "Medical Hall," always staffed by qualified pharmacists.

**COSTS IN IRELAND.** The Irish complain bitterly about the high cost of living in Ireland, but the country is not, for all that, expensive to visit. Some sample costs make the point. For instance, a good hotel in Dublin will set you back no more than about IR£50 to IR£70 a night for two; a large breakfast adds about another IR£7 to the price, though many people find this type of huge meal a little too much so early in the day. For lunch, be modest and go to a pub; you'll get a good meal, sandwiches or a snack say, for about IR£4. Dinner in Dublin is more expensive, with a fancy restaurant, though not an absolutely top spot, charging about IR£18 per person, though this does not include drinks or the tip. All these costs would be at least 10% lower away from Dublin.

Entertainment is inexpensive, with theaters and concerts generally costing about IR£8 for a good seat. But you can also get a great evening's fun for the price of a few drinks and maybe IR£1 entrance fee at a *seisun* (pronounce it seshoon) in a singing pub. Entrance to most art galleries and museums is free, but stately homes and other similar attractions normally charge about IR£2 per person.

Bus fares in Dublin are a minimum of 50p, but that will take you quite a distance. A Dublin cab will charge a minimum of IR£1.80, plus 40p per passenger if there's more than one; thereafter, the charge is IR£1.15 per mile. Taxis are more expensive in country areas, however.

**Irish Currency.** The unit of currency in Ireland is the pound or *punt,* pronounced "poont." It is divided into 100 pence, written simply, as in Britain, as "p." The pound, however, is always written as IR£, to avoid confusion with the English pound sterling.

There are notes of IR£100, IR£50, IR£20, IR£10, IR£5 and IR£1. There are coins of 50p, 20p, 10p, 5p, 2p, 1p and ½p.

Dollars and British currency are only accepted in large hotels and shops geared to tourists. Elsewhere you will be expected to use Irish currency.

At the time of writing (spring 1989), the punt stood at around 70 pence to the U.S. dollar and around IR£1.17 to the pound sterling. However, these rates will inevitably change both before and during 1990, making it essential to keep a sharp eye on the exchange rate during your trip.

For details of changing money in Ireland and bank opening hours, see *Staying in Ireland,* page 17.

**TAKING MONEY ABROAD.** Traveler's checks are still the standard and best way to safeguard your travel funds; and you still usually get a better exchange rate in Ireland for traveler's checks than for cash. In the U.S., many of the larger banks issue their own traveler's checks—just about as universally recognized as those of American Express, Cook's and Barclay's. In most instances there is a 1% charge for the checks. Some banks issue them free if you are a regular customer. The best-known British checks are Cook's and those of Barclay's, Lloyd's, the Midland Bank and the Nat West. It is also always a good idea to have some local currency upon arrival. Some banks will provide this service; alternately, contact *Deak International, Ltd.,* 630 Fifth Ave., New York, NY 10111 (call 212–635–0515 for additional branches).

Britons holding a Uniform Eurocheque card and check book can cash checks for up to £100 a day at banks participating in the scheme and can write checks in hotels, restaurants and shops again for up to £100. Look for the distinctive blue and red symbol in the window. To obtain a card and check book, apply at your bank.

**Credit Cards.** The major credit cards—American Express, Diner's Club, MasterCard (incorporating Access and EuroCard) and Visa—are generally but by no means universally accepted in most larger hotels, restaurants and shops. We give details on which of these cards is accepted by the hotels and restaurants we carry in our Practical Information listings. But always be sure to check before reserving your room or ordering a meal that your particular piece, or pieces, of plastic is accepted.

**PASSPORTS. Americans.** All U.S. citizens require a passport for entry into Ireland. Visas are not required. In the U.S., apply in person at U.S. Passport Agency Offices, local county courthouses or selected post offices. Renewals can be handled by mail (Form DSP-82), provided that your previous passport is not more than 12 years old. In addition to the completed application (Form DSP-11), new applicants will need:

—proof of citizenship, such as a birth certificate;

—two identical photographs, in either black and white or color, on non-glossy paper and taken within the past six months;

—$35 for the passport itself plus a $7 processing fee if you are applying in person (no processing fee when applying by mail) for those 18 years and older, or, if you are under 18, $20 for the passport plus a $7 processing fee if you are applying in person (again, no extra fee when applying by mail);

—proof of identity that includes a photograph and signature, such as a driver's license, previous passport, any governmental ID card.

Adult passports are valid for 10 years, others for five years; they are not renewable. Allow four to six weeks for your application to be processed, but in an emergency, Passport Agency offices can have a passport readied within 24–48 hours, and even the postal authorities can indicate "Rush" when necessary.

If you expect to travel extensively, request a 48- or 96-page passport rather than the usual 24-page one. There is no extra charge. When you receive your passport, write down its number, date and place of issue separately. The loss of a valid passport should be reported immediately to the local police and to the Passport Office, Department of State, 1425 K St. NW, Washington DC 20524; if your passport is lost or stolen while abroad, report it to the local authorities and apply for a replacement at the nearest U.S. Embassy or consular office.

**Canadians.** Canadian citizens apply in person to regional passport offices, post offices or by mail to Bureau of Passports, External Affairs, Ottawa, Ont. K1A 0G3. A $25 fee, a guarantor, two photographs and evidence of citizenship are required. Canadian passports are valid for five years and are non-renewable.

**Britons.** British citizens traveling direct from Britain to the Republic of Ireland do not require a passport to enter the country. It is nonetheless advisable that you bring your passport. It will be useful I.D. and make changing money, hiring a car, checking in and out of hotels, etc., a good deal simpler.

**HEALTH AND INSURANCE.** The different varieties of travel insurance cover everything from health and accident costs, to lost baggage and trip cancellation. Sometimes they can all be obtained with one blanket policy; other times they overlap with existing coverage you might have for health and/or home; still other times it is best to buy policies that are tailored to very specific needs. Insurance is available from many sources, however, and many travelers unwittingly end up with redundant coverage. Before purchasing separate travel insurance of any kind, be sure to check your regular policies carefully.

Generally, it is best to take care of your insurance needs before embarking on your trip. You'll pay more for less coverage—and have less chance to read the fine print—if you wait until the last minute and make your purchases from, say, an airport vending machine or insurance company counter. If you have a regular insurance agent, he or she is the person to consult first.

Flight insurance, which is often included in the price of the ticket when the fare is paid via American Express, Visa or certain other major credit cards, is also often included in package policies providing accident coverage as well. These policies are available from most tour operators and insurance companies. While it is a good idea to have health and accident insurance when traveling, be careful not to spend money to duplicate coverage you may already have ... or to neglect some eventuality which could end up costing a small fortune.

For example, basic Blue Cross-Blue Shield policies do cover health costs incurred while traveling. They will not, however, cover the cost of emergency transportation, which can often add up to several thousand dollars. Emergency transportation is covered, in part at least, by many major medical policies such as those underwritten by Prudential and Metropolitan. Again, we can't urge you too strongly that in order to be sure you are getting the coverage you need, check any policy carefully before buying. Another important example: most insurance issued specifically for travel does not cover pre-existing conditions, such as a heart condition.

Recently, several organizations have appeared which offer coverage designed to supplement existing health insurance and to help defray costs not covered by many standard policies, such as emergency transportation. Some of the more prominent are:

*International SOS Assistance Inc.,* P.O. Box 11568, Philadelphia, PA 19126 (800–523–8930), has fees from $25 a person for one to 13 days, to $195 for a year.

*IAMAT* (International Association for Medical Assistance to Travelers), 417 Center St., Lewiston, NY 14092 (716–754–4883) in the U.S.; or 40 Regal Rd., Guelph, Ont. N1K 1B5 (519–836–0102) in Canada.

*Travel Assistance International,* the American arm of Europ Assistance, offers a comprehensive program offering immediate, on-the-spot medical, personal and financial help. Trip protection ranges from $35 for an individual for up to eight days to $220 for an entire family for a year. Full details from travel agents or insurance brokers, or from Europ Assistance Worldwide Services, Inc., 1133 15th St., N.W., Suite 400, Washington, DC 20005 (800–821–2828). In the U.K., contact Europ Assistance Ltd., 252 High St., Croydon, Surrey CR0 1NF (01–680 1234).

*The British Insurance Association,* Aldermary House, Queen St., London EC4N 1TT (01–248 4477), will give comprehensive advice on all aspects of vacation travel insurance from the U.K.

Another frequent inconvenience to travelers is the loss of baggage. It is possible, though often complicated, to insure your luggage against loss through theft or negligence. Insurance companies are reluctant to sell such coverage alone, however, since it is often a losing proposition for them. Instead, it is most often included as part of a package that also covers accidents or health. Remuneration is often determined by weight, regardless of the value of the specific contents of the luggage. Should you lose your luggage or some other personal possession, be sure to report it to the local police immediately. Without proof of such a report, your insurance company might be very stingy. Also, before buying baggage insurance, check your homeowners policy. Some such policies offer "off-premises theft" coverage, including the loss of luggage while traveling.

The last major area or traveler's insurance is trip cancellation coverage. This is especially important to travelers on APEX or charter flights. Should you get sick abroad, or for some other reason be unable to continue your trip, you may be stuck having to buy a new one-way fare home, plus paying for space on the charter you're not using. You can guard against this with trip cancellation insurance, usually available from travel agents. Most of these policies will also cover last-minute cancellations.

**STUDENT AND YOUTH TRAVEL.** All student travelers should obtain an International Student Identity Card, which is in most instances needed to get student discounts, youth rail passes, and travel insurance. Apply to *Council On International Educational Exchange,* 205 East 42 St., New York, NY 10017 (212–661–1414). Canadian students should apply to the *Association of Student Councils,* 187 College St., Toronto, Ont. M5T 1P7 (416–977–3703).

The following organizations can also be helpful in finding student flights, educational opportunities and other information. Most deal with international student travel generally, but all those listed here also cover Ireland.

*American Youth Hostels,* Box 37613, Washington, DC 20013 (202–783–6161). Members are eligible for entree to the worldwide network of youth hostels. The organization publishes an extensive directory of youth hostels.

*Council on International Educational Exchange* (CIEE)—see above for address—provides information on summer study, work/travel programs and travel services for college and high school students and a free Charter Flights Guide booklet. *Work, Study, Travel Abroad: The Whole World Handbook* ($8.95 plus $1 postage) is the best listing of both work and study possibilities.

*Institute of International Education,* 809 United Nations Plaza, New York, NY 10017 (212–883–8200) is primarily concerned with study opportunities and administers scholarships and fellowships for international study and training. The New York office has a visitors' information center; satellite offices are located in Chicago, Denver, Houston, San Francisco and Washington, DC.

*Educational Travel Center,* 438 North Frances, Madison, WI 53703 (608–256–5551).

**HINTS FOR HANDICAPPED TRAVELERS.** Facilities for the handicapped in Ireland are reasonable, if variable, though where are they not? The Irish Tourist Board produce an annually revised free information sheet, *Accommodations for the Disabled,* which details facilities for handicapped travelers, and lists accessible toilets. A key is needed for most of them, obtainable from the *National Rehabilitation Board,* 25 Clyde Rd., Ballsbridge, Dublin 4 (01–684181). Wheelchairs can be hired from the *Irish Wheelchair Assoc.,* at the same address. There is no charge, but donations are appreciated. Book in advance.

Otherwise, major sources of information are: *Access to the World: A Travel Guide for the Handicapped,* by Louise Weiss, a good but dated book covering all aspects of travel for anyone with health or medical problems; it features extensive listings and suggestions on everything from availability of special diets to wheelchair accessibility. Available from Facts on File,

460 Park Ave., New York, NY 10016 ($14.95). The *Travel Information Service* at *Moss Rehabilitation Hospital,* 12th St. and Tabor Rd., Philadelphia, PA 19141, gives information on facilities for the handicapped in many countries and also provides toll-free numbers of airlines with special lines for the hearing impaired; they can also provide listings of tour operators who arrange vacations for the handicapped. Also helpful is the *Information Center for Individuals with Disabilities,* 2743 Wormwood St., Boston, MA 02210. For a complete list of tour operators, send a SASE to the *Society for the Advancement of Travel for the Handicapped,* 26 Court St., Brooklyn, NY 11242.

In the U.K., contact *Mobility International,* 43 Dorset St., London W1H 3FR; the *National Society for Mentally Handicapped Children,* 117 Golden Lane, London EC1Y 0TJ; the *Across Trust,* Crown House, Morden, Surrey (they have an amazing series of "Jumbulances," huge articulated ambulances, staffed by volunteer doctors and nurses, that can whisk even the most seriously handicapped across Europe in comfort and safety). But the main source in Britain for all advice on handicapped travel is the *Royal Association for Disability and Rehabilitation* (RADAR), 25 Mortimer St., London W1N 7RJ.

**TIME.** Ireland is on Greenwich Mean Time, the same as Britain. Again like Britain, she moves onto British Summer Time—Greenwich Mean Time plus one hour—from the end of March to the end of October. Greenwich Mean Time and British Summer Time are five hours ahead of Eastern Standard Time and Daylight Saving Time respectively.

## Getting to Ireland

**FROM NORTH AMERICA BY AIR.** Flights from major departure points in the U.S. to Ireland are frequent and generally easy to arrange. Flights from Canada are almost equally numerous, but all go via either the U.S., mainly New York or Boston, or other European countries, principally England. And, given the perpetual battle for business among the major airlines flying the North Atlantic, fares are generally inexpensive. We give details of some sample fares below.

However, be warned that though fares may be low and flights numerous, long-distance flying today is no bed of roses. Lines and delays at ever-more-crowded airports, perfunctory in-flight service and shrinking legroom on board a giant jet with some 400 other people, followed by interminable waits for your luggage when you arrive, are the clearest possible signals that the glamor of air travel—if it ever existed—is very much a thing of the past.

Unfortunately, these problems are compounded when flying to Europe by the fact that most flights from the States are scheduled to arrive first thing in the morning. Not only are you in for a night's discomfort on the plane, but you arrive at the start of a new day to be greeted by the confusion (some would say chaos) of a modern airport. To make life even more difficult for the weary traveler, many hotels will not allow you to check in before noon or even 1 P.M. giving you as much as six hours with nothing to do and nowhere to go.

There are a number of steps you can take, however, in order to lessen the traumas of long-distance flying. The first and possibly the most important of all is to harbor no illusions about the supposed luxury. If you approach your flight knowing that you are going to be cooped up for a long time and will have to face delays and discomforts of all kinds, the odds are that you will get through it without doing terrible things to your blood pressure or being disillusioned—but there's no point expecting comfort, good service and efficiency because you won't get them.

The right attitude is half the battle, but there are a number of other practical points to follow. Wear comfortable, loose-fitting clothes and take off your shoes. Try to sleep as much as possible, especially on the night flights; this can very often mean not watching the movie (they are invariably dull anyway) as it will probably be shown during the only period when meals are not being served and you can sleep. If you have difficulty sleeping, or think you might, take along a light sedative and try to get a window seat in order to avoid being woken up to let the person next to you get to the toilet or being bashed by people walking down the aisle. Above all, avoid alcohol, or at least drink only a little. The dry air of a pressurized airplane causes rapid dehydration, exaggerating the effects of drink and jet lag. Similarly, drink as much water as possible. Finally, once you arrive, try to take things easily for a day or so. In the excitement of being in a new place, especially for the first time, you can very often not realize how tired you are and optimistically set out sightseeing, only to come down to earth with a bump. Whatever you do, don't have any business meetings for at least 24 hours after arriving.

**Fares.** With air fares in a constant state of flux, the best advice for anyone planning to fly to Ireland independently (rather than as part of a package tour, in which case your flight will have been arranged for you) is to check with a travel agent and let him make your reservations for you. Nonetheless, there are a number of points to bear in mind.

The best bet is to buy either an APEX or Super APEX ticket. First Class, Business and even the misleadingly-named Economy, though giving maximum flexibility on flying dates and cancellations, as well as permitting stop overs, are extremely expensive. APEX and Super APEX, by contrast, are reasonably priced and offer the all-important security of fixed return dates (all APEX tickets are round trip). In addition, you get exactly the same service as flying Economy. However, there are a number of restrictions; you must book, and pay for, your ticket 21 days or more in advance; you can stay in Ireland no less than and no longer than a stated period (usually six days and six months); if you miss your flight, you forfeit the fare. But from the point of view of price and convenience, these tickets certainly represent the best value for money.

If your plans are sufficiently flexible and tighter budgeting is important, you can sometimes benefit from the last-minute bargains offered by tour operators otherwise unable to fill their plane or quota of seats. A number of brokers specializing in these discount sales have sprung up who can book seats of this type. All charge an annual membership fee, usually around $35 to $50.

Among them are: *Stand-Buys Ltd.,* 3033 S. Parker Rd., Aurora, CO 80011 (800–255–1488). *Moments Notice,* 40 East 49th St., New York, NY 10017 (212–486–0503). *Discount Travel Intl.,* 114 Forest Ave., Narberth, PA (215–668–2182); and *Worldwide Discount Travel Club,* 1674 Meridian Ave., Miami Beach, FL 33139 (305–534–2082).

Charter flights are also available to Ireland, though their number has decreased in recent years. Again, a travel agent will be able to recommend the most reliable. You might also consider, though this too should be done via a travel agent, buying a package tour to Ireland, but using only the plane ticket. As packagers are able to get substantial discounts on fares through block booking seats, the price of the total package can sometimes be less than an ordinary air fare alone.

Typical fares as of mid-1989 for New York to Shannon were: $1,610 one-way First Class (year round); $850 one-way Business Class (year round); from $430 to $633 round trip APEX (depending on season). Fares to Dublin are generally $20 to $30 higher. Charter fares are usually less than APEX.

**FROM NORTH AMERICA BY SEA.** There are no direct liner sailings from either the U.S. or Canada to Ireland, though those with salt in their veins may feel inclined to sail to England on the *QE2* and continue from there—expensive and slow. There are also a limited number of cruises that stop off in Ireland, but these are few and far between; contact your travel agent for details.

**FROM THE U.K. BY AIR.** Ireland has never been served so well by air from the U.K. Not only are there several new operators and routes, but there is also a fare war going on with the ferry companies. Our advice is to shop around for the best deal. There are direct flights to Dublin, Shannon and Cork from both London airports (Heathrow and Gatwick) and from several regional airports. There are, for example, 11 flights daily to Dublin from Heathrow, operated jointly by British Airways and Aer Lingus. Dan Air and Aer Lingus also operate frequent daily flights to Dublin from Gatwick. In addition, Dublin is also served by direct flights from Birmingham, Bristol, East Midlands, Liverpool, Manchester, Leeds/Bradford, Newcastle, Edinburgh and Glasgow. Shannon has at least two flights daily from Heathrow by British Airways/Aer Lingus, while to Cork there are up to three flights daily from Heathrow operated jointly by British Airways and Aer Lingus. There are also flights to Cork from Birmingham, Manchester and Plymouth. Ryan Air fly from Luton (just north of London) to Dublin, Waterford, Knock, Cork and Shannon. Virgin Atlantic also now flies from Luton to Dublin.

**Fares.** A wide range of fares is available on all flights to Ireland from the U.K. At the time of writing (spring 1989) the cheapest unrestricted fare was offered by Ryan Air on the Luton to Dublin route at £85 round trip. Aer Lingus offers a limited number of seats at £62 round trip London–Dublin if you book the day before flying. For the business traveler

Club Class round trip costs £194. Virgin, the newest entrant into this market, offers seats at £35 one-way from Luton to Dublin.

Flying time to Dublin from London is around one hour.

**FROM THE U.K. BY TRAIN.** Getting to Dublin by train and ferry is simple, if slow. There are two principal routes: one, to Dublin from either Liverpool or Holyhead, on Anglesey; the second, from Fishguard/Pembroke Dock in Wales to Rosslare, Co. Wexford; alternatively via Swansea to Cork.

Two companies sail the Dublin routes. B & I Ferries has services from Holyhead to Dublin. Sealink has services from Holyhead and Liverpool which go to Dun Laoghaire, a few miles south of Dublin itself. On all routes there are special bus services into the center of the city from the docks. There are boat trains for Holyhead from London (Euston); the 9.30 A.M. train will have you in Dublin before 8 P.M. In spring 1988 Sealink took over the sailings from Liverpool to Dublin. Check with your travel agent for the latest service information. The Swansea–Cork ferry was reintroduced in 1987 and ran again in 1988; for the convenience of those who wish to start their tour in the south it is hoped that the 10-hour crossing will be available again in 1990 (operates from late March to early January).

Sealink British Ferries operates the route from Fishguard to Rosslare, and B & I sails from Pembroke to Rosslare. To connect with the Fishguard sailings, take one of the direct trains from London (Paddington). A midmorning departure from London serves the afternoon sailing, which berths in Rosslare in the early evening. By connecting train, Waterford can be reached at just after 8.30 and Cork a little before midnight. On this route it's best to take one of the daytime sailings as the overnight boats require you to be up and about at some unearthly hours. To reach Pembroke it is necessary to change at Swansea. For overnight travel go Swansea–Cork. Comfortable Inter-City 125s connect London (Paddington) to Swansea in about 2¾ hours. The 6 P.M. departure, with full restaurant facilities, coincides neatly with the Swansea–Cork ferry, which reaches Cork at 7 A.M. the following morning.

**Fares.** There is an almost bewildering range of fares to Ireland by rail and ship, so the best advice is to contact a good travel agent and compare prices very carefully. Indeed, it may even be cheaper to go by air. The Saver Fare to Dublin is about the best bet, however. In summer this works out at around £75 return; out of season it drops dramatically to £50. Fares to Rosslare are similar. For travel during the high summer, or prior to public holdays, it is essential to book well in advance. During these periods a system of seat regulation operates on the ferries; casual travelers will be disappointed. Your travel agent will obtain a confirmed reservation.

**FROM THE U.K. BY BUS.** Ireland is well served by bus from Britain, but those with young children should beware the long hours and possible delays. There are two main gateways: Dublin and Rosslare. International Express—a consortium of reliable international bus companies—operate up to three buses a day to Dublin during the summer. The daytime Supabus service leaves London's Victoria Coach Station at 9 A.M. and arrives in the Busaras Bus Station at 9.20 in the evening. The sea crossing on this route is by Sealink British Ferries from Holyhead and takes around three and a half hours. From Dublin the Irish State transport authority, C.I.E., run connecting coaches to Donegal, Ballina and Westport. The full round trip fare to Dublin has dropped to around £55 using the new Rapide service.

Rosslare is the main gateway for southern Ireland—Cork, Waterford, Limerick and Tralee. The city of Cork has an overnight Supabus service from Victoria Coach Station which runs via Bristol and makes use of the Sealink crossing to Rosslare. Cork is reached in good time for lunch. Supabus have introduced a service making use of the new overnight Swansea–Cork crossing. Leaving London in mid-afternoon Cork is reached at 7 A.M. the following morning. From Cork there is a connecting service to Limerick. Good value at around £50 round trip. Another new introduction is the Emerald Tripper circular ticket from London to Dublin via Holyhead, then on to Galway, and Cork, and back to London via Rosslare. There is time to spend at least one night—you have to find your own accommodations—in each of the cities, and the fare is only £75.

Details of Supabus services are contained in the International Express brochure for Ireland; only the major destinations have been covered above. The brochure can be obtained from any National Express coach station or appointed travel agent, or direct from *International Express,* The Coach Travel Center, 13 Regent St., London, SW1Y 4LR (tel. 01–439 9368).

Finally, there is an independent Irish operator, Slattery's, who operate bus services to many destinations from London. These include Cork, Rosslare, Killarney, Listowel, Tralee and Wexford. Their London office is at 162 Kentish Town Rd., London, NW5 2AG (01–485 2778), and the Coach Terminal is at 43 North Wharf Rd., London, W2 1LA (01–724 0741). Their fares start at around £55 round trip.

**FROM THE U.K. BY CAR.** Getting to Ireland by car presents no difficulties. There is a wide choice of ferry routes. You can go direct from both Liverpool and Holyhead, landing at Dun Laoghaire a few miles to the south of Dublin. It is possible to choose your route to fit your schedule as all routes offer day and night services which are conveniently timed for motorists. Liverpool, via the M1/M6/M62, at 198 miles from London is the closest both in terms of distance and time. However, the great advantage of the crossings from Holyhead are that they are much shorter, at around three and a half hours compared with seven hours from Liverpool. But the drive via the M6/M56/A55 takes much longer, though recent improvements to the A55 along the north Wales coast have reduced journey times significantly.

If bound for the southern counties of Ireland go via Fishguard/Pembroke to Rosslare, or Swansea to Cork. The overnight service between Swansea and Cork will be reintroduced in 1990—for details contact the Irish Tourist Board—with up to five weekly sailings run by Swansea Cork Ferries. The M4 is continuous from London to the far side of Swansea, some 190 out of 248 miles. But allow extra time for delays on the Severn Bridge in peak summer. Swansea is far more accessible than Fishguard, but the Swansea–Cork crossing is, at 10 hours, the longest.

In terms of price there is little to choose between B & I and Sealink British Ferries. Although slightly more expensive, the longer crossing from Swansea does cut out a tedious drive along the A40 from Swansea onwards. Fares to Southern Ireland are remarkably similar on all routes. As a guide allow around £220 round trip for a car plus driver and passenger.

**CUSTOMS ON ARRIVAL.** Customs regulations for travelers entering Ireland are complex. There are three levels of duty-free allowance: one, for residents of non-European countries; two, for passengers arriving from other E.E.C. countries bringing in goods that have *not* been bought in a duty-free shop; three, for residents of European countries not in the E.E.C. and for passengers arriving from other E.E.C. countries with goods that *have* been bought in a duty-free shop.

In the first category you may import duty free: 400 cigarettes or 200 cigarillos or 100 cigars or 500 grams of tobacco; plus, one liter of alcoholic beverage of more than 22% volume or a total of two liters of alcoholic beverage of not more than 22% volume or sparkling or fortified wine, plus two liters of other wine; plus, 50 grams of perfume and a quarter of a liter of toilet water; plus, other goods to a value of IR£31 per person (IR£16 for children under 15).

In the second category you may import duty free: 300 cigarettes or 400 grams of tobacco or 150 cigarillos or 75 cigars; plus, one and a half liters of alcoholic beverage of more than 22% volume or a total of three liters of alcoholic beverage of not more than 22% volume or sparkling or fortified wines plus four liters of other wine; plus, 75 grams of perfume and three-eighths of a liter of toilet water; plus, other goods to a value of IR£145 per person (IR£41 for children under 15).

In the third category you may import duty free: 200 cigarettes or 100 cigarillos or 50 cigars or 250 grams of tobacco; plus, one liter of alcoholic beverage of more than 22% volume or a total of two liters of alcoholic beverage of not more than 22% volume or sparkling or fortified wine plus two liters of other wine; plus, 50 grams of perfume and a quarter of a liter of toilet water; plus, other goods to a value of IR£31 per person (IR£16 for children under 15).

Note that in all three categories the tobacco and alcohol allowances apply only to those 17 and older. If you have nothing more than the duty-free allowance when you arrive, walk straight through the green "nothing to declare" channel. If you have more than your duty-free allowance, however, you must go into the red channel and declare the goods you are bringing in.

You may also import any quantity of currency, whether foreign or Irish, and non-residents may export any amount of foreign currency provided it was declared on arrival. Otherwise, you may export no more than IR£100, in denominations no larger than IR£20, and no more than the equivalent of IR£500 in foreign currency.

## Staying In Ireland

**CHANGING MONEY.** Irish banks are open Monday to Friday, 10 to 12.30 and 1.30 to 3. In Dublin, banks stay open till 5 on Thursdays; elsewhere in the country, the late-opening afternoon will be the same as the local market day. All banks, except those at Dublin and Shannon airports, are closed on Saturdays and Sundays and public holidays.

The banks at Dublin and Shannon airports are open every day except Christmas Day. At Dublin the bank is open from 7.15 A.M. to 11.30 P.M. April through September, and 7.30 A.M. to 9.30 P.M. October through March. At Shannon the bank is open from 6.30 A.M. to 5.30 P.M. April through September, and 7.30 A.M. to 4.30 P.M. October through March.

Dollars and pounds sterling are not generally accepted in Ireland outside major hotels. Licensed *Bureaux de Change* located in shops or hotels can be used outside banking hours, but the rate of exchange will be less favorable than at a bank.

**HOTELS.** Accommodations in Ireland range all the way from deluxe castles and stately homes through thatched cottages and farmhouses. Standards are high, and rising all the time. Pressure on hotel space only reaches a peak between June and September but it's a good idea to book in advance nonetheless to be sure of getting the hotel you want, and this is especially true of the more expensive spots. An increasing number of Irish hotels can be booked direct from the U.S. Ask your travel agent for details. Similarly, the Irish Tourist Board's Central Reservations Service in Dublin— 14 Upper O'Connell St., Dublin 1 (tel. 01–747733)—can make reservations in many hotels and other accommodations. (The U.S. and Canadian offices of the Irish Tourist Board are not able to make reservations, but can help with inquiries and information.) Local tourist offices can also make reservations for you.

The Irish Tourist Board has an official grading system and publishes a complete list of all hotels every year—*Discover Ireland: Hotels and Guesthouses*—which gives these gradings and the maximum price for rooms. No hotel may charge more than this price without special authorization from the I.T.B., and prices must also always be displayed in every room, so you should have no hesitation in complaining to either or both the hotel manager or the I.T.B. if prices exceed this maximum.

We have divided all the hotels in our listings into four categories: Deluxe (L), Expensive (E), Moderate (M) and Inexpensive (I). These grades are determined solely by price.

Two people in a double room can expect to pay:

| | |
|---|---|
| Deluxe (L) | IR£100 and up |
| Expensive (E) | IR£70 to IR£100 |
| Moderate (M) | IR£50 to IR£70 |
| Inexpensive (I) | under IR£50 |

Expect to pay about 10% more in Dublin. Prices include V.A.T., and in the lower price ranges, breakfast and service. Where breakfast is not included, expect to pay from IR£4.50 to IR£9.50, and look out for non-inclusive service charges of between 12% and 15%. Note also that single occupancy is always proportionately more expensive than double occupancy.

Our hotel listings give details of which of the major credit cards are accepted by each hotel we carry. These appear as AE for American Express,

DC for Diner's Club, MC for MasterCard (incorporating Access and Euro-Card), and V for Visa.

**HIGH LIVING.** Though many Irish castles have been successfully converted into deluxe hotels, Ashford Castle in Co. Galway preeminently, a good many more have remained in private hands. A number of these, among them some of the most celebrated and historic in the country, accept paying guests at certain times of the year, or rent out facilities to them. Probably the most famous is Lismore Castle at Lismore, Co. Waterford, the Irish home of the Duke of Devonshire. Up to six people can stay at the castle for a minimum group charge of around IR£6,000 per week. Among other fascinating places to stay, all with every modern comfort augmenting their richly historical characters, are 13th-century Cloughan Castle in Co. Galway, Springfield Castle in Co. Limerick and Glin Castle, also in Co. Limerick.

The Irish Tourist Board or your travel agent can provide information on staying in these and many other fine buildings. Alternatively, contact *Elegant Ireland,* 15 Harcourt St., Dublin 2 (tel. 01–751665). *At Home Abroad, Inc.,* 405 East 56th St., New York, NY 10016 (tel. 212–421–9165), can also provide information for high lifers of all tastes.

**COTTAGES.** In nearly 30 locations around the Republic of Ireland there are clusters of cottages for rent. The majority are built in the traditional style but with central heating and all the other conveniences of modern life. The demand for these cottages has grown enormously in recent years, but there are never more than a dozen or so in any one place. That's big enough to establish a community, but not so big as to intrude on the area or village.

Basic rental costs for a three-bedroom cottage fully equipped for six adults is around IR£220 in mid-season. Early reservations are essential. For details contact the Irish Tourist Board or your travel agent, or any of the following:

*Irish Self-Catering Assoc.,* Rosslare Beach Villas, Rosslare Strand, Co. Wexford.

*Island Holiday Cottages,* Annagvane, Lettermore, Co. Galway.

*Caragh Village,* c/o M. O'Connor, Caragh Village, Caragh Lake, Co. Kerry.

*Old Deanery Cottages,* c/o Mrs. B. Keane, Killala, Co. Mayo.

*Cruit Island,* c/o C. Ward, Rosses Point, Co. Sligo.

*Rent an Irish Cottage Ltd.,* Shannon Airport House, Shannon, Co. Clare.

**GUESTHOUSES.** Ireland has a wide range of guesthouses, all officially classified by the Irish Tourist Board and listed in its *Hotels and Guesthouses* booklet. The majority are owner-run and offer good standards of cleanliness and hospitality. A number also have private bathrooms, though these are very much the exception rather than the rule. Most also have between five and 10 rooms, though one Dublin guesthouse boasts 90 rooms; again, however, this is exceptional.

Average price for two people in a double room is about IR£30, including breakfast. Local tourist offices have details of guesthouses in their area.

Alternatively, contact *The Irish Guesthouse Assoc.,* c/o Mrs. O'Regan, Madan Heights, Tralee Rd., Killarney, Co. Kerry.

**BED AND BREAKFAST.** Though they may not legally call themselves guesthouses, in effect this is exactly what most Irish bed and breakfasts are. A good many are registered with the Irish Tourist Board—local tourist offices can supply lists of those in their area—and with the *Town and Country Homes Association,* c/o Mrs. McGee, Killeadan, Bundoran Rd., Ballyshannon, Co. Donegal. In rural areas, you will see B & B signs on many houses.

Average charges are around IR£20 per night for two, with, of course, breakfast.

**FARM VACATIONS.** The friendly nature of the Irish and the thoroughly relaxed atmosphere of rural life have long made farm vacations in Ireland extremely popular. Accommodations range from substantial farmhouses to a rather more modest farm bungalow. There is fishing close to most, golf not too far away and horse riding in the area if not on the farm itself. A few farms take guests year round, but the majority are open summer only. The Irish Tourist Board's *Farm Holidays in Ireland* lists all farms that accept guests. Alternatively, contact the *Irish Farmhouse Holidays Association,* Ashton Grove, Knockraha, Co. Cork.

Costs range from around IR£18 a night for two, including breakfast, to around IR£120 per person per week for half-board (lodging and one meal a day in addition to breakfast). There are also often reductions for children sharing their parents' room.

**CAMPING.** If you're hiking or traveling by bike, or even by car, camping provides the cheapest way of seeing the country. The Irish Tourist Board detail all camp sites in their *Caravan and Camping Parks* booklet, but you don't have to camp in an official site, though be sure to ask permission if you plan to camp on private land. Tents and other camping equipment can be hired from *O'Meara Holidays,* 160A Crumlin Rd., Dublin 12, and from outlets in Cork and Limerick.

Rates in camp sites range from IR£1.75 per night for a tent to about IR£20 per week, rising to IR£35 per week in peak season.

**YOUTH HOSTELS.** *An Oige* (the Irish Youth Hostels Assoc., 39 Mountjoy Sq., Dublin 1) has 42 youth hostels in Ireland (and another 11 in Northern Ireland). They range from a castle in Co. Kilkenny to a mountain lodge in Tipperary to onetime coastguard cottages on the edge of the Atlantic at Killary Harbor. You must have an International Youth Hostel Card to stay in an Irish youth hostel; contact your Youth Hostels Association at home (see *Student and Youth Travel* for addresses). Book as far in advance as you can; most hostels get very crowded, especially in the summer.

Charges are around IR£4.50 a night in city hostels, and around IR£3.80 in country areas for those over 21. For those between 16 and 20, rates are about IR£1 lower per night.

**RESTAURANTS.** Despite considerable and continuing improvements in standards overall, Irish food remains ample rather than gourmet, plain rather than fancy. The Irish are still oddly reluctant, or unable, to make the best use of their abundant and rich produce, with the unfortunate result that stodgy, rather overcooked food remains the norm. However, standards are unquestionably rising, and the very top hotels and restaurants offer food the equal of that anywhere in Europe.

Somerset Maugham once complained that the only way you could be sure of really good food in Britain was to eat breakfast three times a day. The same could equally have been said of Ireland, and though, as we say, standards overall have risen, breakfast in Ireland can still put to shame other Irish food. In fact, many people might well find it rather *too* substantial, with a premium on cholesterol, the archetypal "heart attack on a plate." At all events, it has long since ensured that lunch in Ireland is a relatively small meal, with pub lunches predominating.

Restaurants are obliged by law to display their menus outside their premises. In hotels, this generally means just outside the dining room. A number of restaurants offer special tourist menus, providing a three-course lunch or dinner for IR£5.75 or under, IR£7.50 or under, or IR£12 or under, the latter including one glass of wine. Wine, unfortunately, is expensive wherever you go, despite its rising popularity.

We have divided the restaurants in our lists into three categories: Expensive (E), Moderate (M), and Inexpensive (I). These grades are determined solely by price.

Approximate prices, in IR£, per person and excluding drinks:

| | |
|---|---|
| Expensive (E) | IR£25 and up |
| Moderate (M) | IR£15 to IR£25 |
| Inexpensive (I) | under IR£15 |

Our restaurant listings give details of which of the major credit cards are accepted by each restaurant we carry. These appear as AE for American Express, DC for Diner's Club, MC for MasterCard (incorporating Access and EuroCard) and V for Visa.

**TIPPING.** In most hotels and restaurants a service charge of around 12%—rising to 15% in some plush spots—will be added to your bill, so tipping is not really necessary unless you have received particularly good service.

Tip taxi drivers about 10% of the fare, and hotel porters about 50p per case. There are few porters at airports but plenty of baggage trolleys so tipping is not much of a problem. But if you do find a porter, tip him about 50p. Hairdressers normally expect a tip of about IR£1. You don't tip in pubs, but if there is waiter service in a bar or hotel lounge, leave about 10 or 20p. Otherwise, there are practically no other moments when you have to tip in Ireland.

**MAIL.** Air mail rates to the U.S. and Canada are 46p for ordinary letters, and 40p for airletters; postcards are 30p. Mail to all European countries goes by air automatically, so airmail stickers or envelopes are not required. Rates are 28p for letters. All these rates may well change before or during 1990, so be sure to check.

Irish mail boxes are painted green.

**TELEPHONES.** Public payphones are located in all towns and most villages. A local call costs 20p for three minutes, long distance calls within Ireland around 50p for three minutes, and calls to Britain about IR£1.75 for three minutes. Rates go down about a third after 6 P.M. and all day Saturday and Sunday and on public holidays. Calls to the U.S. cost about IR£1.75 per minute, less after 10 P.M., and again on Saturdays, Sundays and public holidays.

Don't make calls from your hotel room unless absolutely necessary. Practically all hotels add 200% to 300% to calls.

**OPENING TIMES.** Most shops are open from 9 to 5.30 or 6, Monday through Saturday. Except in Dublin, they normally shut at 1 for the afternoon once a week, normally Wednesday, Thursday or Saturday. This varies from region to region, so it's best to check locally. Larger shopping malls normally stay open late—generally to 9—once a week; Friday and Saturday are the most popular days.

Pubs are open Monday through Saturday from 10.30 A.M. to 11.30 P.M. June through September, closing at 11 the rest of the year. The famous Holy Hour, which required city pubs to close between 2.30 and 3.30, was abolished in 1988, and afternoon opening is now at the discretion of the landlord; few bother to close. On Sundays, the pubs are open from 12.30 to 2 and from 4 to 10. All pubs are closed on Christmas Day and Good Friday, but hotel residents will be served drinks in the hotel bar.

**ELECTRICITY.** The standard current in Ireland is 220V (50 cycles) AC. Most hotels have 220/110V sockets. Some shavers and hairdryers have a built-in transformer which can be set for 220V or 110V. If you will need a plug adaptor or travel transformer, buy it before leaving home.

**GUIDES.** *Tour Guides Ireland,* Glendinning House, Wicklow St., Dublin 2 (tel. 01–794291) provides qualified and registered guides who cover the whole of the Republic. Rates are around IR£35 for a half-day (up to three and a half hours) and around IR£60 for a full day (up to eight hours).

**ANCESTOR HUNTING.** The late President Kennedy and, more recently, President Reagan are only two among many thousands of Americans who have been drawn to Ireland in an attempt to trace their ancestry. So popular has this become that Ireland today boasts numerous facilities for those in search of their past. It's important, however, to have at least a minimum of information before you begin the search. If your name is Murphy, Kelly or O'Donnell, for example, that in itself is not going to be much help. You'll need a few details: the memories of elderly relatives about the place from which they or their forebears emigrated, for instance, is often a useful starting point. The county name is a help, but the name of their town or village is even more useful. It can lead quickly to parish registers, often going back 200 years or more, which the local clergy will usually be very glad to let you see.

Best of all, however, is to organize some professional help. The Genealogical Office, 2 Kildare St., Dublin 2 (tel. 01–614877), is the best starting point. They do not carry out searches, but offer a professional consultancy service, advising how to start an ancestor-search, for a fee of IR£10, including a document pack.

The Irish Tourist Board's information sheet *Tracing Your Ancestors* (20p) provides essential information for beginners. Certificates of births, deaths and marriages can be obtained for a small fee (cheaper if you apply in person) from The Registrar, Joyce House, 8–11 Lombard St. East, Dublin 2 (tel. 01–711000). Their records go back about 120 years. If you have reason to believe, or indeed know, that your background is either Quaker or Huguenot, or Presbyterian, then the Society of Friends, 6 Eustace St., Dublin 2, and the Presbyterian Historical Society, Church House, Fisherwick Pl., Belfast, respectively, may also be able to help.

There are also a number of private organizations who, for a fee, will be able to undertake detailed investigations. Among them are: *Hibernian Research Co. Ltd.,* 22 Windsor Rd., Rathmines, Dublin 6; *D. Fitzpatrick & Co.,* 17 Dame St., Dublin 2; *Gorry Research,* 16 Hume St., Dublin 2; *Dr. Susan C. Knight,* 32 Grange Park Rise, Raheny, Dublin 5; *David McElroy,* 60 Ivanhoe Ave., Carryduff, Belfast 8; *Terence McCarthy,* 14 Hampton Place, Belfast 7. *Ulster Pedigrees,* 14 Hampton Place, King's Bridge, Belfast BT7 3BZ. You are generally expected to send $5 for preliminary information.

If you just want a copy of your family crest, or the crest of your family name, you can get a hand-painted replica from a number of companies. Among them: *Polycrafts Ltd.,* Ballycasey Workshops, Shannon, Co. Clare; *Historic Families,* 8 Fleet St., Dublin 2; *Heraldic Artists Ltd.,* 3 Nassau St., Dublin 2. The price is generally around IR£40.

**SPORTS.** Whether you are a spectator or a participant, Ireland is the country for you. No matter what part of the country you're in, there'll always be facilities for golf and fishing, Ireland's two principal sporting attractions as far as most visitors are concerned. And there'll always be someone to talk about football—any of three kinds: Gaelic, rugby or soccer—hurling, and the horses—above all the horses. Throw in Ireland's long coastline, her rivers and her lakes, and you'll quickly realize that sailing, swimming, windsurfing or any other of the myriad manifestations of messing about in boats are equally well catered for.

**Racing.** Even if you're not a horse-racing fan, you'll miss part of the special atmosphere of Ireland if you don't go to at least one race meeting. There are two courses in Dublin, at Phoenix Park and Leopardstown, both within five miles of the city center, while the headquarters of Irish racing, the Curragh, is just 30 miles away in Co. Kildare, with buses and trains running right to the track. You can even buy a special "Day at the Races" rail ticket which, for about IR£10, takes two people from Heuston Station in Dublin to the Curragh and includes admission to the track.

There are, in fact, 28 race courses around the country, and about 280 meetings every year, not far short of one a day. Admission to most is normally around IR£3.50, with an extra charge to get into the reserved enclosure. The classic Irish races, all flat races, are all run at the Curragh, among them the 1,000 Guineas, the 2,000 Guineas, the Oaks, the Derby and the St. Leger. The biggest of all, again held at the Curragh, is the Budweiser Irish Derby, reputedly one of the richest races in Europe and attracting a crowd of around 50,000.

Flat racing runs throughout the summer, overlapping in fact in the fall with the start of the jumping, or steeplechase, season. This reaches its peak after Christmas, beginning with the meeting at Leopardstown on December 26 and climaxing with the Easter meetings at Fairyhouse, Co. Meath, about 20 miles from Dublin, when the Irish Grand National is run. The jumping season ends at the end of April at Punchestown, the annual meeting of the Kildare and National Steeplechase Committee, when a carnival atmosphere competes with the cream of Ireland's point-to-pointers.

Hand in hand with racing, of course, is betting, and the Irish dearly love a gamble, betting around IR£90 million every year on the horses alone and another IR£35 million on the dogs. You can place your bets with a bookie, or bookmaker, at the track, usually the most colorful and exciting way of betting, or at the Tote, or Totalizer, a government-run scheme, which is safer and less expensive but not quite entering into the spirit of the thing. Otherwise, there is no shortage of betting shops, usually called Turf Accountants, throughout the country. And they, of course, will accept bets on more or less anything that takes your fancy, from the weather to the date of the next election.

**Golf.** The top participant sport in Ireland for visitors is undoubtedly golf. Indeed, the really hardened addict has the consolation of knowing that there's a golf course no more than 100 yards down the road from Shannon Airport. If you don't think you can wait to get to your hotel before getting your fix, this is the place to fly to. But there are about 170 other courses that welcome visitors in Ireland, so you should have no difficulty in finding one or more to your taste. In most, you'll probably have to pay about IR£20 a day for green fees, caddie car and lunch. But bring your own clubs. Very few courses have them for hire. Professional fees are about IR£12 a round.

There are nine courses in Dublin alone, with a further 19 in Co. Dublin, including the famous Portmarnock links, which has staged the British Amateur Open, the Dunlop Masters, the Canada Cup and the Alcan Championships. Even more celebrated is the 101-year old Royal Dublin club, less than 30 minutes from the city center and venue for the annual Carroll's Tournament, one of the major events on the European golf calendar. But there are at least another 50 championship courses elsewhere in the country. And to keep the off-the-course golfer in form there are two golf ranges just outside Dublin.

A number of hotels have put together attractive package deals for golfers. Full details are available from your travel agent or the Irish Tourist Board; get their *Irish Golfing Holidays* and *Irish Golf Courses* booklets. Combined Irish/Scottish golfing vacations are also available for the serious addict.

**Fishing. Game Fishing.** Ireland has about 920,000 acres of lakes and 9,000 miles of streams and rivers, all waiting for anglers. Salmon and trout are the principal objectives. Remember, however, that both the season and the issuing of licenses are closely regulated, so be sure that you comply with both before setting off with your rod.

The salmon season starts on January 1, though not all rivers can be fished this early, and continues till the end of September. The sea trout, or "white" trout, season runs from the end of April to early-October. You can get a 21-day license, valid for all areas, to fish both salmon and sea trout, for IR£10 from the *Central Fisheries Board,* Balnagowan House, Mobhi Boreen, Glasnevin, Dublin 9 (tel. 01–379206). Alternatively, some tackle shops can also issue licenses. Though some salmon fishing is free, and some held by hotels for their guests, you'll also need a permit to fish waters under club control or privately owned. This is usually about IR£10 a day. If you are interested in longer term rights for salmon fishing, you can rent one of the fisheries controlled by the Department of Fisheries and Forestry for a season or even longer. Every fall, the Department's *Inland Fisheries Division,* Rooms 4–19, Leeson Lane, Leeson St., Dublin 2, issues a list of fisheries available in the coming period. If you'd like to make a bid, your tender must then be sent in by the date specified. Details are available from the Department.

Among the other freshwater fish, brown trout probably has the greatest appeal for most Irish anglers, the season peaking between mid-February and the end of September. A 21-day state license for brown trout costs IR£5 from the Central Fisheries Board. In waters under club or private control, you'll need an additional permit, usually costing between IR£1 and IR£5.

A number of lakes have been stocked with rainbow trout in recent years, and there is much good sport to be had in the season, April 1 (May 1 in some fisheries) to the end of September. The same license is required as for brown trout.

For further information, the Irish Tourist Board's *Freshwater Game Fishing* is an invaluable source of information.

**Coarse Fishing.** Though not as popular as game fishing, coarse fishing has long had its loyal followers in Ireland. The major fish are pike, perch, bream, roach and rudd. There is no close season for any of the coarse fish, but a license is required from the Central Fisheries Board, costing IR£5 for 21 days. Only a few waters are off-limits because they are privately owned; inquire locally. There are, however, two strictly enforced regulations: fishing must be by rod and line, and you may not use more than two rods at any one time.

*Freshwater Coarse Angling,* available from the Irish Tourist Board, details all the principal waters and contains useful lists of tackle and bait stockists.

**Sea Fishing.** With a coastline more than 2,000 miles long, it is hardly surprising that Ireland offers plenty of opportunities for sea angling, both from the shore and offshore. You will meet shore fishermen along the harbor walls in Dublin Bay and along lonely stony beaches from Wicklow to Kerry, while the offshore fishermen have been sailing out of Ballycotton and Kinsale on the Cork coast and harbors like Westport in Co. Mayo for years, returning with shark, cod, skate, monkfish and conger eel of spectacular size.

The major source of information is the *Irish Federation of Sea Anglers,* 67 Windsor Drive, Monkstown, Co. Dublin, though local tourist offices can also help.

**Horseback Riding.** For a country so dedicated to horses, it is only natural that there should be many opportunities for novices and veterans alike to spend a holiday on a horse. A number of equestrian centers offer packages for around IR£220 a week; details from your travel agent or the Irish Tourist Board. Pony trekking is also enormously popular, hardly surprising considering the beauty of the country.

For further information on riding stables and equestrian centers, the I.T.B.'s *Guide for the Equestrian Visitor* is invaluable.

**Hunting.** A number of equestrian centers can provide facilities for visitors to take part in a hunt or watch one, though only experienced riders—and you'll have to prove it—will be able to do the former. Indeed most hunts welcome visitors who know how to follow the hounds and respect the Master's guidance. To be able to report that you have been out with the Galway Blazers, the Killing Kildares, the Scarteen Black and Tans or the Ward Union Hunt is something that marks any horseman or woman as "sound," as the Irish have it.

In several areas, the hunting visitor can arrange an all-expenses package at small hotels, which will organize mounts, transport and special terms for temporary membership. In all, Ireland has 41 recognized harrier packs, one staghound pack, and 32 packs of fox hounds, plus ten groups of foot beagles. A full day's hunting usually costs between IR£35 and IR£50.

**Show Jumping.** To see some of the finest show jumpers in the world, go to the Royal Dublin Society's Horse Show in the first week in August. The competition attracts leading riders from all over the world in a thrilling competition that lasts five days. The Nations Cup, usually held on the Friday of the Horse Show week, creates enormous excitement throughout the country. Smaller but no less exciting show jumping and three-day event meetings are held at a variety of venues, and big international names have shown up at many such occasions.

**Sailing.** The combination of a long and enormously varied coastline on the one hand, plus marvelous inland waterways on the other, has long conspired to make Ireland a natural cruising ground for sailors of all persuasions. There are a number of sailing schools in the country, one of the best of which is the Glenans Irish Sailing Center, with bases at Bere Island and Baltimore on the Cork coast and at Clew Bay in Co. Mayo. A two-week course for those over 18 costs about IR£250. The Fingall Sailing School at Malahide, nine miles from Dublin, offers five-day sailing courses from around IR£160.

Waterskiing, canoeing, windsurfing and even scuba diving are all equally well catered for. For information on all aspects of watersports in Ireland, contact either the *Irish Yachting Association*, 4 Haddington Terr., Dun Laoghaire, Co. Dublin, or the Irish Tourist Board.

## Getting Around Ireland

**BY TRAIN.** Though considerably scaled down in recent years and by no means covering the whole country, Ireland's train services, operated

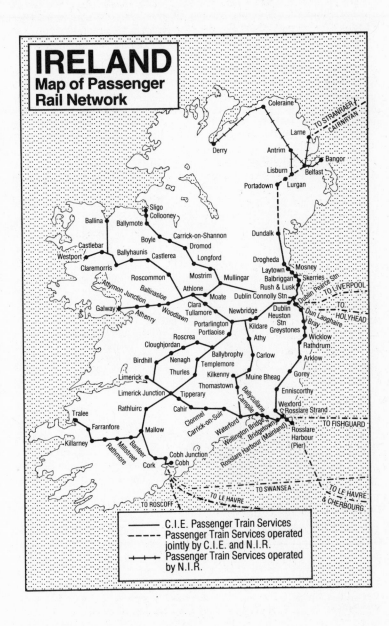

by the state-owned Irish Rail Iarnrod Eireann, the rail division of C.I.E. *(Coras Iompair Eireann),* are generally reliable, reasonably priced, and comfortable. From Dublin at least, all the principal towns are well served, though services between provincial cities are less good: if you want to go from Cork, for example, to Wexford, you have to go via Limerick Junction, a very round about route indeed. However, buses augment a number of services and help to fill in some of the gaps.

Journey times are reasonable. Dublin to Cork is about three hours; Dublin to Galway about three and a half; to Limerick between two and three quarters and three and a half; and to Belfast about two and a quarter. Most mainline trains have two classes: standard and superstandard. It is usually cheapest to buy a round-trip ticket. For example, Dublin to Cork costs IR£27.50 single, and about IR£30 round trip.

There are a number of good-value tourist rail cards for anyone who plans to do much traveling by train. The best buy is the Rail-Road Rambler, good for all trains and buses (excluding city services). There are two types of ticket. The first is valid for eight days travel in a 15-day period and costs IR£66, the second is for 15 days travel in a 30-day period and costs IR£95. Tickets can also be bought for train only or bus only at IR£52 for eight days, and IR£77 for 15 days. So the combined ticket is a much better value. The Overlander ticket is good for unlimited travel on Irish Bus, Irish Rail, Ulsterbus and Northern Ireland Railways and costs IR£109 for 15 days (continuous validity). In addition, the Eurailpass is valid for unlimited rail travel in Ireland as well as in 16 other European countries, though not the U.K. (including Northern Ireland), and also gives discounts on many lake steamers and river boats. However, it is only available to residents of non-European countries and must be purchased before you leave home (contact the Irish Tourist Board in the U.S. or Canada for details). Costs are $298 for 15 days, $370 for 21 days, $470 for one month, $650 for two months and $798 for three months.

For information on Irish Rail services call 01–366222.

**BY AIR.** Ireland is not a large country so air travel plays only a small role in internal travel. Nonetheless, Aer Lingus have flights from Dublin to both Shannon and Cork, flying time being around 30 minutes. There is also a regular air service to all three of the Aran Islands off Galway Bay from Carnmore Airport, Galway, operated by Aer Arann and taking between 15 and 25 minutes. Aer Arann also operate a service between Derry, in Northern Ireland, and Dublin.

**BY BUS.** The long-distance services are operated by Irish Bus (Bus Eireann), a subdivision of C.I.E. Additionally, many inter-town Expressway coaches now compete directly with the train service. Bus Eireann also provides local services in Cork, Galway, Limerick, and Waterford. But a word of warning; many of the destination indicators on bus routes are given only in the Irish language so make quite sure you get on the right bus. For example, you might be surprised to get on a bus in Wicklow, which had "Baile Atha Cliath" on its destination board. But it would in fact be going to Dublin as that is the Irish name for their capital city. Never be afraid to ask.

Expressway bus services cover the major routes throughout the country and are designed to provide a network with interchange points without returning to a terminus. Other bus services are slower, but serve intermediate points. Irish Bus also run day tours from the central bus stations in Dublin (tel. 01–302222), Cork (tel. 021–503399), Limerick (tel. 061–42433), Galway (tel. 091–62141), and Waterford (tel. 051–73401).

In Dublin the large Busarus close to the Custom House is the main station for such services. It is also the main departure point for the bus services to Dublin airport. Although some outer suburban bus routes leave from here the main city services radiate from O'Connell Street where there are several principal bus stops. C.I.E. also operate a bus from the airport to Heuston Station. Check times of this as it runs only in connection with main trains. For details on Dublin bus services call 01–734222.

**BY CAR.** Ireland remains so fundamentally rural a country and so sparsely populated that, despite improvements in public transport, for really successful touring, getting into all the nooks and crannies and off the beaten track, a car is almost essential. Roads are generally good and certainly in comparison to most other European countries, very empty. In addition, the motorway "network" is practically non-existent, meaning that any extended automobile journey almost inevitably provides you with an opportunity for sightseeing in one shape or another.

All the principal roads are designated by the letter "N," standing for National Primary Route. Thus, the main road north from Dublin, for example, is the N1, the main road northwest the N2, and so on. Road signs are generally in both Irish and English, though in the northwest they're in Irish only, so it's as well to take along a good road map if you plan to visit here. Distances on the newer, green signposts are in kilometers; white signposts are older and give distances in miles. Otherwise traffic signs are very much the same as in the rest of Europe.

However, unlike the rest of Europe, except the U.K. of course, you drive on the left. There is a general speed limit of 55 m.p.h. on most roads and 30 m.p.h. in towns. In some areas the limit is 40, always clearly signposted. If there is a yellow box painted on the road at an intersection, don't drive in unless your way is clear to drive out. Roadway markings are of the standard type: note especially, however, that a continuous white line down the center of the road means that you must not overtake or park. Barred markings on the road and flashing yellow beacons indicate a "zebra" crossing, where pedestrians can cross the road and where they *always* have right of way. Yellow lines by the roadside mean you can't park during business hours; double yellow lines indicate no parking at any time. At a junction of two roads of equal importance, the driver to the right of you has right of way. Safety belts must be worn by the driver and front passenger, while children under 12 must travel in the back. It is also compulsory for motorcyclists and passengers to wear helmets.

Despite the relative lack of traffic, parking in towns is a real problem. Signs with the letter "P" indicate car lots, but if there's a stroke through the "P" keep away or you'll likely collect a stiff fine, normally around IR£20. Parking restrictions in Dublin and Cork operate only until 6 P.M., after which you tend to encounter men in nondescript uniform caps guiding you into parking spaces. They're in no way official, but tip them about 20p anyway. Give attendants in official parking lots the same when you leave.

Drunk driving laws are strict. As in the U.K., Ireland has a breathalyzer test which the police can ask any driver they suspect is drunk to take. If you refuse to take it, the odds are you'll be prosecuted anyway. As ever, the best advice is don't drive if you're going to be drinking.

Two particular hazards on Irish roads are cattle and sheep. At night cattle are supposed to be led by a man carrying a lamp and followed by another. This is seldom the case, so be careful. Similarly, sheep are a common occurence on roads, particularly in the hilly regions.

**Car Hire.** If you plan to hire a car, don't forget your driver's license. If you are over 70 years of age, you may be subject to special regulations; be sure to check with the rental firm before you reserve. All the major car hire companies have offices in Ireland, as do a number of Irish firms. We give addresses and telephone numbers of the principal operators in our "Useful Addresses" sections in the *Practical Information* after each chapter. In addition, the Irish Tourist Board in the U.S. and Canada, as well as local tourist offices, can also supply information on car hire. Most of the major firms also have desks at Shannon, Dublin and Cork airports.

There are numerous good value fly-drive vacations available to Ireland, as well as a number of most expensive chauffeur-driven tours. Contact your travel agent or the I.T.B. for further information.

**Frontier Posts.** There are 20 approved routes for crossing the border between the Republic of Ireland and Northern Ireland. If you are going to cross the border in a self-drive car, be sure the rental company gives you the papers.

Border posts are on the following roads (the Northern Ireland town is first):

Newry–Greenore, *Newry–Dundalk (via Killeen),
Armagh–Dundalk (via Newtown Hamilton),
Crossmaglen–Carrickmacross,
Armagh–Castleblayney, *Armagh–Monaghan,
Roslea–Monaghan,
Enniskillen–Clones, Derrylin–Belturbet, Enniskillen–Swanlinbar,
Enniskillen–Manorhamilton, Enniskillen–Ballyshannon (via Belleek),
Kesh–Pettigo,
Castlederg–Castlefin, *Strabane–Lifford,
Derry–St. Johnston,
Derry–Bridgend, Derry–Muff, Derry–Newtown Hamilton

Posts are normally manned 8 A.M. to 8 P.M.; those marked * are manned until midnight.

There are checkpoints on both sides of the frontier, on the northern side by the British Customs and on the south by the Republic of Ireland Customs. On both sides the formalities are quick and friendly. Don't drive on roads near the border marked Unapproved Road, or you're likely to be in trouble with the customs. Sometimes there may be army or police (Royal Ulster Constabulary) checkpoints north of the frontier. Stop on being signaled for a quick check. Bring your passport.

**BY TAXI.** Taxis with meters only operate in Dublin, Cork and Limerick. In all other places, they are known as hackneys or hackney cars. For these, you should agree the price with the driver before starting your journey.

**BY BICYCLE.** Cycling can be a great way to get around Ireland. A "Raleigh Rent-a-Bike" scheme operates throughout the country. Full details are available from the Irish Tourist Board. Rates are around IR£4.50 a day, or IR£6.50 a day for a tandem, or IR£22 a week. You must pay a IR£30 deposit. Insurance is covered in the hire charge. Pressure on rentals is high in July and August, so be sure to book well in advance. If you hire a bike in the Republic you may not take it into Northern Ireland, nor may you take a bike hired in Northern Ireland into the Republic.

**BY INLAND WATERWAY.** Exploring Ireland's lakes, rivers and canals is a delightful way of getting to know the country. Cruises on the Shannon, the longest river in the British Isles, and its associated lakes and canals, are among the most popular. Your travel agent or the Irish Tourist Board have full details of the wealth of operators and trips on offer.

For drifting through the Midlands on the Grand Canal and river Barrow, contact *Celtic Canal Cruisers,* Tullamore, Co. Offaly (tel. 0506–21861).

## Leaving Ireland

**V.A.T. REFUNDS.** A number of Irish stores operate schemes for refunding V.A.T. (Value Added Tax) to foreign visitors. With the top rate of V.A.T. a hefty 25% (10% on clothes), you can make substantial savings by taking advantage of them. The regulations, however, are fairly complicated, so follow them carefully to avoid misunderstandings and delays.

First, goods sent directly to your home by the store are not liable for V.A.T. In all other cases you must pay the V.A.T. when you buy the goods. If you want to reclaim it, you must then export them within two months and they must have a total value of £IR50 (IR£202 for residents of other E.E.C. countries). Ask the retailer to fill out a Cashback voucher at the point of sale. This voucher must be stamped by a customs officer before departure from Ireland. Once the receipt is validated the visitor can go to a Cashback desk at Dublin or Shannon airports and receive the V.A.T. refund in dollars or punts, less a small administrative fee. If there is not time to do this on departure, overseas visitors can send their receipts in a pre-paid envelope to the Cashback headquarters and receive a check at their home address within 21 days.

**CUSTOMS ON RETURNING HOME. Americans.** U.S. residents may bring in $400 worth of foreign merchandise as gifts or for personal use without having to pay duty, provided they have been out of the country more than 48 hours and provided they have not claimed a similar exemption within the previous 30 days. Every member of a family is entitled to the same exemption, regardless of age, and the exemptions can be pooled. For the next $1,000 worth of goods a flat 10% rate is assessed.

Included in the $400 allowance for travelers over the age of 21 are one liter of alcohol, 100 non-Cuban cigars and 200 cigarettes. Only one bottle of perfume trademarked in the U.S. may be brought in. However, there is no duty on antiques or art over 100 years old. You may not bring home meats, fruits, plants, soil or other agricultural products.

Gifts valued at under $50 may be mailed to friends or relatives at home, but not more than one per day of receipt to any one addressee. These gifts must not include perfumes costing more than $5, tobacco or liquor.

If you are traveling with such foreign-made articles as cameras, watches or binoculars that were purchased at home or on a previous trip, either carry the receipt or register them with U.S. Customs prior to departure.

**Canadians.** In addition to personal effects, and over and above the regular exemption of $300 per year, the following may be brought into Canada duty free: a maximum of 50 cigars, 200 cigarettes, two pounds of tobacco and 40 ounces of liquor, provided these are declared in writing to customs on arrival. Canadian Customs regulations are strictly enforced; you are recommended to check what your allowances are and to make sure you have kept receipts for whatever you may have bought abroad. Small gifts can be mailed and should be marked "Unsolicited gift, (nature of gift), value under $40 in Canadian funds." For other details, ask for the Canadian Customs brochure, *"I Declare."*

**British Customs.** There are two levels of duty-free allowance for people entering the U.K.; one, for goods bought outside the E.E.C. or for goods bought in a duty-free shop within the E.E.C.; two, for goods bought in an E.E.C. country but not in a duty-free shop.

In the first category you may import duty free: 200 cigarettes or 100 cigarillos or 50 cigars or 250 grammes of tobacco (*Note* if you live outside Europe, these allowances are doubled); plus one liter of alcoholic drinks over 22% vol. (38.8% proof) or two liters of alcoholic drinks not over 22% vol. or fortified or sparkling wine; plus two liters of still table wine; plus 50 grammes of perfume; plus nine fluid ounces of toilet water; plus other goods to the value of £32.

In the second category you may import duty free: 300 cigarettes or 150 cigarillos or 75 cigars or 400 grammes of tobacco; plus 1½ liters of alcoholic drinks over 22% vol. (38.8% proof) or three liters of alcoholic drinks not over 22% vol. or fortified or sparkling wine; plus five liters of still table wine; plus 75 grammes of perfume; plus 13 fluid ounces of toilet water; plus other goods to the value of £250. (*Note* though it is not classified as an alcoholic drink by E.E.C. countries for Customs' purposes and is thus considered part of the "other goods" allowance, you may not import more than 50 liters of beer.)

In addition, no animals or pets of any kind may be brought into the U.K. The penalties for doing so are severe and are strictly enforced; there are *no* exceptions. Similarly, fresh meats, plants and vegetables, controlled drugs and firearms and ammunition may not be brought into the U.K. There are no restrictions on the import or export of British and foreign currencies.

# IRELAND AND THE IRISH

## *The Gregarious Instinct*

by
**STAN GEBLER DAVIES**

*Stan Gebler Davies is a distinguished Irish journalist and writer. He contributes regularly to many Irish and English newspapers, including the London* Daily Telegraph, The Spectator *and* Punch, *and is the author of an acclaimed biography of James Joyce. He lives in Kinsale, County Cork.*

The Irish are a gregarious people. They cannot bear to be left alone. They must always be talking to their friends. This is a courtesy, or botheration, which is extended also to perfect strangers, so that it is in fact impossible to remain a foreigner in Ireland for longer than it takes to notice that the grass is green or that the airport tarmac is awash in a couple of inches of rainwater.

This is to the taste of some, but not all. Ireland is no place for a man or a woman with a secret, unless it is a secret which is begging to be told. And it is a certain truth that the Irish expect strangers to have tongues in their mouths for purposes other than drinking and ears so firmly attached to their skulls that they will not be blown away by the gales of talk.

It is not, this land of ours, a place for the seeker after privacy. This notably generous people are mean with only one commodity, and that is solitude. If you *are* in search of solitude you'll need a nimble pair of legs on you and a fair skip to your step. You might take yourself to the top of Mount Brandon in a blizzard (I do not recommend it), or out into the Atlantic on a dark night to Skellig Rock, but in either place and under any circumstance you would most likely find some member of the Irish nation had got there before you and was hoping for a little conversation.

The whole of our national life is organized on this principle—that every last thing shall be arranged so as to afford the maximum opportunity for meeting and talking. This is so much characteristic of us that it might as well be written into the constitution. (It is in fact written into the Constitution of the Republic of Ireland, enshrined in several articles of fundamental law, but this is no place to be talking of politics—not at the moment, anyway—and I would not want to deprive anyone of the pleasure of reading that interesting document by giving away what is in it.)

## Being Always with One Another

Providence has been kind to us. We have found ourselves on precisely the right island and it is the knowledge of this sublime and divine gift which makes us so wretched whenever we have to leave it. It is the proper place to be meeting people. Nature has inflicted no impediment to the intention of being always with one another. You may, for example, climb any mountain in Ireland in the space of an afternoon, and I do not suppose there is any offshore island which is so inaccessible that a man cannot be found to take you there in a boat, weather and sanity permitting. (We are suspicious of the sea: it gives you fish, but it might take away your life.)

Each season of the year is arranged by us in such a manner as to accommodate this great gregarious whim of ours. In winter the storms come howling in from the Atlantic and the rain, instead of falling gently, is driven sideways, sometimes in solid drenching sheets that would convince an Olympic swimmer he had never truly come to grips with the element of water before. It is in this season that we take most enthusiastically to the countryside—those of us, that is, who have not the good fortune to live in it in the first place.

This is, in part, because that is where we keep the horses. Those who have horses, take to the horses, and those who do not, follow them. The Irish passion for these animals and the Irish curiosity as to which specific horse can move faster than the other ones, is to be observed at countless hunts, race meetings and fairs.

## The Irish and Their Weather

You have heard of the Irish weather. I have mentioned it already. It consists of rain. There is a lot of it. Nobody ever came twice to Ireland looking for a tan. Few who live there achieve one without booking a trip elsewhere. It has been known for the rain to cease, sometimes for as much as two weeks at a time. But when this happens the Irish complain of drought, pestilence and imminent bankruptcy.

This is because it is water which gives the island its richness and its character. Hence the greenness, the wealth of the land, the incomparable quality of the light, the lakes, the glory of our seasons. This water is also translated, by the kindness and skill of brewers and distillers, into substances which promote the facility of talk.

I do not mean to suggest that our climate is unkind, or that we need any great defence against it. It is never so cold in Ireland as to prevent an outdoor gathering, and even if it were we would gather anyway. When the landscape is unduly damp, as after some several weeks of unremitting downpour we will find that layers of water lend it an extra dimension of drama. It is a good time to take advantage of the sunshine and traipse, well-shod, across the nearest bog on foot, or up the nearest mountain.

The rain brings the flowers after it. Possibly there are tropical islands or equatorial jungles where flowers grow in more splendid profusion and variety than they do in the wild lands of Ireland, but I disbelieve it. Yet I never met an Irish man or woman who made a fuss about flowers, or any plant that could not be eaten, brewed, or distilled. You do not wonder on natural beauty in a country where fuschia and rhododendrons are regarded as weeds which have to be cut back. The rain brings the wealth and the beauty. (It is almost the only thing we do not talk about in Ireland—rain. It is too obvious.)

## The Irish and Their Offspring

Even more ubiquitous (one may not, by the way, describe anything in Ireland as "common": it is a deadly insult) than horses are children. This is not entirely due to the fact that the Republic has the highest population growth rate in Western Europe, more to the wholesome desire of the people to keep their offspring about them as much as they can. Children are brought everywhere.

This should, in theory, lead to the children, under constant parental supervision, behaving in the disciplined manner which W. C. Fields demanded of his juvenile (and canine) co-stars, but the reality is otherwise. W. C. Fields, were he brought back to life in present-day Ireland, would be driven, by the behaviour of Irish children, as he was by the kids and dogs he had to work with, to stock his house from attic to cellar with crates of whiskey.

The Irish child is rumbustuous. The Irish child is all over the place. If bribed to go away, it will oblige. If not, it will not. It is given license to behave as it pleases. It takes full advantage of this freedom, utilising to the fullest extent those enviable vocal and locomotive powers which God has granted to the very young.

This will be bad news to visitors who are used to some peace and quiet in bars and restaurants, but those who are fond of little human beings who have not reached the age of reason, and have no apparent intention of doing so, will discover to their joy that Ireland was not called Tir na n'Og, the Land of Youth, for nothing. Close to half the population of the Republic is under the age of 25, and the proportion is rising. It has been so since the traditional escape valve of emigration was closed. The population of the Republic is growing at about the rate of 15 per cent every ten years.

This would spell trouble to a less optimistic race, but we are not greatly given to worrying about it. We are inclined to regard our own selves, as well as the land we live in, as our greatest resource and it is the opinion of most who come to live among us that we live very well indeed, more so in hope and faith than in resignation. The Irish will go on having children as extravagantly as they please. It is impossible to contemplate Ireland without wishing to people it.

The problem of underfoot, raucous and galloping children is not insoluble and the most valuable piece of advice I have to give to any visitor concerns how to deal with them.

The least efficient method is bribery. This can only provide the most temporary respite. All children are greedy and, once bribed, will come back for more, bringing their friends.

A slightly more efficient source of solace is to bribe the parents. A few civil words (the offer of civil words should always be accompanied in Ireland by the offer of a drink) will always suffice to convince the owners of Irish children to move them somewhere they are not visible or audible. The Irish do not encourage the noise and turbulence of children: they simply do not notice it. It is a curious fact that the Irish, who inhabit a country which has more peace and quiet available in it than almost any other country in Europe, do not in the least value it.

The third possibility is to avoid children altogether. There is always, in any sizeable town, and in many quite small villages, a bar and/or a restaurant where these evidences of God's bounty are simply forbidden entrance, or else exiled to the garden. This is one of the best-kept secrets in Ireland, and the one most worth knowing. It is only necessary to ask where these child-free havens might be, in order to be told.

Ireland, by the way, is still one of the least populated countries in Europe. It is possible to walk or drive for miles on end without seeing a single soul. Honest. The odds are, however, that when you spot a native, it will be a child. Or a horse.

## What the Irish Eat

This island is surrounded by some of the most bountiful seas in the world and there are very few plants that will not grow in its soil. This does not mean that it is easy to get a decent meal in Ireland, because the Irish do not believe in making a fuss about food. Some advice is needed.

The last thing to do is to ask any local person. It does not matter to what rank or station this person belongs, or aspires to. The Irish are commonly brought up with deadened palates and at the first stirring into action of the taste buds the reaction is to batter them into submission with the nearest bland but powerful substance, usually ketchup or some equally vile sauce out of a bottle. The Irish gourmand's idea of a good meal is boiled meat or boiled fish or boiled fowl, with lots of boiled vegetables.

This is the consequence of history, or the lack of it. The Irish have no history of cuisine. Because they are a robust and independent people, they will have no truck with anything imported, unless it is something on a par with the boring stuff they eat themselves, like adulterated hamburger or soggy pasta.

They will not eat any fish they do not like the look of. They do not hang meat or fowl or any type of game, because they think it would "go off" if they did. They think shellfish and crustaceans are probably poisonous.

Where I live, in Kinsale, I am able to pick buckets of mussels off the rocks because no one else wants them, and I am often given monkfish, ling, John Dory and other delicious, but ugly-looking denizens of the deep, because the fishermen who have caught them know they cannot sell them except to restaurants catering exclusively to the weird and probably perverted culinary tastes of foreigners. It is common practice to retain only the claws from a crab and throw the rest of the animal away because every Irishman knows for a sure and certain fact that if you eat the insides of a crab you drop dead on the spot.

Very well, I am exaggerating. The Irish attitude to food which I have been describing is an old one, and it is dying, but it is dying hard. Spanish trawlers come a thousand miles to plunder our waters but our own fishing fleet is tiny, and the refusal of the Irish to eat fish is the despair of what is left of it.

Things change, but slowly. Some years back it occurred to a small but discerning band of restaurateurs (mostly foreigners) that Ireland was uniquely blessed in Europe in the matter of what are called food resources. There is a lot of prime steak walking about in the fields, if only the locals can be persuaded not to boil it or stew it. (Irish stew is the greatest culinary insult ever to be inflicted on one of God's creatures.)

Fish I have already mentioned. As for fowl, I find it profitable to lurk behind the hedge at the bottom of my garden on early winter evenings and wait for the wild duck to come in from the river in flocks to feed in the stubble-fields. A well-aimed rock is sufficient to stun a pheasant (if no one is looking) and the wood-pigeons gather themselves conveniently in clumps.

We know about all this, of course, in the country, but our cousins in the town did not know, or care, about these riches, not until quite recently.

Then came the food revolution, which is still in progress. The insurrectionary idea began to take hold, to the horror of traditionalists, that food might actually be eaten for pleasure. This insidious gospel was greeted by the reactionary element with about the same degree of enthusiasm as George III extended to the proposition that there ought to be no taxation without representation. I am glad to report that the revolution shows every sign of ultimate success. George III was finally sent packing at the battle of Yorktown. Our culinary Yorktown may be in sight.

Why, we have even got an annual gourmet festival in my home town of Kinsale, and very successful it is too. Believe it or not, there was a demonstration mounted against it by the reactionary rear-guard, who thought that the idea of spending a few days on the consumption of food for fun was quite simply disgusting, and revoltingly un-Irish. After they had put their banners and their placards away, the rest of us proceeded to guzzle champagne and lobster, and none of us sickened and died as a consequence, or felt the need to confess the commission of a mortal sin.

One way to deploy a knife and fork to maximum effect in Ireland is to seek the advice of the tourist offices, who keep lists of the revolutionary gastronomic outposts called restaurants. There are now a great many good ones, often to be found in the most unlikely places.

Another is to get hold of the raw material and cook it yourself. Butchers' shops of the old-fashioned sort, where you may order your own cuts, are still everywhere to be found. Fishmongers are regrettably scarce, but it is in any case an excellent idea to go down to the quays in our fishing villages and haggle with the fishermen when the boats come in in the evening. A couple of fresh mackerel or herring can be got in season very cheaply, and more exotic specimens for half of nothing. Besides, it is fun. Long live the revolution!

## What the Irish Drink

We come now to a sore point, and one upon which the entire nation is united, with the exception of the politicians and the tax-gatherers.

The principal social institution in Ireland, after the Church and the home, is the pub. Almost every Irishman will spend some part of every day of the year (except two—I will come to that) in a pub, unless he is terminally ill or incarcerated in a hospital or in prison, because pubs is where they keep the drink and the talk.

The Government knows this. The Government is greedy, like all governments, and like most governments, it has occurred to it that putting a tax on liberty is the easiest way to separate the citizen from his money. Nothing is more precious than liberty and no liberty is more precious to the Irish than the liberty to congregate and talk.

So the Government has put horrendous taxes on the liberty to consume alcohol, and, since alcohol is the medium of exchange in the transaction called conversation, the take is enormous. It is a fact that the public administration of the Republic of Ireland would collapse without the revenue from the taxes on booze as surely as it would if the country were invaded tomorrow morning by a race of super-intelligent malignant beings from outer space. (There are some of us who would welcome this latter development so long as the extraterrestials lifted the tax on drink.)

What the economists call disposable income is what is left over from one's income after one has paid the rent and got one's wallet back from the friendly tax-inspector. It is what the citizen, having satisfied the rapacious demands of the State in the forms of income tax, social insurance tax, and every other damn sort of tax (the Irish have invented some brand new taxes to inflict on themselves, but it requires the twisted brain of a demented economist to understand them, let alone explain them), *and* afterwards assured himself and his family of the basic necessities of life, has left over to spend as he, or she, chooses.

The Irish, at last count, spent 14 per cent of their disposable income on alcohol. The Danes, apparently the next most inebriated nation in Europe, came a very poor second, with four per cent. This does not mean that the average citizen spends most of his life in a condition of drunken stupor, merely that he has to mortgage his house or sell his children into slavery to pay the tax on a pint of beer.

A bottle of Irish whiskey, in Ireland, will set you back about $18. A pint of beer is just this side of $2. Any visitor to Ireland is therefore advised in the strongest possible terms to take advantage of the duty-free drink allowances on entering the country, and bring in every last drop permitted. If you don't want it, I assure you from the bottom of my empty glass, someone else will.

The Government, recognizing that their taxation policy had gone beyond the point of diminishing returns (we stopped buying the stuff in droves because we could no longer afford it) actually reduced the tariff on whiskey in 1984 by about $2 a bottle. A muffled cheer rose from the ranks of the long-suffering only to die away again when the publicans promptly put up their prices to take up the slack.

Our own native remedy for this self-imposed drought is to manufacture the stuff ourselves. It is called poteen (pronounced "pot-cheen") and is readily available in most areas if you ask nicely. It is a bad idea to ask a policeman if he happens to be in uniform at the time, since the Government severely disapproves of any pleasure which it cannot tax, but a policeman out of uniform would be an excellent person from whom to seek advice. He is, after all, in the best possible position to know where to find it.

This poteen is a powerful stuff. It is distilled usually from grain but any organic substance will do. Potatoes were once widely used, but no longer: they are too expensive. It is not whiskey, as many think, but the noble ancestor of whiskey. It can produce the mother and father of a hangover and, unwisely consumed in a raw state, can lead to madness, blindness, paralysis, ruin, and an ignominious death in a roadside ditch. The Russians call it vodka. I am rather fond of the stuff myself. It is best taken in a hot punch, with lemon, cloves and brown sugar.

## The Great Game

To the vexation of taxation is added the vexation of the licensing laws. These are a particularly unwelcome inheritance from the British and stipulate that public houses shall close at 11.30 P.M. in the summer and 11 in the winter. It is a prime example of Government idiocy, one might consider, to send the citizens home early to their beds when their only desire is to stay up a little longer and continue enriching the same Government, but there is no accounting for what passes for thought among legislators. In the meantime, we amuse ourselves with the merry game of playing at not being found on the premises. This sport commences all over the island five minutes after the pubs are supposed to close and the teams are composed of the entire population of Ireland, on one side, and the police force on the other. The police score points for finding citizens on licensed premises at the hour when they are supposed to be home in bed and the citizenry score points by having a pint after they have been told not to by the forces of law and order and the publically elected defenders of the Constitution.

It is a very friendly sport and injuries are rare. Everyone involved knows everyone else and the penalties incurred on either side are very slight. If a policeman breaks the rules by raiding a pub too often, he may find himself refused a drink next time he asks for one when *he* is supposed to be at home in bed. If the citizen loses, he is forced to pay a fine equivalent to the value of about three pints. On the other hand, if he is lucky he will get his name in the local paper, and the publicity is cheap at the price. No visitor to Ireland should lose any opportunity to watch this thrilling and entertaining game. It is the favorite sport of the nation.

(The pubs are closed in the Republic, by the way, on Christmas Day and Good Friday. We can live with this, just.)

## The Irish at Play

I have already mentioned horses. Other sports popular in Ireland, apart from racing, are hurling, Gaelic football and bowling. These are all varieties of sports played by other nations, but we have adapted our own forms of them.

Hurling is a sort of field hockey which we trace back to our Celtic ancestors, but it bears about the same relation to field hockey as ice hockey does to roller-skating. It is extremely fast and frequently ferocious. It is no accident that prowess on the hurling field is regarded as a supreme qualification for election to public office. Indeed a recent prime minister, Jack Lynch, covered himself in glory playing for Cork. A man who has played for Cork, or Kerry, or Tipperary, or Dublin, is thought to be eminently capable of dealing with anything which fate and the spite of other politicians can throw at him.

Quite the most colorful spectacles in Ireland are the regional and all-Ireland finals in hurling and Gaelic football, but local matches, where every person who watches as well as every player, is intimately known to every other, are enthusiastic and heroically convivial occasions.

Gaelic football is rather like a cross between soccer and American football and Rugby all mixed up together. Some say it lacks the finesse of all three but this is not a point of view which would be acceptable to a fan and it is certainly not one which I would care to advance to a player.

The ancestry of the sport is dubious. Some say that it evolved in remote antiquity from certain barbarous practices associated with the beheading of defeated opponents and there are times when, watching the modern manifestation of the sport, it seems that this theory is grounded in solid fact and has not been forgotten by the players.

Our form of bowling (pronounced to rhyme with "howling") is equally idiosyncratic and, incidentally, illegal, though it would be a very unpopular policeman who tried to stop it, and I have never heard of one foolish enough to try.

It is played on country roads (hence the objection of the authorities, who think it may obstruct traffic) and consists of two teams of two men each competing in the throwing of a steel ball around a roughly circular course. The winning team requires the least number of throws.

Bowling is not therefore, on the face of it, a particularly sophisticated sport. But on close examination it becomes clear that a considerable degree of cunning and wit, as well as strength and agility, plus an intimate knowledge of the countryside, is required to win. Modest sums of money can be seen to change hands before and after each game, and a more pleasant way cannot be imagined of spending the afternoon than following the bowlers along four miles of country road, particularly if one has taken good advice and backed the winners.

## The Cultural Life of Ireland

The whole culture of Ireland is based on conviviality. The best works of Irish fiction concern persons of small importance, and not many of them. Painters who have worked in Ireland have most often successfully confined themselves to intimate subjects. Although we are an intensely musical nation, we have no great tradition of grand symphonic or operatic music. The chieftains and kings of ancient Ireland were in the habit of extending hospitality to poets and musicians, who were expected to entertain the assembled company at dinner, and it could be that our taste for culture on a small scale derives from an inherited memory of these festive, and frequently rowdy, celebrations.

Much of this tradition remains. If the Irish neglect the concert hall and the opera house, it could be because it is thought impolite to talk to one's neighbors during the course of performances in those places. We do not neglect the theater, but we may claim to have introduced the world to the concept of audience participation, our theaters having been the scene of notable riots when the gregarious instinct to take part in the proceedings got out of hand.

Other nations have local festivals, but I do not think any people have taken to the idea with our enthusiasm. There is scarcely a town, or even a village, anywhere in the island which has not thought of an excuse for an annual festivity. Some, in fact, manage several, with hardly a pause in between.

Wexford has an opera festival and Waterford, not to be outdone, has a *light* opera festival. Cork celebrates jazz and Dublin the theater. In Killorglin they capture a wild goat from the mountains and stick it in a cage on the top of a pole. No one has the faintest idea of the origin of that festival, but any excuse is good enough. There is a marriage fair in Lisdoonvarna, and there are two rival oyster-eating festivals in Galway. I came across a fishing festival once in a place called Moville, in Donegal. The fishing element consisted of two men sitting forlornly in a boat on the river, while the rest of the place got on with the real business of talking to one another.

We are always celebrating our own private festivals. It is how we live.

# THE IRISH STORY

## *A Fabric of Disharmony*

Ireland was already an island, cut off from Europe, when the first human inhabitants arrived around 8,000 years ago. These pioneers were mere hunters and gatherers of food, squatters on the seashore and the river banks, but they possessed the skill to make boats fit to brave the sea and the courage to set out on a venture of some peril. Before many centuries had passed, they were followed by other settlers with cattle and dogs, with a knowledge of how to clear patches of scrub and forest in order to till the soil and raise crops. These early settlers were derived from the old Paleolithic stocks of western Europe; they have left to the Irish of today the physical heritage of paler skins and a higher proportion of light-colored eyes than the people of any other area in the world. So began the continuous and profitable occupation of a land which offered much to primitive settlers—welcoming beaches, navigable rivers leading deep inland, lakes teeming with fish, woods full of game and with no dangerous animals (except wolves), a fertile soil and a mild climate.

Of the way of life of these Neolithic farmers through some 30 centuries very little is known. The archeologists can tell something about their dwellings and their burial methods, and there are fragments of their pottery and their stone tools and weapons in museums. But even the simplest facts concerning their daily round, even their language, must remain a mystery.

It was discovered that Ireland was rich in copper and in gold—copper for bronze tools and weapons and gold for coveted ornaments and jewelry.

Bronze tools and gold ornaments from Ireland were traded abroad, and the remote and primitive island began to make some stir in the trade and commerce of western Europe, sending out peddlers and merchants and attracting the adventurous, the skilled and the greedy to its shores. Irish bronze and gold objects from this early metal-working period have been found scattered all over western Europe.

## Cult of the Megaliths

About the same time as the first knowledge of metals, there came into Ireland one of the most remarkable phenomena in the history of the spread of culture, something analogous to the coming of Christianity more than 2,000 years later. This was the cult of the megaliths. During a period stretching over many centuries, huge tombs, mighty pillars and great ritual circles of massive stones were erected in all parts of the island, so solid and enduring that they still excite our admiration. These great stone monuments are, without doubt, the most wonderful and revealing relics of Ireland's ancestors. Problems of planning, of engineering, of mechanics, of the organization, direction and support of hundreds of workmen—all of these were met and overcome. Whether they were built by conqueror or native lord, by king or priest or sect, the megaliths demanded a degree of scientific knowledge and a command of material and moral resources only to be found in a vigorous and highly developed community. Sligo has an abundance of these relics in Carrowmore, easily seen from the main roads.

New cultural influences and population elements continued to arrive. Especially noteworthy are the changes in the type and form of weapons and ornaments around 600 B.C. and the coming of a knowledge of iron and of art styles clearly derived from continental Celtic sources around 250 B.C.

When, how, and in what numbers Celtic speaking peoples first came into Ireland is not known. There is no indication of any large-scale invasion. Nevertheless, at some time during the millennium preceding the Christian era, Celtic-speaking people did come into the island in strength sufficient to establish in it, as the ordinary speech of the inhabitants, that branch of Celtic which is the direct ancestor of the Gaelic still spoken today.

Of all the lands of western Europe, Ireland alone escaped invasion by the Romans, although, as Tacitus tells us, the Romans did cast envious glances across the narrow sea from their bases in Britain. One legion, they believed, would be sufficient to conquer Ireland. But no expedition was sent and Ireland was left to develop in its own way.

## Pre-Christian Society

Its society was based upon the small local kingdom, the extent of which was roughly that of a barony and the ruler of which, although he was called *Rí,* king, was no more than a petty lord. Above him was a hierarchy of kings of larger areas, all (in theory) under a High King of all Ireland. A centralized authority seldom was, or could be, enforced, while even the provincial and lesser kings were seldom certain of the support of the small, local kingdoms. Under the local kings were the free landowners, who owed their tribute and loyalty and owned the land in their own right, as individuals or family or other groups. The settlement pattern was dominated by the isolated holding, the homestead and land of the free farmer, of which the "ring-forts" of today are the remains. There were no towns or cities, no urban organizations independent of the countryside. Besides the free farmers, there were bondsmen or peasant tenantry, who may have been as numerous as the free men, but who had a lower place in society.

Ireland at the beginning of the Christian era, although lacking in centralized political authority, was united by a common language, a common culture and a common tradition. Members of the learned and professional classes could pass freely from one kingdom to the next throughout the island. There were schools of poetry, of medicine and of law, with long courses of training and numerous grades of proficiency, and the learned men from these schools seem to have possessed something of a sacred or magical character which raised them far above the status of common men.

Poetry was highly valued, and the reciters of epic tales and of poems in praise of their patrons were richly rewarded. Medicine was based upon sound hygienic rules and much herbal lore, together with some skill in manipulation and surgery; indeed the patients under the care of these ancient physicians had a very much greater chance of survival and cure than the inmates of an 18th-century hospital in a great European city. Law was based on a long series of legal precedents and depended upon public respect for legal forms for its efficacy; there were no court officers, police or prisons, but the sacred character of the law ensured compliance with the judge's ruling or the ostracization of the offender who refused to submit.

Skilled artists and craftsmen were highly respected; a master gold-worker or weapon-smith might dine at the table of a king. Such examples of their art which survive (mainly metalwork) show a very high degree of technical skill and artistic taste.

Outside the professional classes the social standing of the individual depended upon his property and possessions, descending from powerful and wealthy landowners to laborers, serfs and slaves. A woman might own cattle and moveable property in her own right, and retain the ownership after marriage; she could inherit her father's land for her lifetime if he had no son, the land reverting to a male relative after her death. Whether married or single, she could take legal action on her own account, and could testify against her husband in court. Monogamy was usual, although polygamy and concubinage were recognized, with legally-defined rights and privileges for both lesser wife and concubine. The lot of female slaves, however, was hard while paganism lasted—the *cumal* (slave-woman) was a recognized standard of value, equal to three cows.

Wars frequently occurred between the small kingdoms, but were little more than manly sport. In much the same way, cattle-raiding was common, and the prowess of the successful cattle raider was lauded in the tales and poems of the time. Indeed, it appears that a king, on his succession, was largely obliged to prove his leadership and courage by a successful foray on his neighbors' herds. Greater kings tried to ensure the loyalty of their subordinates by taking hostages; a hostage was treated with all the honor due to his social position as long as the pact was kept, but could legally be slain if it was broken.

## Christianity

Into this remarkable blending of culture and residual barbarism, this unique non-Roman civilization of western Europe, came in the 5th century a new force—Christianity. Many aspects of Irish life must have appeared strange to the Roman-trained missionaries, and they, no doubt, had many misgivings in regard to their venturing into a society where the familiar forms of Roman law and organization were unheeded and the prestige and authority of the still-mighty Roman Empire disregarded. Nevertheless, their path proved an easy one, for the conversion of Ireland to the Christian faith was accompanied by two very unusual phenomena. In the first place, the people of Ireland accepted the new religion readily, even with enthusiasm. Not one single Christian martyrdom is recorded in the conversion of Ireland, nor, apparently, was there any persecution of the few reluctant pagans. In the second place, the Christian missionaries showed no hostility to the native forms of learning, and the traditional schools of literature, law and leechcraft continued to flourish side by side with the centers of Christian teaching. Before long, Irish monks and churchmen were composing poetry in the native language and granting their patronage to native artists.

In the centuries which followed, there was a great blossoming of monastic fervor, with hundreds of Irish men and women devoting themselves to the service of God as monks and nuns; while local lords rivaled each other for the prestige of endowing monasteries. These establishments were notable for the rigor and austerity of their discipline, with much prayer, fasting, hospitality and good works. But the things of the mind were not neglected. Far from it—the larger monasteries became great centers of learning with hundreds, even thousands of scholars enrolled. These schools taught not only Christian theology, but all the learning of the time, both Roman and Irish, with literature, classical learning, philosophy, astronomy, cosmography and other sciences.

Soon the tide was flowing outwards again, with Irish monks and scholars pressing into Britain and Europe, preaching the gospel, founding schools and monasteries. Some were to become great bishops and abbots or the friends and counselors of kings, others to be mere wandering scholars disturbing foreign schools with their disputations.

## Enter the Vikings

In the year 795, a terrible band from the sea came ashore on the island north of Dublin which is now Lambay, sailing away again with all the loot and captives they could seize and leaving behind only corpses and smoking desolation. These were the Norse Vikings, and year after year the raids continued, extending farther and farther inland all around Ireland until no place was safe. The monasteries were their special prey, and the precious objects given by pious or repentant kings and lords made a rich booty; Scandinavian museums today show a profusion of such objects excavated from Viking graves.

At first the light weapons and happy-go-lucky fighting methods of the Irish proved no match for the mail-clad and heavily armed raiders, who soon began to establish bases on the coast, some of which developed into towns. Dublin, Cork, Waterford, Wexford and Limerick began as Viking strongholds. Some of these fortresses grew into towns and their occupants began to turn from freebooting to relatively peaceful trading, while around them and up some of the river valleys, Norsemen and Danes began to settle as farmers on land more fertile than any had known at home. Some of these settlements made alliances with local Irish kings, and there was intermarriage between the new settlers and the native population. At times, there was fierce, bloody warfare, with the Irish gaining skill and experience in the fighting methods of the newcomers.

Finally, more than 200 years after the first raids, the Norse attempt to subdue Ireland was broken at Clontarf, in 1014, by King Brian. But so mixed had loyalties and expediencies become by this time that a large part of the Norse army at Clontarf was made up of Irish allies, while the valor of King Brian's Norse contingents contributed much to his victory. Both wings of the Irish army on that day were led by Norse chieftains.

In one sense the victory of Clontarf was a disaster for the Irish, for King Brian, the only leader powerful enough to weld the whole country into one strong unit, was killed in the battle, and for the next 150 years a succession of kings from various provinces and ruling families tried in vain to set themselves up as supreme ruler. Political disunity and intermittent warfare continued. Nevertheless, there was a revival of prosperity, of learning and of the arts. Churches were built and new monasteries established in the continental fashion. A series of synods regulated church affairs; the most important, at Kells in 1152, established the hierarchy as Ireland knows it today.

At the end of the 12th century a provincial king, Diarmuid MacMurrough of Leinster, was driven from his throne because of his evil life. He appealed for help to Henry II, King of England, who gave him leave to enlist volunteers among his followers, and in 1169, bands of Normans arrived in Ireland to support McMurrough's cause. Next year, larger bands followed, and made war with such success that in a few months they had overrun the greater part of Leinster and Munster. Hot upon their heels came Henry II, loudly proclaiming his zeal for the reform of manners and morals in Ireland. He had provided himself with some form of authority from the pope. The authenticity of this has long been questioned, but Henry's acceptance by the Irish bishops indicates some form of papal approval, and most of the Irish kings and lords came to Henry at Dublin and submitted to him.

### The English and Norman Role

Henry claimed feudal lordship, the ownership of the land of Ireland and the right to let it to his nobles, Norman or Irish, in return for loyalty and service, and to deprive them of it if these were withheld. But under Irish law, the land was owned by individuals or groups, and the king or lord had no right whatever to take it from them. English law said that the subject must bow to the king's will and give up his land; Irish law said that the owner should resist, even by force, any such attempt to rob him.

For the next 350 years, Norman families held about half the land of Ireland, acquired by conquest, by marriage, by royal grant or by mere swindling. In some areas, they ejected the old population and settled their own followers on the land. In other places, they accepted the common people as their tenants. These Norman lords had few ties of loyalty or tradition to any country or language and readily adapted to the new environment. Soon the English authorities were passing laws to force them to give up Irish dress, language and manners, and especially forbidding their intermarriage with the Irish, for the most part in vain, for there rapidly developed an Irish-Norman society in which nothing but the family name distinguished the son of a Norman father and an Irish mother from the son of an Irish father and a Norman mother.

Each succeeding English king claimed the Lordship of Ireland, but was too occupied with foreign and civil wars to back the claim with any real force, while on the other hand the quarrelsome lords and chieftains in Ireland could never be brought to unite in a completely independent Irish kingdom. Were it not for their rivalries, they might easily have achieved such a kingdom at almost any time between the beginning of the 13th century and the end of the 15th. A bid for the throne of Ireland was made in 1315 by Edward Bruce, brother of King Robert Bruce of Scotland, but he failed to get sufficient Irish support and was defeated and killed in battle after three years of bloody and devastating war.

Even after the defeat of Bruce, no real peace came to Ireland. The main cause of contention was the possession of lands. The great lords, whether of Norman or Irish stock, were constantly at each others' throats, and peace and order reigned only where the local lord or prince was strong enough to enforce it.

So things went on, with neither side prevailing, with much turmoil, but with much noble patronage of the church and of the arts and sciences. The area under the effective control of the crown shrank until, by the late 15th century, it consisted only of a small territory around Dublin, called the English Pale because it had to be fortified with a great bank and palisade to keep unwelcome visitors out, and the dubious loyalty of a few towns overawed by royal garrisons.

## Henry VII Wins Out

Peace and prosperity were returning to England under the stern rule of Henry VII. His son, Henry VIII, inherited a rich, strong and united kingdom, and was able to turn his attention to Ireland. At first he tried to win over the Irish lords by what he called "sober ways, politic drifts and amiable persuasions." He might well have succeeded but for two obstacles which proved insuperable. In the first place, he claimed the right of a feudal monarch to dispose the land of Ireland to those friendly to him, while ancient Irish law, which now had been adopted by many of the great Norman-Irish families, denied his right to this.

The other great obstacle was the outcome of King Henry's break with Rome. Hitherto, the English kings claimed the lordship of Ireland through the pope's feudal grant, but Henry had sacrificed even the dubious legality of this. He now proclaimed himself King of Ireland by right of conquest, and faced the task of effectively conquering Ireland to make good his claim. His methods were to smash down all opposition and then to drive the "rebel" lords and landholders from their estates and grant these to his own loyal followers, whether Irish or English. This policy was continued by his daughters, Queen Mary and Queen Elizabeth.

The Reformation had made progress in England, and under Elizabeth all effective opposition to it was snuffed out. In Ireland, things were vastly different, for both the Irish and Anglo-Irish remained steadfast in religious allegiance to Rome. During the reign of Queen Elizabeth, her opponents in Ireland were fighting for religious as well as political liberty which, in the atmosphere of the time, added new dimensions of bitterness to the struggle. Because there was still no unity of purpose or action among the great lords of Ireland, they were defeated piecemeal.

Elizabeth's death in 1603 coincided almost exactly with the extinguishing of the last vestiges of Irish independence. The conquest was complete, and the Irish, their land desolated by war and racked by famine, their old lords banished or reduced to the status of petty squires, their trade and commerce destroyed and their religion forbidden, were left to the mercy of the conquerors.

A few years later, the surviving princes and lords of Ulster, who had been restored to their own estates by treaty, became fearful for their lives and secretly fled the country. This gave the government the excuse to seize vast tracts of land in Ulster, to eject the remaining landholders and to replace them with English and Scottish settlers, all stout Protestants and all loyal to the crown. This was the beginning of the Ulster Question which has bedeviled Irish affairs ever since.

## Civil Wars

Ireland settled down to an uneasy peace, rudely broken in 1641 by a long-planned insurrection which had the dual goals of religious freedom and the restoration of the confiscated lands to their former owners. The first victims of the fighting were the new settlers of Ulster; most of these were driven from their holdings and many of them killed. For 12 years war raged, the combatants splintering into numerous factions. There were "Old Irish" who dreamed of independence, "Old English" who would give loyalty to the crown if their religion and their possessions were secure, Royalists and Parliamentarians who supported the rival factions in the English Civil War and Scottish settlers who followed the Covenant. In the various stages of the war, each of these parties was alternately allied to and fighting against each of the others. On no side was there unity of policy or action, until Oliver Cromwell finished the war by bringing his victorious Parliamentary army to Ireland and wiping out all opposition. This final stage of the war sank to a new depth of horror, with famine and massacre, enormous destruction of property, hundreds of homeless men, women and children rounded up and shipped as slaves to the Sugar Islands, and finally with the wholesale confiscation of the lands of all those who had opposed the Parliament.

The restoration of Charles II to the throne of England brought little relief in Ireland. There was a relaxation of active religious persecution, but those who had been loyal to the king's father were dismayed when neither lands nor position were restored to them. The Irish had greater hopes on the accession of Charles's brother, James II, who was a Catholic, and gave him their support in the civil war which developed between him and the other claimant to the throne, William of Orange. William poured troops and material into Ireland while the supporters of James were disappointed in their hopes of massive help from Louis XIV of France and, after two years of resistance, surrendered on terms which became famous as the Treaty of Limerick. This ambiguous document appeared to guarantee many rights and privileges, but within a very few years these were set aside and a code of laws—the iniquitous Penal Laws—was introduced which denied even the semblance of freedom to the Catholics (who formed the great majority of the Irish people), depriving them of all access to property rights, franchise, education, office or appointment, however humble. They bore heavily, too, on the Nonconformists, those Protestants who did not accept the rule and discipline of the state church, denying them privilege, office and education unless they conformed.

## The Ascendancy and Union

The 18th century began in Ireland with all power in the hands of that small section of the population which gave full loyalty to the English crown and the state church—the landowners and officeholders who became known as the Ascendancy and who used religious differences to hold wealth and privilege in their own hands and deny them to Catholics and Nonconformists. However, as the century wore on, a more enlightened attitude spread, partly because of the liberal ideas propagated by such men as Swift and Berkeley, partly because of continued discrimination on the part of Britain against Irish policies and Irish trade. Towards the end of the century, the realization of their treatment as second-class citizens brought a demand for legislative independence and free trade. Faced with the threat of force, Britain yielded. Ireland was declared an independent kingdom under the British crown. Trade, industry and agriculture began to flourish and the worst of the Penal Laws were repealed or relaxed, while some of the Protestant Patriots went so far as to agitate for complete religious freedom for all denominations.

The French Revolution had its effect in Ireland, and a strong movement towards complete independence in an Irish Republic on the model of France began, in which people of all classes and all faiths were involved. This was opposed on all sides, by religious leaders who feared the spread of atheistic liberalism, by the wealthy anxious for their lands and possessions and by convinced or opportunist British loyalists. Matters came to a head in 1798, when the republican party, the United Irishmen, relying on the promise of help from France, came out in open insurrection, only to be defeated and crushed with great severity and much bloodshed. British statesmen now succeeded, by a combination of threats, promises and flagrant bribery, in getting the Irish parliament to vote itself out of existence, and in bringing Ireland under the direct control of the London parliament, in the Act of Union of 1800.

The effects of this upon Ireland were, for a time, delayed, as the Napoleonic Wars ensured a continued demand for Irish products. The coming of peace brought depression in Ireland, with rising population and falling resources and standards of living, culminating in the Great Famine of 1846–49, which caused the death or emigration of two and a half million people. Irish leaders became more convinced than ever that the only hope of their country's well-being lay in some form of separation from Britain.

The majority believed that this could be brought about by constitutional means and agitated for the repeal of the Union and for Home Rule, while a minority held to the doctrine that only physical force could win independence. Irish policies swayed between these two ideas, with constant demands for the one in the British parliament, and a series of insurrections and disturbances to achieve the other, both without success. Indeed, practically the only success enjoyed by the Irish reformers came in 1829 with the passage of the Catholic Emancipation Act, which allowed Catholics to practise their religion freely.

Agitation also continued throughout the 19th century to improve the lot of Irish farmers. They had long suffered under an outmoded landlord system characterized by rackrenting (demanding nearly the full value of the property annually) and eviction. This agitation grew to such proportions towards the end of the century that the British government was forced to yield and to introduce legislation which enabled tenant farmers to buy out their holdings and become independent proprietors of their land.

During the late-19th century, men like Charles Stewart Parnell led Ireland in attempts to achieve Home Rule. But for his involvement in a divorce in 1890, which split the Irish Parliamentary Party in two, Parnell and his followers might have succeeded.

## Partial Independence

The political agitation for independence continued into the 20th century, and finally succeeded, on the eve of the first Great War, in having passed in the British parliament an act giving Home Rule—a limited degree of independence—to Ireland. Opposition to this measure now came to a head, with a strong body of opinion in the eastern counties of Ulster, spearpointed by the Orange Order, actively preparing to resist it by force of arms. This was followed by a movement among the Nationalists of the greater part of Ireland to arm and organize themselves to support the decision of the British parliament, by force if necessary. The months before the outbreak of the 1914–18 war saw three different armies in Ireland—the British army in solid occupation, the Ulster Volunteers pledged to resist Home Rule and the Irish Volunteers determined to enforce it.

Civil war seemed imminent, but the outbreak of the greater conflict gave British statesmen the opportunity of shelving the whole issue on the pretext of the prior claim of the war against Germany. Immediate and massive propaganda was put into effect in Ireland, calling for help for little Belgium and the rights of small nations, and hundreds of thousands of Irishmen of all shades of belief joined the British army.

One body of opinion, however, stood aloof from the war effort and maintained that its loyalty was to Ireland alone. This consisted of the convinced republicans and the socialists who were weary of starvation wages and bad working conditions. At Easter 1916 these, although doubtful of universal popular support, came out in open insurrection, seized the center of Dublin and proclaimed an Irish Republic. Numbering only about 1,000 men, they were defeated in a week of bitter fighting in which a great part of the center of the city was destroyed by fire and artillery. At first the public reaction was one of shocked hostility, but a long-drawn-out series of executions of the leaders, culminating in the shooting of the crippled Sean MacDermott and socialist leader James Connolly, brought the reaction of sympathy and support. (Connolly was dying of gangrene from a leg shattered in the fighting and had to be propped up in a chair before the firing squad.)

For the next two years, the British authorities in Ireland alternated between measures of coercion and conciliation, neither of which bore fruit.

Republican opinion spread and hardened, and was greatly stimulated by a misguided attempt on the part of Britain to force general conscription on Ireland, a measure against which the Catholic bishops and other influential people of moderate leanings pledged their support. Home Rule and the promise of it lost their meaning in the face of such coercion, and in the general election at the end of 1918, republican candidates won 73 out of 105 seats, while the Home Rule party (which had held 80 seats) secured only six, the other 26 being gained by Unionists, nearly all in east Ulster. In the same year, Sinn Féin chose Éamon de Valera as head of a provisional government, confirming the concept of the republic proclaimed in 1916.

## The Irish Revolution

The die was now cast. In January 1919, those of the elected republicans who were not imprisoned met in Dublin, declared themselves to be an Irish parliament, ratified the 1916 declaration of an Irish Republic and pledged themselves to defend it by force if necessary. They appointed delegates to the peace conference in Paris to claim the rights of small nations for Ireland, but these delegates were refused a hearing. Some months later, the republican parliament was declared illegal by the British authorities and driven underground, where its various ministries continued to operate in secret in spite of all efforts to suppress them.

With two rival governments, a state of war was inevitable, and under the circumstances, this was a bitter and bloody little war; on the one side of ambush, assassination and attack on outposts, on the other of reprisals, executions, burning of property and imprisonment without trial. In parts of the country, the populace gave active support to the republican forces. To counter this, the British authorities, in a mistaken policy which only panic can explain, reinforced their armed police in Ireland with terrorist bodies popularly known as the Black and Tans and Auxiliaries, whose murderous savagery and indiscipline nearly put an end to all hope of a settlement. But moderate opinion in England, in growing shame at what was being done in Ireland, prevailed at last. In July 1921, a truce and an invitation to discussion was offered to the Irish leaders and accepted.

A treaty which really satisfied nobody was proposed, and was accepted in the Irish parliament by a small majority. The main cause of dissatisfaction was the exclusion of the six northeastern counties from the jurisdiction of Dublin. These six counties were constituted into the separate state of Northern Ireland, in union with Britain, but with limited local powers. The rest of Ireland became the Irish Free State, with dominion status similar to that of Canada. Uncompromising republican elements would have no part in this and challenged the new state in arms in a civil war which lasted for some months only, but left deep and lasting bitterness.

The two parts of Ireland went their separate ways. Northern Ireland was granted its own parliament at Stormont, subordinate to the parliament at Westminster. The Unionists, who wished to remain an integral part of the United Kingdom, did not ask for a legislature of their own but, having been given one, made vigorous and sometimes ruthless use of it. The Irish Nationalists wanted a united country and would have nothing to do with the Stormont parliament. As a consequence they were discriminated against.

In the Free State of Southern Ireland (the Irish name *Saorstat Eireann* was borrowed from the old Orange Free State, an irony not lost on the

Republicans who opposed its very existence), political divisions formed according to which side people fought on during the civil war that followed the 1921 Treaty of Independence granted by the British.

Two principal parties emerged. Their evolution was complex, but, to put it simply, the party that originally rejected the treaty became, under the leadership of Eamon de Valera, Fianna Fail (Soldiers of Destiny), while the party that accepted it became Fine Gael (which roughly translates as the Tribe of the Irish). Other parties appeared on the political stage, most notably the left-wing Labor Party, which has been in power in coalition with Fine Gael. In 1985 came the formation of a new party, the Progressive Democrats, consisting of elements from all three main parties. Ireland elects its parliamentarians by the electoral process of proportional representation.

## An Uncertain Future

Politics in the Republic is based largely on local issues and squabbles. Since 1932, power has oscillated between Fianna Fail and various coalitions made up of a combination of parties. Fine Gael has a European-oriented Social Democratic wing but also tolerates, with great fondness, an elderly contingent who were the champions of the Spanish and Portuguese dictators Franco and Salazar. Fianna Fail, in spite of its rigorous adherence to constitutional and non-violent politics, contains an element, sometimes noisy, whose principal passion is an extreme nationalism. Both main parties, whatever their faults, have behaved with great responsibility when in government.

Since 1979, the Republic's main tension has been a personal one between Charles J. Haughey and Garret Fitzgerald, respective leaders of the Fianna Fail and Fine Gael parties. As Prime Minister, each has had to face considerable unemployment, an unpleasant national debt and the renewed drain of emigration.

Following the General Election in March 1987, which brought Haughey and Fianna Fail to power again, Fitzgerald resigned as leader of Fine Gael and was replaced by Alan Dukes. A new political grouping, the Progressive Democrats, or Pee-Dees as they are called, got off to a good start in their first election, but their numbers are not yet great enough to affect the balance of power which remains in the hands of Fianna Fail and Fine Gael.

As to Northern Ireland, it is difficult to predict what will happen. The accord of November 1985, known as the Anglo-Irish Treaty, allows the Republic a say in the affairs of the north. It was greeted with rage by northern Unionists and has met with no huge enthusiasm in the south. But it is certainly the hinge upon which the whole future of the island depends.

# A WAY WITH WORDS

*Music—and Blarney—in Irish Literature*

Ireland is one of the few countries in the world where one can happily admit to being a writer. The American travel writer Paul Theroux states, when asked on his travels, that he is a teacher. He should go to Ireland, where to claim you are a writer illicits a nod of acceptance while a management consultant receives the bewilderment and exaggerated respect that a writer or poet could expect elsewhere.

### An Abundance of Authors

Ireland has produced a disproportionately large number of internationally famous authors for a country of her size. Wherever you are in Ireland, the literary heritage is never far away. In Dublin you will find James Joyce's Liffey, Dean Swift's cathedral, and Trinity College, alma mater of the 18th-century Anglo-Irish writers. An anthology of Irish verse is a travel guide in itself: Yeats opens up the county of Sligo; the Aran Islands were the inspiration for J.M. Synge; there's Frank O'Connor's Cork; and Castletownshend, home of Somerville and Ross; Patrick Kavanagh's Monaghan; Oliver Goldsmith's Lissoy; and Brian Merriman's Feakle.

Of course not everyone in Ireland has read James Joyce, but everyone has heard of him. Most people are familiar with at least some of the works of George Bernard Shaw and William Butler Yeats—two of Ireland's Nobel prize winners—while the third, Samuel Beckett, remains something of an enigma to all but the most avid theater-goers among his countrymen.

The works of Dion Boucicault, Oscar Wilde, John Millington Synge, Sean O'Cassey, Hugh Leonard and Brian Friel are frequently staged by both amateurs and professionals, and regularly appear on television.

Today even the smallest bookshop carries a large selection of books under the label "Irish interest." The works of Flann O'Brien, Patrick McGinley, Edna O'Brien and many others compete successfully with imported English and American best-sellers. Whether they read them or not, the Irish buy more books per head of population than any other country in the English-speaking world.

## The Men of Art

Ireland warmly accommodates her artists. Creative writers, artists and composers who can prove that their work is of recognized artistic merit are exempted from income tax. They can be voted a member of *Aosdána,* a self-electing academy of distinguished practitioners of the arts, modelled on the Celtic social order. These *aes dána*—men of letters—are eligible for a government salary if their earnings do not allow them to dedicate themselves full time to creative work. The *Aosdána* includes both well-established writers such as Anthony Cronin, Sean O'Faolain and Mary Lavin and members of the younger generation: Paul Durcan (b. 1944), Paul Muldoon (b. 1951) and Neil Jordan (b. 1951).

## Yeats and the Birth of Modern Irish Literature

W.B. Yeats (1865–1939) has been called "the best poet since Shakespeare" by the contemporary poet Derek Mahon. Yeats' work marks both the beginning of modern Irish literature and the absorption into that literature of the legends and poems of the Celtic past.

Yeats' early lyrics have an immediate appeal. His use of Irish folk and fairy tales stemmed from his decision to write about Ireland for an Irish audience. That the resulting verse is more in tune with the activities of the English pre-Raphaelites than anything Celtic makes it none the less charming:

> Come away, O human child!
> To the waters and the wild
> With a faery, hand in hand,
> For the world's more full of weeping than you can understand.

By 1893 Yeats was making increasing use of material from the Gaelic legends—the Cuchulian saga and the tales of the Fianna—and giving the old material a new dimension. At this time he also discovered the potency of the place names of his native Sligo: the lake isle of Innisfree, the sands of Lissadell, the hill of Lugnagall. He started to use them with an effectiveness that is characteristic of much Irish writing both before and after Yeats.

## The Language Question

"If you would know Ireland—body and soul—you must read its poems and stories," wrote Yeats in 1891. By then he was actively involved in the Gaelic Literary Revival, a movement that led among other things, to the foundation of the Abbey Theater. Pioneering work by Douglas Hyde (who later became the first president of Ireland), George Sigerson, T.W. Rolleston, Lady Gregory and a host of others rekindled interest in the Irish language, its literature and folklore.

The Irish language badly needed such a boost. The Flight of the Earls in 1602 marked the start of 200 years of turmoil during which the Irish and the English languages and ways of life vied for supremacy. The Act of Union in 1800 saw the start of the triumph of all things English.

The 18th century is characterized by the demise of the Gaelic poetic tradition and the far more prolific rise of literature written in English, often by second- or third-generation descendents of English settlers—Jonathan Swift, William Congreve, George Farquhar, Richard Steele, Richard Brinsley Sheridan, Maria Edgeworth and Oliver Goldsmith among others. These "Anglo-Irish" writers contributed considerably to the English language, bringing with them Gaelic idioms and the rhythms of Irish speech.

The rapid spread of English Language National Schools from 1832 onwards consolidated the position of English as the language of the educated classes. Many people continued to speak Irish at home (and did so well into the 20th century) but official policy in the mid-19th century encouraged the mastery of English from childhood. English was the language of politics, law, education and commerce, and those who wished to advance themselves had to use it.

## Poets and Patriots

The close link between the Gaelic Literary Revival (often called the Celtic Twilight) and the uprising against the British at Easter 1916 is no accident, as a generation had became aware of the beauty and power of their heritage. Several leaders executed for their part in the uprising were poets of some note. Thomas MacDonagh, Patrick Pearse and Joseph Plunkett all produced verse of lasting merit. The brief, intense lyrics of Pearse shine with their poignant, prophetic quality.

But their work is overshadowed by that of Yeats. By 1916 the romantic young poet of the early lyrics had become a well-known public figure, and had already rejected a knighthood by the British government (while accepting a civil list pension from the same source). Yeats held a low opinion of the verse of Pearse, Plunkett and MacDonagh, and wrote of having passed them "with a nod of the head or polite meaningless words." In his verse:

> The horse that comes from the road,
> The rider, the birds that range
> From cloud to tumbling cloud,
> Minute by minute they change. . . .

More specifically:

> I write it out in a verse—
> MacDonagh and Macbride
> And Connolly and Pearse
> Now and in time to be,

Wherever green is worn,
Are changed, changed utterly:
A terrible beauty is born.

In that final line, "A terrible beauty is born," Yeats' reaction to the deeds of his fellow poets rises above the events that inspired the poem to become a profound meditation on the ambivalent nature of heroism.

## A Nation Once Again

It is one of the great ironies of history that the men who led the Easter Rising of 1916 were, in the words of their poetic successor, Austin Clarke, "more concerned with the literary problems of the time than with political propaganda."

The execution, or "martyrdom," of these leaders by the British military unleashed a torrent of anti-British sentiment that persisted far beyond the War of Independence and the establishment of the Irish Free State. Not only did the excessive patriotism of the years following 1916 produce much bad literature (including excrutiatingly sentimental ballads), but in certain sections of the community patriotism combined with religiosity and prudish gentility to produce a brand of cultural vandalism that justified the destruction or suppression of any part of the national heritage not conforming to a narrow definition of "Irishness."

The Censorship Act of 1929 is a typical product. It enabled books to be banned on the flimsiest of grounds; usually a vague accusation of indecency by some self-appointed defender of public morals was enough. One such book, *The Tailor and Ansty* by Eric Cross, is a charming, honest and thoroughly inoffensive account of the author's friendship with two Irish-speaking characters, the tailor of Gougane Bara and his wife Anastasia. The tailor's earthy humor, a vital relic of that same Gaelic heritage that the new State sought to promote, was too much for the pious readers of 1942. Not only was the book banned, but the elderly couple of the title were physically assaulted in their cottage by a gang of self-righteous "do-gooders."

So many Irish writers found themselves on the banned list that being banned became a matter of prestige. It also did wonders for book sales abroad, and a smuggled copy of James Joyce's *Ulysses* in Dublin of the '50s was the ultimate status symbol.

Frank O'Connor's translation of *The Midnight Court,* the 18th-century comic masterpiece by Brian Merriman, caused an uproar. The reaction to the uninhibited discussion by a group of witty, articulate women on sex, within and without marriage, caused O'Connor's friend, James Plunkett, to say:

"When some opponents in an effort to clear the good name of Irish literature suggested that the translation was entirely O'Connor's own work, Frank regretted it wasn't true, but remarked that it was the only compliment Ireland had ever paid him. When a fund was started to erect a memorial over Merriman's grave in Feakle, despite the fact that President de Valera was the first subscriber, the Clare County Council wouldn't allow it. When the money collected was spent on publishing a new edition of the translation, that too was banned. Honour-and-Virtue was again triumphant, the suggestion that there was any kind of red blood in the Irish heritage was again stamped out. Things have changed now, I am glad to say, and a Merriman Summer School is attended regularly by the most respectable people."

O'Connor's translation can be read in its entirety in the Penguin Book of Irish Verse.

## Silence Cunning and Exile

James Joyce's reaction to the Censorship Act was "Silence Cunning and Exile." Sean O'Casey and Frank O'Connor found the literary atmosphere less restricting on foreign shores, and as late as 1956 Brendan Behan had to travel to London to find a producer for *The Quare Fellow*.

Joyce was joined in Paris by Samuel Beckett in 1932. The war years intervened, but when *Waiting for Godot* was finally produced in 1953 it became clear that Beckett's voice was to prove as important for contemporary theater as Joyce's had been for writers of prose.

Literary life in Dublin during World War II centered around a magazine called *The Bell.* It was founded by Sean O'Faolain and edited by him until 1946. Many of O'Faolain's and Frank O'Connor's masterly short stories first appeared in the publication, as did the work of Elizabeth Bowen (in the Anglo-Irish tradition) and the contrasting Patrick Kavanagh, who left a small farm in County Monaghan to bring the voice of the "peasant" to the Dublin literary scene. The magazine also fostered the early work of Bryan MacMahon, whose latest collection of stories, *The Sound of Hooves,* gives a vivid picture of rural life in the '80s.

## The Language of Humor

Brian O'Nolan (1911–1966) has many other pseudonyms, but he is best known as novelist Flann O'Brien and newspaper columnist Myles na gCopaleen, whose column *Cruiskeen Lawn* ran for 25 years in the *Irish Times.* O'Nolan's major strength derives from his obsession with words; he was bilingual in English and Irish and had a competent knowledge of several other languages. *The Best of Myles,* a compilation of *Cruiskeen Lawn* pieces, is remarkable for its elaborate puns, linguistic jokes, satirical invention and unforgettable characters (most notably The Brother—the archetypal know-all bore). But it also has a serious purpose in its analysis of the debasement and misuse of language and its spirited crusade against the cliché.

However, it was the novels that established O'Nolan's reputation. *At-Swim-Two-Birds* was hardly noticed when it first appeared in 1939, and he could not find a publisher for *The Third Policeman,* which remained unpublished until after his death. *An Béal Bocht (The Poor Mouth)* appeared in 1941 and was an immediate success, but only among the country's minority of Irish speakers. The enthusiastic reception of *At-Swim-Two-Birds* at its reissue in 1960 spurred O'Nolan to finish *The Hard Life* (1961) and *The Dalkey Archive* (1964). Since then, new generations of readers have discovered his anarchic and highly imaginative world.

## The Irishness of Irish Writing

Irish literature developed its distinctive traits largely because of the country's physical and political isolation. Not even Julius Caesar considered Ireland worth conquering. Centuries later, Ireland remained the only country in Europe uninfluenced by the artistic and intellectual excitement of the Renaissance. Its isolation, combined with the existence of two languages and two cultures, has produced a literature with an exceptionally strong national identity that persists in spite of mass communication and the increasingly cosmopolitan atmosphere of today's Irish society.

The Irish landscape and weather have been a constant and important influence on Irish writing, with characters encountering lashing, teeming pouring rain or silent, creeping, penetrating mist. Consider Brendan Kennelly's translation of an anonymous 8th-century lyric, *The Viking Terror:*

> There's a wicked wind tonight,
> Wild upheaval in the sea;
> No fear now that the Viking hordes
> Will terrify me.

Seamus Heaney's *Exposure* highlights the strong sense of nature in Irish verse:

> It is December in Wicklow:
> Alders dripping, birches
> Inheriting the last light,
> The ash tree cold to look at.

Ireland's past has a place in the country's verse. Stand among the ruined churches, the stunted tower and gravestones innumerable by Shannon side, near Athlone, and recall Rolleston's rendering of *The Dead at Clonmacnois.* Here are its opening and closing verses, from the Irish of Angus O'Gillan.

> In a quiet water'd land, a land of roses,
> Stands Saint Keiran's city fair;
> And the warriors of Erin in their famous generations
> Slumber there.

> Many and many a son of Conn the Hundred fighter
> In the red earth lies at rest;
> Many a blue eye of Clan Colman the turf covers,
> Many a swan-white breast.

Place names, even the most unlikely ones, play an important part. Patrick Kavanagh evokes a far-off Monaghan townland by using its extremely unpoetic name, Mucker:

> In Ealing Broadway, London Town
> I name their several names

> Until a world comes to life—
> Morning, the silent bog,
> And the God of imagination waking
> In a Mucker fog.

Bryan MacMahon has compiled a list of names guaranteed to "fire the poetic imagination":

"Ballyvourney, Kanturk, Labasheeda, Cloone, Toorenamblath, Clonmacnoise, Athboy, Mononia, Tirawley, Corca Baiscin, Desmond, Tír Chonaill, Balashanny, Munster, Aghadoe, the Danish battle axe that is Wexford and the slender Gaelic-Norman blade of Ballyferriter."

## Irish Humor: Wit and Satire

Irish writing thrives on its use of humor. Irish literary humor depends more on wit and satire than on whimsy, and the wit is frequently savage. This is true equally of Gaelic and Anglo-Irish literature and possibly derives from the bardic tradition by which poets were hired to praise their patrons and curse their patrons' enemies; a well-crafted insult that everyone remembers is hard to live down. On being told that an enemy had written a book, James Joyce replied: "I should have been surprised to be told that he had read one." Similarly, Brendan Behan, on hearing that his slim brother Dominic had written a play: "Inside Dominic there is a little me struggling to get out."

Oliver St. John Gogarty was the last bard (if self-appointed). His lyrics won public praise from Yeats, but Gogarty was really better known for the sort of verse that is still circulated privately; even his serious verse is best when it has a bawdy tang.

He could parody Keats' "Silent upon a peak in Darien" with "Potent behind a cart with Mary Anne." But he could do much better than this. There is something of Joyce's gentler genius in Gogarty's poem that begins:

> I will live in Ringsend
>   With a red-headed whore,
> And the fanlight gone in
>   Where it lights the hall-door;

and ends

> And up the back garden
>   The sound comes to me
> Of the lapsing, unsoilable
>   Whispering sea.

In Anglo-Irish literature the first of the great satirists is Swift. The venom he directed at the English on behalf of his own country is equalled only by the savagery he aimed at Ireland. There is a recurring strain in Irish literature of savage criticism of the Irish themselves, who are frequently depicted as lazy, dishonest and incompetent. But because the criticism is usually expressed with sharp wit and a cunning observation of human foible, it is paradoxically regarded as affectionate.

Among the best humorists are Maria Edgeworth *(Castle Rackrent)*, Jonah Barrington *(Personal Sketches)*, Somerville and Ross and, perhaps the most savage of them all, Flann O'Brien.

Irish theater would scarcely exist without the element of wit. Congreve, Farquhar, Goldsmith, Sheridan, Boucicault, Wilde, Shaw, Synge and Behan were all accomplished humorists whose humor was based on wit.

Dublin is an excellent place for theater. The famous Abbey, now installed in a fine modern building, has a company of exceptionally talented actors, though in recent years it has been dogged by financial and artistic difficulties. The appointment of a new artistic director has raised hopes that the Abbey, and its smaller experimental auditorium, the Peacock, will enter a fruitful phase and return to its tradition of combining productions of the Irish classics—Synge, O'Casey, Behan—with exciting work by new playwrights.

The Gate Theater, founded by Hilton Edwards and Mícheál Macliammóir, is shared nowadays by several companies and offers a varied but fairly conventional repertoire. Much good new work has been staged at the Project Arts Center, and several other small venues in and around Dublin are seeking to emulate its formula.

Hugh Leonard is the most successful playwright of recent years, with hit shows on Broadway (a Tony Award for *Da* ) and in London. But at home his popularity is closely rivalled by Brian Friel. The long Broadway run of *Philadelphia Here I Come* established Friel's international reputation in the '60s. In the late '70s he decided to return to Derry where much of the best work outside Dublin is being produced. Friel formed the Derry-based Field Theater Company in 1980 with actor Stephen Rea and its premiere of his brilliant play *Translations* put the Company firmly on the theatrical map.

The most outstanding of the other provincial companies is the Druid Theater in Galway. Director Garry Hynes formed the company in a tiny pub theater in Galway and has now moved it to a larger, though still intimate, theater installed in a warehouse. The company has toured with a variety of productions including Shakespeare, Restoration comedy and little-known Irish works, but their biggest success to date is Synge's *Playboy of the Western World,* which received excellent reviews in London and Dublin in 1985.

The Beltable in Limerick, the Hawkswell in Sligo, and the newly expanded Triskel Arts Center in Cork are all places to watch.

## The New Generation

Seamus Heaney is the colossus of the poetry scene, though many would argue that John Montague is of equal stature. Thomas Kinsella, Brendan Kennelly, Richard Murphy, Sean Lucy, Desmond O'Grady and Derek Mahon have all earned solid reputations, while Padraic Fallon's work is posthumously gaining an appreciative readership.

Perhaps the most promising poet of the younger generation is Eavan Boland, who often exercises her talent on the ordinary events of everyday domestic life with startling effectiveness. Paul Durcan has an enthusiastic following among the young, who enjoy his lively, informal readings. But his use of jazz rhythms is not to everyone's taste.

Links between the Irish poetry scene and American academia are many and fruitful. Heaney teaches at Harvard for part of every year, and Kinsella at Philadelphia. Montague was born in Brooklyn, and O'Grady was friend and secretary to Ezra Pound in the great poet's last years. Academics such as Robert O'Driscoll in Canada and Thomas Flanagan and Eoin McKiernan in America ensure that there is a welcome on the reading circuit for Irish poets.

There is such a wealth of contemporary novelists that any list is bound to be incomplete and biased towards one's own favorites. Molly Keane, who burst into print at the age of 80 after over 30 years of silence, has had well-deserved success on both sides of the Atlantic with *Good Behaviour* and *Time After Time.* Her earlier novels, written under the pseudonym of M.J. Farrell, display the same cutting wit and sharp observation and are proving very popular in reissue. Liam O'Flaherty, another survivor from Molly's generation, is also enjoying a second round of acclaim, both for the early stories set in his birthplace, the Aran Islands, and his historical novel, *Famine.* James Plunkett's historical novels are worth investigating, especially *Strumpet City,* which combines a compelling story with a vivid evocation of life among Dublin's poor in 1913. William Trevor's work was brought to the attention of a wide audience with the television adaptation of *The Ballroom of Romance,* and it is the stories rather than his highly acclaimed novels that are being read and reread.

Jennifer Johnston is much admired for the verbal economy of her well-crafted novels. The best of these—*The Captains and the Kings, The Gates,* and *How Many Miles to Babylon*—are set in the declining world of the Anglo-Irish "big house" in the early years of this century. Aidan Higgins is recognized as the most interesting prose stylist to emerge since Beckett, and belongs as much to the European context as to an Irish one. Dermot Healy, author of the prize-winning *Fighting with Shadows* is a young novelist to watch. Healy, like Bernard Maclaverty, has tackled the theme of "the Troubles" in the north. Healy's approach is the more imaginative, but Maclaverty's short stories are superbly accomplished.

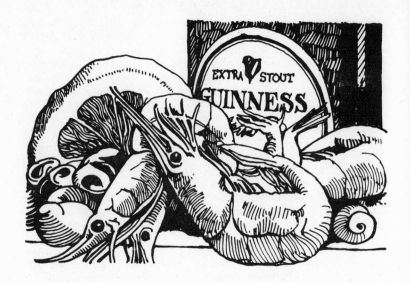

# EATING AND DRINKING

*Food for Thought and Fuel for Talk*

The Irish are justly famed for their hospitality, and you'll find there's no standing on ceremony here. Talking and drinking could be described as the main national pastimes, and the pub is central to Ireland's social life. While most Irish people prefer to drink in bars, indulging both their thirst and their gregarious instinct simultaneously, until quite recently the Irish preferred to do their eating at home. Restaurants were only there for tourists, traveling salesmen and the very occasional special occasion. All this is changing, and Ireland can now claim to have some of the best restaurants in the world. Alas, she also still has some of the very worst. The bad ones are becoming increasingly rare, but do not expect your experience of Irish catering to be without its low spots, though nowadays they should be few and far between.

### The Irish Potato

The Irish have long been known as hearty potato eaters. This stems to a great extent from harsher times, when the humble potato was the staple—and often the only—diet of poor crofters and farming folk. Put simply, when the potato crop failed, the people starved. Indeed, the failure of the potato crop was the principal cause of the Great Famine of 1846–49, which led to untold misery and to so many Irishmen seeking a new life across the ocean in America.

According to legend, when Sir Walter Raleigh originally brought potatoes from the New World, he planted the first European crop in Ireland.

(Sir Walter was also responsible for introducing the first cherry trees into Ireland, when he planted some saplings imported from the Canary Islands at Dungarvan, County Waterford.)

Potatoes boiled in their jackets, steamed dry and piled high on a serving dish are an essential part of the main meal in most Irish homes. The sight of a floury-textured boiled potato bursting out of its skin is quintessentially Irish, as is the tradition of smothering the peeled potato with thick slices of butter before eating it.

Left-over potatoes often appear at the next meal, sometimes in the form of potato cakes. These are made by frying a dough (made of self-raising flour and mashed potato) in butter until the outside is crisp and golden and the interior light and creamy. At its best, the humble potato cake is little short of ambrosial. Irish potato soup, too, is far more subtle and appetising than its name implies—a sustaining blend of potato, onion, bacon stock, cream, parsley and chives.

Irish stew features a combination of winter vegetables—usually onions, carrots and potatoes—simmered slowly in layers with a generous amount of lamb or mutton. Some people believe that it is best made with the cheapest cuts of meat, like neck, while others prefer to use a leg and cube the meat before cooking so that a boneless dish can be served.

Colcannon is another dish which varies from house to house, but is, like potato cakes, essentially a way to use up left-over potatoes. The cooked potatoes are diced and fried in butter with either onions and cabbage, or leeks. A generous portion of thick cream is poured over the pan just before serving.

## Traditional Fare

According to ancient tradition, Colcannon should be cooked at Hallowe'en and served with a gold ring, a thimble, a button and a silver sixpence concealed in the dish. If you find any of these in the portion on your plate they predict respectively that you will either be married, remain a spinster or a bachelor, or become rich. In other parts of the country the same principle applies to barm brack, a special bread which is baked with spices and dried fruits and a single gold ring.

Irish soda bread, or brown cake as it is sometimes called, is one of the healthiest and most simple breads to make. It contains no yeast, but is a combination of wholemeal flour, buttermilk, baking soda and salt.

If you want something really different, try cruibíns (pronounced "croobeens"). These are pickled pigs' trotters (feet) and they are particularly popular around Cork. It is a really succulent dish, owing to the flavor which the meat acquires from being cooked intact with the large amount of bone. More orthodox, and more widely known, is Limerick Ham. This is smoked over oak chips with juniper berries and has a unique flavor.

There are several traditional dishes made out of seaweed, the best known of which is Carrageen Moss Jelly. This is sold in pharmacies throughout the country and is said to contain medicinal properties.

If you want to try cooking some of these dishes, the Irish Tourist Board has a leaflet called *Irish Recipes.* A more comprehensive range of Irish recipes can be found in Theodora Fitzgibbon's *A Taste of Ireland* which also contains interesting old photographs. Another cookery writer who has done much to encourage interest in traditional Irish recipes and fresh seasonal ingredients is Myrtle Allen. Many of the recipes in her *Bally-maloe Cook Book* can be sampled at Ballymaloe House, her hotel near Ballycotton, Co. Cork.

## The Gastronomic Revolution

Since about 1975 Ireland has experienced something of a gastronomic revolution. The soggy overcooked vegetables and tasteless overcooked meat which once characterized Irish hotel and restaurant food are becoming increasingly hard to find. Instead, there is a new generation of chefs determined to take advantage of the fact that Ireland has some of the best "raw materials" in the world for gourmet cuisine. Not surprisingly this change in attitude started at the top end of the market, in the more highly priced establishments, and the "revolution" is by no means complete. Price, however, is not always a reliable indicator. A cheap pub lunch is often a better bet than an expensive hotel lunch.

Some of the finest quality meat in Europe comes from the beasts who graze on Ireland's lush pastures. Perhaps the most reliable option, which appears on almost all Irish menus, is a juicy fillet or sirloin steak. However, if you want it rare, be sure to make a point of asking. Lamb and pork are both of equally high quality. The Irish are fond of traditional plain roast meat served with a selection of vegetables, and the "roast of the day" is usually an excellent (and substantial) choice. Should boiled bacon and cabbage be on the menu it is a specialty not to be missed.

Game has made a welcome appearance on restaurant menus in the course of the gastronomic revolution. The pheasant season starts on November 1 and lasts for about three months, depending on weather conditions. Other dishes locally obtainable in season include woodcock, quail, wild duck, venison and hare.

The same restaurants that specialize in local game in the winter will most likely offer local seafood during the summer. Given that Ireland is a small island on which one is never further than an hour and a half's drive from the coast, it is not only seaside restaurants that can claim to serve seafood on the same day that it is landed. Formerly the best Irish seafood was shipped to the restaurants of Paris, but happily times have changed. Irish lobster served *au naturel* is generally agreed to be unsurpassable. Summer visitors who find fresh salmon on the menu should not hesitate to discover its firm but juicy texture and delicate flavor. Smoked salmon is popular both as a starter and as a light luncheon platter. Smoked trout and the more robust smoked mackeral make interesting alternatives. Irish mussels are small in size but big on flavor, and are usually served in the French style as *moules marinières* or grilled in their shells with garlic stuffing. The more sophisticated restaurants will offer dishes concocted with monk fish, ling, skate and other deep-sea fish, while in less ambitious establishments plain grilled sole on the bone is a good way to sample locally caught fish.

Irish oysters really deserve a chapter all to themselves—this is a subject on which the locals are wont to wax lyrical. In Ireland oysters are only eaten when there's an "R" in the month, and the season traditionally begins in September with the great oyster festival at Clarinridge on Galway Bay, where they reckon they serve the best in the land. Irish oysters are invariably eaten raw, freshly opened, laid out on the shell, enlivened with a squeeze of fresh lemon, or a drop of tabasco, and served on seaweed. The traditional accompaniment to this dish is Guinness.

## Dining Out

If you're traveling in the remoter districts you'll find that the better restaurants are in the hotels. This is not, however, a hard and fast rule, and there should be at least one good restaurant in any place large enough to call itself a town. Those who take their eating seriously should acquire a copy of *Dining In Ireland* which is published annually by the Irish Tourist Board. It contains a detailed list of good restaurants with all the necessary information on price range and opening hours, plus some indication of the menu and ambience. It also lists places that offer a special value Tourist Menu. We do, however, recommend that you splurge at least once to sample one of Ireland's top class restaurants, most of which are included below in the "Practical Information" sections after each chapter.

One tradition which has persisted over the years is the hearty Irish breakfast. If you choose to stay in hotels or B & Bs you will be tempted by the early morning aroma to abandon healthier habits in favor of starting the day with "a good fry" for the duration of your stay. Breakfast will consist of cereal followed by bacon, sausage, tomato and eggs accompanied by toast or soda bread and orange marmalade with a pot of tea or coffee. Many people find that this is enough to keep them going until tea time or later. Others find that a "one-dish" pub lunch makes an adequate midday meal.

Pubs are increasingly assuming the role fulfilled elsewhere in the daytime by cafés and coffee shops. In many pubs one can order a pot of tea or coffee and a plate of sandwiches at any hour during the day. (Outside Dublin and Cork pubs stay open continuously from 10.30 A.M.). At lunchtime many pubs offer "pub grub" which can be anything from a sandwich to more imaginative seafood platters, quiches, salads or hot dish of the day. Requests for tea, coffee and food are not generally welcome in the evenings, when the pub reverts to its traditional role and the main business becomes the provision of alcoholic drinks in convivial surroundings.

## A National Pastime

The Irish national drink is Guinness, a dark stout which is brewed with roasted malt. Those used to lighter lager-type beers may find this rich dark brew, with its thick creamy "head," somewhat unusual at first taste. But once the taste is acquired, it soon becomes an addiction, as any Irishman will tell you!

Guinness has been brewed at the famous one-mile square brewery at St. James's Gate, Dublin, since 1759. The brewery now produces over 60% of all the beer sold in Ireland, no mean feat considering the prodigious size of the national thrist.

The other main drink in Ireland is whiskey (spelt with an "e," to distinguish it from Scotch whisky). "Irish" is a straight pot-still whiskey, and has a characteristic flavor which distinguishes it from Scotch, bourbon or rye. Irish is not drunk until it is at least seven years old—that is, it is not bottled until it has been at least seven years maturing in wooden casks. Powers and Jameson remain firm favorites. Another popular and slightly lighter Irish whiskey is Bushmills, which comes from Country Antrim in the North. The Old Bushmills Distillery also produces a liqueur version known as Black Bushmills which should only be drunk neat.

Irish whiskey is best drunk without a mixer. Try it straight or with water. Remember that the measure used in the Republic is larger than that used in England. The Irish "double," invariably referred to as a "large one" or a "glass," is about equal to three singles in an English pub. The single measure in the Republic is called "a half one."

Illegal distilling of whiskey has long been a tradition in Ireland. The product of this process, Poteen (pronounced "potcheen"), is a powerful moonshine which varies wildly in quality. You are unlikely, in any case, to be offered it, as, due to its illegality, the availability of Poteen in any particular place tends to be a well-kept secret, and any attempts by a "stranger" to procure it will result either in meeting with a brick wall or in being sent off on a wild goose chase. The only truth you are likely to be told about Poteen is that it produces one of the worst hangovers known to man or woman, and it should be avoided like the plague.

A more pleasant local concoction is Gaelic, or Irish Coffee, which was invented just after the war by a bar tender at Shannon Airport. The story goes that in those early days of transatlantic flying, while passengers experienced long delays in the cold wastes of Shannon Airport they needed a drink which would have the double effect of warming them up and keeping them awake. Irish Coffee consists of a warmed goblet-shaped glass of black coffee in which a teaspoonful of sugar has been dissolved. To this is added a double measure of Irish whiskey. A teaspoon is then held face down over the glass and thick cream is poured gently onto the back of the spoon so that it floats on the top of the mixture. You then sip the hot, black whiskey-enriched coffee through the cool thick layer of cream—a truly heartwarming experience! But remember—never stir an Irish coffee.

Even if you never go out for a drink when at home, in Ireland you will find that the pub is an enjoyable experience. Unlike the United Kingdom, children are allowed into Irish bars (at the discretion of the landlord) which makes it possible for a pub lunch or late afternoon drink (non-alcoholic for the under-18s) to form part of a family outing. Understandably most publicans expect the children to disappear by early evening, and to be kept under reasonable parental control while they are there.

In more remote spots, the pub is still sometimes part of the local grocery store, the focus of the whole community, where people are just as likely to drop in for a bag of sugar and a chat as they are for a pint. Country bars tend to be very plain, with little thought for "decor" or "atmosphere," a trend which is encouraged by city folk who have come to appreciate the charms of simple, unadorned bars and find them preferable to urban attempts at modernization involving plastic, garish carpeting and piped music. The genuine pub connoisseur will tell you that a good pub should provide such lively company that you do not even notice your physical surroundings.

Pubs are for conversation and entertainment as much as they are for drinking. If you lose your way on the map, stop and ask at a pub. With any luck you'll find out much more about the neighborhood than you ever expected to know. If you're stuck for a bed for the night, ask the pub to recommend a B & B. In rural areas pubs function as informal information bureaus and it is there that you will most easily find out the time of the next bus, the time of Sunday mass, or the location of the nearest pharmacy, plus anything else you may want to know.

Singing is not confined to so-called "singing pubs," but can break out at any time in any bar, especially on holiday weekends and after weddings. If it is no good it will be ignored. If the song or the singer are local favorites, or the voice is especially good, people will hush each other and silence will reign until the end of the song. Spontaneous "sessions" where everyone in the company contributes a party piece to the entertainment are not easy to find. If you do come across one it is likely to be unforgettable, for any number of reasons. However, a visit to a pub which provides a nucleus of paid musicians to get things going is a good, and qualitatively more reliable, substitute. The local tourist information office will point you in the right direction, as will, of course, any local that you happen to meet in a non-singing pub.

In the cities, many of the pubs still retain their old Edwardian atmosphere, with wooden partitions and long bars. Several of these city bars are historic institutions in their own right. The Brazen Head, down by the Dublin quays, claims to be the oldest pub in Europe. And Davy Byrne's, also in Dublin, has strong literary associations, being mentioned in James Joyce's *Ulysses*. Perhaps the finest example of an old Victorian bar is to be found in Belfast, on Great Victoria Street. This is The Crown, which is preserved by the National Trust—a truly atmospheric spot to savor your pint of Guinness.

# SHOPPING IN IRELAND

## Gifts Galore

There's something to suit every taste in Ireland, so you won't want for souvenirs of your trip. What's more, there are some excellent quality bargains to be had, especially in the clothing line.

### Tweed, Lace and Linen

Tweeds are a must for any visitor—and not just for men. The modern range of tweeds has a wide variety of patterns and textures, from the more masculine hard-wearing kind to the softer light-weight fabrics used for dresses and scarves. Donegal is regarded as the traditional home of tweed weaving, but you'll find that this craft is not confined to that remote county. You can see weavers at work in Dublin and in County Wicklow, as well as in Kerry and around Connemara.

The top shops which specialize in tweeds—such as Kevin and Howlin in Dublin, Martin Standun in Spiddal, County Galway, and McGee's up in Donegal—carry large stocks of sports jackets and suits to meet the most sober or the most exotic of tastes. Tweed hats are coming back into fashion, too. As you'll see, they're both distinctive and comfortable. Tweed ties, as long as they are of the very lightest weave, can make ideal presents for the man back home.

Tweeds are not only for rugged sportswear; look for the jewel-like colors and fashionable cut popularized by Avoca Handweavers, and worn by some of Ireland's most fashionable citizens.

Tweed has moved into the home of recent years. Irish tweed scatter cushions, rugs, table mats, patchwork pictures of Irish scenery, bed covers and curtains are some of the many items that have become popular.

In the more traditional line there's a fine undyed tweed material called *báinín* (pronounced "bawneen"). This attractive hand-woven flannel was originally the material which the Aran island fishermen used for their jackets. Now it has been adapted to finer weaves, and in recent years has begun taking its place in the fashion stakes.

Irish clothing derives its unique style from the clever use of traditional tweed, lace, crochet and linen. The best boutiques are concentrated in a small area around Grafton, Nassau and Kildare streets in Dublin.

Traditional Irish crochet uses a fine cotton and the craft dates back to the 1840s when it originated in the cottage homes of Limerick, Kenmare and Carrickmacross. Today, wool is also used for lace-making, and, apart from blouses and dresses, the cotton crochet is used for collar and cuff sets, wedding veils, hats, scarves and shawls, and for elegant sets of table mats.

Linen weaving is a craft which is now carried out almost exclusively in Northern Ireland, though some printed linens are produced in Dublin. The craft of sprigging, the hand-embroidery of domestic linen and handkerchiefs, was originally introduced as a home craft in County Donegal, though it is now much more widespread. When buying Irish linen remember that double damask is the finest. Good quality Irish linen should last a lifetime.

## Woolens from the Wild West

Another fine buy is an Aran jersey (often called an Aran sweater or "gansey"). These originated in the Aran islands out in the Atlantic Ocean where the harsh weather made warmth and protection vital. The women of Aran long ago discovered the solution to this problem in a strong hand-knit sweater, which is both comfortable and weather repellent.

Aran sweaters are created by a people who are not only hardy but religious, and as a result the raw unbleached wool is knitted into garments that use religious symbols and folk motifs in their patterns. The Tree of Life, the Honeycomb (standing for thrift and thought to be lucky), the Sea-Horse, Blackberry—all are patterns in the almost sculptured, deeply-knitted work that characterizes the Aran method. One of the best places for finding a good range of Aran sweaters is Máirtin Standun's shop in Spiddal (northwest of Galway).

When buying an Aran sweater take care to ensure that you get a hand-knitted sweater if that is what you want. The larger craft shops carry a cheaper range of "hand-loomed" sweaters that have neither the weight nor the durability of the real hand-knits. A colorful belt called a *crios* (pronounced "criss") is hand-crafted in many traditional designs by the Aran women (and others) and makes a useful accessory.

Aran is not the only style of hand-knitting to thrive. Other designs range from home-spun wool dyed with natural dyes and knitted into the simplest shapes, to "picture" sweaters and sophisticated, textured garments.

Rugs for the home come in Irish fleece, Irish calf skin, tweed and Irish mohair. Lumra rugs are made from unspun, undyed wool. Batik wall hangings are one of the newer gift lines; these are based on traditional Irish designs in brilliant colorings. You will also find traditional Celtic designs embroidered on cushion covers of bainin.

## The Last of the Leprechauns

Once upon a time, and it's not such a long time ago, souvenirs from Ireland were usually figurines of little leprechauns, a miniature *shillelagh* with a bit of green ribbon tied around it, or some similar item which the Irish themselves would disown. Some time back the Irish Tourist Board started a drive for better souvenirs, and this has largely been successful. It has also brought a stimulus to craft workers. Now there is a Craft Council of Ireland which gives guidance and organizes training programs for young craftsmen, as well as helping to develop marketing, an area in which craft workers tend to fall short. All this has proved of considerable benefit not only to the workers, but also to the shopper by ensuring much higher standards. Craftwork is usually a solitary occupation, but another development which has proved of benefit to both shopper and worker is the creation of craft centers where a number of people with different skills are gathered in a group of studios. There are about 14 of these throughout the country, including two in the Dublin Bay area, one at Marlay Grange, Rathfarnham, the other at The Tower, I.D.A. Enterprise Center, Pearse St., Dublin.

## Art and Books

Ireland is a land of artists, and their paintings are often of a very high standard. The names of most of these young artists will be unknown to visitors, but if you see something you fancy at a gallery (and there are several in the provinces as well as in Dublin) it's well worth buying. The paintings on show in these galleries are seldom expensive, and the young unknown of today may well pay you dividends later. Apart from paintings, the graphics on display are frequently imaginative and of high quality if you are seeking that little "something different."

Engravings of the Ireland of long ago are a popular buy. Many of them have been removed from old travel books, which is something the booklover will deplore, but there is no doubt that they have an appeal. If you have an interest in antiquarian books there are still plenty to be found in the booksellers. Specialist booksellers can be found in both Dublin and the larger provincial centers.

## Antiques, Silver and Marble

Despite the boom in business in recent years, antique shops still display a remarkable variety of collectors' items, ranging from modest little pieces in silver upwards to fine art and antique period furniture. Here it's worth remembering that American and overseas buyers do not have to pay V.A.T. on items over IR£50. This, coupled with the favorable rate of exchange, can make prices very attractive. If you're interested in what's coming onto the antique market be sure to visit the auctions such as those at Adam's or Allen and Townsend in Dublin, George Mealy's in Castlecomer, County Kilkenny, and Alain Chawner's in Ardee, County Louth. This is where the dealers pick up their bargains.

Irish silver is a prized gift (and an investment), whether antique or modern. The modern silversmiths' or gift shops have a wide range of good souvenir pieces on sale. The silver potato ring—in fact a ring for holding a dish—is a characteristically Irish 19th-century piece, and many are very beautiful examples of the silversmith's art. Other items in this line which make useful souvenirs range from table-napkin rings (which can be bought individually, or as sets) and tie clasps, to ornate bowls and desk lamp standards.

Gifts in Irish marble are another appealing range of craft souvenirs, which can include such ornaments as ashtrays and book ends, statuary and carved pieces. Really beautiful jewelry in Irish silver, inset with Connemara marble, comes made up into cufflinks, pins, rings, brooches, pendants and bracelets in hundreds of designs. Copper work is of high quality, and Irish marcasite and semi-precious stones are widely used by craft workers who specialize in jewelry with a charmingly traditional influence. There are many fine pieces in enamel set in silver-and-copper work, as well as intricately-worked beaten silver designs decorating bracelets and necklaces. Here especially, one cannot help but be impressed by the use of ancient Irish motifs, some taken from the famous *Book of Kells,* others given a very skilful modern interpretation by contemporary craftsmen. The Tara Brooch, a reproduction of the celebrated brooch in the National Museum, is a popular model, and you will find many other variants in different parts of the country.

## Glass, Pewter and Pottery

Ireland is justly proud of its tradition in lead crystal, notably the world-famous Waterford Glass. You can see Waterford Glass being made at the factory, but from here it is only sold for direct export overseas. This beautiful cut glass is on sale all over Ireland, though you'll find the best and most comprehensive range in Dublin's main shopping thoroughfare Grafton Street, where several of the big stores have superb displays. If glass takes your fancy, there is also a good selection of Dublin and Galway crystal; Northern Ireland has its Tyrone crystal. Less formal is Stoneyford uncut handblown crystal from County Kilkenny.

Irish pewter has now made a place for itself among the range of souvenirs. For good examples of pewter work try the Pewter Mill at Timolin, County Kildare, about 40 miles from Dublin. The most popular purchases here are the tankards which you can have etched with your family coat of arms.

China has been made in Beleek, a village just on the border with County Fermanagh, Northern Ireland, since 1857. This local product is a fine-bone china with a delicate green- or yellow-on-white design. It has long been of interest to collectors, and there is now even a thriving Beleek Collectors' Society in the U.S. (Details are available at Beleek.)

Pottery has been known in Ireland for over 3,000 years, and some of the clay found in the country is particularly suitable for this work. Counties Cork, Kerry and Clare have the highest concentration of potters, most of whom encourage visitors to drop in and watch them at work in their studios. As well as tableware, potters also produce decorative ceramics that are increasingly collected by enthusiasts.

The Kilkenny Design Workshops have given a great boost to the craft scene. They were established to enable crafts people from overseas to work beside young Irish men and women and encourage them in craft skills and the development of modern designs. The workshops are located in the former stables of Kilkenny Castle. There is an exhibition center here and a shop on the premises, just opposite the castle gate. There is also a similar set-up in Nassau Street, Dublin (beside Trinity College) which is well worth visiting, whether you are shopping or "just looking."

## Sticks, Clubs and Baskets

Don't be bothered with a *shillelagh,* but if you've a friend who likes a walking stick get a blackthorn—it's stout and smart, particularly when "worn" with tweeds. Briar pipes are a good gift for a smoking man, the Kapp and Peterson brand name being internationally famous.

Hunting and fishing gear, golf clubs, you name it, the Irish sports stores have it. The musically minded can acquire a tin whistle and a teach-yourself book for as little as IR£1, or a four-foot harp for about IR£700.

Basket-weaving does not immediately suggest itself as a craft producing something convenient to carry home; but, apart from baskets, the weavers use rushes or split oak and hazel saplings to produce table mats, dishes and attractive figures. Another popular item in this range is the Cross of St. Brigid, patron saint of all spinners and weavers. Woodcarving is likewise a craft which has returned to favor, and you'll find good-quality carved figures, hand-turned tableware and furniture.

## A Few Last Tips

For general shopping, you'll find that Ireland has many good department stores where it's well worth browsing in search of that little something to take the folks back home. Talking of gifts, you can save yourself a lot of carrying on your return journey by sending your gifts by mail to friends at home in the U.S., as long as you mark the package clearly "Unsolicited gift, under $50 value." But remember, you may only send one package to each address, and you must not include liquor, tobacco or perfume.

One final tip. If you realize just before boarding time that there's something or somebody you've forgotten on your list of souvenirs, you can fill in at the airport shops in Dublin or Shannon. These carry a good range, but the prices tend to be a little more expensive, except of course in the liquor, cigarettes and perfume lines. A bottle of Irish Whiskey is a welcome gift; well-known brands include Powers, Paddy, Jameson and Bushmills. There are also two excellent Irish liqueurs: Irish Mist, which contains whiskey and honey, and Bailey's Irish Cream, a concoction of whiskey and cream so popular that, at the last count, there were 30 copies on the international market. Some are manufactured as far away as Japan.

# DUBLIN

## *The City that Wins Affection*

One of the first things to strike the visitor to Dublin, a city that celebrated 1,000 years of history in 1988, is the large number of children and young people about. While the city is a comparatively small capital, with an official population of just over a million, about another half million live in the greater Dublin area, and 50 per cent of these million and a half people are under 25. Many more, now in their mid-to-late 30s, are the product of the postwar baby boom. As a result Dublin has had to adapt itself to a predominantly youthful population.

Another kind of boom, an economic one, came to Dublin later than to other European cities and coincided with entry into the European Economic Community in the early '70s. This combination of economic and population booms led a totally unprepared government into over-enthusiastic plans for urban renewal. The so-called "picturesque" inner-city tenement slums beloved of playwrights Sean O'Casey and Brendan Behan were virtually eradicated. Slum dwellers were rehoused in the outer suburbs between the late '50s and the late '70s, but inadequate planning gave rise to much protest over the lack of amenities on the new housing developments. Today the policy has been reversed and corporation housing is once more being built in the very heart of the city in the form of well-designed small red-brick houses. (See, for example, the award-winning estate behind Tara Street Station on the south side of Matt Talbot Bridge.)

Another outcome of the ill-judged drive for replanning was the threat to Dublin's heritage of elegant architecture. Had it not been for vociferous protests the area known as "Georgian Dublin" would have been destroyed. In spite of all the uproar, Dublin still has only one "skyscraper," Liberty Hall, headquarters of the Irish Transport and General Workers Union, on the north bank of the Liffey. It is all of 17 stories tall!

Millenium celebrations in 1988 led to many improvements to the city's appearance: a series of varied and imaginative sculptures were installed in the streets and parks, the pedestrianization of central shopping areas was extended, and there was a noticeable rejection by pubs and shops of neon and plastic facades in favor of old-style, hand-painted wooden ones evocative of Edwardian days. In 1991 Dublin will officially be designated "European City of Culture", so such improvements are on-going.

While Dublin is no longer the cozy, provincial city of 35 years ago, it remains a highly individual and atmospheric place. Literary echoes abound, and it is possible for those determined and knowledgeable enough to follow Leopold Bloom's progress as described in James Joyce's great novel, *Ulysses.* Many other writers, from Swift, through Wilde and Shaw to Beckett, are associated with particular corners of the city.

Dublin may have changed, but the characteristics of the Dubliner have not: they love to talk and will have a strong opinion on any topic you care to name, especially if that topic concerns Dublin. If any aspect of city life puzzles you, ask a Dubliner. If you'd like a choice of explanations, ask two or three Dubliners—as long as you have all evening to sit and listen.

Dublin is Ireland's most important port, and wherever one may be in the city, the sea is never far away. This often makes it a breezy place, and also helps to diminish the city's air pollution problem. There is increasing pressure to introduce new laws to control the type of fuel burnt in the area, especially in domestic hearths, following spectacularly heavy smogs in the fall of 1988. The distinctive smell of coal smoke that hangs over the city in the winter months, caused by Dubliners' preference for a real fire in an open hearth, may soon be a thing of the past.

Each city has its season, and Dublin is at its best in the fall, when the students return to Trinity and the whole town seems caught up in the bustle of their arrival. The first open fires are lit in homes and public houses, and the shadowy figures making their way home in the season's long grey twilight acquire a timeless air of mystery and romance.

### The History of the Dark Pool

Dublin was first mentioned by Ptolemy in A.D. 140 when he marked it on the map as a place called Eblana. The name Dublin is derived from the Irish *Dubh Linn,* Dark Pool, a reference to the peat colored waters of the Liffey. Its current Irish name, *Baile Átha Cliath* (pronounced "Bawlaclee"), the Town of the Hurdle-ford, is an even earlier name than *Dubh Linn,* and dates from pre-Viking times. It refers to a ford built of stones overlaid with logs and branches which crossed the Liffey at the site now marked by Father Mathew Bridge.

It is believed that St. Patrick visited Dublin in A.D. 448 and baptized many converts to Christianity at St. Patrick's Well, near the site of which St. Patrick's Cathedral was later to rise.

Viking raiders built a fortress at Dublin in A.D. 840, and 12 years later a Danish force took it over. The continual warfare between the Danes and the Irish kings ended in 1014 when the Irish, led by Brian Boru, were finally victorious, and Dublin was once more in Irish hands.

This state of affairs did not last for long, however. Strongbow (the Earl of Pembroke) landed in Wexford in 1169, and soon had Dublin in his power. Henry II of England came to Dublin in 1171, and granted the city its first charter, making it the headquarters for his conquest of Ireland.

Dublin at this time was a small walled town, with predominantly wooden buildings, and its appearance changed little for the next 400 years. The building of Dublin Castle began in the late 12th century, and it was to figure prominently in the power struggles between English and Irish for the next 700 years. The size of "the Pale"—the area around Dublin under English rule—grew and shrank according to the fortunes of the day. In 1601 the Irish clan chieftains made their last great effort to seize control of the country back from the English, but were forced to emigrate in defeat. Their lands were confiscated and English power in Ireland was consolidated. In 1646 Dublin was occupied by Oliver Cromwell, but remained stubbornly loyal to the king. Cromwell is remembered to this day for his retaliatory gesture to Dublin's Royalists: he stabled his horses in their magnificent St. Patrick's Cathedral.

During the period of relative stability in the late-17th and early-18th centuries Dublin began to expand and flourish, and entered the phase known as "Georgian Dublin." Because its early buildings were wooden and subject to innumerable fires, most of Dublin's famous buildings (with the exception of its two cathedrals, part of the castle and a few churches) date from this period. The 18th century was the heyday of Dublin, when a flamboyant aristocracy built themselves palatial town houses, and the wealthy professional classes established themselves in the terraces that formed elegant new streets and squares. Architecture and the arts in general thrived, with Parliament House in College Green the first of a series of great public buildings.

Ireland was deprived of its short-lived Parliament by the Act of Union in 1800. Political unrest grew once more, and Dublin began a period of slow economic decline. In 1829 Daniel O'Connell secured Catholic Emancipation, allowing Dublin's many Catholics to take a greater part in the city's life. They responded by electing O'Connell Lord Mayor of Dublin.

Dublin was the center of the Gaelic League, formed in 1893 by Dr. Douglas Hyde with the intention of restoring the Irish language and its heritage to the Irish people. This led to the Irish literary renaissance, which, through the early writings of W.B. Yeats and the founding of the Abbey Theater in 1904, established the cultural climate of early 20th century Ireland.

The early years of this century were traumatic ones for Dublin. Poverty and inhuman working conditions gave rise to a struggle for the establishment of trade unionism in Ireland, with James Larkin as its spokesman— vividly described by James Plunkett in his novel, *Strumpet City*. Many Dubliners died of hunger and cold during the Great Lock-out of 1913, a battle of wills between employers and workers.

Easter week 1916 is probably Dublin's most famous historical date. It saw the uprising that led eventually to the formation of the Republic of Ireland. The war of independence that followed the uprising ended in the

Treaty of 1921, but was then followed by the tragic Civil War of 1922–23. Many of the battles were fought in and around Dublin's public buildings, and bullet scars can still clearly be seen today on the pillars of the General Post Office, the figures on the monument to Daniel O'Connell, the portico of the Four Courts and elsewhere in the city, forming a grim reminder of those stormy days. Much of central Dublin was shattered by the fighting, and many buildings were not repaired until the late '30s.

## Exploring Dublin

The river Liffey provides a useful aid to orientation, flowing as it does from the dramatic backdrop of the Wicklow and Dublin mountains, cutting its way through the heart of the city en route for Dublin Bay and the Irish Sea, a couple of miles down river from the city center. If you ask a native Dubliner—a "jackeen," as they are called in the rest of the country—for directions, he or she will most likely reply in terms of "up" or "down," up meaning away from the river, and down towards it. Dublin has no convenient central focal point such as Piccadilly Circus or Times Square, but the center is usually defined as O'Connell Bridge. This is also diplomatic in that it avoids locating the center to the north or the south of the river, as strong local loyalties still divide "northsiders" (who live to the north of the river) from "southsiders," and neither would ever accept that the city's center lay on the other's side of the river. It is even said that true Dubliners can detect a difference in accent between north and south.

Buses headed for the city center are marked An Lar and will deposit you somewhere near O'Connell Bridge, on one side or another of the river. Long (often despairing) lines form at bus stops during peak morning and evening travel times and whenever it rains (or so it seems). A 20- to 30-minute wait is not unusual in those circumstances, and though it may be enlivened by one of those typical Dublin bus-stop conversations so beloved of Myles na gCopaleen (Flann O'Brien), it is always advisable to consult your map and see if it would not be quicker to walk. This is one reason why so many Dubliners prefer to travel by bicycle. Cruising taxis are comparatively rare, especially at the above mentioned times, and are usually hired from a taxi rank or summoned by telephone.

A word about the Dublin pedestrian's attitude to traffic lights: Most traffic lights are equipped with safe sequences for pedestrians, but the only people who wait for the signals are the elderly, the infirm and newcomers to the city. Everyone else waits for a gap in the traffic and dashes across the road. Most Dubliners do not know the meaning of the word "jaywalking." Visitors should treat this local peculiarity as a spectator sport and wait for the lights to indicate that it is safe to cross.

## Up O'Connell Street

O'Connell Bridge, being more or less the center of Dublin, and easily identifiable, makes a convenient starting point and reference point for tours of Dublin. It is one of ten bridges spanning the Liffey between Heuston Station and the sea. O'Connell Bridge is a short bridge, and if you look closely at it you will notice an interesting feature: it is wider than it is long.

On the north side of O'Connell Bridge is the memorial to Daniel O'Connell, "The Liberator," by sculptor John Henry Foley (1818–75). It was erected as a tribute to the great orator's achievement in securing Catholic Emancipation (1829). The four female figures that support it represent both the four ancient provinces of Ireland, and Courage, Fidelity, Eloquence and Patriotism. They bear obvious scars from the fighting of 1916. James Larkin (1876–1947), Father Theobald Mathew (1790–1856) the temperance campaigner, and other figures from Irish history are commemorated by statues in the middle of O'Connell Street's broad thoroughfare. Undoubtedly the most famous of these is Charles Stewart Parnell (1846–91), leader of the Irish Parliamentary Party in the British House of Commons in the 1880s, who could do no wrong in most people's eyes. His political career was suddenly destroyed when he was cited in a divorce suit involving Kitty O'Shea. The ensuing furor has been immortalized by James Joyce in *A Portrait of the Artist as a Young Man,* where it dominates the discussion at Christmas dinner.

Today O'Connell Street (which used to be known as Sackville Street) is the city's main shopping area. On your left-hand side between the bridge and the General Post Office is Henry Street, a pedestrianized shopping area which leads to the colorful Moore Street Market. Here street vendors still call their wares in the traditional Dublin style.

The General Post Office stands on the corner of Henry Street and O'Connell Street. It has an impressive facade in the classical style, and was built by the British between 1814 and 1818 as a center of communications. This gave it great strategic importance, and was one of the reasons why it was chosen by the insurgent forces in 1916 as a headquarters. The Proclamation of the Republic was read from its portico on Easter Monday, April 24, 1916 by Padraig Pearse (1879–1916), the leader of the Rising. The whole building, apart from its facade, was destroyed by fire in the course of the fighting that followed. Part of the text of the Proclamation has been cut in stone and is set into the front of the building. The G.P.O., as it is always called, was re-opened in 1929. In the center of the main hall is a bronze statue by Oliver Sheppard erected in 1934 to the memory of those who gave their lives here. It depicts the death of Cuchulainn, the legendary warrior. The G.P.O. is such a potent symbol of nationalism that it—rather than the seat of government or the presidential residence, as in most other countries—has become the traditional focal point for political rallies and demonstrations.

A new attraction in front of the G.P.O. is the Anna Livia water feature—a large female nude and fountain, representing the River Liffey. Dubliners immediately nicknamed it "the Floozie in the Jacuzzi" and the name has stuck. This was once the site of the 134-ft. Nelson's column, which could be climbed for a fine view of the city. It was blown up in March 1966 by persons unknown, leaving only its very solid base. Oddly enough the original explosion caused hardly any other damage in the area but, when the Irish army decided to blast the base of the statue away, windows were shattered for blocks around.

Before continuing up O'Connell Street to Parnell Square there are two places that every visitor should note. On the opposite side of the street from the G.P.O., just before the Gresham Hotel, is the Irish Tourist Board

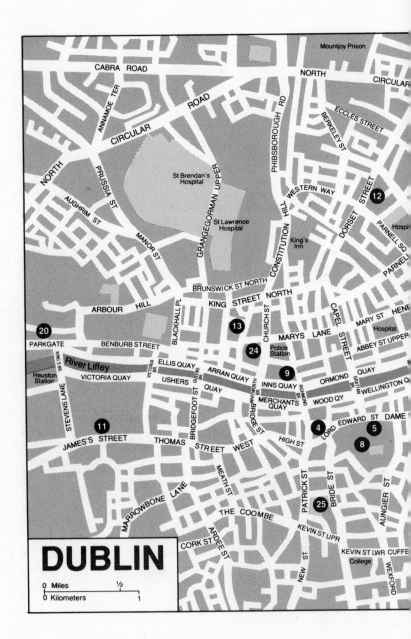

# DUBLIN

```
0 Miles          ½
0 Kilometers          1
```

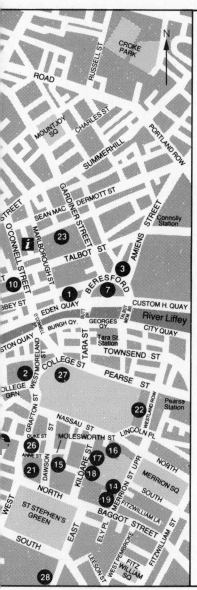

## Points of Interest

1. Abbey Theater
2. Bank of Ireland
3. Central Bus Station
4. Christ Church Cathedral
5. City Hall
6. Civic Museum
7. Custom House
8. Dublin Castle
9. Four Courts
10. General Post Office (GPO)
11. Guinness' Brewery
12. Hugh Lane Gallery of Modern Art
13. Irish Whiskey Corner
14. Leinster House
15. Mansion House
16. National Gallery
17. National Library
18. National Museum
19. Natural History Museum
20. Phoenix Park
21. Royal Irish Academy
22. Royal Irish Academy of Music
23. St. Mary's Catholic Pro-Cathedral
24. St. Michan's
25. St. Patrick's Cathedral
26. St. Theresa's
27. Trinity College
28. University College
    (National Concert Hall)

*i*   Tourist Information Office

Information Office. They will provide you with a map of the city and answer any queries. Should you have any special interest to pursue, from genealogical research to the best traditional singing pubs, they will be able to supply you with a free information sheet. Opposite the Information Center is the C.I.E. (national bus company) tour-booking office offering a selection of local and long-distance guided bus tours. A half-day bus tour of Dublin will provide excellent and friendly orientation.

## The Rotunda and Parnell Square

At the top of O'Connell Street is a large sign advertising the Ambassador Cinema. This establishment now occupies what is left of the once-elegant Rotunda Assembly Rooms. They were built by Dr. Bartholomew Mosse (1712–59) to raise funds for his Rotunda Lying-In Hospital which is beside them. They became the favorite haunt of fashionable Dublin in the 18th and early-19th centuries, and eminent people flocked to see and be seen at the concerts and illuminations held there. John Field, (1782–1837), the famous Irish composer who had an enormous influence on Chopin and the Russian school, gave his first performance here at the age of nine. Later Liszt also performed here.

The buildings at the back of the cinema, which were built as an extension to the Rotunda Rooms, now house the Gate Theater. It was founded by the late Hilton Edwards and Micheál MacLiammóir in 1928 and transferred to these premises in 1929.

The Rotunda was the first maternity hospital in Europe, and opened in 1755. The facade was completed by James Gandon in 1786. Its chapel was designed by Richard Cassels, an architect of German origin who worked extensively in Dublin. It was opened in 1757. It contains some of Dublin's finest Baroque stucco work. The hospital remains an internationally famous training center for gynecologists and midwives.

Beyond the Rotunda the vista of Parnell Square opens up, one of Dublin's first Georgian squares, though originally named Rutland Square. It contains many typical features of Dublin's Georgian architecture. The red brick of the houses is not local, but was made from materials which arrived in ships as ballast—in fact non-indigenous red brick has stubbornly remained the most fashionable domestic building material in Dublin right down to the present day.

The plainness of these brick-faced terraces shows a fine aesthetic sensibility. When looking at a Georgian terrace it is always worth looking upwards beyond the perfect proportions of the facade to note the fantastic shapes made by the chimney stacks on the rooftops. You will also notice immediately that the first-floor windows of these and other Georgian houses are much larger than the others, and that it is easy to see in to them from street level. This is not only a question of aesthetic proportions: these rooms were designed as reception rooms, and fashionable hostesses liked passers-by to be able to observe the distinguished guests at their luxurious candle-lit receptions.

As the houses had no front gardens, the center of the square served as a communal garden, whose keys were held only by the residents of the square. Many of these have now become public gardens, but some squares retain the "key-holders only" tradition.

The top of Parnell Square is dominated by the impressive facade of Charlemont House, and its unfinished Palladian arcade. This is now the

Hugh Lane Municipal Gallery of Modern Art. The building was designed by William Chambers and dates from 1762–65. It houses half of the Lane collection. Sir Hugh Lane (1875–1915) was a nephew of Yeats' patron, Lady Gregory, and a keen collector of early Impressionist paintings. He died when the *Lusitania* was torpedoed in 1915, and left his collection to "the nation." By the time World War I was over, Ireland was fighting for her independence, and once that was won, a long legal wrangle ensued between Britain and Ireland as to which "nation" should be the beneficiary of Sir Hugh's will. This was not resolved until 1960 when it was agreed to divide the collection in half between London and Dublin and exchange halves every five years. But in 1982 the British Government demanded the whole collection, and the matter is still causing controversy. Apart from the Lane collection there are also some interesting works in the gallery by Irish artists such as Roderic O'Conor (1860–1940), Jack B. Yeats (1871–1957) and Louis Le Brocquy (b. 1916).

Just around the corner from the gallery is the Garden of Remembrance "Dedicated to those who gave their lives in the cause of Irish Freedom," as it says in the inscription in English and Irish on the granite wall at the entrance. A large bronze statue by Oisín Kelly of four swans and four humans, depicting the legend of the Children of Lir, was erected in 1971 to mark the 50th anniversary of the signing of the truce with Britain.

## O'Casey, Joyce and Behan

At the top of Parnell Square you are approaching James Joyce territory; he mentions the corner church, "Findlater's Church" (named after the wealthy grocer who endowed it), and nearby is 7 Eccles Street, which was the home of his characters, Leopold and Molly Bloom. Joyce himself went to the Jesuit College, Belvedere, in Great Denmark Street, just across the road from the square. Playwright Sean O'Casey (1884–1964) wrote all his famous Abbey plays: *The Shadow of a Gunman, Juno and the Paycock, The Plough and the Stars* and *The Silver Tassie* at 422 North Circular Road, not far away. The house has been rehabilitated and is now named Sean O'Casey House in honor of the one-time construction labourer who became Ireland's greatest modern playwright. Brendan Behan (1923–1966) the rumbustious house-painter, playwright and raconteur, spent part of his childhood at nearby 14 Russell Street. Today the house is marked by a plaque. His grandmother rented out tenements in Mountjoy Square. Sadly, in spite of its wealth of literary associations, the area is now rather depressed, with Mountjoy Square, the first Georgian Square in Dublin, fallen into a bad state of neglect. However, there are high hopes for a building program which has recently been initiated to revitalize the area.

Returning back down O'Connell Street there is a signpost on the left hand side to St. Mary's Pro Cathedral, the main Catholic church of Dublin. Dublin has two Protestant cathedrals, and one of them, St. Patricks, is the national cathedral for all Irish Protestants, both from the north and south. The Catholic National Cathedral is in County Armagh in Northern Ireland. St. Mary's (built 1816–25) was the scene of John Henry Newman's profession of the Catholic faith in 1851. Its Palestrina Choir can be heard every Sunday at 11 A.M. One of many famous voices to have formed part of this exquisite ensemble is that of Count John McCormack (1884–1945).

Abbey Street, further down O'Connell Street and also on the left-hand side, will lead you to the Abbey Theater, the National Theater of Ireland. It is a new brick building dating from 1966, the original building having burnt down. It also houses the intimate 157 seat Peacock Theater. At lunchtime and early evening the foyer and bar, which display mementoes of the theater's past, are open to visitors.

### South of O'Connell Bridge

It is only a short walk across O'Connell Bridge and down Westmoreland Street to Parliament House. On the way you will pass Bewley's Coffee House (there's another one in nearby Grafton Street), an institution that has been supplying Dubliners with coffee and buns since the 1840s. The richly-decorated interior with marble-topped tables, original wood fittings and stained-glass windows by Harry Clarke, evokes a more leisurely Dublin of the past.

College Green is no longer a green at all, but is the name of a busy traffic-filled intersection outside the gates of Trinity College. Across from the gates is the old Parliament House, now a branch of the Bank of Ireland. The original building was begun in 1729 to the design of Sir Edward Lovett Pearce (1699–1733) to house the Irish Parliament. He did not live to see it completed, but was responsible for its magnificent south colonnade on College Green. The striking Westmoreland Street portico was added by James Gandon in 1785. After the Act of Union in 1800 it was bought by the Bank of Ireland who have owned it ever since. The original House of Lords has been preserved and may be viewed on request. It has a fine coffered ceiling, a Waterford glass chandelier dating from 1788 and containing 1,233 pieces of glass, and the mace of the House of Commons. The main banking hall was previously the Court of Requests, and its character has been sensitively maintained.

### Trinity College

Across the road is the facade of Trinity College, whose memorably atmospheric campus is a must for every visitor to Dublin. In the late summer and at certain other times when pressure of work is not too great, the students themselves operate a rota of guides to show visitors around, a tour which is highly recommended.

Trinity College, Dublin (familiarly known as T.C.D.) was founded by Elizabeth I in 1591, though no trace of that original structure now remains. At that time it offered a free education to Catholics, on condition that they accepted the Protestant faith. A legacy of this condition is the strange fact that right up until 1966 Catholics who wished to study at Trinity had to obtain a special dispensation from their bishop or face excommunication. Today approximately 70 per cent of Trinity's students are Catholic, a clear indication of how far away those days seem to today's generation.

The facade, built between 1755 and 1759, consists of a magnificent classical portico with Corinthian columns. The design is repeated on the interior, so that the view from College Green outside the gates and from the quadrangle inside the gates is the same. The area within the portico contains the only remaining example of Georgian Dublin's wooden footpaths.

These were constructed of oak and mahogany, and became extremely slippery in wet weather.

On the lawn in front of the facade are statues of two of the university's illustrious alumni—statesman Edward Burke (1729–97) on the left and poet Oliver Goldsmith (1728–74) on the right, both by John Henry Foley (1818–75). Other famous students include the philosopher George Berkeley (1685–1753) who gave his name to the University of California's campus at San Francisco, Jonathan Swift (1667–1745), Thomas Moore (1779–1852), Oscar Wilde (1854–1900), John Millington Synge (1871–1909), Henry Grattan (1746–1820), Wolfe Tone (1763–98), Robert Emmet (1778–1803), Bram Stoker (1847–1912), Edward Carson (1854–1935), Douglas Hyde (1860–1949) and Samuel Beckett (b. 1906).

Trinity is built on ground which was reclaimed from the sea many years ago and, as a result, the cobblestones in the main quadrangle shift and have to be entirely relaid every seven years. The buildings, however, have lasted well, and the campus retains a quiet pace of its own, quite removed from the busy commercial bustle of the surrounding streets.

The 18th-century building on the left, just inside the entrance, is the chapel. It has a "twin" on the right-hand side, the Examination Hall, which has an exceptionally graceful interior with ornamental plasterwork and fine acoustics. It is sometimes used for recitals. The Dining Hall, below the chapel on the left-hand side, has been restored following a fire which broke out during examination time in June 1984. When the alarm was raised, students left their desks and combined with staff to form a human chain and remove irreplaceable paintings and works of art before they were engulfed by flames. These treasures are now back in their rightful place, and the Dining Hall again in use.

In the center of the quadrangle is the Campanile or bell tower which is said to mark the center of the priory which occupied the site before Trinity was built. The oldest buildings are the library in the far right-hand corner, and a block of red brick buildings known as the Rubrics, which contain student apartments, both dating from 1712.

## The Book of Kells

Ireland's largest collection of books and manuscripts is housed in Trinity College Library, which is entitled to receive without charge a copy of all books published in Britain or Ireland. At present there are over two and a half million volumes in the library and each year about half a mile of new shelving is needed.

The principal treasure is, of course, *The Book of Kells,* a beautifully illuminated manuscript of the Gospels dating from the 8th century. It was written and painted with outstanding expertise, but it is impossible to identify which monastery carried out the work. It is first mentioned in the year 1007 when it was stolen from the church of Kells in County Meath. It was found three months later buried in the ground and presumably remained at Kells until 1661 when the Bishop of Meath presented it to the college.

There are 680 pages in the book, illustrated with a flamboyant exuberance unique in manuscript art. Originally one large volume, it was rebound in 1953 into four volumes. In order to preserve it from the effect of light, it is screened when no visitors are present and each day a fresh page is turned. There are always two volumes on display, one opened at a completely illuminated page and the other showing pages of the text, with brightly colored birds, animals, faces and figures entwined into the capital letters.

Because of the fame and beauty of the *Book of Kells* it is all too easy to overlook the other treasures in the library. They include the *Book of Armagh,* a 9th-century copy of the New Testament which also contains St. Patrick's Confession, and the *Book of Durrow,* a 7th-century Gospel book from County Offaly. Among the relatively "modern" treasures in the library is an early book printed by William Caxton, a first edition of Dante's *Divine Comedy* and four Shakespearean folios. Among the busts around the walls is that of Jonathan Swift, later to become the celebrated Dean of St. Patrick's Cathedral; he was a student here from 1682–89. The library also has two early Irish harps, one of which is known as Brian Boru's harp, although scientists say it was made in the 15th century—four centuries after Brian was killed at the Battle of Clontarf. Today it is used as the official symbol on Irish state documents and on the obverse side of Irish coins. It is also the trade mark of Guinness's stout!

An original copy of the 1916 Proclamation of Independence hangs on the back wall of the library. While at the end of the room take the opportunity to get an over-all view of the Long Room, as it is called. At 209 feet in length, it well deserves its name. Originally it had a flat plaster ceiling, but the perennial need for more shelving resulted in a decision to raise the level of the roof, so in 1859 the barrel-vaulted ceiling and the gallery bookcases which you now see were constructed.

The new buildings at Trinity—the New Library and the Arts and Social Sciences building—are award winning designs by Paul Koralek, and were opened in 1967. The exit through the new block to Nassau Street takes you past the Douglas Hyde Gallery of Modern Art which regularly holds changing exhibitions of Irish and international art.

## Nassau Street and Kildare Street

Nassau Street, just outside the campus of Trinity College is, as one would expect, well-endowed with bookshops. It also contains the Kilkenny Design Workshops which, besides selling the best in contemporary Irish design for the home, also holds regular exhibitions of exciting new work in ceramics, textiles and metal by Irish craftsmen.

On the corner of Nassau Street and Kildare Street are the premises of the Kildare Street Club, now the Alliance Française. The facade is remarkable for its witty animal carvings which surround each window. A plaque at number 30 commemorates a famous one-time resident, Bram Stoker, the author of *Dracula.*

Further down Kildare Street you will have your first glimpse of Leinster House, the seat of the Irish parliament. The building has a more interesting facade in Merrion Square. The Kildare Street entrance is flanked by two important buildings: the National Library on your left and the National Museum on your right. They are almost symmetrical, each featuring a massive colonnaded entrance rotunda, and built in 1890.

The National Museum houses a remarkable collection of Irish antiquities dating from 6,000 B.C. to the present day. The best pieces include the Tara Brooch and the Ardagh Chalice (both 8th century), the Cross of

Cong, the Lismore Crozier and the Shrine of St. Patrick's Bell (all 12th century). Among the more recent material is some fine Irish silver and glass. The Irish Folk-Life and Military History sections are also full of interest.

Every major figure in modern Irish literature from James Joyce onwards studied in the National Library at some point. Joyce used it in *Ulysses* as the scene of the great literary debate, and it is still thronged with scholars and researchers today. The library preserves a representative collection of first editions and works of Irish authors such as Swift, Goldsmith, Yeats, Shaw, Joyce, etc. It also contains extensive newspaper archives, and is the headquarters of the Genealogical Office.

Molesworth Street joins Kildare Street at this point, and on the north side of the street is the Masonic Hall. It is still used as such, but was previously a home for orphaned children of Masons. A left turn at the end of Molesworth Street into Dawson Street will bring you to the Mansion House. This has been the home of the Lord Mayors of Dublin since 1715. It is one of the best Queen Anne houses in Dublin, but its delicate proportions have been obscured by the addition of balustrade windows and an ornate Victorian porch. The Assembly Rooms behind the Mansion House were the place where the first Dáil Éierann, the Irish Parliament, assembled in 1919 to adopt Ireland's Declaration of Independence and ratify the proclamation of the Irish Republic made by the insurgents of 1916.

## Merrion Square and the National Gallery

If you continue down Nassau Street past Kildare Street you will come to the northwest corner of Merrion Square. The distinctive house on the corner, 1 Merrion Square, was the home of Oscar Wilde's parents, the distinguished surgeon, Sir William Wilde (1815–76), and the writer, "Speranza." Before the birth of Oscar Wilde a scandal in which Sir William was accused of raping one of his patients forced them to move to a more modest house in nearby Westland Row, which became Oscar's birthplace.

This is one of Dublin's most attractive squares. Note the brightly-colored front doors and the intricate fanlights above them. Plaques on the houses indicate famous past residents—W.B. Yeats, George Russell (AE), Sheridan le Fanu and Daniel O'Connell. The public park in the middle of the square, noted for its displays of shrubs and flowers, was given to the people of Dublin by the Catholic church. The site was intended for Dublin's Catholic Cathedral, but proved too marshy. This elegant garden had a very different aspect during the great famine (1845–47) when soup kitchens were set up to feed the starving refugees who had fled from their blighted land.

The east side of Merrion Square and its continuation, Fitzwilliam Street, forms what is known as "the Georgian mile" which, unlike some Irish miles, in fact measures less than a kilometer. On a fine day the Dublin mountains are visible in the distance, and the prospect has been preserved to give an impression of the spacious feel of 18th-century Dublin.

The National Gallery is the first of a series of important buildings on the opposite—west—side of the square. It was opened in 1864 and enlarged and extended in 1968. It is one of Europe's most pleasant and compact galleries. Over 2,000 works are on view, including a major collection of Irish landscape paintings, works of the 17th-century French, Italian and

Spanish schools and a collection of Dutch masters. The collection of watercolors by J.M.W. Turner (1775–1851) is only on public display in January to prevent them from fading, but can be seen on request at other times of the year. The late Sir Alfred Chester Beatty (1875–1968), a New York born Irish-American, gave the gallery an outstanding collection of paintings of the Barbizon school. Sir Alfred became a British citizen, and was knighted while living in England. He finally settled in Ireland, bringing his magnificent art collection with him. (The Chester Beatty Library at 20 Shrewsbury Road, a short ride on buses 6, 7 or 8, contains his collection of Oriental manuscripts and miniatures.)

George Bernard Shaw, another benefactor of the National Gallery is commemorated by a statue at the entrance. Shaw spent many of his schooldays playing hooky in the National Gallery and claimed that he owed his education to the place. He bequeathed to it one third of his estate (the rest went to the Royal Academy of Dramatic Art in London and the British Museum), which happened to include a play called *Pygmalion*. Royalties increased substantially when this became the musical *My Fair Lady*, and the Shaw bequest has helped to finance the purchase of several major works in recent years.

### Leinster House

Further along the west side of Merrion Square is Leinster House, seat of the Irish Parliament, previously glimpsed in Kildare Street. While the Kildare Street facade has the appearance of a town house, the Merrion Square facade, with its sweeping lawn, presents the aspect of a country house. The house was built to the design of Richard Cassels in 1745 for the Duke of Leinster. At the time the fashionable side of Dublin was north of the Liffey. When questioned about the wisdom of his decision to build on the unfashionable side of town the Duke answered that "Where I go, fashion will follow"—and, indeed, it did!

Visitors may be shown over the house when the Chambers are not in session; if you do go through it, take a look at the brilliantly colored Irish handloomed carpets. The Dáil (pronounced "Doyle") is elected by direct vote of the people on a proportional representation basis. The Senate—60 members—is elected on a vocational basis, with six additional members elected by the universities and 11 nominated by the Taoiseach (Prime Minister—pronounced "Tee-shuck"). Members of the Dáil, known as Teachtaí Dála (usually shortened to "TDs"), represent 41 constituencies with 166 representatives. General elections must take place at least every five years; the President is elected by popular vote once in seven years and may run for a second term.

Just past Leinster House is the Natural History Museum. Its most famous curiosity is a huge skeleton of the extinct Irish elk, whose antlers measure ten feet across.

Over the road, Mornington House, at 24 Upper Merrion Street, is the birthplace of the Duke of Wellington (1769–1852). The famous leader of the British army hated being referred to as Irish, and when reminded that he was Dublin born and therefore Irish used to reply "Being born in a stable doesn't make one a horse!"

## St. Stephen's Green

Merrion Square is linked to St. Stephen's Green by Upper Merrion Street, where you will find a small annex to the National Museum. It contains a changing exhibition of artifacts from the site at Wood Quay (near Christ Church Cathedral). The site has provided a wealth of material of archeological interest, having been continuously inhabited since pre-Viking times. Important remains were discovered preserved in peat-like deposits when foundations were being laid for an office block in 1979, and for months controversy raged over whether the block should be allowed on a site of such rich historical interest. Though now two-thirds completed, public opinion has forced the developers to abandon completion of the project indefinitely.

Stephen's Green, as it is always called in conversation, suffered more from the planning blight of the late '60s than did its neighbor, Merrion Square. The nine-hectare public park in the middle of the square is the result of one of many philanthropic gestures by the Guinness family. It was laid out at the expense of Lord Ardilaun, a member of the family, in 1880 and contains flower gardens, an ornamental lake with waterfowl, and an especially fragrant garden for the enjoyment of the blind.

The Shelbourne Hotel, one of the oldest and still one of the most fashionable hotels in Dublin, dominates the north side of the Green. Iveagh House, on the east side, and the largest in the square, was previously owned by the Guinness family who presented it to the state in 1939. It is now the Department of Foreign Affairs. On the same side, 86, a building of fine exterior with some beautiful stucco work, was the original building of the Catholic University of Ireland which was established in 1853 with John Henry Newman (afterwards Cardinal Newman) as its rector. When the university failed to obtain official recognition in Britain most of its faculties declined, but were revived in a University College. Later, the poet and Jesuit priest, Gerard Manley Hopkins (1844–89), was a professor and among its students were Patrick Pearse, Eamon de Valera (later to become President of Ireland), and James Joyce. "86," as it is known to generations of students, is now the home of some of the societies of University College, while most faculties have transferred to a new campus at Belfield, in Donnybrook, about two miles away. University Church, next door, is exuberantly Byzantine in character. The interior fully lives up to the slightly bizarre exterior (which dates from 1856) and has walls lined with colored marble quarried in Mayo, Galway, Armagh, Offaly and Kilkenny.

The only building of any interest left on the west side of Stephen's Green is the Royal College of Surgeons, which was founded in 1784. The College has an international character as one third of its 700 students must come from the Third World, one third from the Developed World, and one third from Ireland.

At the northwest corner is a vast new 70-store shopping complex housed in an intriguing Byzantine-style, glass-roofed building. It was opened in 1988 at a cost of IR£50 million, and its light and spacious interior is well worth a visit. Opposite is the massive South Africa Gate, inscribed with the names of the many Irishmen who died fighting in the British Army in the Boer War (1899–1902). For the first half of this century it was known as "traitor's gate," the implication being that the men should have been fighting for the Irish cause against the British, not with them. Such extreme nationalistic attitudes are no longer perpetuated among Ireland's young cosmopolitan population.

Grafton Street, which runs from this corner of the square to Trinity College, is a fashionable pedestrianized shopping area. Just off it on the left-hand side are two shopping centers worth a visit—the highly elegant, almost brand-new Westbury Center, on the first floor of which is a sumptuously comfortable coffee lounge, and Powerscourt House. This was built in 1771–74 around a central courtyard. In the late '70s it was developed as a shopping center by covering over the courtyard with an attractive glass roof and establishing balconies around this central focal point, thus retaining an unusual 18th-century ambience.

### Marsh's Library and St. Patrick's Cathedral

It is only a short walk from Stephen's Green to St. Patrick's Cathedral, and en route you will pass one of the smaller and most unusual gems of old Dublin, Archbishop Marsh's Library, which is in the Cathedral Close opposite the Dean's house. It was built in 1701 as the first public library in Ireland. Access is through a tiny but charming cottage garden. The interior of the library, with dark oak bookcases, each with carved gables, laden with large leather-bound volumes, has remained almost unchanged for 300 years. The collection of 25,000 books relates to the 16th, 17th and early-18th centuries. Some are annotated by Dean Swift, who was a governor of the library for many years, and there is an exhibition of interesting works (including music used for the first performance of Handel's *Messiah* in Dublin) displayed in glass cases along the central aisle. At the far end of the library are three alcoves enclosed by wire grilles known as the "cages," into which scholars who wished to peruse rare books were locked.

Legend has it that St. Patrick baptized many converts on the site of the cathedral around A.D. 450. A stone marks the spot where it is said he struck the ground with his staff and caused pure water to gush out for the baptizing. The well is about 90 feet north of the cathedral tower.

The cathedral—the national Cathedral of the Protestant Church of Ireland—dates from 1190. The building is mainly Early English in style, though with a 14th-century square tower and a stately 18th-century spire. It originally stood outside the walls of Dublin, while its close neighbor, Christ Church Cathedral, was within the walls and belonged to the See of Dublin. This is why the city has two cathedrals within a short walk of each other.

St. Patrick's is the longest church in the country, at 300 feet, a fact which Oliver Cromwell's troops found useful for stabling their horses. Their visit left the building in a ruinous state, and its current good repair is largely due to the benevolence of the Guinness family, who started to finance major restoration work in 1860.

The great satirical writer, Jonathan Swift (1667–1745) was Dean of St. Patrick's from 1713–1745, and Dean Swift's corner at the top of the north transept contains his pulpit, his specially-designed writing table and chair, his portrait and his death mask. A graduate of Trinity College, much of his polemic was concerned with Irish political life. Outside Ireland he is remembered for *Gulliver's Travels* and *A Tale of a Tub*, a satire on corruption in religion and education. In *A Modest Proposal* he suggested that the

Irish poor should offer their numerous babies for sale to the wealthy English as food, thus relieving themselves of the burden of their education and raising some cash. It is one of the best pieces of polemical writing ever to appear, and even today manages to outrage some readers with its apparent earnestness. Swift died at the age of 78, tormented in his last years by a mysterious disease which caused giddiness and deafness, and in constant terror of mental decline. He left a large bequest to build a hospital for the insane, an entirely new concept at the time. When Swift's Hospital, as it was called, opened in 1757 it was one of the first psychiatric hospitals in the world. When his coffin was disturbed by a flood in 1835, Sir William Wilde (Oscar's father) examined the skull and diagnosed the disease as Menière's Syndrome, a disorder of the inner ear. His tomb is in the south aisle, next to the grave of "Stella" (Esther Johnson), one of his two great loves. His Latin epitaph is inscribed over the door to the robing room. W.B. Yeats declared it the greatest epitaph of all time, translating it thus:

> Swift has sailed into his rest;
> Savage indignation there
> Cannot lacerate his breast.
> Imitate him if you dare
> World-besotted traveler: he
> Served human liberty.

Memorials to important figures from Ireland's past line the walls of St. Patrick's. A curious old door with a hole cut into the middle of it is preserved at the back of the cathedral. It was the chapter door on the south transept and played an important part in a feud between the Earls of Kildare and Ormonde in 1492. Ormonde's faction had bolted themselves into the Cathedral. In order to break the stalemate that ensued Kildare cut a hole in the door and put his arm through it to see if Ormonde would carry on the hostilities or end the feud by shaking his hand. He shook the hand, and so the English language acquired a new expression—"chancing your arm."

A short walk down Patrick Street brings you to a busy road junction, at the far side of which is Christ Church Cathedral, situated on top of one of the few hills in Dublin. It was founded by Strongbow (the Earl of Pembroke) in 1172 and took 50 years to build. Just across the road from Christ Church, steps lead down to the 12th-century Church of St. Audoen. Its crypt has been transformed into a Viking Adventure Center where "real-life" Vikings will take you on a tour of Viking Dublin.

## Dublin Castle and St. Patrick's Blue

From Christ Church there are two choices for further exploration; to the left past the Guinness Brewery and on to the open spaces of Phoenix Park; or to the right past Dublin Castle and back along Dame Street to the gates of Trinity. This is the route we shall follow first. On a fine day it is worth pausing outside Christ Church and enjoying the view of Dublin mountains to the south. Such unexpected vistas are part of the pleasure of a relatively small city like Dublin.

Dublin Castle is well signposted in the area. Guided tours of the lavishly furnished state apartments are offered at regular intervals and provide one of the most enjoyable sightseeing experiences in Dublin.

The castle square is an 18th-century rebuilding of the medieval structure; the only surviving fragments of the original 13th-century building are the Record Tower (on the southeast side) and the base of the Bermingham Tower (southwest), so one is essentially looking at a fine Georgian building. James Malton's (1761–1803) *Views of Dublin,* widely available as prints and postcards, give an excellent impression of the days when Dublin Castle was a bustling and important place.

The State Apartments were formerly the residence of the English Viceroys, and are now used by the President to entertain visiting Heads of State. St. Patrick's Hall, a noble room with a lofty frescoed ceiling, is used for the Inauguration of the Irish President. President Reagan is among the heads of state to have been received in the Banquet Hall. All the rooms in the State Apartments are carpeted with luxurious hand-tufted Donegal wool carpets, whose patterns reflect and complement the elaborate stucco work on the ceilings. The dominant color in the decor is St. Patrick's blue. The flag of St. Patrick features a gold harp on a mid-blue background, and many visitors are surprised to learn that, according to heraldic convention, the official color of Ireland is blue. Green is a modern introduction arising out of 19th-century nationalist movements.

Wander down to the Liffey from Dublin Castle towards two modern office blocks which occupy part of the Wood Quay site. Besides the many artifacts from Viking and Norman times that were preserved in the peat-like soil, outlines of complete Viking and Norman villages were discovered. A decision as to whether the archeological remains will be restored or the building of office blocks will be put on top of the site is pending.

The narrow street on the near side of the office blocks is Fishamble Street, once the location of a magnificent concert hall designed by Richard Cassels and decorated in gold and white. It was opened in 1741. It has long since been demolished, but is remembered by Dubliners with pride as on 15 April 1742 a capacity audience attended the first performance of Handel's *Messiah* there. Handel was in Dublin at the invitation of the Lord Lieutenant, the Duke of Devonshire. He had been working on the oratorio in secret with the joint choirs of St. Patrick's and Christ Church cathedrals, and the event was only announced a few weeks in advance. Dean Swift disapproved of the choir singing the work outside a church and was about to forbid them to perform the oratorio when Handel personally convinced him of the beauty of the music.

## Dame Street and Temple Bar

The impressive Corinthian-style City Hall is on your right as you head back towards Dame Street. It was built in 1769 as the Royal Exchange, and its circular main hall successfully combines classical ornamentation with Georgian simplicity. Opposite the main entrance there is a good example of a Georgian staircase, typical of many in the larger town houses. Dame Street is the main banking and business center of Dublin. The new Central Bank is in the striking modern building on the left-hand side.

Between Dame Street and the Liffey, bordered by O'Connell Bridge and Capel Street Bridge, is an area known as Temple Bar, which anyone interested in discovering "young Dublin" should make a point of exploring. The land was acquired by C.I.E. over the years with a view to building a new central bus terminal. This project has now been abandoned and shops, studios and office space in the area have been rented out cheaply on short (approximately ten-year) leases. The experimental and very successful theater in the Project Arts Center is the best known of these ventures, but there are also second-hand bookshops, imaginative clothes shops, antiques and bric-à-brac, inexpensive restaurants, an art gallery for student exhibitions and other ventures which are creating for Dublin an area of similar appeal to London's Covent Garden or Les Halles in Paris.

## West of Christ Church

From the city center keen walkers can follow the north bank of the Liffey to Heuston Bridge and reach Phoenix Park in some 30 to 40 minutes. There are frequent buses from the city center which will leave you at the gates of the park, but they are not allowed through it (taxis and other traffic are). If, however, you start from Christ Church Cathedral you are already half way there, and can take in the Guinness Brewery (another must on the list of Dublin sights) and other points of interest on the way.

The area to the west of Christ Church is dominated by the Guinness Brewery. In certain atmospheric conditions a strong smell of malt pervades the air, as you pass through the Liberties—an area so named because it stood outside the jurisdiction of the old medieval town. Thomas Street West leads you from Christ Church Place to St. James's Gate, the famous name to be found on Guinness bottles the world over. The brewery now covers 60 acres, and was founded by Arthur Guinness in 1759. This date is carved on the left-hand side of the main gate, and the plaque on the right-hand side is altered annually to display the current date. Guinness invite visitors to attend a 30-minute film show in a converted hop-store next door to the brewery, and to sample a free glass of the famous black beverage. There is also a Guinness museum at the same location. Guinness are proud of their brewery and their reputation for model industrial relations.

Also in Crane Street is the latest in a long list of generous gestures towards Dublin on the part of the Guinness family: the Hop Store. This was converted into an art gallery in 1985 and makes a significant addition to the space available in Dublin for occasional major exhibitions.

A right turn from Thomas Street down Steevens Lane will take you past Swift's Hospital (renamed St. Patrick's Hospital) to Heuston (formerly Kingsbridge) Station and the Liffey. All of Dublin's railway stations are named after signatories of the 1916 Proclamation of Independence and this one commemorates Dublin-born Seán Heuston (1891–1916). It is the terminus for trains from Cork, Kerry and Limerick.

## Phoenix Park

Across the Liffey, a turn to the left brings you to Phoenix Park, 1,760 acres of green open space. The land which constitutes Phoenix Park was seized from the priory of the Knights Hospitaller in the 17th century and turned into a royal deer park. Later, a home for the king's representative, the viceroy, was built here—it is on the right of the main road and is now known as Áras An Uachtaráin and is the official residence of the president of the republic. Its facade can be seen through the trees, and people often comment on its similarity to the White House. Architect James Hoban, who was one of the team that worked on it, later emigrated to the United States and designed the White House which has identical porticos. The residence of the United States ambassador is on the left of the main road and can also be glimpsed through the trees. It was renamed Deerfield by William Shannon, a recent ambassador, whose wife Elizabeth wrote a history of the house which is published in the Irish Heritage series.

Phoenix Park (the name is an anglicization of the Irish *Fionn Uisce,* meaning clear water) was, until 1984, grazed by large herds of wild deer, flocks of sheep and even cows. Today there are only a few Sika deer. The native red deer were joined by the Sika deer which were a gift to the Irish from the Japanese. The red deer strain was being eliminated by cross breeding, so the red deer have been removed to the Wicklow mountains where they still roam free. In 1984 an unsuccessful T.B. eradication campaign led to the removal of the sheep and cows as a public health risk.

The 205-foot-high obelisk, visible from all over the park, is the Wellington Testimonial, a tribute to the first Duke of Wellington and erected in 1817. A towering steel cross marks the site where John Paul II celebrated Mass on his arrival in Ireland in 1979.

The old duelling grounds, known as the Fifteen Acres, now provide playing fields for cricket, soccer, Gaelic games and, on Sunday mornings, polo. Sunday is in fact the best time to visit the park. A large open-air market including bric-à-brac and antiques is held every Sunday from noon on the Phoenix Park racecourse, and the bar and other amenities are open. The Zoological Gardens are the third oldest in the world and are internationally famous for breeding lions, one of whom became familiar to movie fans the world over when M.G.M. used him for their trade mark. As they will tell you at the zoo, he is in fact yawning in that familiar shot: an American lion had to be hired to roar and the "voice" was superimposed. The People's Gardens are the only cultivated part of the park, and their welltended flower gardens make a good place to relax.

### St. Michans

The return trip from the park gives a chance to explore the north bank of the Liffey. The first large building on your left-hand side, set back from the road, is Collins Barracks, headquarters of the Irish army. Many of the picturesque old shops on the quays are currently being demolished, but there is a long-term plan for careful re-vitalization of the area.

A diversion up Church Street to St. Michans (pronounced St. "Mickans") will be relished by those with a macaber turn of mind. Open coffins in the vaults beneath the church reveal mummified bodies, some of which are over 900 years old. The sexton, who can be found at the church gate on weekdays, will guide you around the church and crypt.

The original church dates from 1096 and was named after a Danish saint. Its small sober interior is dominated by its organ and organ gallery. The early 18th-century organ still has its original gilding, and Handel expressed great admiration for it when he played it on his visit to Dublin. The carving in the center of the gallery's balcony was made from a single piece of oak and shows 17 musical instruments intertwined. It is used on £50 banknotes, but cost just £8 when it was commissioned in 1724.

The vaults are entered through a creaking metal trap-door on the outside of the church. Many of the 43 vaults are privately owned and are still used for burials. The clothing of the bodies has long ago disintegrated, but their brown leathery skin remains, and veins, ears, fingers and nails can still be clearly seen. The phenomenon is explained by the dryness of the air and the constant temperature, combined with natural methane gas from the rotting remains of the oak forest underneath the church. If you enter on a wet day, notice how quickly your footprints dry out in the atmosphere of the vaults.

Just behind St. Michan's in Bow Street is the Irish Whiskey Corner. Irish Distillers have converted a 90-year old Jameson warehouse into a museum to introduce visitors to the pleasures of Irish whiskey. Irish whiskey was the original whiskey, and having learnt about its history from the museum and an audio-visual show, visitors participate in a tasting in the Ball O' Malt bar in which five different brands of Irish whiskey are compared with Scotch and bourbon. Up to seven guided tours a day are held.

## The Four Courts and the Custom House

James Gandon (1743–1823) was a London-born architect who made a significant contribution to Georgian Dublin. His Four Courts and the Custom House have been described as among the noblest buildings in Europe. The Four Courts is just a few blocks downriver from St. Michans and Church Street. It is the seat of the High Court of Justice of Ireland, and its library is used as a place of business for barristers (similar to Chambers in London).

The building was completed between 1786 and 1802, and radiates from a circular central hall surmounted by the massive copper-covered dome which gives the building its distinctive outline. The hall is entered through an imposing Corinthian portico which supports a weatherworn entablature with a statue of Moses and figures of Justice and Mercy. Four doors off the central hall give access to the halls that contained the original "four courts"—Exchequer, Common Pleas, King's Bench and Chancery. The circular central hall is flanked by squares which are connected by arcades.

The Four Courts was completely gutted in the Civil War of the '20s, but was later restored. An irreplaceable loss, however, was the adjoining Public Record Office where priceless legal and historical documents were destroyed.

The Custom House lies further down the Liffey on the other side of O'Connell Bridge. It was Gandon's first masterpiece, completed in 1791. Although it is on the north side of the river, an ugly railway bridge obscures the view and it is worth walking across Matt Talbot Bridge to view the main front which has a central portico of four Doric columns from the center of which rises a graceful dome, surmounted by the figure of Hope. The pavilions at each end are joined to the central portico by a series of arcades. The Custom House blazed for five days during the Civil War, and extensive records were destroyed. It now houses government offices.

Gandon's third masterpiece, the King's Inns, lies at the top of Church Street (beyond St. Michans). He designed it in 1795, but there were many delays in its building, and Gandon retired in 1808 leaving it to be finished by his pupil, Henry Aaron Baker. It contains a fine dining hall and has pleasant gardens, but unfortunately is not open to the public.

### The River Liffey

Midway between the Four Courts and the Custom House is the Liffey's only pedestrian bridge, known as the Metal Bridge or Halfpenny Bridge because, until the early part of this century, a toll of a half-penny was charged to cross it. It is a high, arched bridge and offers excellent views up and down the river, the *abha na life,* which James Joyce transcribed phonetically as Anna Livia in *Finnegans Wake.* Here it is near the end of its 80-mile journey from the Wicklow mountains into the Irish sea. It is to the credit of environmentalists that, if you look for long enough into the black waters of the Liffey from the Halfpenny Bridge you have a good chance of spotting a pollack, or even a shoal of mullet swimming past.

### A Little Further Afield

Like any major capital city, Dublin has a seemingly infinite number of attractions for the visitor. Excursions beyond the city center and into the surrounding countryside will be covered in the next chapter, but before you leave the city, here are a few more suggestions.

If you're in town on a Sunday, Kilmainham Jail—a few blocks to the west of Heuston Station—will be open to visitors. The "new" jail was opened in 1792, and accommodated the Fenians in 1886, the Land League prisoners including Parnell and Davitt in 1881, the Invincibles in 1883, and the Volunteers in 1916, many of whom, including Patrick Pearse and James Connolly, were executed here. In 1922 the jail lodged anti-Free State prisoners. It was abandoned in 1924. Voluntary labor has turned it into a historical museum, with some of the cells still intact.

The Royal Hospital at Kilmainham, immediately east of the jail, is considered the most important 17th-century building in Ireland. Completed in 1680, it was designed in the Franco-Dutch style as a hospital for disabled and veteran soldiers. After considerable renovation it re-opened in 1986 to a public wishing to see the 17th-century Great Hall, the vaulted basement containing a 19th-century kitchen, and the Chapel with its magnificent baroque ceiling, wood carvings and stained-glass windows.

A pleasant walk through Georgian Dublin (the area to the south of Trinity College) down the north side of Merrion square (or bus no. 6, 7 or 8) will take you into the residential areas of Dublin's fashionable south side. One of the many annual attractions at the R.D.S. (Royal Dublin Society), such as the Horse Show in August, the Spring Show (May) or a concert may well tempt you in this direction. It's a pleasant walk through leafy streets lined with substantial red brick houses. You will pass the American Embassy, an unmistakable modern circular building, completed in 1964 and surrounded by a shrub-filled moat. Just beyond the Embassy are the grounds of the R.D.S.

The road continues on to Dun Laoghaire, Dalkey and Bray, all of which, along with the rest of the environs of Dublin, will be covered in the next chapter.

# PRACTICAL INFORMATION FOR DUBLIN CITY

**GETTING TO TOWN FROM THE AIRPORT.** Dublin Airport is only six miles from the city center and a bus service (fare IR£2.50) runs every 20 minutes from outside the Arrivals door. The bus leaves you at the Central Bus Station in the city. A new service also calls at major hotels to collect and drop off passengers for around IR£2.50.

There are plenty of taxis at the airport and it's worth checking the schedule of rates (also outside the Arrivals gate) before hiring a taxi.

**TOURIST OFFICES.** There is a tourist information office in the entrance hall of the Bord Fáilte (Irish Tourist Board) headquarters at Baggot St. Bridge, tel. 01–765871. More conveniently located are the offices at 14 Upper O'Connell St., tel. 01–747733.

Other offices are at Dublin Airport, tel. 01–376387, and beside the ferryport at Dun Laoghaire, tel. 01–806984. All these offices are open throughout the year.

**Telephone Code.** The area code for Dublin City is 01.

**HOTELS.** There has been a decline in the number of new hotels built in Dublin in the recent past. A welcome newcomer is the Conrad International, owned by a subsidiary of Hilton Hotels USA. In addition, considerable investment in redevelopment, updating of facilities and refurbishing of some of the older establishments is taking place.

There is a Value Added Tax (V.A.T.) of 10% on hotel charges, and this is included in the room rate quoted on page 18. As in most major cities, there is a shortage of middle-grade accommodations at the peak of the season, but the Tourist Information Office at Dublin Airport, or at 14 Upper O'Connell St., can help late arrivals. The Irish Tourist Board, Baggot St. Bridge, will handle advance reservations if you have any difficulties. We recommend advance reservations through your travel agent, unless you are on a casual type of self-drive tour which can be so enjoyable in Ireland. Try and be sure of your first night and last night reservations before you start.

A service charge of 12% to 15% is included (and shown) in the bills of top-grade hotels, but in other hotels it is best to check if the service charge is included. If it is not, a tip of between 10% and 15% is usual—if you think the service is worth it.

*Deluxe*

**Berkeley Court,** Lansdowne Rd. (tel. 01–601711). 262 rooms, all with bath. Ten luxury suites with Jacuzzis. Attractive conservatory restaurant and grill. AE, DC, MC, V.

**Burlington,** Upper Leeson St. (tel. 01–605222). 472 rooms, all with bath. Dublin's largest hotel, popular with overseas visitors. Conference center. Irish cabaret in season. AE, DC, MC, V.

**Conrad International.** Earlsfort Terrace (tel. 01–765555). 192 rooms with bath. Located just off Stephen's Green, opposite the National Concert Hall, this is Dublin's newest luxury hotel. Two restaurants, health club with sauna and jacuzzi. AE, DC, MC, V.

**Dublin International,** Dublin Airport (tel. 01–379211). 187 rooms with bath. Comfortable, with a pleasant atmosphere not usually associated with airport hotels. AE, DC, MC, V.

**Jury's,** Ballsbridge (tel. 01–605000). 290 rooms, all with bath. Ballroom, bars, conference center. New 100-bed executive wing with exclusive facilities, *The Towers.* Indoor-outdoor pool, hot whirlpool. Irish cabaret in season. AE, DC, MC, V.

**Shelbourne,** St. Stephen's Green (tel. 01–766471). 165 rooms, all with bath. Has been considerably renovated to its original elegance and high standards. Formal, top-quality restaurant. *The* place for diplomats, and very much the top hotel in town. AE, DC, MC, V.

**Westbury,** Clarendon St. (tel. 01–791122). 150 rooms, all with bath, including six luxury suites. Center-city location, underground car park. AE, DC, MC, V.

### *Expensive*

**Buswell's,** Molesworth St. (tel. 01–764013). 68 rooms, all with bath. Located across the street from Leinster House, seat of the Irish Parliament, and popular with Members. Lively bar. AE, DC, MC, V.

**Gresham,** O'Connell St. (tel. 01–746881). 179 rooms, all with bath. Right in the city center. Long-established, but revitalized. AE, DC, MC, V.

**Royal Dublin,** O'Connell St. (tel. 01–733666). 110 rooms, all with bath. Another city-center spot. AE, DC, MC, V.

**Russell Court.** 21–23 Harcourt St. (tel. 01–784991). 22 rooms, all with bath. Centrally located just off St. Stephen's Green. AE, DC, MC, V.

**Sachs,** Morehampton Rd. (tel. 01–680995). 20 rooms, all with bath. Fashionable with the younger set; popular bar. AE, DC, MC, V.

### *Moderate*

**Ashling,** Parkgate St. (tel. 01–772324). 56 rooms, all with bath. Family-operated, with all the warmth that implies. Close to Heuston rail station. Pleasant restaurant. AE, DC, MC, V.

**Clarence,** Wellington Quay (tel. 01–776178). 67 rooms with bath. Unpretentious and central, overlooking the river Liffey. AE, DC, MC, V.

**Green Isle,** Naas Rd., Clondalkin (tel. 01–593406). 84 rooms, all with bath. Off the main road to the south, just out of the city. AE, DC, MC, V.

**Marine,** Sutton Cross (tel. 01–322613). 27 rooms, all with bath. Convenient edge-of-city location; popular with golfers. Heated pool. AE, DC, MC, V.

**Montrose,** Stillorgan Rd., Donnybrook (tel. 01–693311). 190 rooms with bath. About three miles from city center, opposite University College campus. Popular with tour groups. AE, DC, MC, V.

**New Ormond,** Upper Ormond Quay (tel. 01–721811). 49 rooms, most with bath. Newly refurbished, central Liffey-side location. AE, DC, MC, V.

**Skylon,** Upper Drumcondra Rd. (tel. 01–379121). 88 rooms, all with bath. Well-located on the main road out of town to the airport. AE, DC, MC, V.

**Tara Tower,** Merrion Rd. (tel. 01–694666). 84 rooms, all with bath. South side of the city, on the road to the Dun Laoghaire car ferry. Newly refurbished. AE, DC, MC, V.

**Wynn's,** Lower Abbey St. (tel. 01–745131). 65 rooms, most with bath. Central location. AE, DC, MC, V.

*Inexpensive*

**Ariel Guest House,** 52 Lansdowne Rd. (tel. 01–685512). 15 rooms, all with bath. Near U.S. Embassy. AE, MC.

**The Castle,** Gardiners Row (tel. 01–746949). 26 rooms, 18 with bath. Off O'Connell Street near Parnell Square.

**Harcourt,** 60–61 Harcourt St. (tel. 01–783677). 20 rooms, some with bath. Near St. Stephen's Green. AE, DC, MC, V.

**Kelly's,** South Great George's St. (tel. 01–779277). 23 rooms, most with bath.

**Mont Clare,** 13–14 Clare St. (tel. 01–616799). 16 rooms, 8 with bath. Good central location.

**GUESTHOUSES.** Dublin has a number of modestly priced guesthouses, all of which are checked by the Irish Tourist Board and given a graded listing. Most are small with from 10 to 20 rooms, and many are even smaller.

**Egan's,** 7–9 Iona Park, Glasnevin (tel. 01–303611). 24 rooms with bath. On the airport side of the city. Restaurant and T.V. lounge; parking.

**Iona House,** 5 Iona Park (tel. 01–306217). 14 rooms, 12 with bath or shower. Also on the north side. AE, DC, V.

**Kilronan House,** 70 Adelaide Rd. (tel. 01–755266). 11 rooms, all with bath or shower. On the south side.

**Maples House,** 81 Iona Rd. (tel. 01–303049). 21 rooms with bath or shower. AE, DC, MC, V.

**Mount Herbert,** Lansdowne Rd. (tel. 01–648321). 88 rooms, most with bath. Inner suburban location, close to DART. AE, DC, MC, V.

**St. Aiden's,** 32 Brighton Rd. (tel. 01–902011). 10 rooms, 5 with bath or shower. South side of the city. AE, DC, MC, V.

**St. Jude's,** 17 Pembroke Pk. (tel. 01–680928). 8 rooms. At Ballsbridge on south side of city. AE, DC, MC, V.

## Youth Hostels

There are three youth hostels run by **An Oige,** the Irish Youth Hostels Association, in Dublin. Advance booking is recommended, particularly during summer weekends. Bookings for Dublin hostels should be made with *An Oige,* 39 Mountjoy Sq., Dublin 1 (tel. 01–363111/364749), and accompanied by the overnight fee. All places at Mountjoy Street cost IR£6.50, including breakfast. At the other two, the fee for seniors (over 21) is IR£4 per night; for juniors (16–21), IR£3.50; for juveniles (under 16) IR£3, plus return postage.

The Dublin hostels are at 78 Morehampton Rd., Donnybrook, Dublin 4 (tel. 01–680325)—open year-round; 39, Mountjoy Sq., Dublin 1 (tel.

01–364750)—open Apr. to Sept.; Dublin International Hostel, Mountjoy St., Dublin 7 (tel. 01–301766)—open May to Dec.

The **YWCA** has a hostel at Radcliff Hall, St. John's Rd., Sandymount, Dublin 4 (tel. 01–694521). 52 rooms, 21 with bath. Bed and breakfast for around IR£10.

Student I.D. card holders can use Trinity Hall, Dartry Rd., Rathmines (tel. 01–971772) outside term time. Alternatives are **ISAAC'S**, The Dublin Tourist Hostel, 215 Frenchman's Lane, Dublin 1 (tel. 01–749321). 21 rooms with bath, 10 dormitories. IR£6.75 per night, bed only; **Kinlay House**, 2–12 Lord Edward St., Dublin 2 (tel. 01–796644). 38 rooms, 17 with bath. IR£6.50 per night, bed and breakfast.

## Camping

**Cromlech Caravan and Camping Park,** tel. 01–826882. Just off N11 at Ballybrack village. 74 caravan pitches, 7 on-site caravans, 36 camping pitches.

**Donabate Caravan and Camping Park,** tel. 01–450038. On the north side of Dublin City. 80 caravan pitches, 5 camping pitches.

**Shankill Caravan and Camping Park,** tel. 01–820011. Route N11. 112 caravan pitches, 16 on-site caravans, 80 camping pitches.

**RESTAURANTS.** A sample listing of some of Dublin's many restaurants is given here. Most close early and those that stay open late are so indicated. For an explanation of restaurant price gradings, see *Facts at Your Fingertips* on page 21. Unfortunately price is not always a reliable guide to quality, but this list has been compiled with care. Some restaurants have licenses to sell wine only, and not spirits or beer.

### *Expensive*

**Ariel House,** 52 Lansdowne Rd. (tel. 01–685512). Well recommended, small and intimate spot offering seasonal Irish food. AE, DC, MC, V.

**Bentley's,** 46 Upper Baggot St. (tel. 01–682760). Imaginative menu with fresh Irish produce, in an intimate setting. AE, DC, MC, V.

**Berkeley Room,** Berkeley Court Hotel, Ballsbridge (tel. 01–601711). Elegance accompanies good food. The hotel also has an attractive conservatory restaurant. AE, DC, MC, V.

**Braemor Rooms,** Churchtown (tel. 01–988664). A cabaret comes with a meal at this popular spot. AE, DC, MC, V.

**Celtic Mews,** 109A Lower Baggot St. (tel. 01–760796). Gourmet evenings in Georgian surroundings. AE, DC, MC, V.

**Coffers,** 6 Cope St., behind Central Bank Building (tel. 01–715900). Small, but known to people who appreciate good food. AE, DC, MC, V.

**Le Coq Hardi,** Pembroke Rd. (tel. 01–689070). Award-winning French cuisine.

**Ernie's Restaurant,** Mulberry Gardens, Donnybrook (tel. 01–693300). Ernie Evans is a great name among Irish diners-out. AE, DC, MC, V.

**Gallery 22,** 22 St. Stephen's Green (tel. 01–616669). Open fire and seasonal specialties. AE, DC, MC, V.

**Kish Seafood Restaurant,** Jury's Hotel, Ballsbridge (tel. 01–605000). Always busy and that's a sign of good food and service. AE, DC, MC, V.

**Lock's,** Windsor Terrace, Portobello (tel. 01–725025). Good for both classical and nouvelle cuisine. AE, DC, MC, V.

**Lord Edward,** 23 Christ Church Pl. (tel. 01–542420). Renowned old-world seafood spot in the heart of town. AE, DC, MC, V.

**Old Dublin,** 91 Francis St. (tel. 01–542028). In the heart of the old city. Owner-chef; specializes in Russian and Scandinavian fare. AE, DC, MC, V.

**Park Restaurant,** 26 Main St., Blackrock (tel. 01–886177). Family-run restaurant using freshest produce and modern cuisine. AE, DC, MC, V.

**Patrick Guilbaud Restaurant,** 46 James's Pl. (tel. 01–764192). Off Lower Baggot St. In the best French tradition. AE, DC, MC, V.

**Rajdoot Tandoori,** 26–28 Clarendon St. (tel. 01–794274). North Indian cuisine is the specialty here. Good atmosphere. AE, DC, MC, V.

**Shelbourne Restaurant,** Shelbourne Hotel, St. Stephen's Green (tel. 01–766471). Specializes in gourmet food with an Irish twist. *The Hunting Lodge* in the same hotel has an elaborate buffet with hot and cold main dishes. AE, DC, MC, V.

**Shrimps,** 1 Anne's Lane, off South Anne St. (tel. 01–713143). Intimate, continental-style spot serving original dishes of fish, poultry, game and meat. AE, DC, MC, V.

**Whites on the Green,** 119 St. Stephen's Green (tel. 01–751975). Elegant and fashionable venue. AE, DC, MC, V.

### *Moderate*

**Bad Ass Café,** 9 Crown Alley (tel. 01–712596). Great pizzas; cook your own steak; one of the liveliest and loudest places in town. AE, MC, V.

**Beefeaters,** 99–100 Lower Baggot St. (tel. 01–760784). Specializes in prime Irish steak. AE, DC, MC, V.

**Courtyard,** Belmont Court, Belmont Ave., Donnybrook (tel. 01–838815). Pleasant, relaxed atmosphere; carvery at lunch.

**Dobbin's Wine Bistro,** 15 Stephen's Lane (tel. 01–764679). Very popular with people in the arts. AE, DC, MC, V.

**George's Bistro,** 29 South Frederick St. (tel. 01–603177). Fashionable young clientele, live entertainment. Popular spot for a late dinner; best to book.

**Kapriol,** 45 Lower Camden St. (tel. 01–751235). Small, friendly Italian restaurant with good selection of veal and fish. Booking recommended. AE, DC, MC, V.

**Kilmartin's,** 19a Upper Baggot St. (tel. 01–686674). Tasty home cooking in a tiny, elegantly converted bookmaker's shop. AE, DC, MC, V.

**Mitchell's Cellars,** 21 Kildare St. (tel. 01–680367). In the cellars of Mitchell's Wine Shop. Home-style food at lunchtime. AE, DC, MC, V.

**Puerto Bella,** 1 Portobello Rd. (tel. 01–720851). Small and intimate, with an imaginative menu including daily vegetarian specials. AE, DC, MC, V.

**Royal Garden,** Clarendon St. (tel. 01–791397). An attractive up-market Chinese spot. Near Westbury Hotel. AE, DC, MC, V.

**Rudyard's,** 15 Crown Alley (tel. 01–710846). Excellent value three-course dinner in a newly fashionable part of town.

**Silver Lining,** Dublin Airport Terminal Building (tel. 01–372439). Small, but well above average for airport restaurants. AE, DC, MC, V.

**Trocadero,** 3 St. Andrew St. (tel. 01–775545). Bistro-type menu. Popular with theatrical crowd; open till late. AE, DC, MC, V.

**The Waterfall,** Irish Life Center, Lower Abbey St. (tel. 01–788911). International menu, striking modern decor. AE, DC, MC, V.

*Inexpensive*

**Astor's,** 133 Upper Leeson St. (tel. 01–609906). Good value in a small, old-fashioned spot. AE, DC, MC, V.

**Beshoff's,** Westmoreland St. Superior fish and chips in Victorian surroundings.

**Bewley's Café,** 12 Westmoreland St., 78 Grafton St., 13 South St. George's St. Three outlets of long-established tea and coffee shop. A Dublin institution. Own bakery; self-service.

**Brown Thomas,** Grafton St. (tel. 01–776861). Three outlets within an upmarket department store. Two are restaurants (one self-service) and the other is a sandwich bar with continental filled rolls. AE, DC, MC, V.

**Captain America's,** Grafton Court, Grafton St. (tel. 01–715266). Burgers and Tex-Mex in popular shopping area. AE, DC, MC, V.

**Casper & Giumbini's,** Wicklow St. (tel. 01–794347). Lively bar and restaurant, close to Trinity College. AE, DC, MC, V.

**Clery's Rooftop Restaurant,** North Earl St. (tel. 01–740769). On top of Clery's department store. Self-service.

**Flanagan's,** 61 Upper O'Connell St. (tel. 01–731388). Reliable steakhouse, with excellent pizzeria in basement. MC, V.

**The Gasworks** (formerly Murph's), 21 Bachelor's Walk (tel. 01–731420). Simple food and cheerful atmosphere. AE, DC, MC, V.

**Hot Pot,** 10 Burgh Quay (tel. 01–770182). Good-value place near O'Connell Bridge.

**Hugh Lane Gallery of Modern Art,** Charlemont House, Parnell Sq. Pleasant spot for snacks and lunches. Often serves Dublin "coddle."

**Little Lisbon,** 2 Upper Fownes St. (tel. 01–711274). Near Central Bank in trendy Temple Bar. Portuguese and Brazilian seafood. Heavily patronized by budget-minded "yuppies."

**Kilkenny Kitchen,** Nassau St. (tel. 01–777066). Attractive self-service restaurant with emphasis on fresh foods and home baking. Closes 5 P.M.

**Murphy Doodles,** 18 Suffolk St. (tel. 01–711038). Deli-style sandwiches, salads, tacos and pizzas.

**National Gallery,** Merrion Sq. (tel. 01–765268). Self-service with good variety. AE, DC, MC, V.

**Pasta Pasta,** 27 Exchequer St. (tel. 01–792565). Bright and pretty and lots of pasta. MC, V.

**Peacock Theater Foyer,** Abbey Theater, Marlborough St. Always has a cheerful crowd in for lunch. Best get there early.

**The Periwnkle Seafood Bar,** Powerscourt Townhouse Center, South William St. (tel. 01–718165). Bar service, fish specialties.

**Pizzaland.** Has two outlets in O'Connell St., Upper and Lower, also branches at 20 Henry St., 4 North Earl St. and 1 St. Stephen's Green. Freshly baked pizzas.

**PUBS.** To savor the full character of Dublin, it is more or less essential to visit at least a few bars, or pubs as they're called here—short for licensed public houses. Pubs are not just for drinking: conversation and musical entertainment are equally important, and those pubs that serve food make a significant and atmospheric contribution to the dining out scene in Dublin. Nowadays women are just as welcome as men in most bars. There was a time when women stayed in "the snug," walled-off, cabin-like areas which can still be seen in some unrenovated bars. Well-behaved children under the age of 14 are usually allowed in pubs that serve food at lunchtime and up to about 6 P.M., but their presence is entirely at the landlord's discretion, and only over-18s may consume alcohol.

Opening hours are from 10.30 or 11 A.M. to 11 P.M. (11.30 in summer). On Sundays the hours are 12.30 to 10 P.M.

The pubs listed below are divided into three categories: pubs that serve good food; character pubs that are worth a visit for literary, social, historical, or architectural reasons; and pubs that have live musical entertainment. Some overlap between the categories is inevitable.

Food is served at lunchtime and sometimes in the early evening too. A salad or dish of the day at the bar will cost from about IR£3.50 to IR£5. Pubs with separate restaurants fall into the lower part of the moderate price category—about IR£15 for a three-course meal.

**Pubs With Good Food. Davy Byrne's,** 21 Duke St. (off Grafton St.). One of the Dublin pubs immortalized by James Joyce, but modernized beyond all recognition. Offers fresh and smoked salmon salads and a hot daily special both at lunchtime and early evening.

**Paddy Cullen's,** Ballsbridge. Near the U.S. Embassy. Good reputation for lunchtime "pub grub," lively at night.

**Barry Fitzgerald's,** 90 Marlboro St. Salads and freshly cooked house specials at lunchtime in the upstairs bar Mon. to Fri., and pre-theater dinners.

**Lord Edward Bar,** 23 Christ Church Pl. This old-world pub provides a wide range of salads and a hot dish of the day at lunchtime only.

**Old Stand,** 37 Exchequer St. Close to Grafton St. Another well-known eating pub which serves steaks, grills and a daily house special.

**Kitty O'Shea's,** 23–25 Grand Canal St. (tel. 01–609965). Well-known pub-restaurant that recreates the atmosphere of old Dublin. Reservations for lunch and Sunday brunch (with music) accepted.

**Character Pubs.** These pubs tend to be at their liveliest between 5 and 7 in the evening and again from 10 P.M.

**The Bailey,** 2 Duke St. Mentioned by James Joyce in *Ulysses* under its original name of *Burton's.* Nowadays this is a very stylish spot.

**The Brazen Head,** Bridge St. Reputedly the city's oldest bar, dating from 1688.

**Doheny & Nesbitt's,** Merrion Row. Popular with lawyers, journalists and politicians. Has two old snugs.

**Grogan's Castle Lounge,** South William St. Not much to look at, but humming with interesting conversation.

**Henry Grattan,** 47–48 Lower Baggot St. Well-appointed, traditional pub which is a popular rendezvous for the business and sporting fraternity.

**Horseshoe Bar,** Shelbourne Hotel, St. Stephen's Green. You'll pay top prices here, but it's worth it to eavesdrop on Dublin's social elite in this intimate, highly elegant venue.

**Kiely's,** Donnybrook. The place where TV and radio people talk shop.

**The Long Hall,** South Gt., George's St. Atmospheric and unrenovated 19th-century bar.

**Madigan's.** North Earl St. A true cross-section of Dubliners here.

**McDaid's,** Harry St. Another of the real Dubliners' pubs, favored by the literati.

**Mulligan's,** Poolbeg St. Meeting place for journalists and students since 1782.

**Neary's,** Chatham St. (off Grafton St.). Distinguished by two torch-bearing cherubs over the front door. Used to be frequented mainly by actors and retains a theatrical atmosphere.

**O'Neill's Lounge Bars,** 37 Pearse St. (off Grafton St.). The labyrinthine bars of O'Neill's are popular with the students from nearby Trinity College.

**Palace Bar,** 21 Fleet St. You'll learn all about the history of this journalists' bar from the cartoons and paintings on its walls.

**The Plough,** Abbey St. A meeting place for theatrical folk, close to the Abbey Theater.

**Wm. Ryan's,** 28 Parkgate St. This Victorian gem is Dublin's best-preserved traditional pub and has four old-style snugs.

**Stag's Head,** Dame Court. Interesting interior with Victorian glass.

**Music Pubs.** Most sessions are free, but if you happen to choose a night with a big name there will be a charge of between IR£1 and IR£2.50. Organized sessions usually start about 9 P.M.; Sunday lunchtime is also a good bet at some of these venues. Not all music pubs have sessions every night, so it is advisable to check in advance by phone, or in the evening paper. The following are the major venues for traditional Irish music and ballads: **Abbey Inn,** Mary's Abbey, off Capel St. (tel. 01–788790); **An Béal Bocht,** Charlemont St. (tel. 01–755614); **Baggot Inn,** Baggot St. (tel. 01–761430); **Brazen Head,** 20 Lower Bridge St. (tel. 01–779549); **Pat Eagan's Backstage Bar,** East Essex St. (tel. 01–775482); **Hughes,** Chancery St. (tel. 01–726540); **The Merchant,** Bridge St. (tel. 01–793797); **Sean O'Casey's,** Marlborough St.; **O'Donoghue's,** 15 Merrion Row (tel. 01–607194); **Slattery's,** Capel St. (tel. 01–740416).

**HOW TO GET AROUND. By Bus.** There's a good city bus service, most services originating in or passing through the area of O'Connell St. and O'Connell Bridge. If the destination board indicates "An Lar," that means that the bus is going to the city center.

Get a Dublin District Bus Timetable (45p) at the C.I.E. Office, 59 Upper O'Connell St., which gives details of all routes, times of operation and the price code. The minimum fare is 45p, but in the city-center shopping area, there is a standard fare of 24p between 10 A.M. and 4.30 P.M. The Central Bus Station (Busarus), Store St., is the starting point for Expressway and other provincial services, and also the base for C.I.E. tours.

**By Train.** An electric rail commuter service, DART (standing for Dublin Area Rapid Transport), serves the suburbs out to Howth on the north side of the city, and Bray, Co. Wicklow, on the south. Fares are about the same as for buses. Street direction signs to DART stations read Staisiun/Station.

**By Taxi.** Taxis do not cruise, but are located beside the Central Bus Station and the rail stations (Connolly, Pearse, Heuston), as well as on

ranks at O'Connell Bridge, St. Stephen's Green, and near the major hotels.
They are not of uniform type or color. Check that the meter is on.

**By Bicycle.** Bicycles can be hired from *Little Sport,* 3 Merville Ave.,
Fairview (tel. 01–332405); *P.J. Power,* 124D Emmet Rd., Inchicore (tel.
01–532647); *Joe Daly,* Lower Main St., Dundrum (tel. 01–981485).

**TOURS AND EXCURSIONS. City Tours.** C.I.E., the national road
and rail transport company, offers several city sightseeing tours at around
IR£9 for a three-hour trip, or IR£14 for a full day. Book in advance at
the C.I.E. office, 59 Upper O'Connell St. (tel. 01–366111), or on the day
of travel at the Central Bus Station, from which all tours depart. There's
a "Traditional Irish Music Night" tour which takes you to Monkstown
for the purpose and gets back around 11:30 P.M. It costs IR£8.

*Gray Line Sightseeing,* (tel. 01–744466), operates morning, afternoon
and full-day city tours from around IR£9 to IR£14 for the full day.

The Irish Tourist Board has a specially signposted "Tourist Trail" taking in the main sights of central Dublin which can be completed on foot
in about three hours. The accompanying "Tourist Trail" booklet costs 75p
from the Irish Tourist Board, 14 Upper O'Connell St.

Guided walking tours of Old Dublin conducted by native Dubliners
leave from Christ Church Cathedral at 10.30 and 2 P.M. Mon. to Sat., 2
P.M. Sun. Charge IR£1.50. Confirm winter times by calling 01–532407.

*Gogan Tours,* 55 Dame St. (tel. 01–796022) offers a series of afternoon
and evening coach tours of Dublin and district with author and historian
Eamonn MacThomais as guide. Adult fare IR£10. Book in advance.

*Tour Guides Ireland,* Glendenning House, Wicklow St. (tel. 01–794291)
offers a selection of orientation tours including "Literary Dublin," "Georgian Dublin," and "Pub Tours."

**Excursions.** C.I.E. has some good day-long excursions on Sundays and
Thursdays to places such as the Boyne Valley, taking in Tara, Newgrange
and spots of historic interest, priced at around IR£14. Another good trip,
on Fridays, takes in the dramatic Wicklow Mountains as far as Glendalough and the Sally Gap for about the same price. Longer special excursions on Sundays reach Yeats Country, around Sligo; Galway in the west;
Cahir, Cashel and Ballyporeen (home of former President Reagan's forefa-
thers). The fare is about IR£15, but check (tel. 01–366111) because they
don't operate every Sunday.

*Gray Line* covers much the same territory. The "Glendalough Tour"
takes in Russborough House and its superb collection of paintings—fare
IR£17. There's also a tour that goes to the north Co. Dublin coast and
Malahide Castle, with its period furniture and National Portrait Gallery—
an afternoon's trip for about IR£9. Both C.I.E. and Gray Line operate
longer tours embracing a wider area of the country. Pricing depends on
the trip and a seven-day tour covering Cork, Bunratty Castle, Killarney,
the Cliffs of Moher and a return to Dublin by train, topped off with a half-
day touring Dublin and a visit to Russborough House, would be about
IR£200, including hotel, full Irish breakfast and admissions.

*Elegant Ireland,* 15 Harcourt St. (tel. 01–751665) organize customized
tours, for both large and small groups who are interested in architecture

and fine arts, which include visits with the owners to some of Ireland's stately homes and castles.

**HISTORIC BUILDINGS AND SITES. Christ Church Cathedral.** Dates back to Norman times and a leader of that era, one Strongbow, is entombed in the crypt. Open for visiting Mon. to Fri. 9.30–5, Sat. 9.30–4. Choral services on Sun. at 11 A.M. and 3 P.M.

**Custom House,** Butt Bridge. Splendid late-18th-century structure by James Gandon, who designed the Four Courts.

**Dublin Castle,** off Lord Edward St. Parts date back to Norman times, but the State Apartments, where the Republic's Presidents are inaugurated, is 18th century. They are open Mon. to Fri. 10–12.15 and 2–5, Sat. and Sun. 2–5.

**Dublin City Hall,** just outside the Castle walls. Was once the Royal Exchange and now contains the City mace, sword and archives, including the Irish Theater Archive.

**Four Courts,** Inns Quay. Facing across the Liffey, close to where Dublin was founded, this is the center of the administration of justice. Designed by James Gandon in 1815.

**General Post Office.** The G.P.O. to Dubliners, this is the only impressive building in O'Connell St. It was built in the early-19th century, but largely destroyed in the Easter Rising of 1916. The facade, however, remains. Monument inside commemorates the uprising.

**Royal Hospital,** Kilmainham. Built in the 18th century for old soldiers and vacated in 1927. Magnificently restored. Open Sat., Sun. and holidays, 11–6.

**St. Audoen's Arch,** High St., close to Christ Church Cathedral. This is the last surviving gate of the old city walls.

**St. George's Church,** Temple St. Designed by Francis Johnston in the early-19th century. A magnificent piece of ecclesiastical architecture with a fine spire. For information, contact the Rector, tel. 01–305289.

**St. Michan's Church,** Church St. Has mummified bodies in the crypt and a magnificent organ in the church. Open Mon. to Fri. 10–12.45 and 2–4.45.

**St. Patrick's Cathedral.** Founded in the 12th century, but probably best remembered for its Dean, Jonathan Swift, who is buried here. Open for visiting Mon. to Fri. 9–5, Sun. 10.30–4.30. Choral services Mon. to Fri. at 9.45 and 5.45, Sun. 11.15 and 3.15. Marsh's Library (1707) is next door.

**MUSEUMS AND GALLERIES. Chester Beatty Library and Art Gallery,** Shrewsbury Rd. Has a fine collection of Oriental and medieval manuscripts, including the oldest manuscript of the New Testament. Open Tues. to Fri. 10–5, Sat. 2–5. Guided tours Wed. and Sat. 2.30 P.M.

**Civic Museum,** South Williams St. Fine museum, full of interesting sidelights on old Dublin. It's located in what was once the Lord Mayor's Court. Open Tues. to Sat. 10–6, Sun. 11–2; closed Mon.

**Douglas Hyde Gallery,** Trinity College. Enter from Nassau St. Has frequent exhibitions of the work of Irish and other artists. Open Mon. to Sat. 11–5.

**Guinness Museum and Visitors' Center,** James's St. Screens a 30-minute documentary on the history of Guinness and the brewing process, plus a sample of the brew. Open Mon. to Fri. 10–3. The Museum of Brewing, relocated in a neighboring 19th-century hop store, opened in 1986: the building occasionally houses major art exhibits as well.

**Hugh Lane Gallery of Modern Art,** Parnell Sq. Contains part of the famous art collection of the late Sir Hugh Lane and much else. Open Tues. to Sat. 10–6, Sun. 11–2; closed Mon. Sometimes has noon lectures and concerts (free) on Sun.

**Irish Jewish Museum,** Walworth Rd. Reflects the history of the Jewish community in Ireland over 300 years. Open in summer Sun., Mon. and Wed. 11–3.30; winter, Sun. only 10.30–2.30; or by appointment (tel. 01–905689).

**Irish Whiskey Corner,** Bow St., near the Haymarket. Exhibits and audio-visual show on the history of whiskey followed by tastings. By appointment only (tel. 01–725566). Admission IR£2.

**Marsh's Library,** near St. Patrick's Cathedral. Founded in 1707 and has an important collection of old books of theology and medicine, as well as Hebrew, Syriac, Greek and Latin literature. Open Mon., Wed., Thurs. and Fri. 2–4, Sat. 10.30–12.30.

**Museum of Childhood,** Palmerston Park. A fine collection of dolls and a 12-ft., 20-room crystal palace. Open afternoons 2–6.

**National Gallery,** Merrion Sq. Good collection of Old Masters, plus many interesting Irish painters. Lectures on Thurs. and Sun.; conducted tours. Open Mon. to Fri. 10–5, Sat. 10–1, Sun. 2–5; late night viewing on Thurs. till 9.

**National Library of Ireland,** Kildare St. Open Mon. to Fri. 10–10, Sat. 10–1; closed for three weeks in July and Aug.

**National Museum of Irish Antiquities,** Kildare St. Art, Industrial and Natural History sections. See the torques from Tara, the Tara brooch, the famed Ardagh chalice and the Cross of Cong. Open Tues. to Sat. 10–5, Sun. 2–5; closed Mon.

**National Portrait Gallery,** Malahide Castle. Located a few miles north of the city. Frequent guided tours. Open Mon. to Fri. 10–5, Sat. 10–1, Sun. 2–5; late night viewing on Thurs. till 9.

**National Wax Museum,** Granby Row. Open Mon. to Fri. 10–5.30, Sun. 1–6.

**RTE Broadcasting Museum,** 27 Lower Rathmines Rd. Open Mon. to Sat. 2–5.30.

**Royal Hospital Kilmainham.** Important, recently restored 17th-century building. Open Sat., Sun. and Bank Hols. 11–6 for guided tours. Confirm (tel. 01–718666).

**Royal Irish Academy Library.** Open Mon. to Fri. 9.30–5.30, Sat. 9.30–1; closed last three weeks in Aug.

**Trinity College Library.** Exhibits include the famous *Book of Kells,* one of the most beautifully illustrated Gospels in the world. Open Mon. to Fri. 9.30–4.45; Sat. 9.30–12.45. Admission charge Apr. to Sept. Go early to avoid standing in line.

**Viking Adventure Center,** St. Audoen's Crypt, High St. (opposite Christ Church Cathedral). Exciting multi-media reconstruction of a street in Viking Dublin with live "Viking" guides. Open Mon. to Fri 10–3; Sat. and Sun. 10–4.30. Admission IR£2.75, children IR£2.

**PARKS AND GARDENS.** There is no charge for admission to any of the following, except the zoo section of the Phoenix Park. The **Phoenix**

**Park,** all 1,750 acres of it, is open to the visitor. It has fantastic zoological gardens (admission IR£3, children half price) and an extensive Peoples' Park of flowers and shrubs, as well as a herd of deer and polo grounds (watch it and any other game free). **Aras an Uachtarain** (the House of the President) can be seen through the trees; note its resemblance to Washington's White House. The residence of the American Ambassador is also in the Park.

**Herbert Park.** 32 acres in Ballsbridge, beside the American Embassy. The Dublin International Exhibition of 1907 was held here. Nothing remains of the spectacular show, but there are restful and well-kept gardens and a duck pond, bowling greens and tennis courts.

**Marley Grange Park,** Rathfarnham. 300 acres in the foothills of Dublin. Plenty of space to roam and rest. Sculpture park. Aerobic buffs meet here for their exercises and jogging on Sunday mornings. Bus 47B.

**Merrion Square Park,** at Merrion Square. A well-tended flower garden with some modern sculpture and an opportunity for a break in sightseeing.

**National Botanic Gardens,** Glasnevin. Impressive collection of plants, shrubs and trees from all over the world. Open Mon. to Sat. 9.30–6 (sunset in winter), Sun. 11–5. Admission free.

**St. Anne's,** Raheny. Gigantic 3-acre rose garden.

**St. Stephen's Green,** at the top of Grafton Street. An excellent spot to rest and enjoy a picnic lunch; many Dubliners do it. Sometimes there's entertainment in the bandstand. Features a special garden for the blind.

## MUSIC, THEATERS AND MOVIES. Music.
Dublin is alive with music. The Radio Telefis Eireann Symphony Orchestra, in effect the national orchestra, performs regularly in the rather splendid new **National Concert Hall** in Earlsfort Terrace, part of the old University College buildings. The Hall also hosts a wide variety of other musical entertainments from the Vienna Philharmonic Orchestra (on tour), to soloists, the New Ireland Chamber Orchestra and the new National Youth Jazz Band. Monthly programs are available well in advance. Prices are around IR£8 at the most. Hear the Palestrina Choir at the Catholic **Pro-Cathedral** in Marlborough St. every Sunday at 11 A.M.,and the fine male voices in **St. Patrick's Cathedral.** Recitals are frequent during winter months at the **Royal Dublin Society's Hall** in Ballsbridge, and the **Examination Hall** of Trinity College. **St. Ann's Church** in Dawson St. has occasional short concerts at lunchtime on Thursdays.

For pop concerts the **Royal Dublin Society's** auditorium at Ballsbridge is the main spot. Also occasionally at **Goff's Paddock,** Kill, 15 miles out of town, or the **National Stadium,** South Circular Rd. They're all well publicized. Prices up to IR£20, depending on the star.

Traditional Irish music is something you must hear, and some of the best of it is heard in pubs. Inquire as to when and where the regular *seisúns* (pronounced "say-shoons") take place, or ring **Comhaltas Ceoltóira Eireann** (tel. 01–800295)—just say "Co-ultas", they'll understand—about performances in their theater at 32–33 Belgrave Sq., Monkstown.

True ballads go with traditional music, and you can often hear them on Sunday nights in the **Connolly Auditorium** of Liberty Hall, beside Butt Bridge, and even more frequently—if not always in their purest form—in music pubs (see page 102).

**Theaters.** Somebody once said that Dublin is a place where half the people are writing plays and the whole lot of them are acting. Not quite true, but the city has a rich literary and theatrical past and enough theaters to cater for a wide range of tastes, and to compete with television. Prices are low by capital-city standards, around IR£9 for best seats. If you are in town in the fall you can catch some of the new plays by Irish and foreign playwrights at the Dublin Theater Festival. The Irish theater is always in a state of crisis, mostly financial, but it survives in a very lively way.

**Abbey Theater,** Marlborough St. The Irish National Theater was founded by the poet-playwright William Butler Yeats, Lady Augusta Gregory, Elizabeth Horniman from Manchester and others in 1904 in a building which was part Mechanics Institute and part the City Morgue. It flourished with playwrights like J. M. Synge, Yeats and later Sean O'Casey. The old building was destroyed by fire in 1951 and after some years of exile in an old vaudeville theater, the Queen's (now demolished), it was moved to the new building in 1966. It continues to feature works of the older generations of playwrights, but encourages young new Irish writers. Take time out to look at the portraits of Abbeyites of the past which are exhibited in the foyer.

**Focus,** Pembroke Pl., off Pembroke St. Resident company presenting mainly contemporary works.

**Gaiety Theater,** South King St. The city's oldest theater, opened in 1871, had its most recent facelift in 1984. Grand opera, musical comedy, drama, revues.

**Gate Theater,** Parnell Sq. Modern drama and plays by Irish writers. Intimate and lively.

**Lambert Puppet Theater,** Clifton Lane, Monkstown. First-class puppet work by Eugene Lambert, his family and others. Worth a visit. Call first (tel. 01–800974).

**Olympia Theater,** Dame St. Opened as Dan Lowry's Music Hall long ago, but today features drama, comedy, vaudeville, ballet.

**Peacock Theater,** Lower Abbey St., is the Abbey's pocket-basement unit. More experimental than its big brother, although using the same company; occasional one-man shows. Art exhibitions in the tiny foyer.

**Players,** Trinity College. Varied and interesting productions by Dublin University Players.

**Project Arts Center,** East Essex St. Good work, mainly experimental, by young players.

**Movies.** Several movie theaters with multiple-screen units are located around the city center. *The Savoy, Carlton* and *Ambassador* are on O'Connell St.; *Adelphi,* Mid Abbey St.; *Screen on the Green,* Hawkins St. All show new release films. Admission around IR£3.50.

**SHOPPING.** Some of the international names of the world of haute couture are located in Dublin: *Paul Costelloe,* 42 Drury St.; *Michael Mortell,* the Westbury Center, off Grafton St.; *Sybil Connolly* and *Raymond Kenna,* both on Merrion Sq.; *Ib Jorgensen,* 35 Dawson St.; *Thomas Wolfangel,* 99 Lower Baggot St.; *Cleo Ltd.,* 18 Kildare St. Other spots high in the fashion field are *Richard Allan,* Grafton St.; *William Elliott,* Wicklow St., and *Westbury Designs,* Westbury Center.

Best department stores are the upmarket *Switzer's* and *Brown Thomas's*, both on Grafton St., *Arnott's* on Henry St. (there's a smaller branch in Grafton St.), *Clery's* on O'Connell St., *Roche's* on Henry St., and *BHS* on O'Connell St., are in the middle price bracket; lower prices will be found at *Dunne's* (many branches) and *Penney's*, Mary St. Take a look around the ILAC Center just off Henry St. British chain stores *Laura Ashley*, *Next*, *Principles*, and *Marks & Spencer*, all have branches in Grafton St.

For tweeds try *Kevin & Howlin*, Nassau St., *Cleo Ltd.*, 18 Kildare St.; *Irish Cottage Industries*, 18 Dawson St., also good for knitwear. *Joan Doherty* in the Powerscourt Center is another spot for tweeds and the like. Aran knitwear is also to be found in plenty at *Creation Boutique* in Creation Arcade, Duke St., and *The Woollen Mills* at the Ha'penny Bridge. There are a number of boutiques around the Grafton St. area, which embraces the Westbury Center, the Powerscourt Center, and Gaiety Corner. *Donegal Design* is off the main shopping areas at Friarsland Mill, Roebuck Rd., but worth the journey, particularly for mohair fashionwear.

For souvenirs, start looking at *Fergus O'Farrell's*, Duke St. For antiques the area is around Molesworth St. and Dawson St. *Dillon Antiques*, *Dankers*, *J.W. Weldon* and *Fine Art Showrooms* are in South Anne St.; *Gerald Kenyon* is in South William St. Or you might see an auction advertisement by *James Adam's* or *Allen & Townsend*, both on St. Stephen's Green, and that's where an interesting piece of old Irish silver or other antique may be discovered. There are a number of commercial art galleries which offer interesting paintings as souvenirs, among them the *Grafton Gallery* in Anne's Lane, and the small *Arianne Gallery* in Molesworth St., *Tom Caldwell Gallery*, 31 Upper Fitzwilliam St. and the *Oliver Dowling Gallery*, 19 Kildare St.

Souvenir hunting can be a special pleasure in the *Tower Design Center*, Pearse St. Here a number of craftworkers are gathered together in about 30 workshops in a tower that was once a sugar refinery and later an iron foundry. They all use traditional skills and methods to produce jewelry, weaving, woodcarving—you name it. Take the 1, 2 or 3 bus from outside Clery's store on O'Connell St. The entrance is on Grand Canal St.

When you are in Trinity College, visit the *Library Shop;* it provides excellent values for books, prints and jewelry. And when in the *National Gallery*, you will find a good range of prints and reproductions on sale.

For blackthorn sticks the place is *Johnston's* at 11 Wicklow St. On the ground floor of the Norwich Union building in Nassau St. (beside Trinity College), *Kilkenny Design Workshops* have an excellent display of tableware, kitchenware and soft furnishings from all over Ireland; worth a visit, even if you don't buy anything. There's a pleasant restaurant upstairs. Also see the *House of Ireland* at 37–38 Nassau St. for Waterford glass and other good gifts.

Dublin Airport, like all international airports, has its duty-free shop for those last-minute items, or to attract the impulse buyer. It does remove the paperwork of recovering the V.A.T. you may have paid on items bought in the city.

**NIGHTLIFE.** Dublin does not have sophisticated nightclubs in the international sense, but it does have a number of dine-and-dance restaurants and discos, which are often billed as nightclubs.

**Dine-and-Dance. Club Nassau,** Power's Hotel, Nassau St. (tel. 01–605244).

**Flamingos,** Parkes Hotel, Stillorgan (tel. 01–881621). About six miles out of town.

**Green Isle Hotel,** Naas Rd., Clondalkin (tel. 01–593406). Sat. only.

**Cabaret.** Though not exactly on a par with Las Vegas or Paris, the following have good entertainment, but it's best to book.

**The Abbey Tavern** at Howth (tel. 01–322006). Eight miles from the city center, featuring traditional Irish music and song, Mon.–Sat.

**Braemor Rooms,** Churchtown (tel. 01–988664).

**Burlington Hotel,** Upper Leeson St. (tel. 01–605222).

**Clontarf Castle,** Clontarf (tel. 01–332271).

**Jury's Hotel,** Ballsbridge (tel. 01–605000).

**Sheiling Hotel,** Howth Rd., Raheny (tel. 01–314222).

**Discos.** Average admission charges are about IR£5 or IR£6 at weekends. Some are licensed to sell all alcoholic drinks, others wine only. If it matters to you, check first. A modest supper is usually included in the admission price.

There is an ever-changing selection of late-night discos in an area known as "The Leeson Street Strip" which can be found, naturally enough, on Leeson Street and comes to life between 11 P.M. and 2 A.M.

**Chiki's,** Harcourt Hotel, 60–61 Harcourt St. (tel. 01–752013).

**Gigi's,** Russell Court Hotel, 21–23 Harcourt St. (tel. 01–784991).

**New Annabel's,** behind the Burlington Hotel, Mespil Rd. (tel. 01–605222).

**Raffles,** Sach's Hotel, Morehampton Rd. (tel. 01–680995).

**Rumours,** O'Connell St. (tel. 01–741635).

**SPORTS. Golf.** Golf is the major interest of most sporting visitors to Ireland and you will find 16 courses within a radius of 12 miles of the city center. The following are all 18-hole courses, with the exception of the Deerpark, which has 27 holes: **Deerpark Hotel,** Howth; **Castle Golf Club,** Rathfarnham; **Clontarf G.C.; Donabate G.C.; Dun Laoghaire G.C.; Edmondston G.C.; Elm Park G.C.; Grange G.C.,** Rathfarnham; **Hermitage G.C.,** Lucan; **Howth G.C.; Island G.C.,** Malahide; **Newlands G.C.,** Clondalkin; **Milltown G.C.; Portmarnock G.C.; Royal Dublin G.C.,** Dollymount; **Woodbrook G.C.,** near Bray. There's also a driving range at Leopardstown Racecourse.

**Horse-racing.** There are two courses, both within 10 miles of the city center: the **Phoenix Park** course, just outside the Phoenix Park gates, and **Leopardstown.** Frequent meetings, including evening meets in summer.

**Sailing.** Contact the *Irish Yachting Association,* 4 Haddington Rd., Dun Laoghaire (tel. 01–800239).

**Swimming.** Wherever the sea comes in. The most popular spots are Portmarnock Strand on the north side of the city, and Salthill and Sandycove on the south. There is a seawater swimming pool at Blackrock. Several of the hotels have heated pools.

**Tennis.** There are public courts at **Herbert Park,** Ballsbridge and at **Bushy Park,** Rathmines.

**Spectator Sports.** The Gaelic Athletics Association (G.A.A.) games—football and hurling—are well worth watching for speed and excitement, particularly at Croke Park. Check the sports pages for details. Association football (soccer) is played at both professional and amateur level. Rugby football is strictly a winter game, best seen at the Lansdowne Rd. stadium. You can see most spectator sports played on the "Fifteen Acres" in Phoenix Park on Sundays. For track and field, Santry Stadium is the national and international arena.

**USEFUL ADDRESSES. Embassies:** *United States Embassy,* 42 Elgin Rd., Ballsbridge (tel. 01–688777); *Canadian Embassy,* 65 St. Stephen's Green (tel. 01–781988); *British Embassy,* Merrion Rd. (tel. 01–695211).

**Travel operators:** *Aer Lingus,* Upper O'Connell St. (tel. 01–370191); *British Airways,* 112 Grafton St. (tel. 01–686666); *Automobile Association,* 23 Suffolk St. (tel. 01–779481); *Irish Rail* passenger inquiries (tel. 01–366222); *Irish Bus* passenger inquiries (tel. 01–366111); *American Express,* 116 Grafton St. (tel. 01–772874); *Thomas Cook,* 118 Grafton St. (tel. 01–771721).

**Car hire.** *Avis,* 1 Hanover St. East (tel. 01–776971); *Boland's Inter-Rent,* 38 Pearse St. (tel. 01–770704); *Dan Dooley Rent-a-Car,* 5 Lyon House, Cathal Brugha St. (tel. 01–720777); *Flynn Bros. Rent-a-Car,* 151 Lower Drumcondra Rd. (tel. 01–379611); *Hertz,* Leeson St. Bridge (tel. 01–602255); *Kenning Car Hire,* 42 Westland Row (tel. 01–772723); *Murray's Europcar,* Baggott St. Bridge (tel. 01–681777). All have desks in the arrivals concourse at Dublin Airport.

**Emergency.** Garda, Fire, Ambulance, 999.

# THE ENVIRONS OF DUBLIN

*Trips Not Beyond the Pale*

Dublin is an ideally situated touring center with a great variety of attractions all within an hour's drive of the city. To the south are the sandy beaches and richly scenic hills and valleys of the Wicklow Mountains. To the north, in the shadow of the Mourne Mountains, lies Dundalk, the lush plains of County Meath and the Boyne Valley, with its fascinating archeological sites. Inland, the Curragh at Kildare and the National Stud form the heart of the Irish racing world, and offer yet another aspect of Irish life for the visitor to enjoy.

The area is well-served by public transport. Bus tours from Dublin cover County Wicklow as far as Glendalough in the southwest, and the Boyne Valley to the north. Suburban bus services reach into the foothills of the Dublin mountains, while C.I.E. Expressway services take in the outlying towns. Dublin Bay itself is served by a commuter electric train (DART— Dublin Area Rapid Transport) which was extensively modernized in 1984. Fast new trains run along the coast linking the fishing port and sailing marina at Howth in the north with the popular resort and dormitory town of Bray in the south.

### Inside The Pale

Most of the places described in this chapter come within what was once known as the Pale, that part of Ireland in which English law was formally acknowledged. The Pale was created after Henry II subdued the Norman nobles in the 12th century and named his son John, Lord of Ireland. Its boundaries varied, but roughly included Counties Dublin, Kildare, Meath and Louth. As an entity, the Pale disappeared in Elizabethan times, but it long continued in the Irish mind as the stronghold of English rule. The term Pale gave rise to the expression "beyond the pale," an indication that somebody was excluded, outside the law. Ruins of old castles suggest the borders of the area. Interestingly, it never extended into Wicklow, the county to the south of Dublin. Here the wild mountainous country made law enforcement virtually impossible for centuries and there were frequent raids down from the mountains into places like Rathfarnham, which are now suburbs of Dublin. The marauding tribes of Wicklow were the main reason why, until the early-18th century, wealthy Dubliners did not consider it safe to live south of the Liffey.

## The Inner Environs

The best way to explore the inner environs along the coast of Dublin Bay is to do as the Dubliners do, and make use of the DART commuter service. Connolly Station (up Amiens Street from the bus station), Tara Street Station (south of the Liffey opposite the Custom House) or Pearse Station in Westland Row are the three most central stations. Trains run every five minutes or so. The service has become so popular that it has given a new meaning to the verb "to dart," which is now used in Dublin in such sentences as "See you later, I'm DARTing out to Bray."

A northbound DART to Howth (pronounce it to rhyme with "both") will give you unsurpassable views of Dublin Bay. The inner harbor owes its present shape to a figure readily connected in most minds with the mutiny on the *Bounty:* Captain Bligh. He was demoted to the post of Harbor Master at Dublin following the mutiny and built a dike which modernized the port by forming a deep channel in 1790. Its extremity is marked today by a lighthouse. Over the years the dike caused the formation of North Bull Island, which is linked to the mainland by a causeway. The island is the home of the Royal Dublin Golf Club, venue for the Irish Open. It is also a bird sanctuary, and the Brent Geese from Greenland who winter on it hatched their first young there in 1985.

Slightly inland from the coast at Marino is the Casino, which has nothing whatever to do with gambling. Rather, it is one of Dublin's architectural gems, often compared to the Petit Trianon at Versailles. It is a charming Palladian villa constructed between 1762 and 1777 in the gardens of Lord Charlemont's estate. Unfortunately, the main house no longer exists, although the tiny villa still survives today. The building is compact, full of architectural surprises, and is being fully restored in accordance with the plans of its architect, Sir William Chambers, which have fortunately survived intact. Original color schemes and plasterwork in this square building are being painstakingly renewed.

Clontarf, now a suburb of Dublin, was the scene of the famous Battle of Good Friday in 1014 when Brian Boru led the Irish to victory over the Danes. He was later killed in his tent while thanking God for victory in the battle. Clontarf Castle, dating from 1835, is built on the site of an ancient fortification of the Pale.

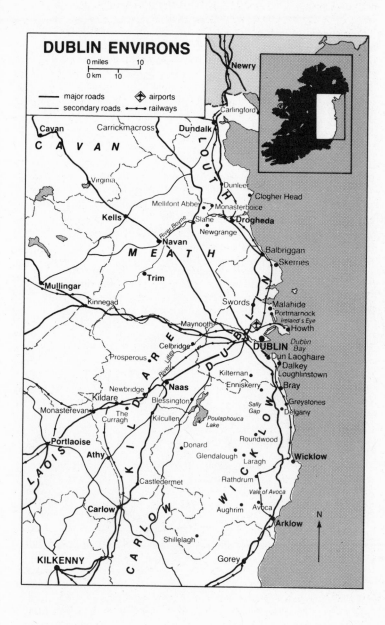

## Howth Head

Howth Head was once an island but is now a peninsular head dominating the north of Dublin Bay. The harbor is on the north side of the headland and was constructed in 1807–9. It is now a popular sailing center as well as a small but active fishing port. Howth Head is noted for its bracing air, and there is a cliff walk to the early-19th-century Bailey Lighthouse which gives panoramic views over Dublin Bay and the Wicklow Hills. The village of Howth still retains a certain character, but modern villas have been allowed to proliferate and cover parts of the headland to its detriment.

Howth Castle, a short distance from the harbor, has a garden famed for its beauty, especially in late-May and early-June when over 2,000 varieties of azaleas and rhododendrons are in bloom on its steep slopes. In 1575 the fabled Irish sea captain, Gráinne Ní Mháille (Grace O'Malley), called at Howth Castle on her return from a visit to Queen Elizabeth in London. Against all laws of hospitality, she and her crew were refused food and shelter on the excuse that the family was at dinner. In revenge, her crew kidnapped the young heir of the St. Lawrence family, and Grace would not release him until Lord Howth promised that in future the gates of his castle would always be open at mealtimes. To this day, descendants of the same Lawrence family always lay an extra place at the dining table.

The island visible off-shore is Ireland's Eye, and can be visited by boat in the summer. Early-Christians had a monastery here believed to date from the 6th-century. An old stone church still marks the spot.

## SOUTH OF DUBLIN

The southern suburbs of Dublin give a preview of the east coast, with the Irish sea rolling in on a mixture of sandy and rocky coastline. This was the site of the first stretch of railway in Ireland, completed at Dún Laoghaire (pronounced "Dunleary") in 1834. In those days the town was known as Kingstown in memory of a visit by King George IV in 1821. It was renamed, along with many other places that recalled the days of the British "Ascendancy," after the establishment of the Irish Free State a century later. The harbor was built in the early-19th century for the mail boat, and is now used for passenger ferry services to and from Holyhead in Wales. It is also Ireland's principal yachting center, and headquarters of the Royal St. George (founded 1832) and the Royal Irish (founded 1846) yacht clubs. Both had regular races and regattas. The National Maritime Museum of Ireland in the Mariner's Church contains a number of historical models, and a French longboat captured at Bantry Bay during an ill-fated attempt to land French forces on Irish soil.

A mile or so beyond Dun Laoghaire, at Sandycove, is the Martello tower in which James Joyce and Oliver St. John Gogarty resided briefly in 1904. It is described in the opening chapter of *Ulysses,* with Gogarty portrayed as Buck Mulligan. Today the tower houses a Joyce Museum opened in 1962 by the remarkable American woman, Sylvia Beach, who first published *Ulysses* in Paris in 1922. Apart from its associations with one of Ireland's most controversial writers, it is worth visiting because it is one of the few Martello towers open to the public. Martello towers are

## NORTH OF DUBLIN

Dubliners are especially fortunate in having not only County Wicklow within easy reach, but also the attractive countryside and coast to the north of the city. Portmarnock, for example, a few miles north of Howth Head, has three miles of golden sandy beach making it a popular summer destination. The beach featured in aviation history as the point of departure for the late Sir Charles Kingsford Smith in his monoplane, *Southern Cross,* on his transatlantic flight from east to west in 1930. To golfers, Portmarnock is known for its championship course.

Malahide Castle, the former home of Lord Talbot de Malahide, dates back to Norman days. Remarkably, it was in the hands of the family until 1976, a total of 791 years. It was here that a remarkable collection of James Boswell's private papers were discovered by American researchers in the '30s. One batch, including the manuscript of Boswell's *Journal of a Tour to the Hebrides,* was found in a box which was supposed to contain croquet equipment, and still later, yet another batch was found when an outhouse was being cleared.

The Talbot family sold the castle to Dublin County Council in 1976, and the National Gallery of Ireland acquired the fine collection of portraits when the contents of the castle were sold. They remain in the building as the nucleus of the National Portrait Gallery's collection. Historic battle, sporting and other pictures have been added to create a panoramic view of Irish life. In addition, the halls and rooms contain one of the best collections of Irish period furniture in the country. In the grounds of the castle there is an extensive exhibition of pieces from the Fry Collection of Irish railway models dating from the 1840s and '50s.

About three miles west of Malahide is Swords, the site of a monastery founded in the 6th century by St. Colmcille. No trace remains of the monastery, but the shell of Swords Castle stands at the northern end of town.

The coast road, the N1, winds north through Balbriggan to Drogheda, situated on the river Boyne which at this point separates Counties Louth and Meath. Drogheda is in County Louth. At only 317 square miles, it is the smallest county in Ireland.

A short detour to Donabate will lead you to Newbridge Demesne, an 18th-century manor and estate. The house, outbuildings, and gardens have been fully restored to give an idea of the demesne as it was run 150 years ago.

The Irish name for Drogheda is Droichead Átha, Bridge of the Ford. The town has bitter recollections of sieges in the 17th century, foremost among them its capture by Oliver Cromwell in 1649, when his troops massacred 2,000 of the garrison and inhabitants and transported others to the West Indies. Only one of the gates of the town walls remains, this being St. Lawrence's Gate in St. Lawrence Street; it is one of the most perfect specimens remaining in Ireland and well worth seeing. The ruin of the 17th-century Augustinian Abbey consists of a tower and an arch spanning Abbey Lane. In Upper Magdalene Street, a two-story tower springing from a pointed arch is all that remains of the Dominican Priory founded in the 13th century.

The imposing Gothic-style Roman Catholic Church, St. Peter's, in the main street, has a shrine housing the head of St. Oliver Plunkett, Archbishop of Armagh, who was hanged, drawn and quartered at Tyburn (London) in 1681; the door of his cell is preserved beside the church. He was canonized in 1975.

Millmount House Museum illustrates the colorful, often violent history of Drogheda. It also houses a collection relating to the linen industry which once flourished in the town.

## The Boyne Valley

Drogheda is a convenient base for exploring the scenery and antiquities of the Boyne Valley. An obelisk on the north bank of the river Boyne about a mile outside town marks the site of the Battle of the Boyne where, in 1690, the Catholic James II's hopes of regaining the English throne were shattered by the victory of William of Orange. The site was purchased by an American, James Delaney, in 1983 and has been handed over to a trust who, in consultation with Mr. Delaney, are considering appropriate uses for the land, including the idea of a park of reconciliation.

Slane Castle, at a crossroads beside the Boyne, is the home of Lord Henry Mountcharles and was built in the late-18th century on the site of an earlier castle. Its grounds form a natural amphitheater and for the last few years have been used for a large open-air rock concert every summer: Bruce Springsteen played at Slane in 1985, Bob Dylan in 1984, the Rolling Stones in 1983. The nearby village of Slane is exceptionally pretty. It was the birthplace of the soldier poet Francis Ledwidge (1887–1917) who died in France during World War I. His home, a stone built cottage, is now a museum.

The Hill of Slane is within sight of Tara, known in popular imagination as the seat of the High Kings of Ireland. Nowadays its summit is crowned by a statue of St. Patrick. The 19th-century ballad by Thomas Moore, *The Harp that Once Through Tara's Halls,* was an important contributing factor in the over-romanticized view of Tara in the late-19th century. Systematic excavation by 20th-century archeologists has led to the less exciting conclusion that the remains are those of an iron-age Celtic fort which had multiple ring forts and a neolithic passage grave, abandoned in the 6th or 7th century. Over 500 years later, in the 12th century, the sites were erroneously identified in the *Book of Leinster* thus misleading generations of scholars. Further confusion was caused by a group of 19th-century religious zealots from England who believed that the Ark of the Covenant was buried at Tara. They were to destroy many important remains in their search for it. Today, there are various earthworks to be seen at Tara, but you will need expert assistance to identify them.

## Newgrange and Knowth

While it may lack the romantic associations of Tara, the site at nearby Newgrange has far more to offer the visitor. In fact, this recently excavated and restored neolithic passage grave is often cited as one of the most spectacular prehistoric monuments in western Europe.

Identified as the Brugh na Boinne (Palace of the Boyne) of ancient Irish tales, Newgrange was constructed as a communal tomb sometime about the year 4000 B.C. The mound is 280 feet in diameter and was originally surrounded by a circle of standing stones, 12 of which remain, the whole covering about an acre. The entrance, a 62 foot-long passage, faces towards the south. At the winter solstice the rising sun hits a roof box above the entrance and creeps up the passageway bathing the inner chamber in light for 15 to 20 minutes. Many of the stones are carved with elaborate patterns. Enthusiastic guides will explain the intricacies of the site, and there is a display center to help you to interpret this prehistoric wonder.

There is much excitement in archeological circles about an even more interesting site at Knowth. The site is closed for excavation, but visitors can watch the work from a platform.

## North of Drogheda

North of the Boyne from Drogheda is the little fishing village of Clogherhead, a good place for sea angling. Inland, the ruins at Monasterboice recall a monastery that was a great seat of learning until about the 12th century. Muireadach's Cross dates from the 10th century and is reckoned by many to be one of the finest in Ireland, both in quality and state of repair. It is one of three elaborately carved High Crosses and is the most important of the monastic remains which include a Round Tower, reputedly the highest in Ireland, and two churches. The south church is 9th century, while the other was built about four centuries later.

Mellifont Abbey, three miles away, was the first Cistercian monastery in the country. Today, fragments and the ground plan alone remain. There are a few arches of the Romanesque cloister, an interesting octagonal lavabo with remarkable decorations, and a 14th-century chapter house. The Cistercians have a modern foundation known as New Mellifont and built in the '30s a few miles away at Collon, the village where the 19th-century admiral, Sir Francis Beaufort, inventor of the Beaufort Scale for wind measurement, was born.

Dundalk, the county town of Louth, is the base for exploring the Cooley Peninsula, which juts out into the Irish Sea, separating Dundalk Bay from the deep inlet of Carlingford Lough to the north. This area was the scene of some of the legendary deeds of the boy hero, Cuchulainn, including the famed Cattle Raid of Cooley, one of the best known of the folk tales of ancient Ireland. This tells of a four-day battle for a great bull coveted by Queen Maeve of Connacht—some say a black bull, some say a red, but all agree that it was a mighty battle. In the Cooley Mountains, the legends tell of the burial place of Bran, the mastiff of the giant Finn McCool, and a signpost points to the Long Woman's Grave. Near Ballymascanlon is the Proleek Dolmen. Dolmens, of which there are many in various parts of the country, were simple megalithic tombs consisting of a large capstone on three or more supporting stones (the capstone at Proleek weighs about 50 tons).

Along the north side of the Cooley Peninsula, there are views of the Mountains of Mourne in Northern Ireland across Carlingford Lough. In Carlingford itself there is plenty of evidence of the town's importance in earlier centuries. King John's Castle here is a fortress dating from the 13th century, while the well-preserved Taafe's Castle dates from the 16th century. The ruins of the 14th-century Dominican Abbey include a fine Gothic arch beneath an impressive square tower. The Mint is typical of a fortified town house of 400 years ago, while the nearby Tholsel, once a gate in the town wall, also served as the town jail at a later period.

## County Meath

County Meath, sometimes called Royal Meath, lies to the northwest of Dublin. This is great hunting country, and indeed has been for centuries. There are many records and depictions of hunting carved on old monuments and stones around the county, including a particularly famous one at Kells. Kells in fact also boasts five High Crosses, ancient carved crosses, the most important being the Market Cross, which is carved with religious scenes and lies in the center of the town. It is generally considered one of the most beautiful of Ireland's many Celtic crosses, though its past has not always been peaceful. In 1798, for example, it was used as a gallows from which to hang rebels.

Kells also boasts a Round Tower. There are about 70 such towers in Ireland, in various states of preservation. They were mainly built between the 9th and 12th centuries by various ecclesiastical establishments for use as watch towers, store houses and places of refuge. The door is usually at least ten feet from the ground. They vary in height from between 50 and 100 feet, and are generally tapered toward the top, often crowned with a conical capstone of masonry. The towers have a number of floors which are reached by a series of trapdoors and ladders.

The other major place of interest in Meath is the little town of Trim, about 15 miles south of Kells. It's dominated by the 70-foot high walls of King John's Castle, the largest Anglo-Norman fortress in Ireland. It was built originally in the 12th century by Hugh de Lacy, but substantially rebuilt after 100 years. It is believed that it was here that Richard II imprisoned the future King Henry V of England.

## WEST OF DUBLIN—County Kildare

St. Patrick's College, Maynooth, some 16 miles due west of Dublin, trains priests who serve in all parts of the globe. These days, however, it is much more than just a seminary. Its campus contains not one, but two universities, in addition to the seminary. Since 1966 Maynooth has been a recognized college of the National University of Ireland, admitting lay students, and since 1896 it has also been a Pontifical University. The entrance to the college is beside the remains of Maynooth Castle, an ancient seat of the Fitzgeralds whose keep dates from the 13th century. The college has a most interesting museum open to visitors during the vacation period. The architecture is varied, as the college has been considerably enlarged since it was founded in 1795.

At the east end of Maynooth is Carton House, country residence of the Dukes of Leinster, whose Dublin house is now the home of Ireland's Parliament. It was designed by the great German architect Richard Cassels, and is a very fine example of mid-Georgian architecture. Unfortunately it is no longer open to the public. However, Castletown House, the largest private house in Ireland, lies just a few miles to the south at Celbridge, and is now in the hands of the Irish Georgian Society who welcome visitors. The village of Celbridge was built at the same time as the house—1721–28—and is designed to give importance to the long avenue of limes that leads up to this perfect Palladian house. It was designed by Alessandro Galilei for William Connolly, Speaker of the Irish Parliament, and decorated by the Francini brothers and other artists. Much of its original furniture is still in place, and it is well worth making the 13-mile journey from Dublin to pay it a visit. It is one of several houses and many monuments which have been saved by the energetic endeavours of Desmond Guinness, founder of the Irish Georgian Society. There is no government money available in Ireland for the preservation of historic buildings, (unless they are designated a "national monument") so the Society fulfills an important function. Chapters in the U.K. and U.S.A. help to raise funds. New members are always welcome, and the annual subscription is a modest IR£5. Contact Desmond Guinness, Leixlip Castle, Leixlip, Co. Kildare.

## Courses for Horses

The main Dublin to Cork road—the N7—takes you through the center of the Irish racing world. Goff's Kildare Paddocks at Kill, for example, 15 miles from Dublin, sells over 50 per cent of all Irish bred horses. Their 1980 turnover of IR£22 million gives some idea of the importance of horse breeding to the national economy. Goff's are a long-established horse auctioneers and continually set and break world records. Kill is also the birthplace of John Devoy (1842–1928), a Fenian who became an American newspaper proprietor and did much to inspire and support the 1916 uprising.

Naas (pronounced "nace") is the chief town of Kildare. It has its own racecourse and is only three miles northwest of Punchestown, famous for its steeplechases. On one part of Punchestown racecourse is a standing stone 24-feet tall which was found to have a bronze age tomb at its base. The Curragh begins about a mile to the west of Newbridge, and is the biggest area of common land in Ireland, containing in all about 12 square miles. On one side is the Curragh Racecourse—the headquarters of Irish racing and the venue for the Irish Derby—and on the other the training depot of the Irish army. If you are out early enough in the day you will see strings of racehorses at exercise; trainers have the right to use the plain, but only for a specified time each morning.

The main road across the plain drops down into the little town of Kildare, where St. Brigid, the patron saint of the county (and, with St. Patrick and St. Colmcille, one of Ireland's patrons), founded her nunnery in the 6th century. The cathedral, although extensively reconstructed in the last century, retains many features of the older buildings on the site, including an unusual carving with skull and crossbones. The nearby 6th-century Round Tower has battlements in place of a conical top—an embellishment certainly not the idea of the monks who built it. After being closed for 20 years the tower is now open to the public.

The main attraction at Kildare is the National Stud and its Japanese Garden; the entrance to the Japanese Garden is not through the elaborate main gate of the Stud, but down a side road. The garden was devised by Lord Wavertree in 1906 and laid out by two Japanese gardeners, Eda and his son Minoru, with the help of 40 assistants, a job which took four years. Lord Wavertree was also a keen horse owner, though something of an eccentric as a trainer: he consulted the birth signs and horoscopes of his horses to determine which he should train and when he should run them. Nevertheless, he won many classic races in Great Britain and Ireland. In

1915 he presented his estate and horses to the British Crown as a National Stud. The British Government in turn handed the Stud over to the Irish state in 1943 and it became Ireland's National Stud. It is the watchdog of standards in what is one of the major Irish industries. In the summer there are two guided tours each day of the extensive stables. The Irish Horse Museum, on the same estate, covers all facets of the horse in Ireland. If you are interested in horses, Kildare is not to be missed.

Beyond Kildare we enter that part of Ireland known as the Midlands which will be covered in the next chapter.

# PRACTICAL INFORMATION FOR
# THE ENVIRONS OF DUBLIN

**TOURIST OFFICES.** The main tourist information office for the area is at 1 Clarinda Park, North, **Dun Laoghaire,** tel. 01–808571. There are other offices at **Arklow,** tel. 0402–32484 (open June to Sept.); **Bray,** tel. 01–867128 (open July to Aug.); **Drogheda,** tel. 041–37070 (open May to Aug.); **Dundalk,** tel. 042–35484 (open year-round); **Dun Laoghaire Ferry-port,** tel. 01–806984 (open year-round); **Newgrange,** tel. 041–24274 (open May to Sept.); **Wicklow,** tel. 0404–67904 (open June to Sept.).

## HOTELS AND RESTAURANTS

**Arklow** (Co. Wicklow). *Royal* (I), tel. 0402–52415. 15 rooms, 10 with bath. On the main street. AE, MC, V.

**Ashford** (Co. Wicklow). *Bel Air* (M), tel. 0404–40109. 10 rooms with bath. Has a good trail-riding center. AE, DC, MC, V. *Cullenmore* (I), tel. 0404–40187. 13 rooms, 10 with bath. Modern, on main route to Wexford/Rosslare. AE, DC, MC, V.

**Aughrim** (Co. Wicklow). *Lawless's Hotel* (I), tel. 0402–36146. 12 rooms. Recently refurbished.

**Avoca** (Co. Wicklow). *Vale View* (M), tel. 0402–5236. 10 rooms with bath. Husband and wife team; excellent hotel in wonderful setting. AE, DC, MC, V.

**Bettystown** (Co. Meath). **Restaurant.** *Coastguard Inn* (M), tel. 041–27115. Country restaurant with good style and admirable cooking. AE, DC, MC, V.

**Blessington** (Co. Wicklow). *Downshire House* (I), tel. 045–65199. 25 rooms, all with bath or shower. Converted mansion in main street of pleasant village near Dublin. Garden, tennis. Very busy at weekends. AE, DC, MC, V.

**Bray** (Co. Wicklow). *Royal* (M), Main St. (tel. 01–862935). 65 rooms with bath. Main street location in seaside town; gateway to Wicklow mountains. AE, MC, V.

**Restaurants.** *Eamon's* (M), Seafront (tel. 01–829072). Specializes in fresh seafood and continental dishes. AE, DC, MC, V. *Hunts* (M), Main St. (tel. 01–863347). Warm, homey atmosphere. MC, V. *Tree of Idleness* (M), Seafront (tel. 01–863498). Traditional Greek/Cypriot restaurant. AE, DC, MC, V.

**Castledermot** (Co. Kildare). *Kilkea Castle* (E), tel. 0503–45156. 51 rooms with bath. Once a Norman castle, but much has been done to it since. Health center, plenty of space for riding. Medieval banquets. AE, DC, MC, V.

**Celbridge** (Co. Kildare). **Restaurant.** *West Wing Restaurant* (E), Castletown House (tel. 01–288502). Dine in the kitchen of an 18th-century mansion. AE.

**Cloon** (Co. Wicklow). **Restaurant.** *Enniscree Lodge* (M), tel. 01–863542. Beautiful rural site between Enniskerry and Glencree.

**Dalkey** (Co. Dublin). *Dalkey Island* (M), tel. 01–850377. 20 rooms with bath. Great views overlooking the sound between the mainland and off-shore islands. AE, DC, MC, V.

**Restaurants.** *Guinea Pig* (E), 17 Railway Rd. (tel. 01–859055). Chef-owner. AE, DC, MC, V. *Barrel's* (M), 108 Coliemore Rd. (tel. 01–858072). Friendly atmosphere. MC, V. *Nieve's* (M), 26 Castle St. (tel. 01–856156). Traditional Irish. AE, DC, MC, V. *Restaurant Baroque* (M), Main St. (tel. 01–851017). Run by friendly owner-chef. AE, DC, MC, V.

**Delgany** (Co. Wicklow). *Glenview* (E), Glen-o-Downs (tel. 01–862896). 23 rooms with bath. Wonderful view over the glen. Restaurant with good reputation. AE, MC, V. *Delgany Inn* (I), tel. 01–875701. 11 rooms, some with bath. Pleasant setting and high reputation for food. AE, DC, MC, V.

**Drogheda** (Co. Louth). *Boyne Valley* (M), Stameen (tel. 041–37737). 20 rooms with bath. Converted mansion in own grounds, just south of the town on the main road from Dublin. AE, DC, MC, V. *Rossnaree* (M), tel. 041–37811. 20 rooms with bath. Owner-managed with popular restaurant. AE, MC, V.

**Dundalk** (Co. Louth). *Ballymascanlon House* (M), tel. 042–71124. 36 rooms, all with bath. Well-deserved top reputation, both for accommodations and food. Leisure center with indoor heated pool, sauna, solarium, squash, tennis, gymnasium; equestrian center. AE, DC, MC, V. *Derryhale* (M), tel. 042–35471. 23 rooms, most with bath. Also a converted mansion, just outside the town. AE, DC, MC, V. *Imperial* (I), tel. 042–32241. 47 rooms with bath. AE, MC, V.

**Dún Laoghaire** (Co. Dublin). *Royal Marine* (E), tel 01–801911. 90 rooms, all with bath. In its own grounds overlooking the harbor. DC, MC, V. *Victor* (M), Rochestown Ave. (tel. 01–853555). 58 rooms with bath or shower. Sauna, solarium. AE, DC, MC, V. *Pierre* (I), Victoria Terrace (tel. 01–800291). 40 rooms, 25 with bath. AE, MC, V.

**Restaurants.** *Digby's* (E), 5 Windsor Terrace (tel. 01–804600). Seafront restaurant that is a leader hereabouts. Has a wine bar on the premises. AE, DC, MC, V. *Restaurant na Mara* (E), tel. 01–800509. Overlooks the harbor. Fish, of course, and excellently presented. AE, DC, MC, V. *Barrels* (M), Mews, 61 Lower Georges St. (tel. 01–809136). Famed for its tender steaks. MC, V. *Salty Dog* (M), 3a Haddington Terrace (tel. 01–808015). One of the few places to feature Indonesian dishes. AE, DC, MC, V. *Bistro Pavani* (I), 2 Cumberland St. (tel. 01–809675). Italian specialties; guitarist at weekends. AE, MC, DC, V.

**Dunlavin** (Co. Wicklow). *Rathsallagh House* (E), tel. 045–53112. 8 rooms with bath. Luxuriously converted farmhouse. Hunting and shooting in season. DC, MC, V.

**Glendalough** (Co. Wicklow). *Royal* (I), tel. 0404–5135. 16 rooms, 13 with bath. In the heart of historic valley. Very busy at weekends. Has restaurant and bar food.

**Restaurant.** *Wicklow Heather* (I), Laragh (tel. 0404–5157). Owner-chef who knows his business; about a mile from the village.

**Greystones** (Co. Wicklow). *La Touche* (I), tel. 01–874401. 33 rooms, half with bath. About half the rooms overlook the sea. Popular restaurant. AE, DC, MC, V.

**Howth** (Co. Dublin). *Deer Park* (M), tel. 01–322624. 35 rooms with bath. Overlooks Dublin, the sea and its own 9- and 18-hole golfcourses. In the park of Howth Castle, beside the famous rhododendron gardens. AE, DC, MC, V. *Howth Lodge* (M), tel. 01–390288. 17 rooms with bath. Overlooks sea with direct access to the beach. Restaurant, "olde world" bars. AE, DC, MC, V. *Sutton Castle* (M), tel. 01–322688. 16 rooms with bath. AE, DC, MC, V.

**Restaurants.** *Abbey Tavern* (E), tel. 01–390307. Maintains its traditional character (stone walls, flagged floors, gas lights) and serves great fish dishes. AE, DC, MC, V. *King Sitric* (E), East Pier (tel. 01–325235). Comfortable and relaxed; excellent fish. Overlooks harbor. *Butler's* (M), Abbey St. (tel. 01–391696). Family-run and specializes in seafood. AE, MC, V. *Russels* (M), Harbour Rd. (tel. 01–322681). Informal seafood place, with good harbor views.

**Kilcullen** (Co. Kildare). **Restaurants.** *The Hide-Out* (I), tel. 045–81232. Good relaxed place to stop for a grill. Has idiosyncratic museum collection. MC, V. *Joe McTernan's* (I), tel. 045–81254. In the main square on the banks of the Liffey.

**Killiney** (Co. Dublin). *Court* (E), tel. 01–851622. 32 rooms with bath. Overlooks Killiney Bay, with private access to beach. Lively bar is a good place to hear jazz on Sundays. AE, MC, V. *Fitzpatrick's Castle* (E), tel. 01–851533. 94 rooms, all with bath. Indoor heated pool, sauna, solarium, squash, tennis. Elegant and popular. AE, DC, MC, V.

**Restaurants.** *Chez Sylvio* (M), Talbot House, Killiney Hill Rd. (tel. 01–855753). French and creole cuisine from Mauritius. AE, DC, MC, V. *Fitzpatrick's Castle Truffles* (M), tel. 01–851533. Elegant. AE, DC, MC, V. *Jester's* (M), in the same hotel is grill bar. AE, DC, MC, V. *Library Grill,* Court Hotel (M), tel. 01–851622. Intimate setting for steaks and burgers. AE, MC, V.

**Kilternan** (Co. Dublin). *Kilternan* (E), tel. 01–893631. 52 rooms with bath. In the foothills of the mountains, nine miles from Dublin. 18-hole golf course, leisure center and new (1985) ILTA-Wright Tennis Center. Garden-style restaurant. AE, DC, MC, V.

**Malahide** (Co. Dublin). *Grand* (M), tel. 01–450633. 48 rooms, all with bath. Beside the sea in sailing center. Has large indoor riding school. AE, DC, MC, V.
**Restaurants.** *Johnny's* (E), 9 James Terr. (tel. 01–450314). Old-time atmosphere and an owner-chef who is one of the best. AE, DC, MC, V. *La Rochelle* (M), New St. (tel. 01–453550). Notable French cuisine. AE, DC, MC, V. *Malahide Castle* (I), tel. 01–452655. Convenient for lunch if you're visiting the castle and its National Portrait Gallery. AE, DC, MC, V.

**Maynooth** (Co. Kildare). *Moyglare Manor Hotel* (E), tel. 01–286351. 11 rooms with bath. Georgian mansion in beautiful setting. Excellent food in restaurant. AE, DC, MC, V.
**Restaurant.** *Country Shop* (I), Mill St (tel. 01–286766). Pleasant downstairs spot for lunches and snacks with craft shop. MC, V.

**Naas** (Co. Kildare). **Restaurants.** *Lawlor's* (M), Poplar Sq. (tel. 045–97085). Pub-restaurant with novelty "Out of Africa" bar. *Manor Inn* (I), Main St. (tel. 045–97471). Pub-restaurant specializing in steaks.

**Navan** (Co. Meath). *Ardboyne* (M), Dublin Rd. (tel. 046–23119). 26 rooms with bath. In hunting country and the famous Boyne Valley area. Restaurant and grill room. AE, DC, MC, V.
**Restaurant.** *Dunderry Lodge* (E), Robinstown (tel. 046–31671). Six miles out of town, but worth searching out. Small, owner-operated. AE, DC, MC, V.

**Newbridge** (Co. Kildare). *Keadeen* (E), tel. 045–31666. 37 rooms with bath. On the edge of the Curragh, headquarters of Irish horse-racing. Lovely gardens. AE, DC, MC, V.
**Restaurant.** *Red House Inn* (M), (tel 045–31516). Old-world atmosphere with turf fire. AE, DC, MC, V.

**Prosperous** (Co. Kildare). *Curryhills House* (M), tel. 045–68336. 10 rooms with bath or shower. A fine Georgian farmhouse that has become a hotel. Husband and wife team are welcoming. Good Tudor-style restaurant. AE, DC, MC, V.

**Rathnew** (Co. Wicklow). *Tinakilly House* (E), tel. 0404–69274. 14 rooms with bath. Exceptionally attractive Victorian decor. Restaurant offers Irish country cooking and nouvelle cuisine. All-weather tennis court.

AE, DC, MC, V. *Hunter's* (M), tel. 0404–40106. 18 rooms, 10 with bath. Old coaching inn with excellent restaurant. AE, DC, MC, V.

**Roundwood** (Co. Wicklow). **Restaurant.** *Roundwood Inn* (M), tel. 01–818107. Irish and continental cuisine in warm 17th-century inn. Also bar food. MC, V.

**Slane** (Co. Meath). *Conyngham Arms* (M), tel. 041–24155. 12 rooms, 10 with bath. Beside the river Boyne. Family operation run by people who care about the guests. Good restaurant.
**Restaurant.** *Slane Castle* (M), tel. 041–24207. 18th-century home of the Earl of Mountcharles. Menu features home-made patés, game (in season) and fish; good food, plus elegance. You can take a tour of the castle (IR£1.50) and if you're dining on Friday or Saturday there's a free night-club. AE, DC, MC, V.

**Sandycove** (Co. Dublin). **Restaurant.** *Mirabeau* (E), Marine Parade (tel. 01–809873). Well recommended nouvelle cuisine in elegant and fashionable surroundings.

**Wicklow Town** (Co. Wicklow). *Old Rectory* (M), tel. 0404–67408. 5 rooms, all with bath. Very small country house. Tranquil setting with gourmet restaurant. *Grand* (I), tel. 0404–67337. 14 rooms with bath. *Raheenmore Stud* (I), tel. 0404–67156. Two miles outside the town. Highly recommended farmhouse for dinner, bed and breakfast.

**Woodenbridge** (Co. Wicklow). *Woodenbridge* (M), tel. 0402–5146. 11 rooms, all with bath. Recently refurbished, but dates back to the 17th century. MC, V. *Valley* (I), tel. 0402–5200. 12 rooms, 5 with bath. Beautiful setting in the Vale of Avoca. Bar lunches and dinner in the evening.

## Youth Hostels

**Aghavannagh House,** Aughrim, Co. Wicklow (tel. 0402–36102). **Ballinclea,** Donard, Co. Wicklow (tel. 045–54657). **Baltyboys,** Blessington, Co. Wicklow (tel. 045–67266).
**Glendalough,** Co. Wicklow (tel. 0404–5143). This hostel is the base of the Association for Adventure Sports, which embraces everything from mountain-climbing to hang-gliding and canoeing.
**Glenmalure,** Greenane, Co. Wicklow. **Graiguenamanagh,** V.E.C., Co. Kilkenny. Open July and Aug. only. **Lackan House,** Knockree, Enniskerry, Bray, Co. Wicklow (tel. 01–867196). **Mellifont Abbey,** Monasterboice, Drogheda, Co. Louth (tel. 041–26127). **Stone House,** Glencree, Enniskerry, Bray, Co. Wicklow (tel. 01–867290). **Tiglin,** Ashford, Co. Wicklow (tel. 0404–40259).
Hostels in County Wicklow should be booked through An Oige's headquarters at 39 Mountjoy Sq., Dublin 1 (tel. 01–363111).

**TOURS AND EXCURSIONS.** C.I.E. operates scenic tours into County Wicklow by bus from Dun Laoghaire Railway Station.
Bicycles can be hired from *P.J. Carolan & Sons,* 77 Trinity St., Drogheda (tel. 041–38242), *Harris & Co.,* Main St., Wicklow Town (tel. 0404–6724).

## PLACES TO VISIT

**Ashford** (Co. Wicklow). **Mount Usher Gardens.** Along the banks of the Vartry River, with over 4,000 shrubs and plants collected from many countries. Open 29 Mar. to 30 Sept., Mon. to Sat. 10.30–6, Sun. 2–6.

**Avoca** (Co. Wicklow). **Avoca Handweavers.** Old mill where tweeds are produced on fly shuttle looms invented in 1740. Mill shop and tea room. Mill open Mon. to Fri. 8.30–4.30; shop open daily 9.30–5.30. Demonstrations most weekends; confirm on tel. 0402–5105.

**Blessington** (Co. Wicklow). **Russborough House.** Palladian house built in the 18th century, with fine plasterwork by Francini brothers. Art collection which includes paintings by Rubens, Goya, Vermeer, Velázquez and others. Also tapestries, silver, porcelain and fine furniture. One of the finest houses in Ireland. Open Easter to 31 Oct., Wed., Sat. and Sun. 2.30–6.30. Last admissions 5.30.

**Celbridge** (Co. Kildare). **Castletown House.** Magnificent Palladian mansion built in 1722. Fine plasterwork; Irish furniture and paintings of the period. Open Apr. to Sept., Wed., Sat. and Sun. 2–6; Oct. to Mar., Sun. only 2–5.

**Donabate** (Co. Dublin). **Newbridge Demesne.** Mid-18th-century manor in 36 acres. Fine interior recently restored; outbuildings include dairy, forge and carpenter's workshop. Off the main road between Swords and Balbriggan. Open Mon. to Fri. 10–5, Sun. and Bank Holidays 2–6. Admission IR£1.75 adults, 75p children.

**Drogheda** (Co. Louth). **Mellifont Abbey.** Ireland's first Cistercian monastery, founded by St. Malachy in association with St. Bernard of Clairvaux, in 1142. Only the foundations remain now, apart from the Chapter House. About five miles from Drogheda off the Collon road.
  **Millmount Museum,** Drogheda (tel. 041–36391). Local folklore and history.
  **Monasterboice.** Irish monastery of the 6th century, dominated by a Round Tower. Has two fine 9th-century high crosses. About four miles north of Drogheda on the road to Dundalk.

**Dún Laoghaire** (Co. Dublin). **James Joyce Museum,** Martello Tower, Sandycove. One of series of Martello towers along the east coast, part of an 18th-century defence against Napoleonic invasion. The tower was once briefly the home of the celebrated Irish writer James Joyce, and the museum contains Joycean memorablia. Open 1 May to 30 Sept., Mon. to Sat. 10–1 and 2–5.15, Sun. 2.30–6; rest of year by special arrangement with Dublin and East Tourism (tel. 01–808571).
  **Maritime Museum,** Haigh Terrace. Maritime exhibits.

**Dunleer** (Co. Kildare). **Rathgorey Transport Museum,** (tel. 041–51389). For veterans and vintage car buffs; also has old motorcycles and fire engines. Open Sun. afternoons.

**Enniskerry** (Co. Wicklow). **Powerscourt Estate and Gardens.** Includes Japanese and Italian gardens, statuary, ironwork and a spectacular waterfall. Open Easter to 31 Oct., daily 10–5.30.

**Howth** (Co. Dublin). **Howth Castle Gardens.** Over 2,000 varieties of rhododendron. Best in May and June. Open 8 to sunset. Admission free outside flowering season.

**Laragh** (Co. Wicklow). **Glendalough.** Remains of monastic settlement founded in 6th century, in a deep valley in the Wicklow Mountains. 100-ft. round tower; dramatic setting. About 1½ miles from Laragh, south of Dublin.

**Malahide** (Co. Dublin). **Malahide Castle and National Portrait Gallery.** One of Ireland's oldest and most historic castles with fine collection of furniture and lovely gardens inside the Malahide Demesne, a 270-acre park. The art collection has battle and sporting scenes as well as portraits in oils. Open Apr. to Oct., Mon. to Fri. 10–12.45 and 2–5, Sat. 11–6, Sun. 2–6; Nov. to Mar., Mon. to Fri. 10–12.45, Sat. and Sun. 2–5.

**Marino** (Co. Dublin). **Casino.** A charming 18th-century Palladian villa designed by Sir William Chambers; full of architectural surprises. Open Sat. 10–5, Sun. 2–5.

**Newgrange** (Co. Meath). **Prehistoric remains.** A massive mound (diameter 280 ft.) containing a passage tomb in which the Stone Age inhabitants of Ireland buried their cremated dead around 3000 B.C. Fascinating geometric decorations on stone. Newgrange is about five miles from Drogheda on the road to Slane. Open mid-June to mid-Sept., daily 10–7; Apr. to mid-June and mid-Sept. to 31 Oct., Mon. to Sat. 10–5, Sun. 2–5; Nov. to 31 Mar., Tues. to Sat. 10–1 and 2–5, Sun. 2–5. Guided tours.

**Rathdrum** (Co. Wicklow). **Avondale Forest Park.** 523-acre forest park with river walks and other signposted nature trails. Avondale House, built in 1777, is associated with Charles Stewart Parnell. The house is open May to Aug., daily; Apr. and Sept., Fri. to Mon. 2–6. Admission free. Park open all year.

**Slane** (Co. Meath). **Slane Castle.** 18th-century home of the Earl of Mountcharles. The ballroom is said to be one of the best examples of Gothic revival design in Europe. Interesting art collection. Tours available every Sunday, Apr. to Oct., 2–6.

**Tully** (Co. Kildare). **Irish National Stud and Horse Museum** (tel. 045–21617). Traces the history of Irish horses and horse breeding since prehistoric times. Also contains the Japanese Gardens (see below).
**Japanese Gardens.** One of the oldest and finest Japanese Gardens in Europe. Open Easter to Oct. 31, Mon. to Fri. 10.30–5, Sat. 10.30–5.30, Sun. 2–5.30. Guided tours on request.

# THE LAKELANDS

*Ireland's Heartland*

As so many of Ireland's best known attractions are located near the coast, there is a tendency to think of the central, inland area of the country as simply a place to drive across in order to reach another coast. In an effort to focus attention on the many scenic and historical aspects of the area, the Irish Tourist Board recently changed the official name of the region from Midlands to Lakelands. This was done principally because the name Midlands automatically conjures up, in both Irish and English minds, images of *England's* Midlands, an area of smokey industrial cities and endless dull suburbs. Lakelands was in fact a natural choice. Parts of the north and west of this central region contain more water than land. And in addition there are numerous rivers and canals bisecting the region and linking up with the lakes, all providing marvelous opportunities for inland cruising as well as swimming and fishing.

Otherwise the region combines rich undulating plains and low-lying bogland in about equal measure. The economy of the area is largely agricultural. Its scenery is pretty rather than dramatic, with a quiet charm that contrasts favorably with the more spectacular and rugged grandeur of the coastal mountain ranges.

Like many things in Ireland, the precise borders of the Lakelands are a matter of contention, but we shall define them as the area above a line drawn from Athy, in County Kildare, to Athlone on the river Shannon in County Westmeath, and bordered in the north by the low hills of County Monaghan and the lakes of County Cavan.

## Canal Country

Our exploration of the Lakelands begins at Monasterevin in County Kildare, seven miles west of Kildare town. Monasterevin has an unusual main street, with houses and shops on one side only, while on the other sadly neglected gardens stretch down to the river Barrow. Otherwise, the town is known chiefly as the home for many years of the famous Irish tenor, Count John McCormack (1884–1945), who became an American citizen in 1919. He lived at Moore Abbey, a neo-Gothic mansion built on the site of a Cistercian Abbey overlooking a marsh. A forest park and picnic site have now been established in the grounds of the house.

Athy, in the southern corner of County Kildare some 15 miles south of Monasterevin, is the largest town in the county. Here we first encounter the Grand Canal. It is still navigable, forming part of the complex of waterways which today serve holiday makers throughout the area. It was built over many years, the work beginning in the 1750s. It crosses Ireland from Ballinasloe in County Galway in the west, terminating at Athy where it joins the river Barrow, which in turn flows south into Waterford. In the first half of the last century, the Grand Canal, like the Royal Canal linking Longford and Dublin, was a vitally important waterway, carrying both passengers and freight. In 1837, for example, the peak of the canal's importance, more than 100,000 passengers were carried. But the arrival of the far quicker railway soon took the passenger business away. (The boats were towed by horses and could average no more than about 20 miles a day.) Nonetheless freight continued to be transported along the canal until as late as 1959—in World War II, a quarter of a million tons of turf were carried—and was officially closed to commercial traffic only in 1960. Today, many of the "harbor" villages which sprang up along the canal have the air of ghost towns, with their seemingly disproportionately large hotels left derelict. (There is one such in Athy). But as the freight disappeared, so the canals were given a new lease of life with the rapid growth in popularity of canal-boat vacations. The relaxed pace and out-of-the-way places they pass have won many converts in Ireland to the cause of canal preservation. Its main economic potential of course is as a recreational facility, but with soaring transportation costs there is even talk of bringing the canal system back into commercial use for freight.

Athy itself, strategically located on the Barrow, was fortified during the Middle Ages and into the Elizabethan age. White's Castle, overlooking the bridge across the Barrow, was built in the 16th century by the Earl of Kildare to defend the river crossing. Both more peaceful in intent and more modern is the Dominican church, downriver from the castle. It's a fine new building designed in an unusual fan shape that from the front resembles a prehistoric dolmen. Athy has also gained a place in photographic history, the result of the work of John Minihan. He is a native of the town who emigrated to London at the age of 15 to pursue a photographic career. Over the last 25 years or so he has built up a superb portfolio of pictures of daily life in Athy, taken on his visits home. His pictures are not only of high artistic merit but form a valuable and fascinating record of a fast disappearing way of life. A selection of his work has been exhibited in London and New York and in book form.

## County Laois

Stradbally, over the border in County Laois (pronounced "leash"), is the venue for an annual steam engine rally on the first weekend of August. The narrow gauge railway at Stradbally Hall features a steam locomotive originally used in the Guinness Brewery in Dublin in the 19th century. The train runs every weekend from March to October. The Stradbally Traction Engine Museum in the town can be visited.

The main road from Stradbally, the N80, takes you to Portlaoise just a few miles away. On the way, you pass by the Rock of Dunamase. Though no more than 150 feet high, the rock, crowned by the remains of a castle, well illustrates the territorial struggles that bedeviled this part of Ireland. It was originally a Celtic fortress, but was plundered by the Vikings in 845. Aoife, daughter of the king of Leinster, then received it as part of her dowry on her marriage to the Norman lord, Strongbow. Thereafter, it passed by marriage into the hands of the Mortimers and the O'Mores, remaining an Irish stronghold until it was besieged and then blown up by Cromwell's men in the middle of the 17th century. The views from the top are superb.

Portlaoise—previously known as Maryborough—was built as a fortified town at the time that the O'Mores held Dunamase in the hopes of pacifying them. Nothing remains of these fortifications now but the outer wall of one tower. Today the town is the location of Ireland's top-security prison, the reason the town's name crops up so often in news bulletins.

Abbeyleix, to the south of Portlaoise, takes its name from a Cistercian abbey founded here in the 12th century by a member of the O'More family. As it stands today, the town owes much to the Viscount de Vesci who redesigned it in the 18th century, and built many of its charming stone houses. The de Vesci family still own an Adam-style manor built in the late-18th century on the traditional site of O'More's abbey. The terraced gardens of the Abbeyleix estate were laid out by Emma, wife of the third Viscount. The gardens, with a 13th-century monk's bridge, are open to the public in summer.

Heading north from Portlaoise is Mountmellick, seven miles up the N80. It's a small town, almost encircled by the little Owenmass river. It was originally a Quaker settlement and became famous in the last century for its lace, samples of which are today in the New York Public Museum. Its elegant 18th-century houses are a reminder of its prosperous past.

Nearby is Coolbanagher, whose exquisite church of St. John the Evangelist makes the slight detour to reach it well worth while. It was designed in the late-18th century by James Gandon, architect of the Four Courts and the Custom House in Dublin. The original 1795 Gandon plans for the building can be seen inside the church. There is also an elaborately carved 15th-century font. Gandon also designed the nearby Georgian Inn.

Beyond Coolbanagher is Emo Court, just off the main Dublin–Cork road, the N7, from which the house can be glimpsed. This too is the work of Gandon, who designed it for the first Earl of Portarlington, though it was not finished until the middle of the 19th century. The gardens, but not the house, are open to the public.

## Into County Offaly

Continuing north from Emo Court and just over the border into County Offaly is Portarlington itself. The town was founded in 1666, soon afterwards becoming a major center for Huguenot refugees. St. Michael's Church here is still known as the French church. Similarly, many of the tombstones are engraved in French, and services were conducted in French until the end of the 19th century. Some evidence of Huguenot architecture is also found in Patrick Street, but the days are long gone when the sons of the wealthy would be sent to Portarlington to learn French.

Tullamore, 17 miles northwest of Portarlington, is another Grand Canal port. It is also the home of Irish Mist, a fine liqueur whiskey. Just to the north of the town on the Kilbeggan road, the N80, are the remains of Durrow Abbey. This was one of St. Colmcille's (St. Columba) foundations, and remains a place of pilgrimage on his feast day, June 9. It was here that the *Book of Durrow*—a copy of the Gospels now in the library of Trinity College, Dublin—was written in the 10th century. The late-10th-century High Cross and St. Colmcille's Well can be seen in the churchyard. Two stones, known as the Headache Stone and the Backache Stone, are reputed to ease these troubles!

In Kilbeggan itself, local enthusiasts have restored a giant water wheel 20 feet high and weighing in at about 20 tons. It is turned by the millrace of an abandoned whiskey distillery. The distillery was built in 1880, and the restoration project will eventually include a museum of industrial archeology.

Away to the southwest of County Offaly is Birr, 23 miles from Tullamore on the N52. The town itself is predominantly Georgian and has retained many of its elegant tree-lined malls and buildings. Sir William Petty, a 17th-century surveyor, designated the town the geographic center of Ireland, but as there are at least three other places in Ireland that have also laid claim to the distinction, the award is regarded as somewhat dubious. (The controversy is the result of Ireland's irregular coastline, not the incompetence of Irish geographers). The Hill of Unagh in County Westmeath, ancient meeting place of the four great provinces of Ireland—Ulster, Leinster, Munster and Connacht—has been given the title, as has a hill two miles northeast of Glasson in the same county. Yet another Westmeath hill, Knockcosgrey, near Kildare, also claims the honor.

Originally, Birr was known as Parsonstown after the Parsons family. One of their descendants, a distinguished astronomer, was made Earl of Rosse. In 1845 he built what was then the world's largest telescope, which can be seen in the small museum associated with the astronomer in the grounds of Birr Castle. The present Earl of Rosse has plans to expand the museum considerably. The splendid gardens of Birr Castle are open to the public.

Dooley's Hotel in Emmet Square is one of Ireland's oldest coaching inns, the original building dating from 1747. It was here, in 1809, that the famous Galway Hunt acquired their even more famous nickname, the Galway Blazers. Having been invited to hunt in the area, an over-exuberant celebration by the guests from Galway at Dooley's resulted in a blaze that burnt the building to the ground. It has long since been rebuilt, and is one of the principal centers of activity during Birr Vintage week, held every August, when the people of the town turn back the clock to Georgian days.

Leap Castle, in southern Offaly, is still visited by optimistic ghost hunters, eager to get a whiff of its unusual elemental: Ireland's smelly ghost! The ghost was described by both the poet W.B. Yeats and the distinguished surgeon, wit and writer, Oliver St. John Gogarty. The castle was burnt out in 1922; today it is a picturesque ruin, and the ghost has not been "smelled" for many years.

There are numerous earthworks in the Leap district: ringforts, hillforts, and so on, evidence of continuous settlement dating back many thousands of years.

## Across the Boglands

Traveling west from Birr, you reach Banagher, ten miles away, a picturesque town on the Shannon. One of its most famous residents was Anthony Trollope, the 19th-century novelist. He was, for some years, Post Office Surveyor here, and was to comment on his move to Banagher: "Since that time, who has had a happier life than mine?"

The road through Cloghan, 11 miles to the north, takes you across extensive bogland. This is red bog, as opposed to the blacker and wetter mountain bog more commonly found in Ireland, and supports different forms of wildlife. Within its apparently monotonous stretches of brown, green and mauve, botanists will be able to identify various heathers, the orange spikes of bog asphodel, bog myrtle and a wide variety of lichens and moss. The giant power stations in the region, all "turf" fired, make clear the continuing importance of the bogs to modern, industrial Ireland. Indeed, turf remains a vitally important fuel source in oil- and coal-less Ireland. You'll still find a good many farmers cutting their own turf in this region, though more and more people buy their turf direct from Bord na Mona, the Irish Peat Development Authority, in the form of cleaner and more compact turf "briquettes."

A mile or so to the northeast of Banagher lies Shannon Harbour, dominated by the ruins of the Grand Canal Company Hotel. Motor cruisers and row boats can be hired both here and at Banagher. There is also good brown trout fishing on the river Shannon and the neighboring Brosna, and numerous pike, perch and bream in the deep pools of the Shannon. Shannonbridge, a little to the north, is a village with a single street and an imposing stone bridge of 16 arches over the Shannon and leading to the west.

## Clonmacnois

Clonmacnois, on the banks of the Shannon a few miles north of Shannonbridge, is one of Ireland's most important early monastic settlements. It was founded about A.D. 548 by St. Ciaran, who died a few months later when only 33. The first settlement grew rapidly into a large monastic city and then into a medieval university. None of the original buildings remains; the earliest structures to be seen were built in the 9th century, among them Temple Ciaran, a cell just over 12-feet long, reputed to be on the spot where Ciaran built his original oratory.

On the right is the South Cross, dating from the 11th century. Walking to the right, the first building is Temple Doulin, a restored 9th-century church, and adjoining it, a 17th-century church, Temple Hurpain. Next is the 12th-century King's Church, Temple Ri, which is on a rise in the ground and has an interesting east window.

To the north is Temple Ciaran, where the saint is reputedly buried at the end most distant from the door. The largest building of the group (facing towards the entrance again) is the cathedral, originally founded in 904 by Abbot Colman and King Flann. There has been considerable restoration work in later centuries.

Nearby there is a remarkable gallery of ancient carved grave slabs, and beyond them a refuge tower, O'Rourke's Tower, built between the 10th and 12th centuries. About 500 yards to the east of the main settlement is the Nun's Church, built in the 10th century and an outstanding example of early Irish Romanesque architecture at its best.

The monks of the settlement produced many famous books, including *The Book of the Dun Cow,* now in the Bodleian Library at Oxford. Metalworkers created great works and the masons have left the results of their skill as stone carvers for the traveler to see centuries later. Because of its artistic and material wealth, Clonmacnois was raided many times in its history, by everybody from the Vikings to the English, before being finally supressed in 1552 by Henry VIII.

There is a pilgrimage to Clonmacnois on September 9 each year. Pope John Paul II paid a helicopter visit to the site during his Irish visit in 1979.

## Athlone

Athlone, a few miles north up the Shannon from Clonmacnois, is a busy port serving Ireland's inland waterways system, and an important road and rail junction as well. Athlone Castle, on the west bank of the Shannon, has been a famous military stronghold since the 13th century, changing hands several times during the Cromwellian Wars in the 17th century. It was declared a National Monument in 1969 and now houses a museum in its central keep with a collection of historical and antiquarian items relating to the Athlone district.

When waterbus tours are operating on the river they will be found at the pier below the castle. While Athlone is a major point on the Shannon, most of the cruiser hire operators are based up-river, but there are some here from whom boats may be hired on a weekly basis.

From Athlone an armada of a hundred or more small craft sets out every July for the north, passing through Lough Ree to the Shannon Boat Rally, but there is so much space on the Shannon that the waterway never becomes crowded.

On the eastern bank the old character of Athlone is shown in the narrow streets approaching the river and its bridge. The 19th-century St. Mary's Church, in the center of the town, stands beside the tower of an older church which, according to tradition, has one of the bells from the old ecclesiastical settlement at Clonmacnois. Near the riverside is the Franciscan Friary and the remains of a 13th-century foundation of the same order. On the outskirts of the town are the remains of fortifications built in the early-19th century in preparation for a French invasion which never happened.

Famous sons of Athlone include Count John McCormack, the tenor, whose birthplace on The Bawn, off Mardyke Street, is marked with a plaque. There is a fine bronze portrait bust of the singer by Cork sculptor

Seamus Murphy on the promenade beside the Shannon. T.P. O'Connor (1848–1929), Nationalist member of parliament, journalist and litterateur, was born in the house marked with a plaque in The Square. The modern poet, Desmond Egan, winner of the National Poetry Foundation of America Award in 1984, was born here in 1936.

Athlone is a good base for exploring the shores and islands of Lough Ree, an expansion of the Shannon which forms a lake 15 miles long and between one and six miles wide. Its shoreline varies from deep bays to shallow inlets and most of it is pleasantly wooded. Some of the larger islands have remains of ancient churches. The ruins on Hare Island are said to be those of a church founded in the 6th century by St. Ciaran.

## Poet's Country

About seven miles north of Athlone is Lissoy and the start of an area associated with the poet and playwright Oliver Goldsmith (1728–74) which has become known as Poet's Country. Goldsmith was actually born in neighboring County Longford, but was brought to Lissoy at the age of two when his father was appointed rector here. Glasson, a couple of miles south of Lissoy, is believed by some to be the village he immortalized as "Sweet Auburn" in his poem *The Deserted Village.* In fact, there is much controversy in academic circles about the extent to which the area is really represented in Goldsmith's work, a controversy which is largely ignored by the local tourist authority, however. Nevertheless, both Glasson and Lissoy are extremely pretty villages, with roses entwined over their stone cottages. The Goldsmith home, on the other hand, though one of the few authenticated "Goldsmith" buildings, is now in ruins.

Most of Goldsmith's life was passed in hardship and poverty, even though his literary productions, which include the classic *Vicar of Wakefield,* enjoyed, as they still do, considerable popularity. He studied at Trinity College, Dublin, but ran away several times. His family subsequently attempted to send him to America, but he spent all the money they saved for the journey on his way to Cork Harbour.

Poet's Country extends north to Ardagh, near Longford. Ardagh House (today the School of Rural Domestic Economy) was formerly the residence of a landowner named Fetherstone. It was this building that Goldsmith mistook for an inn one night in 1744, the ensuing fiasco forming the basis for his enduringly popular play *She Stoops to Conquer* (subtitled "Mistakes of a Night").

## Edgeworthstown

The road north from Athlone through Lissoy joins the main Dublin–Longford road, the N4, at Mostrim, which has still not quite shed its old Ascendency name of Edgeworthstown. The town has a long association with the Edgeworth family who settled here in 1583. Among its best-known members were Richard Lovell Edgeworth (1744–1817) and his daughter, Maria, the novelist, who was but one of his 24 children (by four wives). The small Georgian mansion at the eastern end of the village where they lived is now a nursing home run by the Sisters of Mercy. Richard Edgeworth was an inventor, somewhat before his time. He designed and installed a central heating system for his friend and neighbor, the Earl of Longford, and invented a semaphore system, a velocipede, a pedometer, a horse carriage with sails (which scared the horses), a species of early caterpillar wheel, a pebbled road surface, and an umbrella to keep haystacks dry.

His devoted daughter Maria (1767–1849) was only four feet seven inches tall in spite of his efforts to elongate her by hanging when young. She became her father's chief assistant in running the property, and educating his numerous other children. But she was also a literary figure of note. Her satirical novel, *Castle Rackrent,* is still read with glee by those familiar with Irish country life. Sir Walter Scott and William Wordsworth were among her admirers, and her fame even spread as far as Russia, where Turgenev once claimed that his own writing was inspired by hers.

### Mullingar

Eighteen miles southeast of Mostrim down the N4 is Mullingar, the center of an important cattle raising area. The town is dominated by its twin-towered cathedral, a Renaissance-style structure built in the '30s. It contains some interesting mosaics of St. Patrick and St. Anne by the Russian artist, Boris Anrep. The town is almost encircled by the Royal Canal which is also being developed as a recreational waterway for cruising. When the restoration work is complete it will provide a leisurely route from Dublin to the Shannon. Mullingar is a good center for exploring the lakes of County Westmeath. Lough Ennel, just south of the town is one of the most attractive in the area, and three other major lakes, Lough Owel, Lough Derravaragh and Lough Lene are all within ten miles of the town, and offer a variety of water sports and fishing.

Castlepollard, near Lough Lee, is a well-laid-out 19th-century village with a central village green, an unusual feature in Ireland. The principal interest here, however, is Tullynally House, seat of the Earls of Longford, the Pakenhams, a family who have long combined literary talent with an endearing brand of eccentricity. The house itself is an early-19th century Gothic castle with a fanciful facade of turrets and towers containing more than 1,200 feet of battlements. It has been much added to over the years, but still contains the original central-heating system designed by Richard Edgeworth, as well as an immense kitchen and servants' hall. The house, park and walled gardens are all open to visitors.

Two miles east of Castlepollard is Fore Abbey, an important ecclesiastical establishment which was built in a valley under limestone bluffs. The monastery was founded by St. Fechin in A.D. 630 and grew to be a community of 300 monks. St. Fechin's church is the oldest structure in Fore, dating from the 10th century and it probably marks the site of the original monastery. The Benedictine priory was founded early in the 13th century by the de Lacy family, and is the only Irish Benedictine foundation of which significant remains survive. There are many quaint legends associated with Fore concerning the miraculous achievements of St. Fechin when building it.

### Longford

Heading northeast from Longford to Granard, the main road, the N55, passes through Ballinamuck—the Place of the Pig, as it is otherwise unromantically known—remembered chiefly because of the battle here in 1798 between the combined French and Irish forces under General Humbert and the English under General Lake, the latter emerging victorious. Two monuments commemorate the battle, one erected in 1928, the other in 1983. This later monument was inspired largely by the success of Thomas Flanagan's novel, *The Year of the French,* and its T.V. adaptation. Thomas Pakenham, one of the Pakenham's of nearby Tullynally House, has written an excellent history of the 1798 uprising called *The Year of Liberty.*

There is an impressive stone circle at Toberfelim just outside Granard, evidence that the area was inhabited at least 3,000 years ago.

The prominent Motte of Granard, at the southwest end of town, was fortified by the Normans in about the year 1200. A statue of St. Patrick was erected on top of it to mark the 15th centenary of his arrival in Ireland; one of the first episcopal sees to be established after the mission of St. Patrick was based at Granard. Nowadays the town is associated with an annual harp festival, held in early August. This was a regular event throughout the 17th and 18th centuries, and has proved a popular attraction since its revival in 1981, combining traditional music and pageantry.

## Counties Cavan and Monaghan

Cavan and Monaghan, the most northerly counties of the Lakelands, contain innumerable small lakes, and anglers soon get accustomed to having a lake all to themselves. There are at least 180 lakes in Monaghan, and as many again in Cavan, where the lake system links up with Lough Erne across the border in Northern Ireland. There are about 40 coarse angling centers, yet the banks of the lakes are never crowded. Pike, perch, rudd, bream, tench and others exist in abundance. Game fishing is also available, and several lakes and rivers have been developed and stocked by the Inland Fisheries Trust. Local tourist offices can suggest the ideal lake for you.

Virginia in County Cavan, on the main N3 road from Dublin, has no connection with its American namesake, but was built as a garrison town in the 17th century. It is now a quiet attractive town on the shores of Lough Ramor.

Ballyjamesduff, a few miles northwest of Virginia, also has literary associations. It was from here that the grandfather of novelist Henry James and philosopher William James emigrated to America in 1789. Most people, however, associate Ballyjamesduff with another emigrant, Paddy Reilly, whose sweetheart, in Percy French's song, *Come Back Paddy Reilly,* entreats him to come back home to Ballyjamesduff. French in fact spent much time in Cavan while employed by the government as Surveyor of Drains. (The drains in question were not of the domestic variety, but were intended to drain the boglands.)

Of major architectural interest is the Palladian villa of Bellamont Forest, just outside Cootehill. The building was designed by Edward Lovett Pearce and has remained virtually unaltered since its completion in 1728. It has been called the purest example of a Palladian villa in the British Isles.

Cavan town, 20 miles northwest of Virginia, is an important center for the manufacture of crystal; tours of the factory are available. Monaghan town, by contrast, the principal town of County Monaghan, is a thriving agricultural center. The elegant 18th-century courthouse now houses an attractive local museum which was set up in 1974 to collect and display historical objects and examples of traditional local crafts.

Inishkeen in the southern corner of County Monaghan was the home of poet Patrick Kavanagh (1904–67). He worked on his father's small farm and was the local shoemaker. In 1938 he published his first books, *The Ploughman and Other Poems* and an autobiography called *The Green Fool.* Their success led him to Dublin where he supported himself by journalism while continuing to pursue his career as a poet. He caught the essence of the hard, simple pastoral life of Inishkeen, and his work is as highly thought of today as it was in his lifetime. His birthplace is signposted.

Annaghmakerrig, near Newbliss in County Cavan, exists to encourage today's poets, writers, artists and musicians. It was the home of theater director, Sir Tyrone Guthrie (1900–71), and when he died he left it to the state to be used as a retreat for creative artists who need a period of seclusion. It is administered jointly by the Irish Arts Council and the Arts Council of Northern Ireland.

# PRACTICAL INFORMATION FOR

# THE LAKELANDS

**TOURIST OFFICES.** The main tourist office for the area is in **Mullingar,** tel. 044–48761. There are other offices at **Athlone,** tel. 0902–72866 (open year-round); **Birr,** tel. 0905–20206 (open June to Aug.); **Cavan,** tel. 049–31942 (open June to Sept.); **Clonmacnoise,** tel. 0905–74134 (open May to Sept.); **Longford,** tel. 043–46566 (open June to Aug.); **Monaghan,** tel. 047–81122 (open June to Aug.); **Portlaoise,** tel. 0502–21178 (open June to Aug.).

## HOTELS AND RESTAURANTS

**Athlone** (Co. Westmeath). *Prince of Wales* (M), tel. 0902–72626. 42 rooms with bath. In the center of town. Good restaurant. AE, DC, MC, V. *Royal* (M), tel. 0902–72924. 55 rooms, half with bath. AE, DC, MC, V.

**Restaurant.** *The Jolly Mariner* (M), (tel. 0902–72892). Riverside restaurant on banks of the Shannon.

**Birr** (Co. Offaly). *County Arms* (M), tel. 0509–20791. 18 rooms with bath. Near the famous Birr Castle and its gardens. Good restaurant. AE, DC, MC, V.

**Borris-in-Ossory** (Co. Laois). *Leix County* (I), tel. 0505–41213. 19 rooms with bath. A pleasant stopover place. DC, MC, V.

**Carrickmacross** (Co. Monaghan). *Nuremore* (M), tel. 042–61438. 39 rooms, all with bath. In woodland setting with 9-hole golf course and own lakes providing good coarse fishing. Heated indoor pool, sauna, spa, squash, restaurant and bars. AE, DC, MC, V.

**Cavan** (Co. Cavan). *Kilmore* (M), Dublin Rd. (tel. 049–32288). 40 rooms with bath. In the heart of the fishing district. Dining room; nightclub at weekends. AE, MC, V.

**Clones** (Co. Monaghan). **Restaurant.** *Hilton Park* (M). Informal restaurant in large country house. Imaginative use of fresh local produce. MC.

**Cootehill** (Co. Cavan). *White Horse* (M), tel. 049–52124. 30 rooms, most with bath. Located between the rivers Dromore and Annalee, so there's plenty of choice for fishing. Restaurant and weekend entertainment. MC, V.

**Durrow** (Co. Laois). *Woodview* (I), tel. 0502–36286. 10 rooms, 5 with bath. Convenient stopping place just off the main Dublin–Cork road. Well-recommended restaurant open 7.30 AM to 11 PM daily. AE, DC, MC, V.

**Longford** (Co. Longford). *Longford Arms* (M), tel. 043–46296. 51 rooms with bath. A convenient spot for exploring the Lakelands. *Annally* (I), tel. 042–46253. 34 rooms, 18 with bath. Good restaurant with French chef.

**Monaghan** (Co. Monaghan). *Hillgrove* (M), Old Armagh Rd. (tel. 047–81288). 43 rooms, most with bath. Recently extended and updated. Comfortable and friendly. DC, MC, V.

**Mullingar** (Co. Westmeath). *Bloomfield House* (M), tel. 044–40894. 33 rooms with bath. In parkland on the shores of Lough Ennel. Well-appointed, with character. AE, DC, MC, V. *Greville Arms* (M), tel. 044–48563. 33 rooms with bath. In the middle of town. Has a very good snack bar. AE, DC, MC, V.
**Restaurants.** *Crookedwood House* (M), tel. 044–72165. Family-run cellar restaurant which maintains its standards. AE, MC, V. *Gramby* (M), 9 Dominic St. (tel. 044–40280). Homey, with an open fire to greet you. MC, V.

**Portlaoise** (Co. Laois). *Killeshin* (M), tel. 0502–21663. 44 rooms with bath. Attractive conservatory-style restaurant. On the Dublin side of town. AE, DC, MC, V. *Montague* (M), Emo (tel. 0502–26154). 70 rooms with bath or shower. East of town in own grounds. AE, DC, MC, V.

**Tullamore** (Co. Offaly). **Restaurant.** *Moorhill House* (M), Moorhill, Clara Rd. (tel. 0506–21395). In converted stables of old country house. Game in season; Irish and continental cuisine. AE, DC, MC, V.

**Tyrrellspass** (Co. Westmeath). *The Village* (I), tel. 044–23171. 10 rooms, all with bath. In a charming village on the main road to the south and southwest, run by an excellent hotelier. AE, DC, MC, V.

**Virginia** (Co. Cavan). *Lake* (I), tel. 049–47561. 13 rooms, some with bath. Close to the fishing waters. *Park* (M), tel. 049–47235. 22 rooms, 19 with bath. Overlooks both a golf course and the lovely Lough Ramor.

**HOW TO GET AROUND.** The Lakeland area is crossed by the National Routes to the south, west and northwest, and by railway services. Expressway bus services also provide a useful network. Services are not frequent, but are adequate, and drivers are helpful with advice on points at which to change buses if you are not making a direct journey.

If you are driving in the north of the counties Cavan and Monaghan, be sure to avoid unapproved roads which cross the border into Northern Ireland: they are marked. If you wish to make a visit to the North, or to take a shortcut to Donegal, cross at a frontier post. The approved routes in this area are Monaghan–Aughnacloy; Castlefin–Castlederg; Swanlinbar–Enniskillen; Clones–Newtownbutler; Monaghan–Rosslea. If you are driving a rented car, make sure it has been cleared for cross-border journeys when you pick it up.

Bicycles can be hired at *Hardiman's,* Irishtown, Athlone, Co. Westmeath (tel. 0902–72951); *Edward Denniston & Co.,* Longford, Co. Longford (tel. 043–46345).

**TOURS AND EXCURSIONS.** This is very much a go-as-you-please area, but local tours are organized from Mullingar. Check with the tourist office for the latest arrangements.

Cruises on Lough Ree (part of the river Shannon) take place from the Jolly Mariner Marina, Athlone, June to end Aug., daily. They cost about IR£2.75. Check with *Aloma Cruises,* tel. 0902–72894, for times. If there is a cruise downriver to Clonmacnois available, take it, because it provides the best overall impression of the remarkable monastic settlement in the area.

## PLACES TO VISIT

**Athlone** (Co. Westmeath). **Athlone Castle Museum** (tel. 0902–72191). Folklore and local archeology.

**Birr** (Co. Offaly). **Birr Castle Demesne.** Home of the Earl and Countess of Rosse. The 17th-century castle is open only by special arrangement, but the gardens are worth seeing, covering over 100 acres and containing many species of tree, shrub and plant. In the park are the remains of a huge 72-inch reflecting telescope, the world's largest in the 19th century. There's a scale model of the original and astronomical displays. Open all year, daily 9–1 and 2–6 (or dusk if earlier).

**Carrickmacross** (Co. Monaghan). **Carrickmacross Lace.** See the beautiful traditional Carrickmacross lace being made at the St. Louis Convent, Carrickmacross. Mon. to Fri. only.

**Castlepollard** (Co. Westmeath). **Tullynally Castle and Gardens.** The home of the Earls of Longford since the 17th century. 30 acres of woods and walled gardens. Garden open 1 June to 30 Sept., daily 2–6. Castle rooms open mid-July to mid-Aug., daily 2.30–6.

**Fore Abbey.** Part of what was once a small walled town of the 13th century. The abbey was a Benedictine foundation and looks, in part, like a fort. One of the "Seven Wonders of Fore" is St. Fechin's Spring. A couple of miles east of Castlepollard.

**Cavan** (Co. Cavan). **Cavan Crystal.** Visitors can see the glass being blown and cut.

**Killykeen Forest Park.** 600 acres of planned walks, near Cavan Town, on one of which, the Derinish Nature Trail, a number of ancient dwellings, or *crannogs,* can be seen. There are four fishing locations by the lake. Restaurant and car park.

**Clonmacnois** (Co. Offaly). **Monastic settlement** of the 6th century which became a famous seat of learning. The well-preserved remains include two Round Towers, six churches and two high crosses, as well as the finest collection of old Irish gravestones in the country. Pope John Paul II visited here in 1979. Ten miles south of Athlone on the river Shannon. Open mid-June to mid-Sept., daily 9–7.30; mid-Apr. to mid-June and mid-Sept. to 31 Oct., Tues. to Sat. 10–5, Sun. 2–5; 1 Nov. to mid-Apr., Tues. to Sat. 10–1 and 2–5, Sun. 2–5.

**Glaslough** (Co. Monaghan). **Castle Leslie.** Originally a medieval stronghold, it has been rebuilt several times, most recently by Sir John Leslie, grandfather of the present owner, in 1870. Fine art collection and interesting interior design, with particular Italian associations. Seven miles northeast of Monaghan Town. Open 19 June to 19 Aug., daily 2–6. Tours every half-hour.

**Kingscourt** (Co. Cavan). **Dun a Ri Forest Park.** 558 acres of an ancient forest. About a mile north of Kingscourt on the Carrickmacross road.

**Monaghan** (Co. Monaghan). **Monaghan County Museum,** St. Mary's Hill, (tel. 047–82928). Recent winner of the Council of Europe museum prize. Archeology, folklife, lace and other craftwork.

**Mullingar** (Co. Westmeath). **Military Museum,** Columb Barracks, (tel. 044–48391). Visiting by arrangement only, so phone before you go.

**Multyfarnham** (Co. Westmeath). **Multyfarnham Friary.** A Franciscan friary of the 14th century restored to its original state. Life-size Stations of the Cross are located in the grounds.

**Stradbally** (Co. Laois). **Stradbally Traction Engine Museum,** The Green. As well as permanent exhibits related to steam engines, there's usually a rally of steam traction engines on August Bank Holiday Monday. Check, tel. 0502–25136.

**Tullamore** (Co. Offaly). **Irish Mist Building.** Video on the making of Irish Mist liqueur and samples. For details tel. 0506–21586.

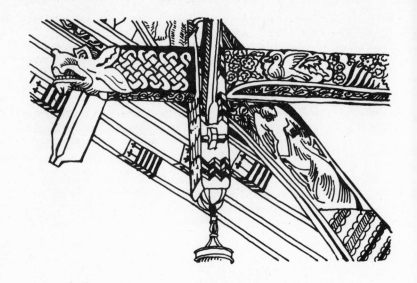

# THE SOUTHEAST

## *Wexford, Waterford, Kilkenny and Carlow*

South of the hills of County Wicklow, the Counties of Carlow and Wexford provide a gateway to the undulating river plains and sandy beaches of Ireland's "sunny southeast." The label is by no means merely fanciful: the weather station of the Irish Meteorological Service at Rosslare has established that the southeast is, beyond any doubt, the sunniest and the driest part of Ireland.

Miles of sandy beaches stretch along the coasts of Counties Wexford and Waterford, making them popular vacation areas. Wexford itself is an ancient town of narrow, winding streets dating back to the Viking period. But the whole area is rich in history, having been occupied at various times by Celtic, Norse, Anglo-Norman, Welsh and Cromwellian settlers. Like Wexford, Waterford too was founded by Viking invaders. Most of the ancient walls the Vikings built around Waterford are still standing. Similarly, Carlow town was a stronghold of the Anglo-Normans, and still has the remains of its 13th-century castle.

While the history of the area stretches back to pre-Christian times, in the eyes of most Irishmen at least, its past is dominated by the Rebellion of 1798, which had its origins in Wexford. The rebel forces, most armed only with pikes, fought heroically against great odds, with over 50,000 Irishmen killed in the space of a few weeks. Stories of those days are told and retold as if they had happened only yesterday, and are commemorated in popular ballads such as *The Croppy Boy* and *The Rising of the Moon*. The rebellious sentiments expressed in such ballads also suited the mood

# Trinity College Library Dublin

Admit one
Long Room and Book of Kells

402312

of the country in the years following the 1916 Easter Rising, and they are still sung with great fervor to this day.

The coast of the southeast has always had strong links with Wales, which lies across the St. George's Channel, and these links are maintained today by the passenger and car ferry running from Rosslare to the Welsh port of Fishguard.

## Kilkenny—The Marble City

Kilkenny, on the banks of the river Nore, is a good place from which to start exploring the southeast.

A large proportion of County Kilkenny is formed of limestone rock, which turns black when polished. Extensive use of this polished rock in the walls and buildings of the city of Kilkenny has given it the name of the "Marble City." Looking across the river Nore, the skyline of the city reminds us of its history—the great bulk of the castle and the towers and spires of the churches overshadow the 20th century, yet down in the narrow streets of the city, the old buildings do not look out of place among their newer neighbors.

The city has existed in the Valley of the Nore since the 6th century, when St. Canice founded a monastery where the cathedral stands today. St. Canice in fact gave his name to the city: in Irish it is Cill Chainnigh, literally Canice's Church. The Normans came in the 11th century and subsequently anglicized the name to Kilkenny and it was the Normans who built the castle overlooking the river on the site of an earlier fortress erected by the warrior Strongbow. From the 14th century the castle was the seat of the Butlers, Earls and Dukes of Ormonde. 17th- and 18th-century additions gave the castle the imposing form which dominates the town today. The Marquess of Ormonde gave the castle into the care of the city of Kilkenny in 1966, prior to its restoration. It is now open to the public, and plays host to visiting exhibitions.

The castle stables have become the Kilkenny Design Workshops, a government-sponsored project in which designers from overseas work with and train Irish designers. The workshops produce ceramics, woven textiles, woodturning, printed textiles and silver and metal work. So successful has the project been that today Kilkenny has become a byword for all that is best in modern Irish design, as can be gathered from a glance at the work on exhibition. It is well worth browsing around their shop in search of an unusual gift or two.

Kilkenny's castle was the hub of activity in medieval times when several parliaments were held in the city. One of these, summoned in 1366 by the Duke of Clarence (son of Edward III of England), passed the infamous Statute of Kilkenny. It forbade the Anglo-Normans to intermarry with the Irish, use the Irish language, dress or surnames, or allow Irish clergy into their churches. The Irish were banished from the city (there is still a district across the river known as Irishtown).

The General Assembly of the Catholic Confederacy made Kilkenny its capital in 1642. Dissensions and compromise broke up the Confederation, and Kilkenny became a Royalist stronghold. After a five-day siege, Kilkenny surrendered to Cromwellian forces in March 1650. Cromwellian soldiers sacked the town with their usual brutality. The Irish expression "fighting like Kilkenny cats" originates from those days. Cromwell had a special dislike of cats, and his officers, hoping to curry favor with their general, devised a torture in which two cats were tied together by their tails. The tails were then set alight and the cats left to fight to the death.

The Cathedral of St. Canice remains one of the finest in Ireland, despite Cromwellian damage. It was begun in 1250 and completed ten years later. In 1332 the central tower collapsed and was rebuilt in the squat style that stands today. There are also remains of a 100-foot Round Tower in the churchyard. The 12th-century Kilkenny marble font is worth seeing, and there are a number of medieval tombs. The library (founded 1693) has an impressive collection of ancient books, including a *Sarum Missal* (1498) printed by William Caxton. Contact the Librarian to see this priceless library.

### The Witch that Got Away

Rothe House in Parliament Street is a well-preserved Tudor merchant's house with cobbled courtyards and an ancient well. It now contains a museum with period furniture, costumes, pewter ware and prehistoric weapons from the local countryside. While looking round the house, glance upwards to see the fine workmanship of the roof timbers. The Courthouse across the street dates back to the 16th century; it was later the city jail.

Where Parliament Street meets St. Kieran's Street, you will find Kyteler's Inn, the oldest house in Kilkenny, once the home of the 14th-century witch, Dame Alice Kyteler. In 1324 she was charged with witchcraft, heresy and the assault of her four husbands. The sentence was whipping through the streets and burning at the stake. However, the nobility took Dame Alice's part and helped her to escape to England, uncharitably leaving her maidservant Petronilla to be burnt at the stake.

Nearby are the ruins of the 13th-century St. Francis Abbey, which has given its name to the adjoining brewery. This abbey was at the northeast corner of the old city wall; over at the northwest junction is a Dominican friary of the same period, called the Black Abbey. Restoration work on it was finally completed in 1979 and there are many remarkable relics of its historic past to be found there. A short distance away is Trinity Gate, the only remaining gate of the old walled city. Shee's Almshouse (1594) is another representative building from the past; it is in Rose Inn Street on the way to St. John's Bridge, which provides the most imposing view of Kilkenny Castle.

Kilkenny College (1780), on the right of John Street, is the successor of St. John's College, where Jonathan Swift (1667–1745), William Congreve (1670–1729) and the philosopher Bishop George Berkeley (1685–1753) were educated. Berkeley, whose name is commemorated by the University of California, was born at Thomastown, 11 miles to the south.

### South from Kilkenny

Southwest of Kilkenny city is the market town of Callan, an important fortified town in medieval times. There is a memorial in Kilkenny limestone in the main street dedicated to Edmund Ignatius Rice (1762–1844) who was born here. He was the founder of the Irish Christian Brothers, an influential teaching order in Ireland, who have colleges spread throughout the English-speaking world. James Hoban, the architect who designed the White House in Washington, was also born near Callan in 1762, the same year as Brother Rice. He emigrated to Philadelphia in 1785, after training as an architect in Dublin.

Ten miles across country to the east is Thomastown, named after a 12th-century Welsh mercenary, Thomas FitzAnthony Walsh, who became Seneschal of Leinster. His fortified castle was destroyed by the Cromwellians in 1650, but there are some interesting monuments among the ruins of a large 13th-century church. The present Catholic church contains the old high altar from the great Cistercian Abbey of Jerpoint.

Jerpoint Abbey is about a mile outside Thomastown across the old stone bridge, and should not be missed. The ruins of this 12th-century Abbey have been carefully restored. The oldest sections are the chancel and transepts, built in Hiberno-Romanesque style. But in fact the architecture spans several centuries, and includes a 14th-century window, 15th-century cloisters and a battlemented square tower built at about the same time.

Just a few miles north of Thomastown is Bennettsbridge, on the river Nore. The river has been providing power for Mosse's Flour Mills since 1503. It is not only the smallest mill in Ireland but its products include a mix which makes the famous Irish brown bread. One of the family, Dr. Bartholomew Mosse, founded the Rotunda Hospital in Dublin in 1751.

## North of Kilkenny

Dunmore Cave, about seven miles north of Kilkenny, is one of very few limestone caves in Ireland to have been made safe for visits from the general public. Lighting and walkways have been introduced to enable visitors to view the vast stalagmites and stalactites. Dumore Cave was the scene of a massacre by the Vikings in 928.

The county town of Carlow, the neighboring county to Kilkenny, lies 27 miles northeast of Kilkenny city. Carlow is pleasantly situated on the banks of the river Barrow, which offers salmon, trout and coarse fishing. Once an Anglo-Norman stronghold, Carlow is now a thriving industrial center, and was the site of the first beet sugar factory in Ireland.

Its history has been particularly stormy, as it was an outpost of the English Pale and a fording place of the river Barrow. The last great battle was fought here during the Rising of 1798, when over 600 of the insurgents were killed, most of them being buried in a nearby gravel pit which is marked by a Celtic-design memorial cross.

Captain Myles Keogh, who died with General Custer at Little Big Horn in June 1876, was born at Orchard House, Leighlinbridge, nine miles from Carlow; there is a small museum to his memory at Clifden Castle nearby.

## County Wexford

Across country to the southeast lies the aptly-named town of Gorey in County Wexford, a major battleground of the 1798 Rebellion. Here the road from Dublin (the N11) is joined; it continues south to Enniscorthy, a town which developed beside a castle on a hill which guarded the limit of the navigable waters of the river Slaney. The English poet Edmund Spenser (1551–99), author of *The Faerie Queene,* lived here at one time; at another, the castle was a jail. Its square turreted keep was rebuilt in 1586 and is open to the public. It contains an important folk museum.

The capture of Enniscorthy by the insurgents of 1798 inspired a major revolt in the country. The most important battle took place at Vinegar Hill on the eastern side of the town. About 20,000 rebels armed only with pikes were bombarded by the cannon of the British army, and very few survived. Vinegar Hill offers a panoramic view of the surrounding countryside and river.

Enniscorthy's 19th-century cathedral, St. Aidan's, was designed by the English architect, Augustus Pugin, a pioneer in the revival of Gothic architecture. Its tower is built largely of stones from a ruined Franciscan Friary in the neighborhood. The statue in the Market Square of Father John Murphy, a pikeman of 1798, is the work of Oliver Sheppard, and bears the inscription of "1798," which says enough for any Wexfordman.

The N11 road south runs parallel to the river Slaney into Wexford, passing by Ferrycarrig, a narrow river gorge which still bears signs of its one-time strategic importance, guarding the river entrance. Ferrycarig Castle, on the north bank of the Slaney, is a 16th-century keep built on a rock. The monument on the south bank is often mistaken for an early monastic tower. It is in fact a 19th-century memorial to those Wexford soldiers who died in the Crimean War.

## Wexford Town

Wexford has been on the map for a long time: the Roman geographer Ptolemy put it there in the 2nd century, marking it as Menapia after a tribe believed to live in the area. Its Irish name is Loch Garman, but the Vikings called it Waesfjord, the harbor of the mud flats, which passed into English as Wexford.

It is a town brimful of history, and very proud of its long traditions. Volunteer members of the Old Wexford Society will conduct visitors on walking tours of the town and can be contacted at The Talbot and Whites Hotel. But in fact it is easy enough to find your own way around the compact town center. The Quay runs from the new bridge along the full length of the town. About mid-way along the quay is a crescent which is dominated by William Wheeler's bronze statue of Commodore John Barry (1745–1803), the "Father of the American Navy." Barry was born nearby, and the statue was presented by the United States' Government in 1956.

Wexford Harbor has now largely silted up, and Waterford on the river Barrow has become the principal port in the region. However, a few small trawlers still fish out of Wexford, though never on November 10, Martinmas Eve. The reason is simple. St. Martin is the patron saint of these Wexford fishermen. In the last century they once defied the tradition and the night brought disaster—over 80 men were drowned.

Down on the Quay, near the point where the trawlers tie up, there is a floating maritime museum aboard the former Arklow lightship, *The Guillemot*.

Moving inland from the Quay up Wexford's narrow hilly streets, you will discover the Westgate Tower, the only one of Wexford's five fortified gateways still standing. Nearby are the ruins of Selskar Abbey. The importance of the Normans in Wexford's history can be gauged by the fact that the first treaty between the Irish and the Normans was signed in Selskar Abbey in 1169.

At the center of the town on a corner of Main Street is the site of St. Doologue's Parish. This is generally believed to be the smallest parish in the world, consisting of no more than three acres. In the building nearby known as Kelly's, William Cody, father of Colonel William "Buffalo Bill" Cody, was born. Also in this part of town are two 19th-century Gothic churches: The Assumption and the Immaculate Conception. They are known as the "twin churches" as their exteriors are identical, their foundation stones were laid on the same day, and their spires both reach a height of 230 feet.

Hemmed in by shops and a market building in the center of the town is a square which still bears the name Bull Ring, because it was here that the Normans staged their bull-baiting competitions.

The Franciscan Church in John Street, St. Francis, is on the site of Wexford's Franciscan Friary which was founded in 1230. Beneath the altar of St. Francis are the relics of a Roman boy martyr, St. Adjutor, who was murdered by his own father; they were presented to an Irish family by Pope Pius IX in 1856.

### Music, Mussels and Slobs

Music lovers will immediately associate the name of Wexford with opera. Its famous opera festival was founded in 1951. Every year three full-scale productions of unusual and rarely performed operas are presented in the tiny 440-seat Theater Royal during the last two weeks of October by top international singers and musicians. The festival organizers take full advantage of the extraordinary amount of musical talent which gathers in the town at that time of year and the operas are supplemented by a full recital program running from mid-morning until after midnight. Even if you do not care for opera it is worth visiting the town at festival time to enjoy the convivial atmosphere and to observe one of the highlights of the Irish social calendar. If you do plan to take in an opera, full evening dress is strongly recommended.

Wexford boasts another festival in late-August, the mussel and seafood festival. Wexford is the home of Ireland's mussel industry, and has the country's largest fish-farming operation.

The mud flats which gave Wexford its Viking name are called slobs. The slobs on the northern shore of Wexford Harbor, a short walk across the new bridge, form the Wexford Wildfowl Reserve. Half the world's population of Greenland white-fronted geese winter at Wexford; shelducks, mallard and tufted duck all breed there. Screened approaches and an observation tower are provided for visitors, and a collection of the various species of duck, geese and swans who live on the slobs has been established near the reception area.

Johnstown Castle, three miles south of Wexford, contains the Irish Agricultural Museum with a collection of Irish agricultural tools and farming instruments on display. Reconstructed stables, a dairy and typical cottage interiors give a good idea of a way of life which has only recently disappeared.

Rosslare is a well-known seaside resort 11 miles southeast of Wexford which can offer six miles of firm sandy beaches. Five miles down the road from Rosslare is Rosslare Harbor, departure point for ferries to Fishguard in Wales, and Cherbourg and Le Havre in France.

## Forth and Bargy

The area southeast of Wexford contained in the triangle of land between Wexford town, Bannow and Carnsore Point is known as Forth and Bargy and was the first area in Ireland to be settled by the Anglo-Normans. The people of the Baronies of Forth and Bargy (or the English Baronies, as they are sometimes called) spoke a strange dialect, which in its decline was known as *Yola* from their word for old, in which many early English words and forms were preserved. Until the middle of the last century, the peoples of the Baronies retained many of the domestic manners and customs of their Norman ancestors, including a siesta taken at noon, called an *enteet,* which caused much mirth among the neighboring Irish. This was how the people of Forth and Bargy began the Lord's Prayer in *Yola* around the year 1900:

"Oure vaader fho yarth ing heaveene, ee-hallowet bee t'naame. Thee kingdomw coome, thee weel be ee-doane, as ing heaveene, zo eake an ear-the."

The language has, alas, now died out completely, but surnames such as Parle, Codd, Devereux, Lambert and Rossiter identify the Anglo-Norman people of Forth and Bargy.

The last stronghold of *Yola* was Lady's Island, five miles from Rosslare. It is on an almost totally enclosed inlet of the sea, and is linked to the mainland by a causeway. It has been a place of pilgrimage for many centuries, and pilgrimages are still made between August 15 and September 9. The ancient monastery on the island was dedicated to the Blessed Virgin—hence the name, Lady's Island.

The flashing light six miles out to sea off this coast guards the notorious Tuskar Rock, a danger to shipping but a great place for anglers, sharing the latter role with the Splaugh Rock off the same coast. The latter is noted for its bass fishing, while men who fish around the Tuskar not only bring back stories of the big fish that got away, but the big fish themselves—usually skate, plaice, cod, tope and mackerel.

Kilmore Quay, not far from the rather dismally named Forlorn Point (the Irish alternative is better, Crossfornoge), is an increasingly important fishing port. Its development, however, has not spoiled its quiet character. For the visitor the main interest is the facilities it provides for sea anglers and the boat service, weather permitting, to the Saltee Islands, which lie five or six miles south and contain Ireland's largest bird sanctuary.

There is a name hereabouts which may puzzle visitors who have visited the famous Tintern Abbey on the river Wye in the Welsh border county of Gwent. There is a Tintern Abbey in this part of County Wexford, named after the more famous abbey in Wales from which it was founded many centuries ago. Stones from the old abbey have since been used to build a local bridge and a church, and part of the old building is embraced in the residence still known as Tintern Abbey.

## New Ross and J.F. Kennedy Park

New Ross, 23 miles northwest of Wexford town, is an important inland port on the river Barrow and, to the pleasure of the growing number of people who take their vacations cruising on inland waterways, is linked to Dublin and the Shannon through the Grand Canal and the Barrow Navigation Canal. A short cruise can be made on the Barrow from New Ross with Galley Cruising Restaurants while lunch or dinner is served. The Barrow itself rises near the village of Clonaslee up in the Slieve Bloom mountains of Laois and wanders for 120 miles before it reaches the sea at Waterford.

The road south on the left bank of the river Barrow leads to Dungans-town and the cottage where the great-grandfather of President John Fitz-gerald Kennedy was born. Kennedy relatives are still living in the house. Two of the President's direct forebears fought as rebels in the 1798 siege of Ross.

The late President is commemorated by the park that bears his name at Slieve Coillte near Dunganstown. The park has not yet been completed but its 270 acres will eventually contain some 6,000 different species of plants from around the world. Already, however, it has become a training center of repute for botanists and foresters and the venue for international conferences. There are fine panoramic views from the top of the park.

Campile, about ten miles from Dunganstown, was settled originally by English monks in the 12th century. There they built Dunbrody Abbey. Although it was suppressed in the 16th century, the buildings are still suffi-ciently well-preserved to warrant a visit. The tower is typical of religious establishments of its kind, and there are some elaborately shaped windows of considerable beauty.

The small fishing village of Ballyhack, just to the south of Campile, has an interesting ruined castle which was occupied between the 13th and 16th centuries by the Knights Templar. The village itself, on the shores of Wa-terford Harbor, is extremely picturesque, as is its nearby "twin," Arthurs-town. Ballyhack has a car ferry to Passage East that greatly shortens the journey to the neighboring county of Waterford, which must otherwise be approached across the bridge at New Ross.

Waterford harbor forms an estuary ten miles long in which the rivers Nore, Barrow and Suir converge. Its most easterly point is called Hook, while in Cromwell's day its most westerly point had a village called Crook, which is why Cromwell vowed that he would capture the city of Waterford "by Hook or by Crook."

## Waterford

Whether you come into County Waterford across the bridge in New Ross or by the Ballyhack–Passage East ferry, the main road, the N24, will take you to Waterford City. As the road enters the town, it makes a sharp turn over the river Suir to the quays which front the city itself; on the way part of the old defenses may be seen near the railway station. Water-ford is a prosperous port with a number of industries, including bacon and meat processing, furniture-making and iron-founding. It is best known, however, for the Waterford Glass Factory, now the biggest crystal factory in the world.

It was almost 1,000 years ago that Reginald the Dane landed in Water-ford and built a circular guard tower with walls ten feet thick and a low conical roof. Reginald's Tower is still standing, having served in succeed-ing centuries as a fort, a royal residence, a mint, an ammunition magazine, a prison and a police barracks. Since 1955 it has been a civic museum of considerable interest, displaying many of the city's archives.

The Danes, who gave the city its name, were pushed out by the Anglo-Normans. It was in Waterford that the Norman leader, Strongbow, allied himself to the Irish by marrying Aoife, the daughter of Diarmuid Mac-Murrough, king of Leinster, thus considerably increasing his personal power in the country. Strongbow and Aoife are buried in Christ Church Cathedral, Dublin.

Waterford's charter dates from 1205 when it was granted by King John—ten years before he signed the Magna Carta in England.The City Hall, built on the Mall in 1788, has a group of unusual exhibits, including two of the flags carried by the Irish Brigade at Fredericksburg and the uniform, sword and medals of Brigadier-General Thomas Francis Meagher (1823–67). Meagher was born on the Quay (a plaque on one of the buildings marks the site); he was an active "Young Irelander" and one of the founders of the Irish Confederation. Captured in the Rising of 1848, he was sentenced to death, but the sentence was commuted to transportation to Tasmania, or Van Diemen's Land as it was then called. He escaped to America in 1852 and fought in the Civil War at Fort Sumter and Fredericksburg. Later he was appointed Governor of Montana. He drowned in the Missouri at Fort Benton in 1867. There is an impressive equestrian statue of Meagher in the Capitol Grounds at Helena, Montana.

In the City Hall, after looking at the Meagher Collection, look up at the Waterford glass chandelier. There's an exact replica of it in Philadelphia's Independence Hall.

A tour of the Waterford Glass Factory is a must. (Check with the tourist office for the times of free tours.) Informative guides lead the way so that you can see the skill of glass blowing, polishing and cutting. There is an excellent lobby display, and orders can be placed for delivery overseas. There are also numerous shops in Waterford with good selections of the crystal, and most of them will organize tax-free overseas mail orders.

The Catholic Cathedral in Barronstrand Street is a graceful neo-Classical building, completed in 1796. It has a richly decorated interior and its treasures include a collection of cloth of gold vestments dating from pre-Reformation times. They were found during the demolition of the old Christ Church Cathedral nearly two centuries ago and presented by the Church of Ireland bishop to his Roman Catholic counterpart. The altar plate includes fine silver and gold craftsmanship from the 17th and 18th centuries. The Church of Ireland Christ Church Cathedral in Cathedral Square near the City Hall is mainly 19th century, but there are some remnants of the ancient crypt which can be seen if the verger is contacted. St. Olaf's, in the same area, was a Danish church, later rebuilt by the Normans. It has some beautifully carved black oak in its pulpit, and a bishop's throne.

A tower is virtually the only remnant of the 13th-century Franciscan Friary, which retains the name French Church since its use by a Huguenot colony in the 18th century. The tower of the Dominican Priory (St. Saviour's) is the only major surviving part of the original foundation which dates back to 1266, but its treasures include a small oak figure of the Blessed Virgin, known locally as Our Lady of Waterford.

## Around County Waterford

Nine miles inland to the west of Waterford City is the small town of Portlaw on the Clodagh river. Curraghmore, adjoining the town, is the seat of the Marquis of Waterford. The house is a lovely 18th-century building, and is generally considered to stand in one of the most beautiful estates in Ireland. The gardens are open to the public on Thursdays during the summer only.

From Waterford City there is a pleasant but leisurely coastal route which will lead you south towards Cork. The first place of interest is Passage East, seven miles east of the city. This quaint village at the foot of a hill looking out over Waterford Harbor was at one time fortified against invaders. Nowadays it is the embarkation point for the car ferry to Ballyhack in County Wexford.

Passage East was the landing place of Strongbow, who arrived in 1170 with over 1,000 men. In the following year the local waters must have been even more crowded, for Henry II arrived with a fleet of 400 ships and 4,000 troops.

Not far south of Passage East are the ruins of Geneva Barracks, infamous in Irish hearts since the 1798 rebellion. The Barracks got its name from its original use; a home for a colony of immigrant goldsmiths and silversmiths from Geneva, who were invited to Ireland under a government sponsored scheme in 1785. The scheme was a failure and the buildings were converted to military use and as a prison for the insurgents. The ruins, which overlook Waterford Harbor, are marked with a tablet and its part in the 1798 uprising is remembered in *The Croppy Boy:*

> "At Geneva Barracks the young man died,
> And at Passage they have his body laid.
> Good people who live in peace and joy,
> Give a prayer and a tear for the Croppy Boy."

The pleasant fishing village of Dunmore East lies nine miles southeast of Waterford City. It is a village in name, but in actuality is a thriving fishing port, whose harbor is crowded with boats during the herring season. Most of the catch is exported, as are the substantial catches of lobsters and crayfish, but there is invariably a lobster or some other attractive fish dish to be enjoyed by the visitor.

Across the bay is the lively seaside resort of Tramore, with a three-mile-long beach, suitable for bathing at all states of the tide. At the west end of the beach, the coast takes a sharp turn to form an arm of the bay and changes from a sandy shore to rocky cliffs, the Doneraile Cliffs, with a well-surfaced pathway barred to cars. The path leads on to the setting for one of Ireland's most popular legends. On the Great Newtown Head, at the end of the Doneraile Walk, stand three white pillars, on one of which is The Metal Man, an iron figure of an old-time sailor with an arm pointing out to sea. It is said that if a young woman hops round the base of the pillar three times on one foot, she will be married within the year.

Heading east along the coast you come to the smallest Gaeltacht, or Gaelic-speaking area, in the country. It is centred around the village of Ring, just a few miles southeast of Dungarvan. The people here are especially proud of their distinctive County Waterford accents. There is also an Irish Language College here, to which young people flock for residential summer courses.

The last town on the Waterford coast before entering Cork is Ardmore, eight miles east of Youghal. It is well worth making the short detour from the main road to visit the town, which is renowned for an attractively located group of early-Christian remains. The Round Tower is 96-feet high, and is one of the best preserved of its kind. Projecting stones in the interior are carved into grotesque heads. St. Declan's Oratory is a very small early church. The Cathedral contains work of various periods from the 10th to the 14th centuries and is noted for the curious carvings on its western gable end.

Ardmore itself is a quiet seaside resort, built on an imposing cliff, and was traditionally the place where wealthy landowners of the inland Blackwater Valley maintained their summer residences. The much-loved Irish novelist Molly Keane lives in Ardmore and it was here, in her secluded cliff-top house, that she wrote her two most recent works, *Good Behaviour* and *Time After Time*. Another distinguished resident is Patricia Cockburn, widow of the writer Claud. Her shell pictures, which employ a little-used 18th-century technique, have been exhibited internationally.

Before leaving Waterford, drive inland through Cappoquin towards the Knockmealdown mountains to enjoy the splendid scenery of the Blackwater Valley. Lismore, near Cappoquin, has a magnificent castle standing on a cliff above the Blackwater. It was built by King John in 1185, and was much extended in later centuries. Today, it is the Irish home of the Duke of Devonshire. His uncle, Lord Charles Cavendish, lived here from 1932 until his death in 1944 with his wife, Adele Astaire, sister of Fred. When the castle is not in use by the Duke, it can be rented for a substantial weekly sum, though this naturally includes the use of a butler.

Finally, a visit to the modern Cistercian monastery at Mount Melleray in the Knockmealdown mountains can be recommended. Mount Melleray was founded in 1832 by Irish monks expelled from France in 1822. Visitors are still welcome to this extraordinary place of prayer, contemplation and work. There is a guesthouse at the Abbey for men, and a neighboring one for women. No charge is made, but the guest leaves whatever offering seems appropriate. The monks are bound by a rule of silence, but the guest master is absolved from the rule during his period of office. Virtually all the needs of guests and community are met by the produce of the monks' mountain farmlands.

# PRACTICAL INFORMATION FOR
# THE SOUTHEAST

**TOURIST OFFICES.** There are tourist offices at **Carlow,** tel. 0503–31554 (open July to Aug.); **Dungarvan,** tel. 058–41741 (open July to Aug.); **Gorey,** tel. 055–21248 (open July to Aug.); **Kilkenny,** tel. 056–21755 (open Jan. to Oct.); **New Ross,** tel. 051–21857 (open July to Aug.); **Rosslare Harbor,** tel. 053–33232 (open mid-Apr. to Sept.); **Tramore,** tel. 051–81572 (open July to Aug.); **Waterford,** tel. 051–75788 (open year-round); **Wexford,** tel. 053–2311 (open year-round).

## HOTELS AND RESTAURANTS

**Ardmore** (Co. Waterford). *Cliff House* (I), tel. 024–94106. 16 rooms, 8 with bath. Owner-run hotel overlooking bay. AE, DC, MC, V.

**Ballyhack** (Co. Wexford). **Restaurant.** *Neptune* (M), tel. 051–89284. Small, attractive riverside restaurant by the ferry; specializes in local seafood.

**Carlow** (Co. Carlow). *Carlow Lodge* (M), Kilkenny Rd. (tel. 0503–42002). 10 rooms, all with bath. Woodland setting just out of town. AE, DC, MC, V. *Royal* (M), Dublin St. (tel. 0505–31621). 30 rooms, 26 with bath. In the heart of town. AE, DC, MC, V.

**Dunmore East** (Co. Waterford). *Candlelight Inn* (M), tel. 051–83239. 11 rooms with bath. Exceptional family-run hotel overlooking the estuary. Outdoor heated pool. AE, MC, V. *The Haven* (M), tel. 051–83150. 14 rooms with bath. AE, MC, V. *Ocean* (M), tel. 051–83136. 14 rooms, some with bath. AE, V.
**Restaurant.** The Ship (M) tel. 051–83144 Overlooking sea, fresh local fish. V.

**Enniscorthy** (Co. Wexford). *Murphy-Flood's* (M), tel. 054–33413. 22 rooms, most with bath or shower. Central location in historic town. AE, DC, MC, V.

**Foulksmills** (Co. Wexford). *Horetown House* (I), tel. 051–63633. 12 rooms. Georgian manor and riding center.

**Gorey** (Co. Wexford). *Marfield House* (L), tel. 055–21124. 12 rooms, all with bath. Lovely Regency house on the Gorey–Courtown road. The restaurant (E) here has a well-deserved top reputation.

**Kilkenny** (Co. Kilkenny). *Hotel Kilkenny* (E), tel. 056–62000. 60 rooms with bath. Development of old country house. Health center. AE, DC. *Newpark* (M), tel. 056–22122. 60 rooms with bath. Pleasant setting off the main road. Friendly and efficient. AE, DC, MC, V. *Springhill* (M), tel. 056–21122. 44 rooms with bath. Lively, modern hotel with cabaret and dancing; real log fires. AE, DC, MC, V. *Lacken House* (I), Dublin Rd. (tel. 056–61085). 10 rooms. Owned and operated by an award-winning chef and his wife. Restaurant closed Sun. AE, DC, MC, V.
**Restaurants.** *Newpark Hotel* (M), tel. 056–22122. Irish and continental dishes. AE, DC, MC, V. *Flannery's* (I), tel. 056–22235. Informal wine bar and restaurant. *Mulhall's* (I), 6 High St. near Kilkenny Castle (tel. 056–21329). Family-owned; grills, snacks. MC, V.

**Lismore** (Co. Waterford). *Ballyrafter House* (I), tel. 058–54002. 14 rooms, some with bath. *Lismore* (I), tel. 058–54219. 15 rooms.

**New Ross** (Co. Wexford). *Five Counties* (M), tel. 051–21703. 35 rooms, all with bath. Pleasant grounds overlooking the river Barrow. AE, DC, MC, V. *New Ross* (I), tel. 051–21457. 12 rooms all with bath.
**Restaurant.** *Galley Cruising Restaurant* (M), tel. 051–21723. Based at Bridge Quay. Lunch or dine on the beautiful sister rivers Nore and Barrow. Sailings not affected by weather. Booking essential.

**Ring** (Co. Waterford). **Restaurant.** *Seanachie* (M), tel. 058–46285. Thatched bar and restaurant with traditional live music and Irish dancing daily. On the main Waterford–Cork road, three miles outside Dungarvan. An Irish-speaking district.

**Rosslare** (Co. Wexford). *Casey's Cedars* (M), tel. 053–32124. 34 rooms with bath. New leisure center, exercise facilities. *Emmet Restaurant* is particularly good for lobster. *Great Southern* (M), tel. 053–33233. 96 rooms, all with bath. On clifftop overlooking the harbor. Heated indoor pool, sauna, tennis. AE, DC, MC, V. *Kelly's* (M), tel. 053–32114. 89 rooms with bath. Has long family ownership and concentrates on family holidays. Indoor pool, solarium, tennis and other sports facilities. *Rosslare* (M), tel. 053–33110. 25 rooms, 22 with bath. Clifftop position. Cheerful atmosphere, top-rate bar food at the *Portholes Bar.* AE, DC, MC, V. *O'Leary's Farm* (I), at Kilrane (tel. 053–33134). 10 rooms, 8 with shower. Fronts the sea.

**Tramore** (Co. Waterford). *Grand* (E) tel. 051–81414. 50 rooms, all with bath. Family-run, overlooking Tramore Bay. AE, DC, MC, V. *Seaview* (I), tel. 051–81244. 11 rooms, 6 with bath. AE, DC, MC, V.

**Waterford** (Co. Waterford). *Waterford Castle* (L), Ballinakill (tel. 051–78203). 19 rooms with bath. Luxuriously converted castle on an island just outside the town. Opened in 1988; indoor pool, tennis, shooting and fishing. AE, DC, MC, V. *Ardree* (E), tel. 051–32111. 100 rooms, all with bath. On a height overlooking the city. AE, DC, MC, V. *Bridge* (E), 1 the Quay (tel. 051–77222). 40 rooms, all with bath. Restaurant, cocktail bar and nightclub. AE, DC, MC, V. *Granville* (E), Meagher's Quay (tel. 051–55111). 66 rooms, all with bath. The original house was the birthplace of Thomas Francis Meagher, founder of the "Fighting 69th." AE, DC, MC, V. *Tower* (M), the Mall (tel. 051–75801). 81 rooms, all with bath. Good restaurant. AE, DC, MC, V. *Dooley's* (I), tel. 051–73531. 36 rooms, 33 with bath. Family-run, and well-run. Good restaurant and bar food. AE, DC, MC, V.
**Restaurants.** *Annestown House* (M), tel. 051–96160. About 16 miles out of town at Bonmahon, but worth the trip. AE, DC, MC, V. *The Reginald* (M), the Mall (tel. 051–55087). Bar-restaurant in a building which features part of the old city walls. AE, DC. *Oak Room* (I), Bailey's, New St. (tel. 051–74156). Friendly relaxed atmosphere. MC, V.

**Wexford** (Co. Wexford). *Ferrycarrig* (M), Ferrycarrig Bridge (tel. 053–22999). 40 rooms with bath. In its own grounds overlooking the river Slaney. AE, DC, MC, V. *Talbot* (M), Trinity St. (tel. 053–22566). 104 rooms with bath. Indoor heated pool and leisure center. Top-class restaurant, as well as grill and good bars. AE, DC, MC, V. *White's* (M), George St. (tel. 053–22311). 74 rooms, all with bath. Pleasant lounge, restaurant and bars.

Convivial atmosphere. AE, DC, MC, V. *Wexford Lodge* (I), The Bridge (tel. 053–23611). 20 rooms, 14 with bath. DC, MC, V.

**Restaurants.** *Captain White's* (M), George St. (tel. 053–22311). Seafood is tops here. *Oak Tavern* (M), Ferrycarrig (tel. 053–22138). Charcoal grilled steaks and seafood; local salmon. *The Bohemian Girl* (I), North Main St. (tel. 053–23596). Tudor-style pub with award-winning owner-chef. MC, V. *Chan's* (I), North Main St. (tel. 053–22356). Szechuan and Cantonese cuisine. MC, V.

### Youth Hostels

**Arthurstown,** New Ross, Co. Wexford (tel. 051–89186). Open May to Sept. **Foulksrath Castle,** Jenkinstown, Co. Kilkenny (tel. 056–67674). **Glengarra,** Lismore, Co. Waterford (tel. 058–54390). **Rosslare Harbour,** Co. Wexford (tel. 053–33399). The YWCA have 24 rooms at **The Cliff,** Church Rd., Tramore, Co. Waterford (tel. 051–81363).

**HOW TO GET AROUND.** Local bus services from Wexford serve Rosslare and neighboring areas. Similar services from Waterford serve Tramore. C.I.E. rail services operate north to Dublin (through Wexford) and to Waterford, Limerick Junction, Cork, Killarney and Tralee.

A car ferry from Ballyhack, Co. Wexford to Passage East, Co. Waterford, across the river Suir, cuts driving time between Wexford and Waterford by about an hour. Crossing time is 10 minutes and it costs about IR£4 per car.

Bicycles can be hired from *J.J. Wall,* Maudilin St., Co. Kilkenny (tel. 056–21236) and *Hayes,* 108 South Main St., Co. Wexford (tel. 053–22462).

### PLACES TO VISIT

**Ardmore** (Co. Waterford). **Round Tower.** One of the most complete of its kind in Ireland, the tower is 96 ft. high. Seven miles east of Youghal.

**Enniscorthy** (Co. Wexford). **Enniscorthy Museum,** Castle St., Enniscorthy. An excellent regional museum with folklife and archeological exhibitions. Located in the castle.

**Lismore** (Co. Waterford). **Lismore Castle Gardens.** Beside the river Blackwater. Lismore Castle is the Irish home of the Duke of Devonshire. Has walled and woodland gardens and a remarkable Yew Walk. The Riding House, built in 1631, connects the upper and lower gardens. Open 6 May to 13 Sept., Sun. to Fri. 1.45–4.45; closed Sat.

**New Ross** (Co. Wexford). **John F. Kennedy Park.** Eight miles southeast of New Ross, overlooking the late president's forebears' home at Dunganstown. Park covers 620 acres on the slopes of Slieve Coilte and supports over 4,000 shrub and plant species. Fabulous view from the top of the park.

**Portlaw** (Co. Waterford). **Curraghmore Gardens,** Portlaw. Landscaped gardens surrounding the house, decorated in 1754 in exquisite taste. May and June are the best months to appreciate the flowers. 10 miles from Waterford City. Open 1 Apr. to 30 Sept., Thurs. and public holidays 2–5. Open to groups by appointment, tel. 051–87101/2.

**Tramore** (Co. Waterford). **Metal Man,** Great Newtown Head. A sailor's figure atop one of the three pillars marking the eastern end of Tramore Bay. Legend says that marriage will come to any girl hopping around it three times.

**Waterford City** (Co. Waterford). **French Church.** A medieval Franciscan friary given to the Huguenot refugees as a place of worship.

**Reginald's Tower Museum,** the Mall (tel. 051–73501, ext. 408). Items from the city archives, memorabilia of Thomas Francis Meagher, maritime exhibition.

**Waterford Crystal Factory.** See the famous Waterford glass being crafted. Call 051–73311 to check tour times.

**Wexford City** (Co. Wexford). **Agricultural Museum,** Johnstown Castle. The castle itself is a research center, and only the ornamental 19th-century gardens and the museum in the grounds are open to the public. Displays of machinery and many aspects of Irish rural life. Three miles south of Wexford. The museum is open June to Aug., Mon. to Fri. 9–5, Sat. and Sun. 2–5; May and Sept. to 5 Nov., Mon. to Fri. 9–12.30 and 1.30–5, Sun. 2–5; 6 Nov. to 30 Apr., Mon. to Fri. 9–12.30 and 1.30–5.

**Irish National Heritage Park.** Two miles from Wexford, at Ferrycarrig. Newly opened (1988), open-air museum reflecting 9,000 years of history with full-scale replicas of homesteads, burial sites and places of worship. Tel. 053–2311 for opening times.

**Maritime Museum.** On board the lightship *Guillemot,* moored at the Quay. For information, call 053–2311.

**Rathmacknee Castle.** Well-preserved 15th-century tower house. Five miles south of Wexford City, just off the Wexford–Rosslare road. Freely accessible to the public.

# TIPPERARY

## *The Heart of Ireland's Dairyland*

Tipperary is the largest inland county in Ireland, though it also lays claim to some notable waterways. In the northwest, Tipperary borders on the shores of Shannon's Lough Derg. Similarly, the river Suir, which flows through the county from north to south, and which was once an important transport artery, today provides much appreciated recreational assets. The hills and mountains, plains and river valleys of Tipperary provide a rich variety of scenery. In the south are the Galtee mountains, extending into County Cork, and the Knockmealdown range, topped by the conical landmark of Slievenamon.

The middle of the county, bisected by the Suir, consists of rich limestone-based grasslands—notably around the Golden Vale—that provide excellent pasture for the region's thriving herds of cattle. It is also a great county for the breeding of horses, gundogs and greyhounds, and Tipperary's football and hurling team regularly win national honors on the sporting field. There are several interesting historical sites in Tipperary, of which the most important, and by far the most famous, is the Rock of Cashel, with its magnificent ecclesiastical ruins.

### Roscrea

The main road from Dublin to the south and southwest—the N7—passes diagonally through Tipperary, and will take you past the Rock of Cashel. It would, however, be a mistake to hurry through an area that is both scenically and historically so satisfying. Indeed, Tipperary's historical background is emphasized almost as soon as the traveler crosses the county line: on driving in from Dublin, the remains of St. Cronan's Abbey, built in the 12th century on the site of a monastic settlement founded five centuries earlier, dominate the entrance to the prosperous little town of Roscrea. The west door of the abbey wall is a particularly good example of Hiberno-Romanesque architecture—three arches within each other, and with sculptured heads and an ecclesiastical figure over the center (reputedly St. Cronan, the original founder of the monastery). One of the treasures of his original abbey is the illuminated gospel book, the *Book of Dimma,* which is now in the library of Trinity College, Dublin. Just across the road from the abbey, there is a characteristic Irish round tower, but without its top; this was blown off during the 1798 Rebellion when a cannon was hoisted up the tower in order to command a better field of fire. There is an unexplained carving of a ship about 25 feet from the base.

The principal feature of the town, however, is its partly-ruined 13th-century Norman castle, located, appropriately enough, in Castle Street. The imposing tower of the castle is currently being restored, but if it is open the view from the top illustrates effectively how the castle dominated the surrounding countryside in its heyday. Inside the castle grounds is Damer House, an attractive early-Georgian house built from about 1715. The house is open from Easter to September and contains a splendid carved wooden staircase, paintings, period furniture and a regional museum charting the history of the area. You might also like to visit the Franciscan Friary in Abbey Street, founded in 1490. Its buildings were incorporated into the Roman Catholic church of St. Cronan's in the 19th century, the gateway, for example, being part of the original building.

Not far from Roscrea (about two miles east), there are remains of another church on what was once an island in a strange lake which disappeared just over two centuries ago—Loch Cré, the lake from which Roscrea, or Ros Cré, got its name. The one-time island was a land of mystery and legend for centuries: to the Irish it was Inis na mBeo, "Island of the Living;" to the Anglo-Normans it was Insula Viventium, the island on which there is no death, a reference to the belief that on the island the dead could not decay.

### Thurles

Journeying south to Thurles about 20 miles away is pleasant driving. The town is bounded by the Silvermines and Devil's Bit mountains—there is a gap in the hills, clearly seen from the main road, which they say was bitten out by the devil in a fit of anger who later spat it out, thereby forming the famed Rock of Cashel 22 miles to the south. Thurles is the seat of the Roman Catholic archbishop of Cashel, and his cathedral is a 19th-century Irish architect's interpretation of the Romanesque style, reputedly inspired by Pisa Cathedral.

Thurles is the birthplace of the Gaelic Athletic Association, Ireland's biggest sporting body, which was founded at a meeting in Hayes's Hotel on November 1, 1884, during which Archbishop Thomas William Croke (1824–1902), a priest who was born in Cork and became bishop of Auckland, New Zealand, before returning to Ireland as archbishop of Cashel and Emly, was named patron. He is honored by a memorial in Liberty

Square and by the naming of the G.A.A.'s main stadium in Dublin as Croke Park.

The one-time military importance of the town is recalled by the 15th-century castle keep guarding the south side of the bridge over the river Suir and another near the center of the town. There is another castle which was never completed two miles north of the town. It is actually a 19th-century building, modeled on the imposing Warwick Castle in England. However, the project came to an untimely end when a piece of falling masonry landed on the man building it, one H.G. Langley.

Near Newport and close to the Slieve Felim mountains are the Clare Glens (named after the family, not the county), an interesting plantation of trees) and strange rock formations.

The remains of Holy Cross Abbey, beside the river and just over four miles from Thurles on the road to Cashel, are worth an excursion for historic and scenic interest. The abbey was founded in the 12th century by Donagh Cairbreach O'Brien, king of Munster, for a community of Cistercian monks, and had in its keeping a reputed fragment of the True Cross. The shrine became a place of pilgrimage for centuries and the buildings were constantly being reconstructed. There is an east window of fine craftsmanship in the chancel, and on the right side of the chancel is a *sedilia,* a wall seat used by the celebrant and his assistants during High Mass, of finely carved black marble. The age-old interest in hunting is seen in a mural in the transept, which shows three men on a stag hunt. When the monastery was suppressed in 1536, the lands became the property of the Earl of Ormonde. His family (the Butlers) were given the relic which gave the abbey its name; today it is in the Ursuline Convent at Blackrock, Cork. Holy Cross Abbey has been restored to preserve the ancient character of the building.

## Cashel of the Kings

The Rock of Cashel rises imposingly to a height of 200 feet above the surrounding plains, and is crowned with a magnificent group of ruins. Distant views of the rock can be glimpsed traveling south on the main road from Dublin, the N8. They give a good idea of the strategic importance of Cashel in bygone days.

The town-name Cashel derives from the Irish *caiseal,* meaning a stone fort, and that was the basic concept which led to the establishment of the group of buildings on the rock. The kings of Munster held it as their seat for about seven centuries, and it was here that St. Patrick reputedly plucked the shamrock to hold up in explanation as he preached the doctrine of the Trinity, an action which has given Ireland the shamrock as its universally recognized symbol.

At the base of the rock is the Dominican Friary. Most of the ruin dates from the late-15th century, but the beautiful east window is part of an earlier building, dating from the 13th century. However, the most prominent feature among all the ruins is the Round Tower, a perfect 11th-century example of the type. It stands 92 feet high, and has the distinction of a doorway 12 feet above ground level. The tower is built of sandstone and has the usual distinctive conical cap.

The buildings on the rock are in the care of the Office of Public Works, and their guides will ensure that you do not miss any of the outstanding features of the various styles of architecture and carving contained in the main enclosure. The first building to be seen on entering the modern gateway of the rock enclosure is the 15th-century Hall of the Vicar's Choral, an extensive building in two parts of two stories, each of which accommodated minor officials of the Cathedral. St. Patrick's Cross, on the green inside the entrance gate, is an unusual form of Irish cross. The stone at its base is reputed to be the coronation seat of Brian Boru and other great kings of Munster.

Cormac's Chapel was built by Cormac, who was both a king and a bishop in the 12th century; it is stone-roofed, vaulted and richly carved. Some of its features are unusual in Irish church architecture of the period and may be the result of continental European influence, notably a carving of a beast being attacked by a centaur.

The cathedral is 13th-century, a cruciform building with high lancet windows typical of the period and an adjoining building which was probably the archbishop's residence. There is a roof walk on the top of the central tower, 127 steps up.

The cathedral was burned down in 1495 by Gerald, Earl of Kildare, who explained his action to King Henry VII with the excuse that he had thought the archbishop was inside! Cromwellian troops damaged the cathedral, and it was repaired, although subsequently abandoned in 1748 because the archbishop of the time could not reach it in his coach from the town below.

Don't hurry through the buildings on the Rock of Cashel. Absorb the atmosphere and picture the men who lived here long ago. It is also relaxing to rest on the short grass outside and look out across the quiet plains of Tipperary.

Cashel Town itself is a pleasant place, kept busy by its popularity as a half-way stopping spot on the main Cork–Dublin road. The Cashel Palace Hotel in the town center is a handsome mansion, originally the archbishop's palace, dating from 1730. Its hall still has the original paneling and plasterwork decoration, and the red-pine staircase has an ornately-carved balustrade which compares well with that of Damer House in Roscrea. The Catholic Church of St. John the Baptist has a colorful display of statuary, while the 18th-century Church of Ireland Cathedral of the same name is a sober place of quiet beauty. The town's park is called Larkspur after the winner of the 1962 Epsom Derby. It was donated to the town by Larkspur's owner, Raymond Guest, who was the American Ambassador to Ireland from 1965 to 1968. Larkspur was trained nearby at Vincent O'Brien's stables at Ballydoyle.

Cashel also has some well-preserved examples of the typical Irish divided shop front. Meany's Pub, for instance, has a four-part window with timber pilasters, wrought-iron decoration and a brass rail. Indeed, there is a run of six such windows to be spotted in Main Street. Rossa pottery, with its delicate glazing, is one among a flourishing set of modern crafts in Cashel, the best known of which is the silver and gold jewelry workshop of Padraig O'Mathuna. Much of O'Mathuna's work uses designs inspired by the carvings at the Rock of Cashel and has been internationally acclaimed.

One of the most exciting archeological discoveries of recent years is the Killenaule Hoard, found 11 miles northeast of Cashel. It consists of 8th- and 9th-century religious vessels and includes the *Derrynaflan Chalice*.

These have now been cleaned and added to the collection of antiquities in the National Museum, Dublin.

## Cars and Castles

Cahir, the next town on the road south (pronounce it "Care") is a busy market town built on the river Suir at the eastern end of the Galtee mountain range. The Suir offers good salmon and trout fishing, as does the Aherlow river which joins it above the town. The visitor's attention will immediately be attracted by Cahir Castle, dating mainly from the 15th century and the largest of its period in Ireland. It has a massive keep, high enclosing walls and spacious courtyards. It is now used as an "interpretive center" charting matters architectural, historic and environmental. The center is equipped with an audio-visual unit and its program *Stone Upon Stone,* lasting 12 minutes and including many color slides, tells the story of man's impact on the Irish landscape and shows the evolution of architecture in Ireland. The castle may look familiar to movie-goers: *Excalibur* was filmed here.

Cahir was the first town to which the Italian immigrant Charles Bianconi (1786–1875) operated his transport service. The development of the railways in Ireland in the 19th century was slow and erratic and Bianconi's wagons, known as Bians, together with more conventional stage coaches, carried people around Ireland for the greater part of the period. Bianconi was inspired by the expense and the scarcity of ordinary mail coach routes to set up his own transport business. His first trip in July 1815 carried the mail and a couple of passengers the 12 miles from Clonmel to Cahir on a jaunting car, or "outside car" as it was called in those days. His operation developed until he was using coaches carrying up to 19 people (driver included) and drawn by four horses, with an aggregate daily mileage on his route network of 4,000 miles. Bianconi built his own wagons at a factory in Clonmel, all on the jaunting car model. An 1878 guide book had this advice for visitors to Ireland who planned to travel by Bians, or public cars as they became known after Bianconi's death:

"Ascertain which way the wind is blowing if the weather is likely to be bad, and choose your seat accordingly, as the tourist will find it no slight comfort to hear the rain beating on the other side while the well and the luggage shelter him. Aprons are provided in the car; at the same time a private waterproof apron is a great convenience; added to which the traveller should obtain a strap by which he may buckle himself to the seat during the night journeys and thus go safely to sleep without fear of being jerked forward . . . "

Bianconi's home, Longfield House, is preserved by the Irish Georgian Society at Goold's Cross, five miles north of Cahir. Look out for period aquatints of Bianconi's coaches by M.A. Hayes. They make an interesting souvenir of Cahir.

## East to Clonmel

Despite a population of only 11,000, Clonmel is Tipperary's chief town. Sited on the Suir it suffered many a water-borne raid in its early history. Later it became a walled town (its rebuilt West Gate still straddles a main road), and part of the old wall still surrounds St. Mary's (Church of Ireland) Church.

The author of *Tristram Shandy*, Laurence Sterne (1713–68), was born in Clonmel, the son of an English officer serving in the town. George Borrow (1803–81) was another English novelist who lived in Clonmel while his soldier father was on duty there; Borrow's work reflects rather more of the atmosphere he absorbed in Ireland than that of Sterne. The Town Hall on Mitchell Street has some very interesting civic regalia, including swords and silver maces and a gold mayoral chain. Every new mayor is bound to add a fresh link.

A once-famous Wesleyan chapel designed in the Greek style by Victorian architect William Tinsley, a native of Clonmel, has been converted into a little theater. The building had been unused for some years and the purchase and conversion have both preserved a beautiful building and provided an entertainment center.

Horse and greyhound breeding are two considerable industries in the area and within the town there is a large cider plant which uses the apples from the orchards of the south. Not for nothing is the Irish name of the town Cluain Meala, "honey meadow."

## Ballyporeen

Clonmel makes a good base for exploring the Knockmealdown mountains which form the border with County Waterford. The road south from Clonmel rises through the village of Clogheen to the famous Vee Road which follows a zig-zag course up the Knockmealdown Gap, 1,114 feet above sea level, before descending to Lismore in County Waterford.

A diversion north of Clonmel on the main road to Cashel will provide an opportunity to visit the Fethard Folk Farm and the Transport Museum, housed in an old railway goods store. This project has brought together horse-drawn agricultural machinery and hand tools, mill stones, a blacksmith's forge and dairy equipment of long ago. The transport section includes such things as Victorian perambulators and a penny-farthing bicycle.

Carrick-on-Suir, 13 miles east of Clonmel, has a fine Elizabethan fortified mansion, with the keep of an earlier castle beside it. The mansion was built by an Earl of Ormonde, known as "Black Tom," for a proposed visit by Queen Elizabeth I. Nobody knows why the visit was called off, but "Black Tom" spent his money for nothing, except to provide a mansion which is still worth seeing.

The village of Ballyporeen in the southwest corner of Tipperary is well signposted these days, thanks to the visit of President Ronald Reagan in 1984. President Reagan's paternal great grandfather, Michael Reagan, was born at Templetenny just outside the village and baptized in Ballyporeen church on September 3, 1829. A graveyard now occupies the site of the Reagan cabin. The records of the Reagan family are contained in the church register. You will hear all about the '84 event in the Ronald Reagan Lounge, which also sells souvenirs of the President's visit, including a handsomely-produced family tree and history. A Ronald Reagan Museum was opened in the center of the village in 1985. In spite of having been described by the world's press at the time of the Presidential visit as "the original one-horse town in the back of beyond" Ballyporeen is an attractive little village whose friendly inhabitants give a warm welcome to the unexpectedly large number of tourists who pass through it these days. Its wide main street was so designed to accommodate the open-air cattle markets which were held there as recently as the late '60s, and its broad spread gives a certain dignity to this quiet mountain place.

Turn right in Ballyporeen past its church for a side excursion to the Mitchelstown Caves, three and a half miles away. They contain some of the finest natural subterranean limestone formations in Ireland, three of which have been christened, respectively, the House of Commons, the House of Lords, and the Cathedral. In another, the Old Cave, the Earl of Desmond—known as the Sugaun or "straw" earl—took refuge after an unsuccessful rebellion in 1601, only to be betrayed by a relation and removed to the Tower of London, where he died. During the War of Independence (1921), the caves were again used by men on the run and the local landowner's house was burned down by the military because they suspected him of allowing the insurgents to shelter there. The caves form a fascinating network, extending for some miles, with interest for the amateur and plenty to attract the attention of the expert. The guide lives nearby, and his family has been associated with the caves for generations. He will be happy to provide an amusing and informative tour to anyone who knocks on his door.

## Through the Glen of Aherlow

Return to Cahir through Ballyporeen in order to approach Tipperary Town through the beautiful and historic Glen of Aherlow. The road winds around the eastern end of the Galtee mountains, passing the secluded glen on the left and the long wooded ridge of Slievenamuck on the right. The glen is famed for its woodcock and snipe. It was once an important pass between Tipperary and Limerick and the scene of many ancient battles. It later became a favored hiding spot for outlawed Irishmen.

At the head of the glen near the village of Galbally are the ruins of Moor Abbey, a Franciscan foundation established in the early part of the 13th century. The ruined church dates from the 15th century, was used as a fortress during the Elizabethan Wars and burnt out by English cavalry in 1569. The road through the glen meets the main road to Tipperary—the N24—in the village of Bansha where Canon John M. Hayes (1888–1957), founder of *Muintir na Tire* (The People of the Countryside), the important Irish movement for rural development, was parish priest from 1946 until 1957. He is buried in the graveyard beside the church.

Turn northwest to Tipperary, the great dairy center of the rich pasture lands of the Golden Vale. Tipperary's history is unspectacular, but the town nonetheless has the distinction of having been the birthplace of a number of famous Irishmen, including the Fenian leader John O'Leary (1830–1907). William Hazlitt (1778–1830), the essayist, lived for a time nearby before his family moved to America and then back to England.

To the west of Tipperary is the village of Emly, which at one time had considerable ecclesiastical significance; an important church was founded here by a contemporary of St. Patrick, St. Ailbhe, whose name was joined with that of Patrick in the original naming of the Rock of Cashel. Ailbhe's Well is in the neighborhood, while an ancient cross in the graveyard beside the Roman Catholic church is supposed to mark the saint's burial place.

## North of Tipperary

For centuries the existence of silver, lead and zinc in the appropriately named Silvermine Mountains, south of Nenagh, has been well known; the lodes have been mined with varying degrees of success through history and are now being successfully exploited by an Irish-Canadian company operating under a license from the Irish Government, which controls all mineral rights in the country.

Nenagh is the principal town of north Tipperary. The dominant feature of the town is the 100-foot-high circular keep of Nenagh Castle, one of the best examples of its kind in Ireland and once part of a much larger castle dating from the 13th century. Part of the castle was reconstructed in about 1860, but characteristic features remain, including the spiral staircases, built right inside the walls, that climb to the battlements.

Four miles northeast is a three-ringed prehistoric earth fort, its stone gate piers still in position.

Southwest of Nenagh the village of Ballina, next to the town of Killaloe, (not to be confused with Ballina in County Mayo) is one of Tipperary's contact points with the river Shannon at the southern end of Lough Derg, the longest of the Shannon lakes.

The most important of the Lough Derg harbors in this area is at Dromineer, a few miles to the north of Ballina and five miles from Nenagh. The ruin of a medieval castle dominates the harbor. In the era of canals and Shannon navigation Dromineer was known as the Port of Ormond. Today it is a mecca for swimmers, anglers, dinghy sailors, yachtsmen, water skiers and wind-surfers. The Lough Derg Yachting Club at Dromineer is one of the oldest in Ireland and the village is noted for its amiable hospitality to visitors who are interested in water sports. There are frequent cruises on Lough Derg from Dromineer, Garrykennedy Quay and Killaloe; the lough is an inland sea 25 miles long from Portumna in Galway to the limit of inland navigation at Killaloe at the southern end. Scenically, the shores and the many lake islands are beautiful, offering plenty of picnic sites. Warnings are issued by the Lough Derg yachtsmen to the inexperienced; they ask that the advice of the local men be heeded, as they know the waters and such things as the Scarriff Breeze, which blows across from the Clare shore and can be dangerous. There is more advice to be got from the local fishermen—at the north end of the lake, for example, coarse fishing from the banks is particularly good at Munster Harbor, Connacht Harbor and Hayes's Island. The size of Lough Derg pike is legendary; there's a story of one found dead, choked by a salmon!

# PRACTICAL INFORMATION FOR TIPPERARY

**TOURIST OFFICES.** There are tourist offices at **Cahir,** tel. 052–41453 (open July to Aug.); **Cashel,** tel. 062–61333 (open Apr. to Sept.); **Clonmel,** tel. 052–22960 (open July to Aug.); **Nenagh,** tel. 067–31610 (open May to Sept.).

## HOTELS AND RESTAURANTS

**Aherlow.** *Aherlow House* (M), tel. 062–56153. 10 rooms with bath. Overlooks the famous Glen of Aherlow. AE, DC, MC.

**Birdhill. Restaurant.** *Matt the Thresher* (M), tel. 061–379227. Old-style spot which serves good food all day. Traditional Irish music in the evenings. AE, MC, V.

**Cahir.** *Kilcoran Lodge* (M), tel. 052–41288. 25 rooms, 22 with bath. Just outside town in own grounds, on the southern slope of the Galtees. A hunting, shooting and fishing center. AE, DC, MC, V. *Keane's Cahir House* (I), tel. 052–41207. 14 rooms. This was once the Georgian mansion of the Earls of Glengall. AE, DC, MC, V.

**Cashel.** *Cashel Palace* (L), tel. 062–61411. 20 rooms with bath. For 200 years the palace of the bishop, this is an elegant Palladian mansion, built in the 1730s; well-run. AE, DC, MC, V. *Grant's Castle* (I), tel. 062–61044. 12 rooms, 10 with bath.
**Restaurant.** *Horseshoe Room* (M), Dundrum House Hotel (tel. 062–71116). Pleasant setting in early Georgian mansion. AE, DC, MC, V.

**Clonmel.** *Clonmel Arms* (E), Sarsfield St. (tel. 052–21233). 35 rooms, 25 with bath. In town center. *Gate Buttery* for quick-service meals. AE, DC, MC, V. *Knocklofty House* (E), tel. 052–38222. 15 rooms with bath. Excellent restaurant with French cuisine. MC, V. *Hearn's* (M), tel. 052–21611. 25 rooms, 16 with bath or shower. This was the base of Charles Bianconi's famous 19th-century coaching service. DC, MC, V. *Minella* (M), tel. 052–22388. 30 rooms, all with bath. Modernized stately home in own grounds on banks of the river Suir; good views. AE, DC, MC, V.

**Dromineer.** *The Waterside* (I), tel. 067–24114. 11 rooms, most with bath. On the banks of the river Shannon, with a good restaurant and cheerful company. AE, DC, MC, V.

**Dundrum.** *Dundrum House* (E), tel. 062–71116. 30 rooms with bath; 4 rooms designed for wheelchair guests. In beautiful Georgian mansion on extensive grounds. Restaurant is very good. AE, DC, MC, V. *Rectory House* (M), tel. 062–71115. 10 rooms, 7 with bath. As the name suggests, located in a former rectory; owner-chef presides over restaurant. AE, DC, MC, V.

**Nenagh.** *O'Meara's* (I), tel. 067–31266. 43 rooms, 14 with bath. AE, DC, MC, V. *Ormond* (I), tel. 067–31404. 17 rooms, 11 with bath or shower. AE, DC, MC.
**Restaurant.** *The Derg Inn* (M), tel. 067–22037. Intimate, family-run restaurant. *The Hibernian Inn* (M), tel. 067–31253. Home-cooked food in a bar lounge/steak bar.

**Roscrea.** *Pathe* (I), tel. 0502–21301. 20 rooms, 9 with bath. AE, DC, MC, V. *Racket Hall* (I), tel. 0505–21748. 10 rooms, 5 with bath. Recommended family-run hotel with good restaurant.

**Thurles.** *Hayes* (M), Liberty Square (tel. 0504–22122). 32 rooms, 26 with bath. On the main square. DC, MC, V. *Anner* (I), tel. 0504–21799. 14 rooms, 8 with bath. AE, DC, MC, V. *Munster* (I), tel. 0504–22305. 13 rooms with bath. Restaurant.

**Restaurant.** *Castle House* (I), Friar St. (tel. 0504–21015). Plain cooking, tourist menu.

**Tipperary.** *The Glen* (M), Glen of Aherlow (tel. 062–56146). 24 rooms, 21 with bath. Good restaurant. AE, MC, V. *Ballyglass House* (I), tel. 062–52104. 10 rooms, 1 with bath. *Royal* (I), Bridge St. (tel. 062–51204). 16 rooms with bath. AE, MC.

## Youth Hostels

**Ballydavid Wood House,** Bansha (tel. 062–54148). **Mountain Lodge,** Burncourt, Cahir (tel. 052–67277). Open Apr. to Sept.

**HOW TO GET AROUND.** Provincial and inter-town bus services operate through the major towns, inquire locally for times. Bicycles can be hired from *M. McDermott,* Irishtown, Clonmel (tel. 052–21869).

## PLACES TO VISIT

**Cahir. Cahir Castle.** In the center of Cahir. A medieval fortress with the only working portcullis (a heavy iron-grating doorway that slides up and down) in the country. An audio-visual presentation of local monuments can be seen in the castle complex. Open mid-June to mid-Sept., daily 10–7.30; mid-Apr. to mid-June and mid-Sept. to 31 Oct., Tues. to Sat. 10–5, Sun. 2–5; 1 Nov. to 31 Mar., Tues. to Sat. 10–1 and 2–5.

**Carrick-on-Suir. Carrick-on-Suir Castle.** Built about 1600 and regarded as the best example of an Elizabethan mansion in Ireland. Gabled and mullioned exterior, some fine plasterwork inside. Open mid-June to mid-Sept., daily 10–6. Rest of year, key with caretaker.

**Cashel. Holycross Abbey,** tel. 0504–43241. Cistercian abbey of the 12th century, named after a relic of the "True Cross." Very well-preserved; the Abbey has been restored and is in use as a parish church. On the Cashel–Thurles road, nine miles north of Cashel.

**Rock of Cashel.** Ireland's most impressive monument, perched on a hilltop in the town of Cashel. This was the seat of the kings of Munster for several centuries, before becoming a religious foundation in the 12th and 13th centuries. Its central point is the 13th-century Gothic cathedral, beside which is the Romanesque Cormac's Chapel. There is also a round tower and a 12th-century cross—an impressive story in stone. Open 1 Apr. to 30 Sept., daily 9–7.30; 1 Oct. to 31 Mar., Mon. to Sat. 10–5, Sun. 2–5.

**Fethard. Fethard Folk Farm.** Features antique farm equipment and vehicles; picnic facilities. Ten miles from Clonmel. To check if it's open phone 052–31516.

**Mitchelstown.** **Mitchelstown Caves.** Three large caverns, the largest of which is 200 x 160 ft., with a roof rising to 60 ft. and innumerable columns formed through the centuries. Two miles off the Cahir–Mitchelstown road. Mitchelstown is in County Cork, but the caves are in County Tipperary. Open throughout the year, daily 10–6.

**Nenagh.** **Nenagh Heritage Center,** tel. 067–32633. Opened in 1985 and located in an old-time jail. Features displays of material of archeological and historical interest from this part of the country. Open mid-May to 31 Oct., Mon. to Fri. 10.30–5, Sat. and Sun. 2.30–7.

**Nenagh Keep.** Well-preserved cylindrical tower of four storeys built around 1200. Has walls up to 16 ft. thick. Key with caretaker. Admission free.

**Roscrea.** **Damer House.** Restored 18th-century Georgian house, built within the walls of 13th-century Roscrea Castle, now being restored. Features a Heritage Center with a collection of local artifacts and the largest exhibition of traditional furniture in the country. In the center of Roscrea. Open mid-May to 31 Oct., Mon. to Fri. 10–5, Sat. and Sun. 2–5.

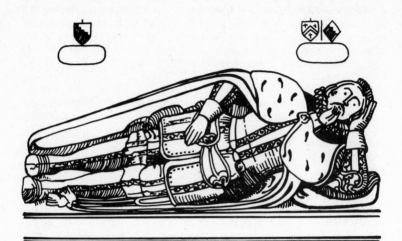

# THE CHARM OF THE SOUTH

## *Around County Cork*

Cork is the biggest county in Ireland. And as any of its inhabitants—who are noted for their loyalty and their boastfulness—will tell you, it is also the most beautiful. It contains some of Ireland's richest agricultural land, and some of its most stunning scenery.

The north and east of the county, bordering on Tipperary and Waterford, contain the best agricultural land, while the coastal areas of the southwest offer beautiful scenery and facilities for visitors. Tourism is an important industry in Cork and visitors from both home and abroad will always receive a warm, if somewhat inquisitive, welcome.

The Cork accent takes some getting used to. The communication problem is not confined to visitors from overseas either: even Dubliners find Corkonians incomprehensible at times, and vice versa. But after a day or two, visitors become attuned to the Cork lilt and often find they pick up certain intonations themselves.

### Cork City

Cork City is the major metropolis of the south, indeed, with a population of about 135,000, it is the second largest city in the Republic. But rather than thinking of their city in terms of size, Corkonians prefer to refer to it as "Ireland's cultural capital." Poet and writer Robert Gibbings encapsulates the sentiments of his fellow citizens thus, "Cork is the loveliest city in the world. Anybody who does not agree with me either was not born there or is prejudiced."

Whether or not it merits the accolade of "loveliest city in the world," Cork does have plenty to recommend it. It received its first charter from Prince John in 1185, and in 1985 it celebrated 800 years of existence with an impressive display of civic pride. The city grew rapidly in the 17th and 18th centuries with the expansion of its butter trade. Many of its buildings have attractive Georgian facades with interesting features such as wide bow windows.

The name Cork derives from the Irish (or Gaelic) *Corcaigh,* meaning a marshy place. The river Lee, on which the city is built, was the cause of the marsh. When the marsh was drained the river was divided into two main streams which flow through the city, giving it a profusion of picturesque quays and bridges. The river also gave Cork that beautiful old song, *On the Banks of my Own Lovely Lee,* which is guaranteed to bring tears to the eyes of expatriate Corkonians.

The population figure for Cork is slightly misleading. Many people, especially those with young families, prefer to live outside the city. Places like Carrigaline and Ballincollig, mere villages ten years or so ago, are now thriving dormitory towns. Shopping centers—modest versions of an American mall—at Douglas, Wilton and Bishopstown on the periphery of the city, have proved a popular innovation. Their establishment has also eased Cork's once chronic traffic congestion.

## Exploring Cork City

The main business and shopping center of Cork lies on the island created by two diverging channels of the river Lee, with most places within walking distance of the center. (The buses tend to be overcrowded and the one-way traffic system is fiendishly complicated.)

Patrick Street is the focal point of Cork and the best place from which to take your bearings. Here you will find Cork's most famous statue, that of Father Theobald Mathew (1790–1861). Father Mathew led a nationwide temperance crusade, no small feat in a country as fond of its "pints" as this one. In the first year of his campaign he enrolled a startling 151,000 people, with the movement later spreading to Scotland, England and the United States. Even today, many Irish wear the "Pioneer's Pin" in their lapels to show that they have "taken the pledge."

Patrick Street leads to St. Patrick's Bridge and the north side of town. Cross over the bridge and turn left along Camden Quay to Pope's Quay and St. Mary's Dominican Church. Inside St. Mary's, on the Lady's Altar, is a 14th-century Flemish figure of Our Lady of Graces. This small statue was originally in the Dominican church at Youghal, having been found on the beach near there, embedded in a piece of wood which had apparently been part of the mast of a wrecked ship (possibly one of the ships of the Spanish Armada).

In this hilly area of the city is the famous 120-foot Shandon Steeple, the bell tower of St. Anne's Church, built on the site of a church destroyed when the city was besieged by the Duke of Marlborough (then John Churchill) for William of Orange in 1690. The steeple, a popular landmark, is shaped like a pepper pot and houses the bells immortalized in the song *The Bells of Shandon,* written by the 19th-century wit and priest, Father Prout. Visitors can climb the tower and read the inscriptions on the bells, and, on request, have them rung out over Cork.

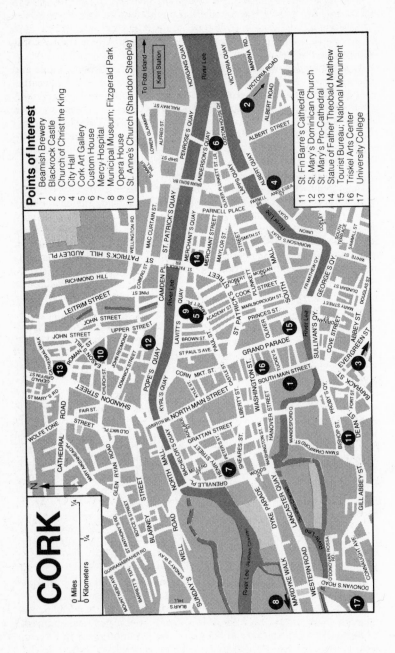

## CORK

0 Miles    1/4
0 Kilometers    1/4

### Points of Interest

1 Beamish Brewery
2 Blackrock Castle
3 Church of Christ the King
4 City Hall
5 Cork Art Gallery
6 Custom House
7 Mercy Hospital
8 Municipal Museum; Fitzgerald Park
9 Opera House
10 St. Anne's Church (Shandon Steeple)

11 St. Fin Barre's Cathedral
12 St. Mary's Dominican Church
13 St. Mary's Pro-Cathedral
14 Statue of Father Theobald Mathew
15 Tourist Bureau; National Monument
16 Triskel Arts Center
17 University College

St. Mary's Pro-Cathedral, in the same area, is both less interesting and newer than St. Anne's, having been begun in 1808, though much of the interior decoration is good. Incidentally, if you think you have Cork forebears, you might care to check at the presbytery here, for their records of births and marriages date from 1784.

Back across the river Lee, down Patrick Street to Grand Parade and across the second branch of the Lee, lies the city's Church of Ireland cathedral, St. Fin Barre's, an imposing 19th-century building in the French Gothic style. Inside there is a strange memorial. It recalls the only woman Freemason, Elizabeth Aldworth, a girl who hid behind a curtain in the library of Doneraile House in north Cork, and overheard the secret Masonic proceedings conducted by her father. When discovered, she had to be made a member of the Masonic Order.

At the top of Patrick Street, on either side of the intersection with Grand Parade, Cork's two markets can be found. Neither market caters specifically for tourists, but those who enjoy the atmosphere of a real working market will appreciate their charm. The open-air Coal Quay market is a genuine "flea market," with trestle tables full of old clothes and household effects, among which attractive bits of bric à brac can sometimes be found. The English Market, as it is known, is a covered market in the area between Patrick Street, Grand Parade and Oliver Plunkett Street, with old-fashioned displays of meat, game, shellfish, fruit and vegetables and a few clothes stalls. Its elegant Victorian architecture is more interesting than its produce.

The Crawford Art Gallery is signposted from Patrick Street and is well worth a visit. It has an excellent collection of topographical landscape paintings showing views of Cork in the 18th and 19th centuries and mounts adventurous exhibitions by contemporary artists. Contemporary works can also be seen, and purchased, at the Cork Art Society on Lavitt's Quay, just around the corner, a private gallery that also holds exhibitions.

The campus of University College is a 15-minute walk up Washington Street from Grand Parade. U.C.C., as it is known, standing for University College, Cork, currently has over 5,000 students, though its future population is expected to rise to 7,000. The main quadrangle is a pleasant example of 19th-century university architecture in the Tudor Gothic style. An exception, however, is the Boole Library, opened in 1985. It commemorates the eminent mathematician George Boole (1815–1864), generally considered the father of modern computer logic. He was also the first Professor of Mathematics at the College.

One block across from the Western Road entrance of the campus is the Mardyke, a popular riverside walk leading to Fitzgerald's Park. The Georgian mansion in the park houses Cork's public museum which has a well-planned exhibit of Cork's history from ancient times to the present day.

## Exploring the Harbor

The fashionable residential districts of Cork City overlook the harbor. The hilly suburbs of Tivoli and Montenotte look across from the north at the marina and Blackrock in the south. Blackrock Castle is the dominant landmark, whose quaintness is much admired. Originally a 16th-century fortification, it was rebuilt in the 19th century. William Penn (1644–1718), the founder of the Pennsylvania colony, was born in Cork and it is believed that he stayed in the castle before sailing for America. He spent his youth in Cork, becoming a Quaker at the Meeting House in Cork City.

William Penn was, of course, only one of thousands who sailed from Cork hoping for a better life in the New World. The point of departure in most cases was not Cork City itself, but the Cove of Cork on Great Island, 15 miles down the harbor. Cove was renamed Queenstown in 1849 to commemorate a visit by Queen Victoria, but has now reverted to its original name, albeit in Irish transliteration, Cobh (pronounced "cove"). Cobh can be reached by rail on a regular service from Kent Station on the Lower Glanmire Road, or by following the main road to Waterford, the N25. The train journey gives excellent views of the harbor.

Seen from the water, Cobh is an attractive hilly town dominated by its 19th-century cathedral, St. Colman's, built in the Gothic revival style with an elegant spire. In World War I, it was an important base for the Royal Navy, and after 1917 for the U.S. Navy. Many of the buildings on Haulbowline, one of the islands off Cobh, were built by convict labor for the Royal Navy. Today they are the headquarters of the Irish Navy.

Earlier this century Cobh was also the first and last European port of call for transatlantic liners and gave many passengers a tantalizing and memorable view of Ireland. One such was the ill-fated *Titanic.* Cobh has other associations with shipwreck as it was from here that destroyers were sent out on 7 May, 1915, to search for survivors from the *Lusitania,* torpedoed off the Old Head of Kinsale by a German submarine with the loss of 1,198 lives. Many of the victims are buried near Cobh and the tragedy is commemorated by a memorial on the quay. Cobh Museum has a display of contemporary photographs and newspaper reports giving graphic details of the disaster.

## Fota Park

The road and rail links with Cobh both pass through Fota Island, eight miles east of Cork City. Fota is one of Cork's newest and best tourist attractions. The 750 acres of park and farmland are owned by University College, Cork, and an experimental farm using solar and wind energy has been established on part of it. The Royal Zoological Society of Ireland has also created a 70-acre wildlife park here—one of the animals, the wallaby, has developed an unexpected liking for the climate of Fota and is reported to be breeding prolifically. The Arboretum is also open to the public. It was started in the 1820s and contains rare trees and shrubs from Japan, China, New Zealand, Australia and South America, as well as well-tended native specimens.

But the star of Fota Island is Fota House itself, now restored and redecorated thanks to the imagination and generosity of a young Cork businessman, Richard Wood. Originally an 18th-century hunting lodge, the house was redesigned and extended in the 1820s for the Smith-Barry family (once Earls of Barrymore) by Sir Richard Morrison, and is a splendid example of Irish Regency architecture. It was a family home until the late 1970s and the neo-Classical interior has been restored to give the impression that the house is lived in still.

The most important feature of Fota House is Richard Wood's collection of 18th- and 19th-century Irish landscape paintings. Next to that of the

National Gallery of Ireland, this is the most important collection of its kind and provides an easily assimilated introduction to the development of landscape painting in Ireland. The setting of 18th-century Irish furniture, period wallpapers and curtains and intricately painted ceilings greatly enhances the beauty of the pictures.

## Blarney

Most visitors to Ireland want to kiss the famous Blarney Stone in the hope of thus acquiring the "gift of the gab." Blarney itself, five miles from Cork City, should not, however, be taken too seriously as an excursion. All that is left of Blarney Castle is its ruined central tower, or keep, containing the celebrated stone. There is more to see next door in Blarney House, a late 19th-century mansion opened to the public in 1988, which contains a collection of ancestral paintings and heraldic decorations. The village has an abundance of craft shops offering knitwear, Irish crystal, pottery, tweed and linen. While some may find the exploitation depressing, it does make the prices competitive, so those who plan to do some shopping for Irish goods might as well take advantage of the commercialization.

The castle itself dates from the mid-15th century, and the keep is a square structure 120 feet high, standing on limestone rock. It was built by Cormac MacCarthy and destroyed some 100 years later by Cromwell's forces. Queen Elizabeth I of England is credited with giving the word "blarney" to the language when, commenting on the unfulfilled promises of Cormac MacCarthy, Lord of Blarney at the time, she is reported to have remarked: "This is all Blarney; what he says, he never means." Whether you intend to kiss the stone or not, the view from the battlements of the square tower is most impressive. The Kissing Stone is set in the battlements and to kiss it you must lie on the walk within the walls, grasp a guard rail, lean your head back and touch the stone with your lips. It sounds dangerous, but it isn't and it makes a first-class picture. Nor is it unhygenic—so many tourists have become wary of the Stone lately that it is now scrubbed with disinfectant four times a day. Moreover, an Irish doctor has stated that it is impossible to catch AIDS from this or any other stone.

Nobody is certain how Elizabeth's comment developed into the legend that the gift of eloquence may be derived from kissing the Blarney Stone, but it is not unlikely that the stone had some significance in the MacCarthy clan. The castle is open daily all year.

## East Cork

The one-hour drive to Youghal (pronounce it "yawl") is a popular excursion with the people of Cork City, who go there to enjoy its sandy beaches, its seaside amusement facilities and its seafood restaurants.

The road from Cork takes you straight past the turning for Cobh and on through Carrigtwohill to the thriving distillery town of Midleton. Midleton's distillery contains the world's largest pot-still for making whiskey: it holds 36,000 gallons of spirits. Father Mathew would not be amused. There is a craft center to visit in the headquarters of the town council. This area has a long tradition of pottery and many contemporary potters have come here to work from England and the States. They usually sell direct from their studios, as well as through normal retail outlets, and roadside signs inviting passersby to drive in and visit are worth following up.

A slight detour at Midleton will take you to Cloyne and Ballycotton. Cloyne is associated with St. Colman, founder of its first church. The present (Church of Ireland) cathedral dates from the 13th century, but has been extensively restored. The famous 18th-century metaphysician, Bishop Berkeley (1685–1753), was once the Bishop of Cloyne and there is a monument to him in the cathedral. Next to the cathedral is the 100-foot Round Tower. The view from the top amply repays the effort of climbing it.

Ballycotton is a pretty fishing village and a well-known center for deep-sea angling. A walk down to the harbor will give you the chance to inspect its fleet of small trawlers and their catch. Offshore is a steep island dominated by a lighthouse, where the open sea sweeps around the headland into the calm waters of Ballycotton Bay.

Youghal, by contrast, has a far larger bay, the estuary of the river Blackwater. The most famous figure from Youghal's past is an Englishman: the Elizabethan explorer and adventurer Sir Walter Raleigh, once the mayor of the town. Youghal holds an annual potato festival to commemorate the (probably apocryphal) local legend that the great man himself planted the first Irish potato in the garden of his Youghal home. That house, Myrtle Grove, a good example of Elizabethan domestic architecture, is still occupied as a private residence and is not open to the public. Information on Sir Walter can be found in the town's museum in Main Street, housed under a distinctive clock tower which straddles the road.

## North Cork

The inland reaches of the Munster Blackwater (so-called because Wexford and Meath both have rivers of the same name) can be explored by traveling north from Cork City on the main road to Dublin, the N8. The Fermoy stretch of the river is popular both for fishing and canoeing. Further up the same road is Mitchelstown, an important center for butter and cheese. An old-fashioned country market is held in its main square every Thursday.

Mallow, to the west of Mitchelstown, has regular meetings at its race track, and between the two lies Buttevant. It was here that cross-country racing—steeple-chasing—began in 1752, when Edward Blake challenged a neighbor to race across country from Buttevant church to St. Leger church, four miles distant. By keeping the steeple of St. Leger in sight, the riders could see their finishing point, and so the term "steeple-chasing" was added to racing. Buttevant retains its links with the world of horses on 12 July every year when the Cahermee Horse Fair is held in its streets. Thousands of pounds worth of horses and ponies change hands to the accompaniment of much old-style haggling about the price.

### West to Kinsale

Kinsale, a largely 18th-century port 18 miles west of Cork City, marks the beginning of scenic West Cork. From June to September, distinctive hedges of dark-red fuchsia are in bloom and the roadsides are adorned with a profusion of wild flowers. The further west you go, the less traffic you meet, and the more slowly it moves. The whole of West Cork is ideal for leisurely motoring.

Some of the back roads are so quiet that they are still used for the game of road bowling. If you come across a large group of men on the road, leaping and cheering for no apparent reason, the explanation will most likely be that a bowling match, known as a "score," is in progress. The game now survives only in County Cork and parts of County Armagh in Northern Ireland. It consists of a contest between two players to throw a heavy iron ball, either under or overarm, along the road for a distance of one mile. The lowest number of throws taken to complete the distance wins. There is much betting, both by and on the participants, and a celebration afterwards in the nearest bar.

A fine view of Kinsale awaits you at the end of the main road from Cork. The town is built at the top of a wide fjord-like harbor where the river Bandon flows into the sea. Grey-slated 18th-century houses with wide bay windows dominate the hilly streets of the town.

The navy has long since departed from Kinsale, but it is still an important fishing center with excellent facilities for deep-sea angling. Cod, ling, monkfish and shark are among the more interesting fish to be caught off the Old Head of Kinsale. The yachts clustered around Kinsale's new marina race regularly, often competing against boats from neighboring Crosshaven. The Royal Cork Yacht Club in Crosshaven is the world's oldest, and lays claim to having founded the sport of ocean racing.

One of the best-remembered dates in Irish history is 1601. It was then that the Irish and Spanish armies joined forces against the English in the Battle of Kinsale. The harbor sheltered the whole Spanish fleet for 10 weeks and 4,000 Spaniards seized the town. However, the Spanish were forced to surrender early in 1602 and Kinsale became an English town as a consequence, with the Irish forbidden to live within the walls. The battlefield was near the old highway to Cork and is well signposted.

The date 1703 is less well known, but it was in this year that one Alexander Selkirk set sail from Kinsale on board a 90-ton vessel, *The Cinque Ports.* He was to be marooned on the lonely Pacific island of Juan Fernandez, providing Daniel Defoe with the story for his famous novel *Robinson Crusoe.*

Until about 20 years ago, widows in Kinsale wore long black hooded cloaks known as Kinsale cloaks. Examples of these, and relics of Kinsale's naval and military past, can be found in the museum which occupies the town's 17th-century courthouse. There are also mementoes of the *Lusitania* wreck, and some of the victims are buried in the graveyard of the 12th-century St. Multose Church, a pretty Norman construction with an imposing tower. The town stocks, where wrong-doers were confined, can be found in its porch.

Two miles outside Kinsale, on the edge of the harbor, is Charles Fort, dating from 1611. It is a fine demonstration of the "science" of 17th-century fortification and was still in use as recently as 1920. One of the best-preserved examples of the "star fort" in Europe, Charles Fort compares favorably with Ticonderoga in New York State. Twelve acres of land are enclosed within its walls and moats, and in its heyday it had a population of over 2,000. Extensive restoration is still in progress, making it one of the most spectacular historical sites in Ireland. Guided tours are available from June to September.

Kinsale has gained a well-deserved reputation as a gourmet center, and every October the town holds a "gourmet festival." The Old Head of Kinsale, nine miles away, provides magnificent sea views and can be reached by road across the new bridge at the west end of town. Just off the road from Kinsale to the Old Head is Ballinspittle village, well signposted since the summer of 1985 when it hit international headlines because of its "moving statue." A plaster statue of the Virgin Mary, set in a roadside grotto, was seen by thousands of pilgrims to move her hands and to sway back and forth. She has not moved since then, but visitors still frequent the roadside grotto in the hope that they may witness a renewal of activity.

## The Roads West—Bantry and Glengariff

Bantry and Glengariff are the most popular destinations in West Cork, gateways to the dramatic mountains of the southwest. There are several routes to choose from, either mountainous or coastal.

The best mountain route takes you up the valley of the river Lee, past the spreading lakes of Inchigeela to the Pass of Keimaneigh. The summit of the pass is only 700 feet above sea level, but the steep rocky hills provide majestic views. Beyond Macroom, until you emerge on the coast at Ballylickey, you will be passing through part of West Cork's *Gaeltacht,* where Irish is the first language of most of the residents.

Not far from the Pass of Keimaneigh is Gougane Barra, the little lake in which the river Lee has its source. It is now a national park. On an island in the lake, reached by a causeway from the mainland, was the cell of the 6th-century monk, St. Finbar, who founded Cork. There is still a pilgrimage to the 18th-century church which now stands on his island. It's held on September 29 every year.

As the road from Keimaneigh nears the head of Bantry Bay, it divides into two. The right fork takes you to Glengariff, the left to Bantry, lying at the end of Bantry Bay itself, at between six and eight miles wide one of the largest natural harbors in the world. It was here that the French attempted to land a force of some 14,000 men in 1796, during the Napoleonic Wars. A combination of foul winds and naval incompetence proved their undoing, however.

Bantry House, on the shore of the bay, was built about 1750 and is open daily throughout the year. Lawns and flowerbeds in front of the Georgian house emphasize the lush vegetation of the district. The house was the seat of the Earls of Bantry and is now owned by their descendant, Egerton Shelswell-White. Before he inherited this magnificent property in 1978, he was farming in Alabama. Of special interest are the furniture, tapestries (including some reputedly owned by Marie Antoinette) and objets d'art collected from all over Europe by the second Earl. The furniture includes pieces from the Louis XV period, as well as examples of Chippendale, Hepplewhite, Sheraton and Old Irish styles.

## The Coastal Route

The longer coastal route from Cork to Bantry has been gaining in popularity recently. It can be done in a day, but there are so many tempting detours that a leisurely two-day meander, including a visit to Cape Clear or Sherkin Islands, is recommended.

There is a fast main road, the N71, from Cork to Clonakilty that runs via Bandon. There are still people in this part of the world who never mention the name of Clonakilty (13 miles west of Bandon) without adding the words "God help us." Clonakilty—God help us—acquired this tag in the days of the great famine when thousands of starving people from all over West Cork dragged themselves to Clonakilty in the hope of finding relief. Many died in the workhouse; others struggled on to Cobh to take the "coffin ship" to Ellis Island and the New World. That West Cork was one of the most severely affected areas of Ireland in the 19th-century famine is hard to believe today. Anyone looking at its prettily decorated cottages, flourishing hedgerows and tidily cultivated fields, or sampling the abundant produce of its coastal waters, would be hard put to it to imagine the desperate poverty and terrible hardships of that time.

At Rosscarbery there is a delightful detour along the coast through Glandore, Union Hall and Castletownshend to Skibbereen. Glandore and Union Hall are small fishing villages on a sheltered bay, the former an unspoilt holiday resort favored by yachtsmen and English visitors in the summer months.

Castletownshend is unusual for this area in that, though only a village with a population of 104, it contains several substantial stone-built houses of some architectural merit, and even has its own (inhabited) castle. Many descendants of its Ascendancy (Protestant English) settlers, who arrived with Cromwell in the late-17th century, live here in quiet harmony with the descendants of the Clan MacCarthy, who originally owned the land. The village still evokes the world of Edwardian Ireland, immortalized by Violet Martin (1862–1915) and Edith Somerville (1858–1949) who wrote their *Irish R.M.* stories here. Edith's memory is still very much alive locally. Her great-nephew now lives at her home, Drishane House.

Connections between Castletownshend and Boston were forged through one of Edith's lesser known pastimes: breeding and breaking hunters and selling them through her Boston cousin, Mrs. Sylvia Warren, at great profit. The West Carbery Hunt, of which she was Master for many years, still meets twice weekly in winter. Skebawn, the fictional town in which the Resident Magistrate—the "R.M."—of her stories presided, is based on Skibbereen. A glimpse at the hilarious court reports in its local paper, the *Southern Star,* will show how little some things have changed.

Beyond Skibbereen is Ballydehob, an attractive mountain village which has become something of a haven for writers and artists and has a surprisingly cosmopolitan population. What appears to be a Roman aqueduct on your left-hand side as you enter the village is in fact a viaduct left over from the days of the immortal West Cork Railway. Nowadays it takes less than two hours to drive direct from Cork to Ballydehob. The railway took six hours if you were lucky, and you seldom were.

Schull and Baltimore on the coast of the appropriately named Roaring Water Bay both offer facilities for deep-sea fishing. From Schull and other points along the bay the Fastnet Rock Lighthouse is visible on the horizon. Mount Gabriel (1,339 feet), which towers above Schull, has two egg-shaped beacons on top of it to guide transatlantic jets in and out of Irish airspace.

Sherkin and Cape Clear Islands in Roaring Water Bay can be visited by ferry or mailboat from Baltimore. Sherkin is close to the mainland and has the ruins of a Franciscan Friary and castle. Bad sailors should only attempt the crossing to Cape Clear—it takes about an hour—in good weather. Ornithologists will find it a rewarding experience. Cape Clear is three miles long by one and a half miles broad at its widest point, and is the southernmost extremity of Ireland. The population of Clear (which is a Gaeltacht area) is dwindling below the 100 mark, and most visitors are campers, youth hostelers and yachtsmen.

If the rugged cliffs and hidden coves of Roaring Water Bay appeal, then the village of Crookhaven, the lighthouse at the Mizen Head and the road between Durrus and Kilcrohane will also be worth exploring before pushing on through Bantry to Glengariff.

The 12-mile drive between Bantry and Glengariff provides breathtaking views of the wide expanse of Bantry Bay. Glengariff itself is a small village lying in a thickly wooded glen. The principal attraction here is Garnish Island, accessible by boat, and there are many on offer. Warmed by the Gulf Stream and enclosed by sheltering trees, Garnish was planted with tropical and sub-tropical trees and shrubs over 50 years ago, and its unusual vegetation is still thriving.

Glengariff is a portal to the dramatic scenery of the southwest (to be explored in the chapter on *The Southwest*) and travelers to Kerry can continue northwest by the Tunnel Road (it passes through a short mountain tunnel) or, less directly, by heading southwest and making the crossing of the mountains by the long Healy Pass and exploring the lonely, impressive country of the peninsula.

# PRACTICAL INFORMATION FOR CORK CITY

**TOURIST OFFICE.** Tourist House, Grand Parade (tel. 021–273251).

**Telephone Code.** The area code for Cork City is 021.

## HOTELS

### *Expensive*

**Arbutus Lodge,** Montenotte (tel. 021–501237). 20 rooms, all with bath. Comfortable, overlooking city and river Lee. Outstanding restaurant. AE, DC, MC, V.

**Imperial,** South Mall (tel. 021–274040). 101 rooms, all with bath. Founded on this spot in 1943, interior recently redecorated. Good restaurants and the pleasant *Orange Lounge* for snacks. The *Captain's Bar* is invariably busy. AE, DC, MC, V.

**Jury's,** Western Rd. (tel. 021–276622). 185 rooms, all with bath. Pavilion complex with restaurant and bars. Garden site on river, five minutes' walk to city center. Indoor and outdoor pools, gymnasium and sauna. Plenty of parking. AE, DC, MC, V.

**Silver Springs,** Tivoli (tel. 021–507533). 110 rooms with bath or shower. Modern building five minutes' drive from city center. Major refurbishing in 1989. Health club with indoor pool. AE, DC, MC, V.

*Moderate*

**Ashbourne House,** Glounthaune (tel. 021–353319). 26 rooms, 24 with bath. Heated pool, sauna; gardens. AE, DC, MC, V.

**Country Club,** Montenotte (tel. 021–502922). 37 rooms with bath. AE, DC, MC, V.

**Metropole,** MacCurtain St. (tel. 021–508122). 91 rooms, all with bath. Considerably updated in recent years. In the city center; plenty of activity. AE, DC, MC, V.

**Moore's,** Morrisons Island (tel. 021–271291). 39 rooms, most with bath or shower. Close to city center. AE, DC, MC, V.

*Inexpensive*

**Glengariffe,** Orchard Rd., Victoria Cross (tel. 021–541785). 10 rooms, 7 with bath. Pool. AE.

**John Barleycorn Inn,** Riverstown, Glanmire (tel. 021–821499). 17 rooms, all with bath. On the edge of the city, 4 miles from Cork. Former 18th-century stage-coach halt, in own grounds by river. AE, DC, MC, V.

**Powdermill,** Ballincollig (tel. 021–870700). 10 rooms with bath. Just outside town on the Killarney road.

**Sunset Ridge,** Killeens (tel. 021–385271). 28 rooms with bath. On the edge of the city, near Blarney.

**Vienna Woods,** Glanmire (tel. 021–821146). 18 rooms with bath. Picturesque setting on main Dublin–Cork road, 10 minutes from center.

## Guesthouses

**Gabriel House,** Summerhill, St. Lukes (tel. 021–500333). 20 rooms, all with bath or shower. MC, V.

**Garnish,** 1 Aldergrove, Western Rd. (tel. 021–27511). 6 rooms, 2 with bath. Five minutes from the center. Recommended. AE, DC, MC, V.

**Glenvera,** Wellington Rd. (tel. 021–502030). 34 rooms with bath.

**Lotamore House,** Tivoli (tel. 021–822344). 20 rooms with bath. 3¼ miles east on route N25. Has good views and a garden. AE, DC, MC, V.

**Roserie Villa,** Mardyke Walk, Western Rd. (tel. 021–272958). 7 rooms, 5 with bath. Near university and park. AE, DC, MC, V.

## Youth Hostel

There is a youth hostel at 1–2 Redclyffe, Western Rd. (tel. 021–543289).

## RESTAURANTS

*Expensive*

**Arbutus Lodge,** Montenotte (tel. 021–501237). Top of anybody's list, this is one of Ireland's greatest eating spots; excellent wine list. Run by the Ryan family. AE, DC, MC, V.

**The Barn,** Lotamore, Glanmire (tel. 021–866211). Family-run restaurant in a rural setting, 10 minutes from the center. Serves fresh local produce.

**Fastnet Restaurant,** Jury's Hotel (tel. 021–276622). Seafood specialties. Live entertainment nightly.

**Lovett's,** Churchyard Lane, Douglas (tel. 021–294909). Deserves its high reputation among Corkonians. Specializes in light dishes, particularly fresh fish. AE, DC, MC, V.

## *Moderate*

**Glandore,** Jury's Hotel, Western Rd. (tel. 021–276622). First-rate hotel restaurant. AE, DC, MC, V.

**Glassialley's,** 17 Drawbridge St. (tel. 021–272305). Relaxed dining in city center. MC, V.

**Huguenot,** French Church St. (tel. 021–273357). Fashionable place for classic French cuisine. MC, V.

**Jaques,** 9 Phoenix St. (tel. 021–502387). Behind Imperial Hotel, near the G.P.O. Interesting cooking. MC, V.

**Oyster Tavern,** Market Lane, just off Patrick St. A Cork favorite. DC, MC.

## *Inexpensive*

**Beecher's,** Faulkners' Lane, off Patrick St. (tel. 021–273144). Bar with excellent lunchtime food.

**Crawford Art Gallery,** Emmet Place. Outstanding cafeteria run by the award-winning team from Ballymaloe House.

**Halpin's,** Cook St. Substantial portions of salads, curries and daily specials. MC, V.

**Mary Rose.** Has good spots in both the Savoy Center and Queen's Old Castle. AE.

**Paddy Garibaldi's,** Carey's Lane, off Patrick St. (tel. 021–277915). Cheerful spot for pizzas and burgers.

## Bars

Recommended bars where you can meet the people of Cork are the **Chateau,** near the *Cork Examiner* office on Patrick St., a newsmen's spot; the **Long Valley,** near the General Post Office; the eccentric **Hi-B** on the second floor opposite the G.P.O. in MacCurtain St.; and the wonderfully old-fashioned **Vine,** in Market Pl., off Patrick St.

**HOW TO GET AROUND.** There is a limited bus service into Cork City from Cork Airport (IR£2), but there are always taxis available. Check the rate. Taxis are also available at the rail station, and on call throughout the city.

The Father Mathew statue in Patrick St. is the major starting point for city and immediate suburban bus services, with a fixed fare of about 50p. The main bus and coach terminus is at Parnell Place.

The rail terminus is Kent Station, which has mainline trains and a suburban service to Cobh. For passenger enquiries about trains and buses, tel. 021–504422.

If you're driving yourself around Cork, beware of the one-way system, it is complicated, so check your route on a city map before starting a journey.

Bicycles can be hired from *D.M.D. Cycles,* 18 Grafton St. (tel. 021–21529).

**TOURS AND EXCURSIONS.** C.I.E., Ireland's transport company, operate a number of trips from the Parnell Place terminus. Telephone for current information: 021–503399, ext. 300, or contact the Tourist Information office.

**HISTORIC BUILDINGS. The Courthouse.** The façade has a rise of steps to a Corinthian portico. The figures on the pediment represent Justice, Law and Mercy.

**Honan Collegiate Chapel,** University College. Built in the Hiberno-Romanesque style of the 12th century, it's worth a detour to see.

**St. Anne's Church,** Shandon. Home of the famous Bells of Shandon, which visitors may have rung, by arrangement. Built in 1722.

**St. Fin Barre's Cathedral.** Built 1865–1870; statues of the Wise and Foolish Virgins flanking the Bridegroom (west front).

**St. Mary's Pro-Cathedral.** Built in 1808; has a prominent tower.

**MUSEUMS AND GALLERIES. Cork Arts Society Gallery,** 16 Lavitt's Quay (tel. 021–277749). Has frequent exhibitions by Irish artists. Open Tues. to Sat., 11–2 and 3–6.

**Cork Public Museum,** Fitzgerald Park (tel. 021–270679). Collection of national and local history since prehistoric times; also Cork silver and glass. Look for such items as the Gold Bird of Garryduff.

**Crawford Municipal Art Gallery,** Emmet Place (tel. 021–273377). Permanent collection of Irish and European painting, as well as sculpture, silver and glass, and adventurous contemporary exhibits. Open Mon. to Fri. 10–5, Sat. 9–1.

**Fota House,** Fota Estate, Carrigtwohill (tel. 021–812678). Collection of Irish landscape paintings, 1750s to the 1870s, the most comprehensive such private collection and containing many works of national importance, as well as furniture of the 18th and early-19th century. Open mid-Mar. to end-Sept., Tues. to Sat. 11–6, Sun. 1–6.

**Triskel Arts Center,** Tobin St., off Grand Parade (tel. 021–272002). Exhibits, poetry readings, movie club, performance art and more.

**MUSIC AND THEATERS. Father Mathew Hall,** Father Mathew St. Houses visiting companies.

**Granary Theater,** Greenville Place. Own theatrical productions, as well as visiting companies.

**Opera House,** Emmet Place. Presents a wide range of entertainment, including drama and musicals. Its main opera season in the spring presents work of very high standard. The Irish National Ballet also has its headquarters in Cork and usually premieres new work in the Opera House.

Concerts are also held in the **City Hall** and in the auditorium of the **Municipal School of Music,** Union Quay.

**SHOPPING.** Patrick St. is the city's main shopping thoroughfare with some good department stores, notably **Cash's,** which also has an international mail order operation, and **Roche's.** The most exciting shops in town are to be found in the newly pedestrianized Paul St. area behind Patrick St. near the City Center Car Park. The **Stephen Pearce Shop** is a converted warehouse stocking the best in modern Irish design, including tableware, decorative ceramics, knitwear, hand-woven tweeds and high fashion in its boutique. The **Donegal Shop** next door specializes in made-to-measure tweed suits for export and has outstanding rainwear.

The new (1989) Merchant's Quay Center on the corner of Patrick St. and the river is a shopping mall with a good selection of high-street chain stores including **Marks & Spencer** and **Laura Ashley.** Across St Patrick's Bridge, Macurtain St. has an interesting selection of antique shops. **Mercier Press,** Bridge St., publishes a range of books on Ireland and works by Irish authors. Locally produced statues and plaques (reproductions of Celtic masterpieces of the past) are good souvenirs, and don't ignore the wide selection of locally made pottery and ceramics.

**SPORTS. Angling.** Take your choice of game angling for salmon and trout, sea fishing or coarse angling. Tackle dealers can supply everything you need, as well as giving advice on where the big ones can be found.

**Sailing.** The world's oldest sailing club, the Cork Water Club, was founded in 1720 and later became the Royal Cork Yacht Club, now based in Crosshaven.

**Cruising.** Yachts are available for charter in Kinsale in the 1990 season. Call Kinsale Chamber of Tourism, 021–774026 for details.

**Golf.** There are eight 18-hole courses and 12 nine-hole courses within easy traveling distance of the city.

**Greyhound racing.** You can watch greyhound races three nights a week in Cork.

**Bowling.** Not the game you know, but the throwing of an iron ball for long distances on roads. This is a novel spectator sport for visitors. Inquire locally when and where matches are taking place. The **Fox and Hounds,** near the end of the Carrigrohane Road, or the **Waterloo,** a little further on, are places where they usually know about fixtures. There are sometimes big wagers.

# PRACTICAL INFORMATION FOR THE SOUTH

**TOURIST OFFICES.** Apart from the main tourist office for the south at Cork, there are also offices at **Bantry,** tel. 027–50229 (open July to Aug.); **Clonakilty,** tel. 023–33226 (open July to Aug.); **Cork Airport,** tel. 021–964347 (open mid-June to mid-Sept.); **Fermoy,** tel. 025–31110 (open July to Aug.); **Glengarriff,** tel. 027–63084 (open July to Aug.); **Kinsale,** tel. 021–772234 (open July to Aug.); **Skibbereen,** tel. 028–21766 (open year-round); **Youghal,** tel. 024–92390 (open July to Aug.).

## HOTELS AND RESTAURANTS

**Ballinascarty.** *Ardnavaha House* (E), tel. 023–49135. 36 rooms, all with bath. Georgian house in spacious grounds of lawns, woods and meadows. Modern bedroom block. AE, DC, MC, V.

**Ballycotton.** *Bay View* (I), tel. 021–646746. 18 rooms, some with bath. Seaside hotel with good views of the harbor. Angling, golf, swimming. DC, V.

**Baltimore.** *Baltimore House* (I), tel. 028–20164. 10 rooms, some with bath. AE, MC, V. *Beacon Park* (I), tel. 028–20361. 34 rooms with bath. MC, V.
**Restaurant.** *Chez Youen* (M), tel. 028–20136. Famous for its fish. DC, V.

**Bantry.** *West Lodge* (M), tel. 027–50360. 90 rooms, all with bath. AE, DC, MC, V. *Bantry Bay* (I), tel. 027–50289. 12 rooms, most with bath. MC, V.
**Restaurant.** *The Admiral* (M), New St. (tel. 027–51350). Small and elegant with authentic French cuisine. MC, V.

**Barleycove.** *Barleycove Beach* (M), tel. 028–35234. 11 rooms, all with bath. Golf links, indoor pool. AE, DC, MC, V.

**Blarney.** *Blarney Park* (M), tel. 021–385281. 70 rooms, all with bath. Special facilities for handicapped visitors. AE, DC, MC, V. *Christy's* (M), tel. 021–385011. 25 rooms with bath.

**Castletownroche.** *Blackwater Castle* (L), tel. 022–26333. 12th-century castle on river's edge converted into a hotel in 1989. Fishing, tennis, rafting, putting. Excellent restaurant.

**Cobh.** *Commodore* (M), tel. 021–811277. 39 rooms, most with bath. 25 minutes from Cork City center, 10 minutes from Fota Park; train services to both. AE, DC, MC, V.

**Courtmacsherry.** *Courtmacsherry* (I), tel. 023–46198. 16 rooms, some with bath; in spacious garden and woodland.

**Restaurant.** *Dunworley Cottage* (M), Butlerstown (tel. 023–40314). German owner-chef makes imaginative use of organically grown vegetables and the best local, fresh produce.

**Durrus. Restaurants.** *Blairs Cove House* (M), Durrus (tel. 027–61127). Overlooks the famous Dunmanus Bay. AE, DC, MC, V. *Shiro Japanese Dinner House* (M), Ahakista, Durrus (tel. 027–67030). Japanese food in idyllic setting overlooking Dunmanus Bay.

**Glandore.** *Marine* (M), tel. 028–33366. 16 rooms, 8 with bath. Quayside hotel in a pretty, fishing and holiday village.

**Glengarriff.** *Casey's* (I), tel. 027–63010. 20 rooms, some with bath. Seasonal. *Eccles* (I), tel. 027–63003. 35 rooms, all with bath. Lovely setting overlooking Bantry Bay; sub-tropical gardens. AE, DC, MC, V. *Mountain View* (I), tel. 027–63103. 20 rooms, 7 with bath. Seasonal.

**Innishannon.** *Innishannon House* (M), tel. 021–775121. 13 rooms with bath or shower. Beautiful situation on the banks of the river Bandon. AE, DC, MC, V.

**Kanturk.** *Assolas Country House* (L), tel. 029–50015. 10 rooms, 9 with bath. A 17th-century country house with lovely gardens, which maintains its atmosphere and a top cuisine. AE, DC, MC, V.

**Kinsale.** *Acton's* (E), tel. 021–722135. 55 rooms, most with bath. Period building overlooking harbor. Indoor pool, gym and sauna. AE, DC, MC, V. *Blue Haven* (M), Pearse St. (tel. 021–772209). 10 rooms, 7 with bath. Good family-run hotel with pleasant bar and good restaurant. *Trident* (M), tel. 021–772301. 40 rooms with bath. Newly refurbished modern hotel on the water's edge. AE, DC, MC, V. *Folk House* (I), tel. 021–772382. 18 rooms, one with bath. Simple accommodations above a popular bar.
**Restaurants.** *Blue Haven* (E), Pearse St. (tel. 021–772209). Seafood; has won awards for its cooking. AE, DC, MC, V. *Vintage* (E), Main St. (tel. 021–772502). Outstanding cuisine. AE, DC, MC, V. *Jim Edwards* (M), Short Quay (tel. 021–772541). Excellent steaks, seafood and duck. MC, V. *Man Friday* (M), Scilly (tel. 021–772260). Cozy restaurant with international reputation. MC, V. *Armada House* (I), Pearse St. (tel. 021–772255). Good value in a town where eating can be expensive. MC, V. *Max's Wine Bar* (I), Main St. (tel. 021–772443). Pleasant old-style town house and patio. MC, V.

**Mallow.** *Longueville House* (L), tel. 022–47156. 18 rooms, all with bath. A Georgian mansion on the road to Killarney, with a 500-acre estate and a restaurant well worth making a detour for. AE, DC, MC, V.
**Restaurant.** *Keppler's* (I), Bank Place (tel. 022–21946). Atmospheric basement in town center. Good value.

**Shanagarry.** *Ballymaloe House* (E), tel. 021–652531. 29 rooms with bath. One of the most famous of Ireland's country house hotels. Has a restaurant, run by Myrtle Allen, which is outstanding. Heated swimming pool, tennis, riding. AE, DC, MC, V.

**Skibbereen.** *West Cork Hotel* (M), tel. 028–21277. 42 rooms with bath. Popular modern hotel with restaurant that serves outstandingly generous portions. AE, DC, MC, V.

**Youghal.** *Hilltop* (I), tel. 024–92911. 50 rooms, all with bath. AE, MC, V. *Monatrea House* (I), Ferry Point (tel. 024–94301). 14 rooms, half with bath. Country house style on the banks of the Blackwater estuary, over-looking Youghal Bay. Good restaurant with fresh local produce. DC, MC, V.

**Restaurants.** *Aherne's Pub and Seafood Bar* (M), 163 North Main St. (tel. 024–92424). Has a fine reputation for its seafood. AE, DC, MC, V. *The Yawl Inn* (I), North Main St. (tel. 024–93190). Award-winning bar food served in nautical surroundings; live traditional music. DC.

## Youth Hostels

**Allihies,** Cahermeelabo, Bantry (tel. 027–73014). **Cape Clear Island,** South Harbor, Skibbereen (tel. 028–39144). **Summer Cove,** Kinsale (tel. 021–772309).

**TOURS AND EXCURSIONS.** *Bernard O'Keeffe,* 126 North Main St., Youghal (tel. 024–92820), organizes cruises on the river Blackwater for groups and private parties. Bicycles can be hired from *N.W. Roycroft,* Ilen St., Skibbereen (tel. 028–21235) and *Mylie Murphy,* Pearse St., Kinsale (tel. 021–772122).

## PLACES TO VISIT

**Bantry. Bantry House.** Former home of the Earls of Bantry, built in the 1750s overlooking Bantry Bay. Has furniture and objets d'art from all over Europe, collected by former owners. 56 miles from Cork. Open daily 9–6; in spring and summer until 8 P.M.

**Blarney. Blarney Castle.** Famous for the Blarney Stone beneath the battlements which is traditionally kissed for the gift of eloquence. Five miles from Cork. Open May, Mon. to Sat. 9–7; June and July, Mon. to Sat. 9–8.30; Aug., Mon. to Sat. 9–7.30; Sept., Mon. to Sat. 9–6.30; Oct. to Apr., Mon. to Sat. 9–sundown. Also open on Sun., summer 9.30–5.30; winter 9.30–sundown. Last admission 30 mins. before closing.

**Blarney House.** Late 19th-century mansion in the Castle grounds which contains a collection of ancestral portraits and heraldic decorations. Open 1 June to mid-Sept., Mon. to Sat. 12–5; closed Sun.

**Castletownroche. Anne's Grove Gardens.** Extensive Robinsonian gardens surrounding 18th-century house, overlooking the river Awbeg. Has many rare trees and shrubs. A mile north of town on the main Fermoy–Mallow road. Open Easter to 30 Sept., Mon. to Fri. 10–5, Sun. 1–6. Closed Sat. Other times by arrangement.

**Cork. Fota Island Wildlife Park and Arboretum.** Estate owned by University College, Cork, eight miles east of the city and easily reached by road, rail or boat (the latter in summer from Passage West). Has about

780 acres of farmland, parkland and woods, some of which is open to the public. The Arboretum is possibly the finest in the country and has collections of plants from all over the world. Wildlife Park is open 6 Apr. to 8 Sept., Mon. to Sat. 10–5.15, Sun. 11–5.15; 8 Sept. to 28 Oct., Sat. and Sun. only. The Arboretum is open Apr. to Oct., Mon. to Sat. 10–6, Sun. 11–6. Admission free.

**Glanmire. Riverstown House.** Originally built in 1602, rebuilt in 1745. Beautiful old furniture and fine interior plasterwork. Four miles from Cork on the Dublin road. Open 1 May to 30 Sept., Thurs. to Sun. 2–6.

**Glengarriff. Garinish Island.** Also known as Ilnacullin and Bryce's Island. An elaborate Italianate garden begun in 1910, and a joy to explore. Reached by boat from Glengarriff—check the rate. Open 1 Mar. to 31 Oct., Mon. to Sat. 10–5.30, Sun. 1–6; other times by special arrangement.

**Gougane Barra. Forest Park.** This was where the patron saint of Cork, St. Finbar, founded his monastery; it's also the source of the river Lee. Has nature trails and car trail. Two miles off route T64 at the dramatic Pass of Keimaneigh on the Cork–Kenmare road.

**Kinsale. Charles Fort.** The biggest and best-preserved star-shaped fort in Europe. Built in the reign of Charles II to protect the sea approaches to Kinsale. Still in use up until the 1920s. Two miles southeast of Kinsale. Open mid-June to mid-Sept., daily 10–6.30; mid-Apr. to mid-June and mid-Sept. to 31 Oct., Tues. to Sat. 10–5, Sun. 2–5; rest of year, Mon. to Fri. 8–4.30.

**Mallow. Doneraile Forest Park.** Formerly the St. Leger Estate, now owned by the Irish government.
**Doneraile Court.** On the grounds, built in 1725 and remodelled in the early-19th century. A fine period building. Six miles northeast of Mallow.

**Timoleague. Timoleague Abbey.** A Franciscan friary built about 1240 and well-preserved. Near Courtmacsherry, 30 miles from Cork.
**Timoleague Castle Gardens.** Gardens laid out and maintained by the Travers family for 160 years. Contains the ruins of a 13th-century castle. Open June, July and Aug., daily 12–6.

# THE SOUTHWEST

## *Around the Ring of Kerry*

The scenery of the extreme southwest of Ireland might have been designed with the tourist in mind. Ever since Killarney was first "discovered" by travelers in the late-18th century, visitors have come away searching for superlatives to describe the vistas afforded by its heather-clad sandstone mountains, deep blue island-studded lakes and lush lowland vegetation. Killarney and the Ring of Kerry provide two of Europe's most scenic driving routes, combining mountainous splendor with a spectacularly varied coastline. Its facilities for anglers and golfers are legendary. There are world class 18-hole golf courses at Waterville, Killarney, Ballybunion and Tralee.

The southern extreme of County Kerry reaches into the sea in the form of three long peninsulas. The Beara is partly in County Cork and provides a minor prelude for its neighbor, the Iveragh, around which the road known as the Ring of Kerry runs. The northernmost peninsula, the Dingle, contains the wild Atlantic seaboard and is altogether more rugged in character. These peninsulas offer an alternating selection of long sandy beaches, wild rocky headlands and sheltered wooded coves, all of which are enhanced by views across the estuaries dividing them to the serried mountain ranges of their interiors.

In the north of the county a smaller lowland area of rich pasture stretches towards the Shannon estuary, and contains the towns of Tralee and Listowel. Characteristic of Kerry's agricultural land are the distinctive Kerry Black cattle, a compact and hardy short-horn breed native to the area rapidly regaining favor following an influx of the ubiquitous black-and-white Fresian earlier this century.

The main reason for visiting Kerry is to enjoy its scenery. But a word of warning from the Cork-born writer, Frank O'Connor, is needed here: "Kerry is remarkable for its scenery—when you can see it, which owing to the appalling weather the county enjoys, is very rarely." Being a Corkman, he is exaggerating a little. Rain in Kerry is often only a shower, over in a few minutes. Even if the day is not perfect, mist-shrouded mountains can be just as beautiful as sun-lit ones and there is no need to postpone an outing. However, there is no denying that if you are fortunate enough to have good weather in Kerry, your visit will be especially memorable. Incidentally, because of the mildness of its climate Kerry is just as beautiful in winter as in summer, and far less crowded.

Tralee, with a population of just 15,000, is Kerry's largest town. Indeed the vast majority of Kerry people are rural dwellers. This bucolic lifestyle has led to Kerrymen becoming the butt of what are known in Ireland as "Kerryman jokes." In Britain these same stories circulate as Irish jokes, while in the United States they will be familiar as either Irish or Polish jokes. For example—How do you confuse a Kerryman? Show him two shovels and ask him to take his pick.

Do not be misled by this local banter into believing that Kerrymen are stupid. The people of Kerry are among the wittiest and most astute in Ireland, and have a naturally poetic way with words which is apparent in even a short exchange. This is not surprising given Kerry's strong traditions in Irish poetry. The bardic tradition of traveling poets died out in the rest of Ireland soon after the Flight of the Earls following the Battle of Kinsale in 1601. In Kerry, however, this bardic tradition persisted well into the late-18th century. The tall stories that you will hear from the "jarveys" (as the guides offering jaunting car and boating trips in Killarney are called) are heirlooms and will greatly enliven your visit.

Over 2,000 archeological sites, coastal settlements, megalithic tombs, monastic sites and forts have been identified in this area, and much exciting excavation is still under way. St. Brendan, the 6th-century navigator who probably discovered the American continent long before Christopher Columbus was born, is remembered near his birthplace in names like Mount Brandon. Moving into the realm of historical fact, there have been strong links between the people of Kerry and the United States for generations. The emigration rate from the county was very high until as recently as the '50s, although today it has fallen to a trickle. Some who left earlier this century have managed to fulfill the emigrant's dream, and have returned to enjoy their retirement here. Many Kerry people have relatives in the States, and they are proud of the association. A bar in the village of Asdee, for example, the Jesse James Tavern, is named after *the* Jesse James, whose family lived in the district until they emigrated to Missouri, where Jesse was born.

## Killarney

Killarney itself is an undistinguished market town, but provides good facilities for exploring the surrounding countryside, which is the objective of the visit. Be sure to book in advance in the summer, as the peak season is very busy.

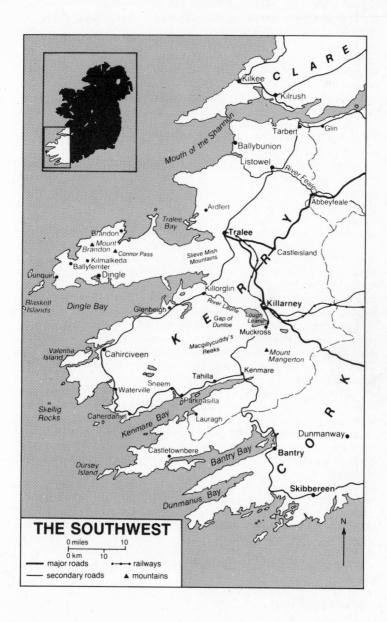

## THE SOUTHWEST

0 miles 10
0 km 10

— major roads ·—•— railways
— secondary roads ▲ mountains

C L A R E

Kilkee
Kilrush
Mouth of the Shannon
Tarbert
Glin
Ballybunion
Listowel
River Feale
Abbeyfeale
Ardfert
Tralee Bay
Brandon
Mount Brandon ▲ Connor Pass
Slieve Mish Mountains
Tralee
Castleisland
Kilmalkeda
Ballyferriter
Dunquin
Dingle
Killorglin
Blasket Islands
Dingle Bay
Glenbeigh
River Laune
Gap of Dunloe
Lough Leane
Killarney
Muckross
K E R R Y
Macgillycuddy's Reeks
▲ Mount Mangerton
Valentia Island
Cahirciveen
Tahilla
Kenmare
Skellig Rocks
Sneem
Waterville
Parknasilla
Caherdaniel
Lauragh
Kenmare Bay
Dunmanway
Castletownbere
Bantry Bay
Bantry
C O R K
Dursey Island
Dunmanus Bay
Skibbereen

N

In the 17th century the town of Killarney (from the Irish *Cill Airne,* Church of the Sloe) was not even on the map. But by the late-18th century the English observer Arthur Young discovered the then tiny hamlet and praised its scenic beauty, arousing the interest of travelers. By the time the Romantic movement was into its considerable stride in the mid-19th century, the lakes and mountains of Killarney were considered as exhilarating and as awe-inspiring as anything in Switzerland. County Kerry's fame had arrived.

Among the principal sights in the town itself is the Catholic Cathedral of St. Mary, a fine example of the work of the great English Gothic revivalist, Pugin. It was completed in 1855 in the Early English style, using local limestone. The parish church of St. Mary (Church of Ireland) is in the same style and has a richly decorated interior.

Opposite the Franciscan Friary (near the railway station) is an impressive monument called An Speirbhean (literally "Sky Maiden," implying the Muse) erected in 1940 to commemorate four famous Kerry poets, Pierce Ferriter (1616–53), Geoffrey O'Donoghue (1620–90), Aodhgan O'Rahilly (1670–1726) and Eoghan Ruadh O'Sullivan (1748–84). But to find the famous scenery one must head out of town towards the lakes. Killarney's three main lakes lie in a valley running south between the mountains. The Lower Lake, largest of the three, is nearest to the town. Lower Lake (Lough Leane) has many islands and Muckross Abbey and Ross Castle are situated on its eastern shore. It is separated from the Middle Lake by the peninsula of Muckross. A narrow channel connects the Middle and Upper lakes. Smaller lakes and tarns can be discovered in the folds of the mountains, and four miles to the southeast is Lough Guitane.

The lakes are surrounded by luxuriant woods which thrive in Killarney's mild oceanic climate. The Arbutus, or Killarney Strawberry Tree, is a Killarney native otherwise only widely found in the Mediterranean. Wild orchids are widespread. Birch, holly, mountain ash, and oak are complemented by a wealth of ferns and mosses. Rhododendrons were introduced to Killarney from Turkey in the last century and have adapted so well to the climate that, in spite of their colorful contribution to the local flora, they are now seen as something of a menace. Their growth in the wild is so vigorous that it is damaging the native oak woods and yew trees, and a campaign to control the spread of rhododendrons has been initiated.

The effects of the Ice Age are largely responsible for the scenery of Killarney. The mountain mass is made of old red sandstone, while the limestone of the valleys around the Lower and Middle Lakes has been eroded into strange shapes by the action of the lake waters. Perched boulders, smooth rocks and deep corries excavated by glacial action (at the Devil's Punch Bowl, for example, or the Horses' Glen) add drama to the scene, as do the gigantic volcanic rocks, some as big as houses, which are perched around the district.

## Muckross Estate

Part of Killarney's lake district is within Killarney National Park. At the heart of the National Park is the 10,000 acre Muckross Estate, previously known as the Bourn Vincent Memorial Park. This was presented to the Irish nation by its American owners, Mr. and Mrs. William Bowers

Bourn, and their son-in-law, Senator Arthur Vincent, in 1932. Purchases and gifts in subsequent years have increased the Killarney National Park to 19,380 acres.

Cars are not allowed in the Muckross Estate, but if you don't want to walk, you can either hire a bicycle—they're available in the town—or take a trip in a jaunting car, a little two-wheeled horse-drawn cart, still very much a traditional way of getting around in Kerry. Be prepared for a non-stop stream of patter from the jarvey, or driver. He considers his commentary an important part of the deal, whether you like it or not (though you probably will). But at the very least he will give you a few good laughs.

After entering the Estate, the route runs along the shore of the Lower Lake to Muckross Abbey, one of the best preserved ruins in the country, made all the more delightful by its idyllic site. Originally a Franciscan Abbey, it was founded by the Macarthy Mor, a famous chieftain, in the mid-15th century. It was then formally supressed by Henry VIII in 1542, but the friars returned, only to be burnt out by Cromwell's men in 1652. The Abbey comprises both church and monastery. A massive tower separates the nave from the choir and its east window. Chiefs of the clans Macarthy, O'Donoghue and O'Sullivan are buried here along with a number of Kerry poets. Three flights of stone steps give access to the upper floors and the living quarters of the monks where you can visit their dormitory, kitchen, refectory and infirmary.

Not far away is the ruined cottage which you will be told was the home of Danny Mann, the boatman in the story of *The Colleen Bawn;* the Colleen Bawn rock will also be pointed out. The Colleen Bawn (Ellen Hanly) was murdered many miles away and her body was found on the north bank of the river Shannon at Killimer, County Clare, in 1819. When Gerald Griffin (1803–40) used the story as the basis of his novel *The Collegians* (one of the best Irish novels of the 19th century), he transferred the locale to Killarney—a much more romantic spot—and Dion Boucicault (1820–90) did the same for his melodrama *The Colleen Bawn.* The German composer Julius Benedict (1804–85) followed on, when using the plot for his opera, *Lily of Killarney.* (But why spoil a good story for the sake of a fact?)

Next stop on your tour will be the 19th-century manor, Muckross House, which now contains the Kerry Folklife Center. The traditional crafts of the blacksmith, weaver, potter and basketmaker are demonstrated by skilled workers. Kerry's musical and poetic past forms a separate exhibition, and there is a third one of farming machinery from bygone days as well as a craft shop. The informal gardens are noted for their rhododendrons and azaleas, the water garden and an outstanding rock garden on natural limestone. There is a special entrance to the estate for cars visiting Muckross House three miles outside Killarney on the Kenmare road, the N71 (though remember that cars themselves are not allowed in the Estate).

## The Gap of Dunloe to Ross Castle

This day-long tour which takes in the Gap of Dunloe, the Upper Lake, Long Range, Middle and Lower Lakes and Ross Castle is highly recommended. As the middle stretch is not accessible to motorists, an organized tour leaving town by jaunting car makes an ideal way to explore the region, providing the perfect pace at which to digest the scenery.

You leave town by a pleasant tree-lined avenue, and cross the river Laune. From here there is a view of Dunloe Castle between the trees. The road then takes you south to Kate Kearney's Cottage, the entrance to the Gap of Dunloe, which runs for four miles between the Macgillicuddy's Reeks and the Purple Mountains. This narrow defile is not suitable for cars, and they must be left at the Cottage from whence visitors can continue on foot, on horseback or by jaunting car.

Five small lakes are strung beside the road, and the valley is crossed by a rushing stream. Massive glacial rocks form the side of the valley, and strange echoes reverberate among the hills. At the head of the Gap the Upper Lake comes into view with the Black Valley stretching into the hills at the right. From Lord Brandon's Cottage a path leads to the edge of the lake and the journey is continued by rowing boat. Traditionally the boatman carries a bugle and uses it to demonstrate the echoes obtained from the wooded crags of the Eagle's Nest. Beyond the Old Weir Bridge and across the rapids you enter a calm stretch of water leading to Dinis Island, on which sub-tropical plants and shrubs can be admired.

Look out for caves on the north shore while crossing the Middle Lake. The boat passes under Brickeen Bridge into the Lower Lake, whose 30 islands have inspired many a local legend. The journey ends at Ross Castle, a well-preserved 14th-century ruin.

### Other Side-trips from Killarney

Innisfallen Island on the Lower Lake is worth a special trip. It's a small island near the northern shore of the Lower Lake with some unusual vegetation including a four-in-one tree—holly, ash, hawthorn and ivy growing as if from a single step—and a holly tree, reputed to be Europe's largest. There was a monastery established here in the 6th or 7th century and the ruins of Innisfallen Abbey may still be seen near the landing stage. Between 950 and 1350, the *Annals of Innisfallen* were compiled here by a number of monks. The book is now in the Bodleian Library at Oxford, England. Another relic of the abbey, the Innisfallen Crozier, was found in the river at Killarney towards the end of the 19th century and is in the National Museum, Dublin. Innisfallen Island was presented to the Irish nation by its American owner, John McShane, in 1973, and in 1977 the Irish government bought about 30 other islands from Mr. McShane to protect the amenities from development.

The view from Aghadoe Hill, less than three miles outside Killarney on the Killorglin road, is remarkable. The Lower Lake is in the foreground with Innisfallen Island in the distance, Mahoney's Point just below the hill, and, away to the southwest, the Gap of Dunlow. Close by to the east is Aghadoe Castle and the site known as Aghadoe Cathedral, which contains the ruins of a small church with a 12th-century Romanesque doorway.

Climbers will be attracted by Carrantwohill and Mangerton Mountains, where the tracks can also be ascended by pony. Just over 2,000 feet up Mangerton Mountain is the Devil's Punch Bowl, a deep dark pool which feeds the Torc Waterfall, and a short distance beyond it the full panorama of Killarney is spread out before you. For more serious climbers there are rock climbs on the cliff range on the southern side of the glen. The Killarney Mountaineering Club in the town's High Street will supply essential local information and advise on weather conditions as mist is a hazard in the area.

Few people leave Killarney without wanting to return, and it is the character of the climate that whenever a return visit is paid, there is always a change in the scenery—not a physical change, but that of the light and shade of the clouds, perhaps of a mist on a mountain. Long after you've left Killarney, long after you've gone from Ireland, the memory will flash back to a view, maybe a corner or perhaps a great panoramic sweep, and the image will come clear in the mind to renew the pleasure of one of the world's most beautiful spots.

## Ring of Kerry

The Ring of Kerry is about 110 miles in all. To travel it clockwise you leave Killarney heading south on the Kenmare road, returning to Killarney via Killorglin. To travel anticlockwise you leave Killarney by the Killorglin road. But the best way to decide which way round to go is to toss a coin; both routes are equally good, and those who know the Ring well are equally divided on their merits. Because many visitors approach Killarney from Glengarrif, in County Cork, via Kenmare and take in the Ring before arriving, the clockwise route will be followed here.

Kenmare is a small market town 21 miles from Killarney at the head of Kenmare Bay. On the eastern shores of Kenmare Bay is the Beara Peninsula. Keen birdwatchers will enjoy an excursion to the Dursey Island at its tip, accessible only by a tiny cable car licensed to carry five passengers or one cow. Derreen House, near the hamlet of Lauragh, has mature subtropical gardens open to the public with a profusion of rare fern trees from New Zealand and other interesting specimens.

The Beara Peninsula is O'Sullivan country and the ruins of their stronghold are at Dunboy near Castletownbere. Magnificent seascapes can be found at Eyeries and Allihies. The latter has, not surprisingly, become the headquarters of a talented group of young artists including Tim Goulding and Cormac Boydell, whose landscape paintings and ceramics are exhibited internationally.

The Beara Peninsula, with its grey-blue mountain ranges, the Caha and the Slieve Miskish, will be on your left hand side as you drive out along the Iveragh Peninsula on the Ring of Kerry. The village of Sneem, on the estuary of the river Ardsheelaun, is one of the prettiest in Ireland, although its English-style central village green is untypical. Two miles south is the beautiful hotel and wooded estate of Parknasilla. The road then runs inland for a few miles until emerging at the coast again at Castlecove.

Staigue Fort, about one and a half miles north of Castlecove is one of many important archeological sites in the area. The fort is surrounded by an 18-foot stone wall and encloses a circle about 90 feet in diameter. The rough stones are held in position without mortar of any kind. The only entrance is through a tiny doorway with sloping sides.

Beyond the next village, Caherdaniel, is Derrynane House, which was the home of Kerry's most famous son: lawyer, politician and statesman, Daniel O'Connell (1775–1847), "The Liberator," who successfully campaigned for Catholic emancipation. The house, together with its 298-acre park, now forms Derrynane National Park. Additions to the house were completed by Daniel O'Connell in 1825 and the south and east wings are open to visitors. They still contain much of the original furniture, and other items associated with the great man, who was immensely proud of his Kerry ancestry. His grandparent's generation were well known in the area as smugglers, bringing in brandy, fine wines, spices and silks and smuggling out butter, sheepskins and, most importantly, young Irishmen recruited to fight for the Catholic cause in Europe. The village of Waterville, just a few miles north, is famous as an angling center, and the atmosphere of its old-fashioned hotels recalls the village's heyday in Victorian and Edwardian times.

A detour from the main Ring at Waterville leads to Ballinskelligs, an Irish-speaking village with a fine sandy beach, and Valentia Island. Valentia is now joined to the mainland by a bridge and has good facilities for deep-sea angling and skin diving. The island was formerly the Western Union cable station and terminal for the first transatlantic cable. The first transatlantic message was sent from Valentia to Heart's Content, Newfoundland, in 1858.

From Valentia you will get one of many tantalising glimpses of the Skellig Rocks. Boat trips can be made from Knightstown on Valentia in suitable weather. Landing conditions on the Skelligs are tricky. June, July and early-August are the best times to try.

The larger of the conical shaped Skelligs, Skellig Michael, rises sharply 700 feet out of the Atlantic. Some 600 steps, shaped out of solid rock, lead up to the remains of a settlement of early-Christian monks. 1,000 years of Atlantic storms have left the rock structure of their beehive-shaped living cells, their church and two oratories surprisingly well preserved. Little Skellig is an Irish Wildlife Conservancy preserve and landing is not permitted. Puffin Island, to the north, is also a nature reserve with a large population of shearwaters, storm petrels and about 7,000 pairs of puffins.

The main Ring is joined again just outside Caherciveen (accent on the last syllable: pronounce it "Cah-her-sigh-veen," and take it slowly!) which is the main shopping center for this part of Kerry. The road between here and Glenbeigh is one of the highlights of the Ring, with a wholly different character from the road on the Kenmare Bay side. The road skirts the edge of Dingle Bay and gives fine views across it to the rugged peaks of the Dingle Peninsula.

Glenbeigh offers magnificent mountain scenery and excellent trout fishing on Lough Coomasaharn. A three-mile excursion inland leads to the angling and climbing center at Glencar, and the wide expanse of Carragh Lake.

Killorglin, the next stop on the Ring and no more than a few miles from Glenbeigh, is a small town on a hill, scene of the famous Puck Fair, a three-day stint of merrymaking of obscure origin, which takes place in mid-August. The central event, the enthroning of a goat, has been suggested as a survival from pagan times, but whatever the truth of it, the he-goat, invariably a big one with be-ribboned horns, heads a procession in a large cage on a truck. In the town center a high tower is built and the goat in his cage hoisted up to preside over the fair, well supplied with food and water. There is a big cattle, sheep and horse fair with dancing and entertainment to follow far into the night, and on the third day down comes King Puck and the fun is over for another year. Book accommodations early if you plan to stay.

The Ring is completed by following the main road beside the Laune river back to Killarney.

## The Dingle Peninsula

While the Dingle Peninsula does not have a complete main road loop around it like the Ring of Kerry, it can be explored in a figure of eight loop which begins by following the coast road from Killorglin to Dingle via Inch.

The head of Dingle Bay is cut off by two sand spits which enclose the harbor of Castlemaine. The sand spit on the Dingle side forms the sheltered seaside resort of Inch which has a four-mile-long sandy beach backed by sand dunes. Five miles down the coast road from Inch is the village of Annascaul. Its South Pole Inn was named by its owner, Thomas Crean, who accompanied Scott on his disastrous and ultimately tragic expedition to the South Pole in 1912. Crean himself may well have considered himself fortunate not to have been picked for the final Polar Party, though as a member of one of the support teams, he did get to within 100 miles of the Pole.

Dingle is the chief town of the Peninsula, lying at the foot of a steep slope on the northern side of Dingle harbor and bounded by hills.

The western end of the Peninsula, beyond Dingle, is an important Gaeltacht area—Irish speaking area—where traditional music and crafts are very much alive. It will not be difficult to find a "session" in one of the bars in this area, and it is an experience not to be missed. The term session is derived from the Irish *seisiún,* and implies an informal and usually boisterous gathering of singers and musicians who improvise together on the same air, each giving solo performances when inclined.

Between Dingle and Dunquin the ocean pounds on the towering cliffs of Slea Head, one of the most magnificent sights in the area. Dunquin is the base of the Irish artist, Maria Simonds-Gooding, who divides her time between her studio here, Dublin and New York, where she has held several successful exhibitions. Many of her paintings are based on features of the Kerry landscape such as *clocháns* (unmortared beehive huts or cells), of which 414 have been detected on the southern slopes of Mount Eagle between Dunquin and Slea Head.

Off Dunquin is the group of islands known as the Blaskets. One of these, Innishvicallaune, is the property of the well-known Irish politician, C.J. (Charlie) Haughey, leader of the Fianna Fail party. The others can be visited by boat from Dunquin. The largest island, the Great Blasket, is about four miles long, and its last inhabitants moved to the mainland in 1953. The Blasket islanders were great storytellers, and were encouraged earlier this century to write their memoirs. *Twenty Years a-Growing* by Maurice O'Sullivan gives a fascinating picture of a way of life which has only recently disappeared.

One of the most recent and most exciting finds in an area rich in archeological remains is the wreck of the *Santa Maria de la Rosa,* one of the ships of the Spanish Armada (1588) which foundered in the Blasket Sound. There is reputed to be a large amount of gold on board and plans are being made to raise the wreck from the sea bed.

Beyond Ballyferriter, about two miles south of Kilmakaedar, is Gallarus Oratory, one of the best preserved buildings of the early-Christian period.

This area abounds in archeological remains—Ogham stones, standing stones, *clocháns,* and dolmans (burial chambers)—which can often be spotted from the road through binoculars.

## From Dingle to Tralee

The best route to choose from Dingle to Tralee 40 miles away is via the Connor Pass which crosses the center of the Peninsula between the Brandon and Central Dingle mountain ranges. At the summit of the pass, some 1,500 feet high, the bays of Brandon and Tralee can be seen to the north with Dingle Bay visible in the south.

Brandon Bay and mountain are named after St. Brendan (484–577), who began his astonishing wanderings from this point. He was 59 when he made his first journey from what is now Brandon Bay in a *curragh* of wood and skins. From the records of the trip, it seems he reached the Shetland Islands off the coast of Scotland in three months, after landing at one time on the back of a sleeping whale, mistaking it for an island.

The next trip took several years and carried him as far north as Iceland. On his return he built a new ship and sailed in it with 60 companions from one of the Aran Islands off Galway. The records indicate an encounter with an iceberg and a landfall which was almost certainly Newfoundland or Labrador. Voyaging again to the west, Brendan made a landfall on white sandy beaches—was it Florida? Back in Ireland two years after his departure, he was appointed a bishop and established a monastery at Clonfert, County Galway, before making further short voyages to Wales and to the north of France, where he died in Brittany at the age of 93.

Brendan's discovery of land far to the west of Ireland was recorded in medieval maps as an island: did he discover America? It seems quite likely that he did. In 1977 Tim Severin, an Englishman who now lives nearby in Courtmacsherry, County Cork, and two companions sailed in a replica of Brendan's *curragh* from Brandon creek to Musgrave Harbor, Newfoundland, a distance of 3,500 miles. Severin had demonstrated that it was at least possible for St. Brendan to have sailed to America. Whether he actually did, of course, is another matter.

## Tralee to Listowel

Tralee is a busy, if unprepossessing town, which is immediately associated with the song, *The Rose of Tralee,* composed by William Pembroke Mulchinock (1820–1864) at Cloghers House, Ballymullen, just outside the town. The song was the inspiration of the annual Rose of Tralee International Festival, still held every September. Irish communities in America, Canada, Australia, and Great Britain send young women to join Irish competitors in the final. Emphasis is on personality and achievement rather than just good looks, though there is of course no lack of the latter. Festival week attracts musicians and entertainers from all over Ireland. There is also a race meeting and the town is literally packed out during festival week. The televised highlights of the competition are compulsive viewing all over the country.

Tralee is closely associated with the Desmond family, a branch of the Anglo-Norman Fitzgeralds. An Earl of Desmond introduced the Dominicans into Tralee in 1243 and some of the sculptured stones from their original foundation of Holy Cross Abbey are in the priory of the 19th-century

Gothic Dominican Church on Princes Quay. St. John's Roman Catholic Church is another 19th-century church, with a fine set of Stations of the Cross by Sean Keating and a modern statue of St. Brendan the Navigator.

Tralee is also the home of *Siamsa Tire*—the Folk Theater of Ireland— and it is worth catching one of the lively and colorful productions of this talented group.

Five miles northwest of Tralee is Ardfert, with its ruined 13th-century cathedral. The village was a great ecclesiastical center from the time St. Brendan founded a monastery there seven centuries earlier. The cathedral, named in honor of Brendan, has examples of the Romanesque style in its architecture, while a short distance away, Teampall na Hoe has some unusual ornamentation in the early Irish manner. Teampall Griffin, also nearby, dates from the 15th century. The Franciscan Friary is another well-preserved ruin.

The many ring forts in the district are an indication of the one-time importance of the center. It was at one of these forts (McKenna's Fort, also known as Casement's Fort), a mile west of Ardfert, that Sir Roger Casement was captured in April, 1916, on the eve of the Easter Week Rising, after landing from a German submarine on Banna Strand, a short distance away. Casement, who remained in the fort overnight, was captured by the local police and tried and executed for high treason in London on August 3, 1916. Robert Monteith, who had landed with Casement, evaded capture and escaped to America, where he died in Detroit in 1956. In 1965 Casement's body was returned to Ireland from England and buried with full military honors.

Ballybunion, on the coast to the northeast of Listowel, is a popular seaside family resort, with sandy beaches and caves to explore under the cliffs. It has two 18-hole golf courses, the most recent of which opened in 1985.

The main road runs inland to Listowel. The prolific and ebullient writer, John B. Keane, owns a bar in Listowel. Brian MacMahon, a local schoolteacher, keeps a lower profile and produces work of high quality. The stories in his most recent collection, *The Sound of Hooves,* are among the best written about Kerry for many years. Listowel hosts an annual invasion of writers every June who indulge in a week-long session of workshops and informal get-togethers.

At Listowel's race week in October you are likely to encounter the Wren Boys, a noisy group of men and women, masked and in fancy dress, who are accompanied by musicians through the streets. Persecution of the wren was a common tradition in many countries because the chattering of the bird is said to have betrayed St. Stephen, and in the south of Ireland it became a custom for groups of youths to visit houses on St. Stephen's Day (December 26). In the old days they carried a dead wren, but today it is a bunch of feathers or ribbons tied to an evergreen branch. The traditional Wren song ends with a hint for money with which to "bury the wren." Nowadays the song is likely to be any popular Irish ballad, and the money collected is often (but not always) donated to charity.

The road from Listowel to Newcastle West takes you on to Limerick, 47 miles away, and Shannon Airport. The car ferry from Tarbert, 12 miles north of Listowel, provides a convenient short cut to County Clare across the river Shannon. The ferry crosses from Tarbert to Killimer in County Clare every hour on the half hour and takes about 20 minutes.

# PRACTICAL INFORMATION FOR
# THE SOUTHWEST

**TOURIST OFFICES.** There are tourist offices at **Ballybunion,** tel. 068–27202 (open July to Aug.); **Cahirciveen,** tel. 0667–2141 (open July to Aug.); **Dingle,** tel. 066–51188 (open July to Aug.); **Kenmare,** tel. 064–41233 (open July to Aug.); **Killarney,** tel. 064–31633 (open year-round); **Tralee,** tel. 066–21288 (open year-round).

## HOTELS AND RESTAURANTS.

Many of the hotels and restaurants in the southwest are seasonal and therefore closed during the winter months. But closing periods vary, so be sure to check. All of the following places are in County Kerry.

**Ballybunion.** *Ambassador* (M), tel. 068–27111. 85 rooms with bath. Rooftop restaurant. AE, DC, MC, V. *Greenmount* (I), tel. 068–27147. 11 rooms, 3 with bath. *Marine* (I), Sandhill Rd. (tel. 068–27139). 10 rooms with bath. Restaurant with French and Irish cuisine. V.

**Ballyferriter.** *Ostan Dun An Oir* (M), Dingle Peninsula (tel. 066–56133). 22 rooms, all with bath. Also a group of 10 cottages to rent, accommodating 6–8. Heated swimming pool, pony-trekking, nine-hole golf course. Good restaurant. AE, DC, MC, V.

**Caherciveen. Restaurant.** *Old Schoolhouse* (M), Knockeens (tel. 0667–2426). Family-run in a converted school. Offers seafood, steaks, fresh vegetables and home baking.

**Caherdaniel.** *Derrynane* (M), tel. 0667–5136. 51 rooms with bath. Heated pool. AE, DC, MC, V.
**Restaurant.** *Dominique's* (M), tel. 0667–5215. Owner-chef has a high reputation. Seafood and French cooking.

**Dingle** *The Skellig* (M), tel. 066–51144. 50 rooms with bath. Wonderful location at entrance to Dingle Harbor. A great place to hear some of the folklore of the region. Outdoor seawater pool, tennis. Exceptional seafood restaurant. AE, DC, MC, V.
**Restaurants.** *Doyle's Seafood Bar* (M), John St. (tel. 066–51174). Deserves its high reputation as one of Ireland's best fish restaurants. AE, DC, MC, V. *The Half-Door* (M), John St. (tel. 066–51600). Family-run fish restaurant. AE, DC, MC, V. *The Singing Salmon* (M), The Harbour (tel. 066–51359). Imaginative menu in comfortable waterfront location.

**Glenbeigh.** *Glenbeigh* (I), tel. 066–68204. 18 rooms, 12 with bath. On the ring of Kerry; fishing (own waters) and other sports. AE, DC, MC, V. *Towers* (M), tel. 066–68212. 22 rooms, all with bath. Also on the Ring. Good restaurant. AE, DC, MC, V.

**Kenmare.** *Park* (L), tel. 064–41200. 48 rooms, all with bath. One of the country's top hotels. Elegant and fine food. DC, MC, V. *Kenmare Bay* (M), tel. 064–41300. 100 rooms, all with bath. MC, V.

**Restaurants.** *The Anchorage* (M), Killaha East (tel. 064–41024). Pleasant nautical atmosphere. MC, V. *Jug's* (M), Gortamullen (tel. 064–41099). Has a Dutch-American owner. Specializes in fresh seafood. AE, DC, MC, V. *The Lime Tree* (M), tel. 064–41225. Informal setting in old stone building; fresh produce with light sauces.

**Killarney.** *Great Southern* (L), tel. 064–31262. 180 rooms, all with bath. Set in large gardens; heated indoor pool. AE, DC, MC, V.

*Aghadoe Heights* (E), tel. 064–31766. 60 rooms, all with bath. Overlooks Lower Lake. AE, DC, MC, V. *Cahernane* (E), Muckross Rd. (tel. 064–31895). 52 rooms with bath. Former manor house in pretty setting. AE, DC, MC, V. *Dunloe Castle* (E), tel. 064–44111. 140 rooms, all with bath. AE, DC, MC, V. *Europe* (E), tel. 064–31900. 174 rooms, all with bath. Indoor pool. AE, DC, MC, V.

*Castleross* (M), tel. 064–31144. 40 rooms with bath. AE, DC, MC, V. *Killarney Ryan* (M), Cork Rd. (tel. 064–31555). 168 rooms with bath. AE, DC, MC, V. *Three Lakes* (M), tel. 064–31479. 70 rooms with bath. AE, DC, MC, V. *Torc Great Southern* (M), tel. 064–31611. 96 rooms, all with bath.

*Arbutus* (I), tel. 064–31037. 35 rooms with bath. Well established in a central location. *Imperial* (I), tel. 064–31038. 40 rooms with bath. *International* (I), tel. 064–31836. 88 rooms with bath. AE, DC, MC, V. *Royal* (I), tel. 064–31533. 28 rooms with bath. AE, MC, V.

**Guesthouses.** *Glena House,* tel. 064–32705. 15 rooms with bath. *Kathleen's Country House,* tel. 064–32108. 10 rooms with bath. Just outside town on the Tralee road. *McSweeney Arms,* tel. 064–31211. 18 rooms with bath.

There are over 130 I.T.B.-registered bed and breakfast houses in and near Killarney charging between IR£10 and IR£15 per person. Details from Killarney Tourist Information, tel. 064–31633.

**Restaurants.** *Malton Rooms* (E), in the Great Southern Hotel (tel. 064–31262). Worth a visit for the ambience and food. AE, DC, MC, V. *Foley's* (M), 23 High St. (tel. 064–31217). Good food and atmosphere. AE, DC, MC, V. *Fossa Rooftop Restaurant* (M), Fossa (tel. 064–31497). Good atmosphere and friendly service. MC, V. *Gaby's* (M), 17 High St. (tel. 064–32519). Seafood, simple and fresh. AE, DC, MC, V. *The Strawberry Tree* (M), Plunkett St. (tel. 064–32688). Intimate restaurant with talented owner-chef. *Sugan Bistro* (I), Michael Collins Pl. (tel. 064–33104). Near railway station. Wholefood menu popular with young travelers.

**Killorglin.** *Bianconi Inn* (I), tel. 066–61146. 19 rooms, some with bath. Family-run guesthouse on the Ring of Kerry. MC, V. *Castleconway* (I), tel. 066–61178. 5 rooms. MC, V.

**Restaurant.** *Nick's Steak and Seafood* (M), tel. 066–61219. Family-run establishment with a good old-world atmosphere. MC, V.

**Listowel.** *Listowel Arms* (M), tel. 068–21500. 35 rooms, most with bath. AE, DC, MC, V. *Stack's* (I), tel. 068–21094. 20 rooms, some with bath.

**Restaurant.** *The Spinning Wheel* (M), tel. 068–21128. Main St. Small, with wine bar. AE, DC, MC, V.

**Parknasilla.** *Great Southern* (L), tel. 064–45122. 60 rooms, all with bath. Set in extensive sub-tropical gardens by the sea. Heated indoor pool, sauna, other sports facilities. AE, DC, MC, V.

**Sneem.** *Avonlea House* (I), tel. 064–45221. 4 rooms, 1 with bath. Well-run B & B in a modern home. *Stone House* (I), tel. 064–5188. 5 rooms. Guesthouse in an attractive village on the estuary of the Kenmare river. Good steak and fish restaurant. AE, DC, MC, V.

**Tahilla.** *Tahilla Cove* (I), tel. 064–45204. 9 rooms, 8 with bath. Admirable guesthouse in quiet cove. AE, MC, V.

**Tralee.** *Ballyseede Castle* (L), tel. 066–25799. 14 rooms, 10 with bath. Atmospheric, turreted castle; golfing holidays arranged. AE, MC, V. *Ballygarry House* (M), Leebrook (tel. 066–23305). 16 rooms with bath. Own grounds just outside Tralee. MC, V. *Benner's* (M), Castle St. (tel. 066–21422). 42 rooms with bath. AE, MC, V. *Earl of Desmond* (M), tel. 066–21299. 50 rooms, all with bath. Rustic setting, two miles from Tralee. AE, DC, MC, V.

**Restaurants.** *Cordon Bleu* (M), The Square (tel. 066–21596). Centrally located, serving steaks and seafood. *Oyster Tavern* (M), the Spar (tel. 066–36102). Just out of town; for a sing-along and seafood. *Slatt's Bar and Restaurant* (M), Boherbee (tel. 066–21161). Three minutes' walk from town center. Cheerful, with piano bar. AE, DC, MC, V. *The Tankard Bar and Restaurant* (M), Kilfenora, Fenit (tel. 066–36164). Intimate restaurant outside town on the shores of Tralee Bay. MC, V.

**Valentia Island.** *Valentia Heights* (I), tel. 0667–6138. 8 rooms, 6 with bath. Guesthouse near the Grotto with lovely sea views, good food.

**Waterville.** *Butler Arms* (E), tel. 0667–4144. 29 rooms with bath. Over three generations of the Huggard family have run this hotel, to a high standard. AE, DC, MC, V. *Waterville Lake* (E), tel. 0667–4133. 50 rooms with bath. Heated indoor pool, 18-hole championship golf links. Chef-manager has an international reputation. AE, DC, MC, V. *Jolly Swagman* (I), tel. 0667–4272. 20 rooms with bath. *The Smugglers' Inn* (I), Cliff Rd. (tel. 0667–4330). 6 rooms with bath. Guesthouse on the beach with a good restaurant. AE, DC, MC, V.

**Restaurants.** *Chez Marie* (M), tel. 0667–4231. Bistro-style with a wine bar. MC, V. *Huntsman* (M), tel. 0667–4124. Owner-chef. AE, DC, MC, V.

## Youth Hostels

**Aghadoe House,** Killarney (tel. 064–31240). **Ballinskelligs,** Prior House (tel. 0667–9229). **Carrán Tuathail,** Gorthboy, Beaufort, Killarney (tel. 064–44338). Open 1 Apr. to 31 Oct. **Dun Chaoin,** Dunquin, Dingle (tel. 066–56121). **Glanmore Lake,** Lauragh, Killarney (tel. 064–83181). **Loo Bridge,** Clonkeen, Killarney (tel. 064–53004). **Valentia Island,** Knightstown (tel. 0667–6154).

Independents: **Waterville Leisure Hostel,** Waterville (tel. 0667–4400). **Sugan,** Michael Collins Pl., Killarney (tel. 064–33104).

**HOW TO GET AROUND.** Buses linking most centers are scheduled, but infrequent. C.I.E. operates day tours by coach from Killarney and Tralee railway stations, from Ballybunion town center, and from Listowel, Kennelly's Travel Agency. They don't operate every day so check locally for details.

Taxis are not available, but you can hire cars known as "hackney cars"—agree on the charge before starting the journey. Bicycles can be hired from *O'Callaghan Bros.*, College St. Killarney (tel. 064–31465); *D. O'Neill*, Plunkett St., Killarney (tel. 064–31970); *John Moriarty*, Main St., Dingle (tel. 066–51316).

If you would like to get around on horseback in Killarney National Park, contact *Killarney Riding Stables*, Ballydowney, Killarney, Co. Kerry (tel. 064–31686). They also offer residential riding holidays.

## PLACES TO VISIT

**Caherdaniel. Derrynane Historic Park.** Consists of Derrynane House and 298 acres of grounds, once the home of the great 19th-century parliamentarian Daniel O'Connell. Contains furniture and memorabilia. Park open all year. House open mid-June to 30 Sept., daily 10–1 and 2–5; Oct. to mid-June, Tues. to Sat. 10–1, Sun. 2–5.

**Casteltownbere. Dunboy Castle.** Ruins of the 16th-century O'Sullivan stronghold and of the 19th-century home of the Puxley family.

**Dingle Peninsula. Ballyferriter Museum.** Exhibits relating to Brendan the Navigator, currachs and Dingle folklife.
**Gallarus Oratory.** The best-preserved of Ireland's primitive churches; it looks like an upturned boat of unmortared stone. About five miles north of Dingle.
**Kilmalkeder Church.** Has an early sundial worth seeing in the graveyard.

**Killarney. Killarney National Park.** Formerly the Bourn Vincent Memorial Park, named after the American donor of much of the land. Has 19,955 acres of forests and mountains embracing the lakes of Killarney. Cars can only enter the park by the main gate on route N71. There are signposted nature trails and jaunting carts, pulled by horses, may be hired. The center of the park is Muckross House (see below) and its beautiful gardens. Open Easter to 31 May and 1 Sept. to 31 Oct., daily 8–7; 1 June to 31 Aug., daily 9–9.
**Muckross House.** 19th-century manor house in lovely setting close to Muckross Lake. Gardens are noted for their fine collection of rhododendrons and azaleas. The house contains an excellent museum of Kerry folklife and is the main visitor center for Killarney National Park. Has craftsmen engaged in making traditional crafts. Open 17 Mar. to 30 June, daily 10–7; 1 July to 31 Aug., daily 9–9; 1 Sept. to 31 Oct., daily 10–7. Rest of the year, Tues. to Sun. 11–5; closed Mon.
**St. Mary's Cathedral.** Designed by the famous 19th-century architect Augustus Pugin.

**Lauragh. Derreen Gardens.** Woodland garden by the sea with magnificent views. The most famous feature of the garden is a grove of New Zealand tree ferns. Open 1 Apr. to 30 Sept., Tues., Thurs. and Sun. 2–6.

**Sneem. Staigue Fort.** One of the largest and best-preserved stone forts in Ireland, about 2,000 years old. The wall rises to 18 ft. high and is 13 ft. thick. Can be seen from the road (about eight miles southwest of Sneem). Private land must be crossed to make a close inspection and a small "fee" is often requested by the owner.

**Tralee. Ardfert Cathedral.** 12th-century church about five miles northwest of Tralee. An impressive structure with two smaller churches nearby—Romanesque and 15th century.

**Waterville. Blasket Islands.** Europe's most westerly point, now uninhabited (it was once used as a vacation home). The Great Blasket may be visited, in good weather, by boat from Derrynane, Dunquin or Waterville.

**Skellig Michael.** An early monastic settlement of about the 10th century on a rocky island seven miles off the Kerry coast. Two oratories, six dwelling huts and a church. Can be reached by boat from Portmagee or Knightstown, if the weather's right. Twelve miles west of Waterville.

# SHANNON

## *Gateway from the Atlantic*

Until the late '30s, Shannon meant little more to most people, if it meant anything at all that is, than the name of the longest river in the British Isles, running for 170 miles from County Cavan to Limerick City in County Clare. But mention Shannon nowadays and people are more than likely to think of the airport here (and/or its famous duty-free shop) rather than the river or even, indeed, the little town that has grown up since the airport was opened.

The primary purpose of the airport, which was enormously successful, was to provide a convenient stop-over for planes making the then slow and uncomfortable flight between North America and Europe. Today, with giant jets treating the north Atlantic run as little more than a long hop, this role has largely been made redundant. Nonetheless, Shannon remains the principal gateway to western Ireland and, because of its substantial duty-free complex, an attractive destination in itself. Interestingly, Shannon was the first airport in the world to open a duty-free shop, back in 1945. The duty-free zone has since been extended to include the nearby industrial estate. A significant number of foreign companies have taken advantage of this tax-free status to import raw materials, process them here and export the finished article. It is this more than anything that has led to the rapid growth of the new town of Shannon, today the second largest in County Clare, albeit with a population of only 8,000 souls.

The airport claims another first: Irish Coffee. Passengers arriving at the airport in those early days after the long flight from North America needed something to warm them up and keep them going for the next leg of their journey. The airport's barman came up with a concoction of black coffee and whiskey (Irish of course) topped with cream. This delightful discovery alone, in some eyes, has long since justified the existence of the airport.

## Castles, Cliffs, Caves and Crafts

The combination of easy access to the region and the extensive range of attractions and activities offered by Counties Clare and Limerick have today conspired to make Shannon one of the most popular regions of Ireland, a fact that the local tourist industry has been fast to exploit. Indeed you can be sure of a warm and memorable welcome here, in addition to a wealth of well-organized and unusual activities.

The principal attraction of the region is its castles, nearly 900 in all. They range from the dignity and splendor of the fully-restored Bunratty Castle to crumbling and ancient ruins which loom up dramatically all over the area.

In addition, the Atlantic coast of County Clare is wonderfully varied, with towering cliffs, warrens of caves, and long sandy beaches. To the north of the county the coast rises in a sheer mass to nearly 700 feet, creating the breathtaking beauty of the cliffs of Moher. More caves will be found in the Burren, a strange rocky limestone district which many visitors say reminds them more of the surface of the moon than of anything they have seen on earth. It is in fact a superb nature reserve, with a profusion of unique wild flowers that attracts numerous botanists.

Old crafts have been preserved throughout the region, and a stopover at Shannon will give you the chance to see craftsmen young and old at work, from roofthatchers to spinners and weavers, woodturners and potters, wheelwrights and blacksmiths, as they continue traditional ways of working.

## Bunratty Castle

The organized tours out of Shannon are an admirable way of getting a quick, comprehensive view of the area. Bunratty is the premier attraction.

Bunratty Castle, as you'll discover from the top of the keep, dominates a considerable area of Counties Clare and Limerick. That's why it was built, located on the edge of a river which formed one side of its defense and filled the moat around it. Bought by Viscount Gort in the '50s, it was restored to medieval splendour under the guidance of John Hunt (1900–1976)—Ireland's leading expert on the period—to give the place true character. The castle is most famous now for its nightly medieval banquets. You'll be welcomed by colleens in 15th-century dress, bearing the traditional bread of friendship (Irish brown bread and salt), before donning bibs and sitting down at the long tables under the presidency of an Honorary Earl chosen from among the visitors. Beakers of honey mead wash down unusual and very palatable food based on authentic medieval recipes, while the serving wenches break off to sing a few ballads or pluck the strings of a harp; high pageantry prevails. Banquets should be booked well in advance as they are extremely popular.

Just behind the Castle the little village of "old" Bunratty has been created. It's a folk village that came into being by chance when a thatched farm-

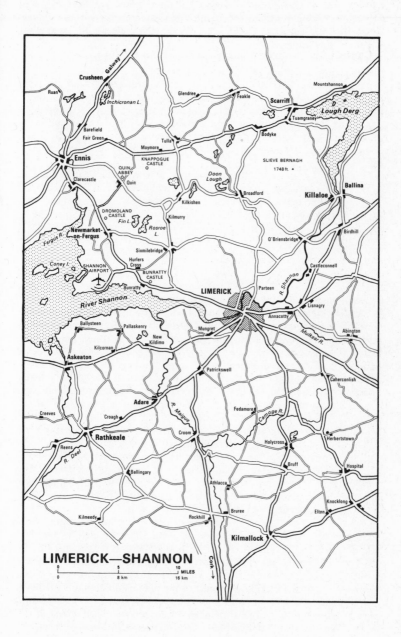

**LIMERICK—SHANNON**

house, once typical of the area, was moved here when it was in the way of a runway development at Shannon airport. It was reconstructed and furnished in its period and soon other houses were added to the village, which now has every area of the Shannon region represented, from West Clare to the Golden Vale.

The forge is a replica of one from Athea in County Limerick, and the blacksmith a skilled member of his ancient craft, still working to meet the needs of the neighborhood. There are other old crafts to be seen: the making of butter by hand in a "dash" churn, baking of delicious soda bread in a pot-oven on an open turf fire (you can get to taste the soda bread at one of the party-time tours) and lace-making. The Dean Talbot collection of over 500 antique farm implements was given to Bunratty in 1977 and some of these may be seen in action, illustrating the development of farming technology.

While old Bunratty village is a replica of 19th-century rural Ireland, just a few yards away is another village, a replica of 20th-century Ireland in the pre-War days. It's not just a museum piece, however. The shops are well-stocked and the post office fully functional. The whole place looks and feels alive. Just across the bridge from the castle is Durty Nelly's, a lively pub with imaginative old-style decor. Indeed, the pub is nearly as famous as Bunratty Castle itself, and should not be missed.

### Castles Galore

Knappogue Castle at Quin, about eight miles northwest of Bunratty, is another highlight on the Shannon castle-circuit. Knappogue, literally The Hill of the Kiss, was built in 1467 by an Irish chieftain: it now belongs to an American couple who have restored it. The Shannon people have leased the castle for 50 years specially for the presentation of medieval banquets and an entertainment in the form of a pageant of Irish history. The menu differs from that of Bunratty, but is well in line with the traditional meals served at the castle 400 years ago. Fresh garden fruits and a mild cheese of a type first made in Knappogue long ago round off the meal. To drink? Mead from fermented honey, apple juice, clover and heather for a start, and then Beaujolais from casks in the Banqueting Hall.

The third outstanding attraction on the Shannon castle-circuit, 16th-century Dunguaire Castle, is 40 miles north of Shannon at Kinvara in County Galway. Medieval banquets are held here nightly between May and September, and afterwards guests are entertained with Irish music and dancing, and readings from writers with local connections, such as W.B. Yeats, Lady Gregory, and blind Raftery, the poet.

Among the region's other principal castles is Craggaunowen, built from 1550, and situated just a few miles north of Bunratty. Erected by the Macnamaras as a fortified house, it was abandoned after it was confiscated by the Cromwellian forces in 1653. In 1965 the castle was bought from the Land Commission by John Hunt, who carried out restoration work and furnished the interior. It is now open to the public and contains medieval art objects from the Hunt collection. Hunt also created a bronze-age complex in its grounds, and this includes a full-size replica of a *crannog,* a bronze-age lake dwelling complete with replicas of bronze-age furniture, tools and utensils. The Craggaunowen Project, as it is called, also contains a reconstructed ring fort of the early-Christian period with a *souterrain,* or underground chamber.

One extremely interesting item has recently been added to the collection. This is a replica of the type of boat sailed by the 6th-century saint, Brendan the Navigator, who may have discovered the American continent many hundreds of years before Columbus. The *Brendan* was donated to the Cràggaunowen Project by Tim Severin, who not only designed and built it, but also sailed it himself to North America in 1977 to prove that Brendan's feat was possible. It is housed in a special building to ensure that the leather hull will be permanently preserved.

On the other side of the Shannon estuary, at Rathkeale, 15 miles outside Limerick City, is another of the region's 900 castles: Castle Matrix. It was built in 1440 and subsequently confiscated by Elizabeth I. It was at Castle Matrix in 1580 that the poet Edmund Spenser first met Walter Raleigh. They were both unknown 28 year-olds at the time. When Raleigh returned from his expedition to "Virginia" (nowadays North Carolina) he presented Lord Southwell of Castle Matrix with potato tubers, and Southwell carried out the first cultivation of the potato on these lands. The following year he was able to distribute tubers throughout South Munster. The castle was bought in 1962 by Colonel Sean O'Driscoll, an Irish-American architect, who restored it. It is now open to the public, and possesses a very fine library, noted for its collection of documents relating to "The Wild Geese," Irish mercenaries who served in European armies in the 17th and 18th centuries.

## The Palatinate

The area between Rathkeale and the village of Adare is still known as the Palatinate, a throwback to the days when Calvinist refugees settled there in the 18th century after the French conquest of the German Palatinate. Some of the old names still exist, but in an Irish form as the community became absorbed with the people of Limerick. Adare itself has an unusual appearance for an Irish village, largely due to the developments carried out by a 19th-century Earl of Dunraven (the family seat, Adare Manor, was sold in 1984). The town is attractively laid out with characteristics which suggest the English rather than the Irish countryside. There is also a castle here, in addition to the well-preserved ruins of a 15th-century Franciscan friary.

North of Adare, on the Askeaton–Limerick road is the Currahchase Forest Park. Currahchase House, an 18th-century building, was once the home of the poet Aubrey de Vere, whose song *The Snowy Breasted Pearl* is still popular with Irish folk singers. It is now a picturesque ruin, having been destroyed by fire in 1941. Forest walks, nature trails, a lake, an arboretum and a camping park now occupy its grounds.

## Limerick City

Limerick is the third largest city in the Republic of Ireland, with a population of 60,000. Limerick-cured hams and bacons enjoy a world-wide reputation, and the famous Limerick lace is still made in the town. It might be thought that the town's most famous "export" is the limerick itself. Intriguingly, however, there appears to be no connection whatever between the satirical five-line verse, popularized in the mid-19th century by Edward Lear, and Limerick City.

Limerick was founded in the 9th century by the Danes. In 1210 King John visited Limerick and ordered a castle and a bridge to be built. King John's castle, beside Thomond Bridge, is an imposing piece of 13th-century architecture, still pock-marked by shot from the guns of the Williamite artillery in the sieges of 1690 and 1691. The restored interior is used for Irish entertainments during the summer season.

October 1691 is an important date in Irish history, being the date of the signing of the Treaty of Limerick. The Irish forces had retreated to Limerick after defeat at the Battle of the Boyne in 1690, pursued by William of Orange at the head of a large army. William laid siege to the city, making three unsuccessful attempts to destroy it. Eventually he raised the siege, but a year later another of William's armies appeared before the walls of Limerick. After nearly two months of siege the Irish opened negotiations. These culminated in the Treaty of Limerick. Under the terms of the treaty the Irish garrison marched out and 11,000 of them later gave their allegiance to King Louis of France and fought under his standard. This was the start of the exodus known as the "Flight of the Wild Geese" in the course of which thousands of Irish soldiers entered the service of France and Spain to fight for the Catholic cause in Europe.

During the summer season Limerick's history is vividly brought alive by a *son et lumière* presentation in St. Mary's Cathedral. This was built in the 12th century when Donal Mor O'Brien donated his palace for the purpose. Parts of the palace were incorporated into the building, giving it a curious hybrid appearance. The pilasters and the Romanesque doorway of the western front, for example, were part of the original palace. The 15th-century misericords on the choir stalls are among the most interesting features of its interior; these grotesque carvings in black oak are believed to be the only pre-Elizabethan ones in the country. Limerick does, however, boast a more conventional church: St. John's, the city's Catholic Cathedral, a 19th-century Gothic building with a 280-feet high tower.

Do not be confused by talk of the "old town" and the "new town". In Limerick, much as in Edinburgh, Scotland, "Newtown" refers to an area dominated by Georgian buildings which have been there since the mid-18th century. One of these, The Granary, built in 1774 for grain storage, has been carefully restored and is now used as the main tourist office for the area. There are other fine Georgian residential buildings nearby, and an impressive Custom House.

Pery Square suggests the Limerick of a century ago, and the museum and art gallery in the nearby People's Park deserve a visit. The gallery has a good collection of Irish paintings, and the museum covers the story of Ireland as far back as the stone and bronze ages. Included among the relics of the later centuries is the Limerick "Nail," a pedestal which formerly stood outside the Exchange (now part of St. Mary's Cathedral boundary wall) in Nicholas Street, on which Limerick merchants paid their debts, giving currency to the expression "Paying on the nail" as indicating prompt payment.

Probably the most colorful of Limerick's sons and daughters, certainly the one who achieved most international fame, was Lola Montez, born Maria Dolores Eliza Rosanna Gilbert in 1818. She became a Spanish dancer; captivated King Ludwig I of Bavaria; exercised remarkable influence over the Bavarian court; appeared in New York in a couple of flops in the 1850s; married for the third time; made a theatrical tour of Australia

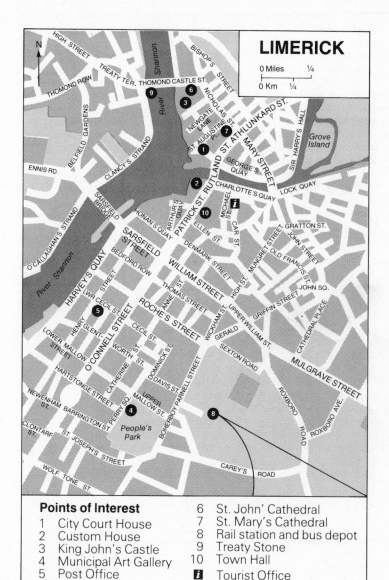

**LIMERICK**

0 Miles ¼

0 Km ¼

**Points of Interest**

1 City Court House
2 Custom House
3 King John's Castle
4 Municipal Art Gallery
5 Post Office
6 St. John' Cathedral
7 St. Mary's Cathedral
8 Rail station and bus depot
9 Treaty Stone
10 Town Hall
**i** Tourist Office

(horse-whipping a newspaper editor for questioning her character); returned to America in a few more non-successes; and then started a new career as a lecturer and writer, penning the likes of *The Art of Beauty*. She ended her days as a reformed character visiting the poor and sick, and died in Astoria, New York, in 1861, where she is commemorated by a tablet in the Greenwood Cemetery.

Among the literary figures from the Limerick area is Gerald Griffin (1803–1840) whose novel *The Collegians* was the inspiration for the Boucicault drama *The Colleen Bawn*. Griffin came across the story while attending the trial of John Scanlon in Limerick's Court House. Scanlon was charged with the murder of his wife, Ellen, and was found guilty and executed. Kate O'Brien (1897–1974), whose novels have regained popularity in recent years (*Without my Cloak* and *The Ante-Room* being the best known) was also a native of Limerick.

## Up the Shannon to Lough Derg

Fourteen miles inland from Limerick to the north, at the town of Killaloe, the Shannon widens into Lough Derg, 25 miles long and between two and three miles wide. County Clare forms its western shore, Tipperary its eastern.

Outside the city, just off the road to Killaloe, is Ard na Crusha, Ireland's first hydro-electric power station, built to take advantage of the fall in the river between Lough Derg and the sea. When it was completed in 1929 it supplied electricity to the entire country—or rather to those lucky enough to be on the national grid. Many villages in Ireland did not receive electricity until the '50s.

Plassy House, the National Institute of Higher Education, is three miles north of Limerick. It is home for a large collection of Irish antiquities—bronze-age and early-Christian pieces, medieval artifacts and 18th-century silver—donated to the nation by John Hunt, restorer of Bunratty Castle. Admission to the collection is free.

Castleconnell, just a few miles northwest of Limerick, is the place to head to for a pleasant riverside walk. It is a pretty village in a delightful setting on the Shannon. Just below Castleconnell, near an old castle originally owned by the de Burgos family, the course of the river is interrupted by a series of limestone shelves which create a long stretch of swirling shallows until the river resumes its placid course at the rock promontory of Doonass.

The marine recreation area begins at Killaloe, connected to the village of Ballina in County Tipperary by a 13-arched bridge at the point where the Shannon widens into Lough Derg. As well as being a fishing center for Lough Derg, Killaloe is a noted cruising and sailing center with over 200 berths on its marina. Motor cruisers offer day trips on Lough Derg, and in addition there are many opportunities for water-skiing, dinghy racing and sail-boarding.

Although Killaloe is little more than a village today, in the 12th century it was the ecclesiastical center of the diocese of that name. Accordingly, it boasts a fine cathedral, St. Flannan's. However, this was by no means the first church to occupy this site; indeed it is possible that the first church to have been built here stood on the site now occupied by St. Flannan's Oratory, a small 12th-century church with a high pitched stone roof and intricately-carved capitals. It is located in the churchyard of St. Flannan's. The richly carved doorway of the cathedral, restored in 1966, is thought to have been the entrance to the tomb of King Murtagh O'Brien, a Munster monarch who died in 1120. There is a fine 12th-century (east) window, while the most recent restoration has exposed an unusual medieval barrel staircase.

Another fascinating old church in Killaloe, St. Molua's Oratory, is located in the grounds of Killaloe's Catholic church. It originally stood on the little island of Inis Lua in the Shannon. When it became apparent that the island would be submerged as a result of the Ard na Crusha hydroelectric scheme, the Oratory was removed stone by stone and re-erected in its present position. The building probably dates from the 9th or 10th century.

The road north from Killaloe along the County Clare shore of Lough Derg gives good views of the lake itself and the surrounding hills. Scarriff is a noted angling center, situated on one of the prettiest parts of Lough Derg, catering for both game and coarse anglers, and Mountshannon, five miles northeast of Scariff, is a popular center in the mayfly season.

The most interesting of the islands in Lough Derg is Inis Cealtra, Holy Island, about a mile beyond Mountshannon and half a mile from the mainland. There was a monastic settlement here in the 7th century. The unusual early-Christian ruins here suggest that Holy Island was a place of rigorous self-mortification.

Feakle is a small village six miles west of Scariff, whose name will be familiar to readers of W.B. Yeats as the headquarters of the witch Biddy Early. Its churchyard contains the grave of Brian Merriman (c.1749–1805), one of the most curious figures in Irish literary history. He cultivated a small farm near Feakle to supplement his meager income as a schoolmaster. Local tradition describes him as a master of Greek, Latin and English as well as his native Irish. It is quite probable that he picked up his knowledge from the last of the wandering scholars and poets. His reputation rests on a poem of 1,206 lines, *Cúirt an Mheán Oíche (The Midnight Court),* which attacks marriage and clerical celibacy, and advocates the pleasures of "free love." It was written around 1780. His satirical gift and earthy humor made the poem widely popular in his lifetime. When it was translated into English in 1946 by Frank O'Connor it was immediately banned by the government of Eamon de Valera, the Censorship Board claiming that the poem was the product of O'Connor's "filthy imagination," and not the work of Merriman at all. Fortunately we live in more enlightened days, and Merriman's unique place in Irish literature is recognized by the Merriman Summer School, a literary event held annually in his home county.

## Ennis and West Clare

Ennis, the county town of Clare, was once linked to the seaside resorts of the Clare coast by the West Clare Railway, which was immortalized in Percy French's ballad *Are Ye Right There, Michael?* French compares the journey from Ennis to Kilkee to Columbus's crossing of the Atlantic, implying that Columbus's feat was nothing compared to the train journey. Michael was the driver of the West Clare Railway, which had a terrible reputation for punctuality and breakdowns, but a great reputation for the friendliness of its staff.

The last of the engines of the West Clare Railway, the "Slieve Callan," is now preserved in Ennis, and on taking a look at it there is almost a likelihood of truth in the tale that the guard sometimes called out: "First-class passengers keep your seats; second-class passengers, please get out and walk, third-class passengers get out and shove." Today, a bus service covers the area rather more efficiently.

Located on the banks of the river Fergus, Ennis Abbey, founded in 1241, has been very well restored and contains some fine sculptures. The key can be borrowed from Mulqueen's shop, beside the abbey grounds.

Ennis was the campaigning base of Eamon de Valera (1882–1975), the New York-born politician whose character and views dominated the Republic of Ireland in its early years, and who was later elected for two terms as President of the Republic. After the death of his Spanish-born father in America he was reared in Bruree, County Limerick, the village from which his mother, Kate Coll, had emigrated to America. His association with Ennis began in 1918, two years after he had escaped execution and been sentenced to life imprisonment for his part in the 1916 Easter Rising. He was released in 1917, and the following year elected Member of Parliament for East Clare, though he did not take his seat in the House of Commons in London. When Ireland came through its fight for independence and the subsequent civil war, de Valera displayed his skill as politician and statesman both at home and abroad.

Heading up the road northwest from Ennis for about six miles, there is an interesting stop about one and a half miles off the main road at Dysert O'Dea. The church here was founded by St. Tola, and among its impressive survivals is the fine Hiberno-Romanesque doorway and a sculptured high cross.

The Clare Heritage Center can be found at the next village on the way northwest; Corofin. It portrays the traumatic period of Irish history between 1800 and 1860 under such headings as famine, land tenure, culture, etc. Between 1851 and 1860, for example, over 100,000 people left the county, most of them to emigrate to the United States.

Just north of Corofin, on the left of the road, there is a pre-Christian cross, known as the Killinaboy Tau Cross, believed to be 2,000 years old. It is a short stump with a transom across the top, on which are two carved heads looking up at the sky, the necks meeting in the center.

In the same area is the partly-ruined Lemaneagh Castle. It consists of the tower of the original 15th-century castle and an impressive house built two centuries later. The house is beautifully proportioned with mullioned and transomed windows. The story is told that when Conor O'Brien, then the castle's owner, was killed by Cromwell's soldiers, his widow, Maíre Rua, married a Cromwellian officer to retain the castle and its land for her son. The Cromwellian is said to have had a nasty end: he fell from one of those mullioned windows with the help of a push from Maíre Rua.

## The Clare Coast

From Corofin the best plan is to head for the coast of Clare, which, with its combination of sandy beaches, dramatic cliffs, limestone caves and first-class golf courses, has provided recreation and amusement for generations of Irish vacationers. The region is much celebrated in song, indeed the area is noted for its fiddle players and step-dancers. There is excellent music to be found here, usually in the informal setting of a bar. Young musicians from Dublin and elsewhere still travel to this part of the world for the summer, learning their profession from the virtuosos of County Clare.

Lahinch has a fine sandy beach, and two 18-hole golf courses. Spanish Point, to the south of Lahinch, is a small resort with a good sandy beach and a reputation as a venue for surfing. It is named in memory of the Spaniards who were buried here when the ships of the great but doomed Spanish Armada, despatched to England by Philip II in 1588 to deal his Protestant enemies a fatal blow, were blown off course by a gale and swept around the coasts of Britain, many being wrecked along this coast. More than 1,000 men were lost, and many of their bodies were washed ashore at Spanish Point. A ship from the Armada which was wrecked on the reefs surrounding Mutton Island can be visited by *currach* from the fishing village of Quilty.

Midway between Lahinch and the cliffs of Moher is the small fishing village of Liscannor. Glahane Shore, west of the village, is a popular bathing place. The inventor of the submarine, John P. Holland (1841–1914), is Liscannor's most famous son. He was born there, but emigrated to Paterson, New Jersey in 1872. Seven years later he tested the first submarine on the Passaic River.

Northwest of Liscannor are the dramatic cliffs of Moher which rise vertically out of the sea in a five-mile wall that varies in height from 440 to 700 feet, reaching its highest point at O'Brien's tower, a circular structure erected in 1835. There is now an Information Center for visitors in the tower which is open from mid-March to October. On a clear day the Aran Islands are visible from the cliffs, the closest being Inisheer, the smallest. Inishmore, the largest, is the most distant, while Inishmaan lies between the two. There are large seabird colonies of guillemots, puffins, razorbills and kittiwakes on the cliffs.

## Lisdoonvarna and the Burren

Lisdoonvarna, 10 miles up the coast and slightly inland from Lahinch, is a spa town with several sulfurous and iron bearing springs, all containing iodine and all with radioactive properties. The principal sulfur springs are at Gowlane on the south side of town, one of the area's "Twin Wells," where a sulfur and an iron water spring flow out of the rocks within a few inches of each other.

Lisdoonvarna is thronged with young visitors on the first weekend in August when a large open-air folk music festival takes place. Its traditional season, however, is in the fall, after the harvest is gathered in. The town has always had a great reputation for matchmaking, and still fosters the idea that it is a good place to find a prospective mate. Their annual personality and talent contest for bachelors provides the whole country with great entertainment when the televised finals are broadcast.

Lisdoonvarna is a handy base from which to explore both the coast and the Burren. Five miles southeast of Lisdoonvarna in the town of Kilfenora is the Burren Display Center, a visit to which will greatly enhance the nonspecialist's appreciation of a unique natural phenomenon. This extensive region of over 100 square miles is noted for its extraordinary rock formations. At first glance the region appears barren and lifeless—a kind of lunar landscape. One visitor who was taken in by its appearance was General Ludlow, who led the Cromwellian forces into Clare in 1651. He said that the Burren was a "country where there is not water enough to drown a man, wood enough to hang one, or earth enough to bury him." In fact below the carboniferous limestone surface lie spectacular caves, streams and potholes with many *turloughs,* seasonal lakes which appear and disappear. The flowers and plants of the Burren have made it famous among botanists, who are particularly intrigued by the co-habitation of Mediterranean and arctic-alpine plants. The flora of the Burren is at its best about mid-May.

Ailwee Cave, signposted off the road to Ballyvaughan, is situated in one of the most beautiful parts of the Burren. The cave was discovered as recently as 1944 by a local farmer, and it is the only cave of the many in the region which has been developed for tourist purposes and made accessible to those without spelunking expertise. The caves are paved and lit throughout and the visitor can penetrate 1,120 yards into the mysterious underworld of the Burren.

The road from Ballyvaughan to the west hugs the coast of Galway Bay and swings away from the Burren over the county line into Galway and the beginning of another journey of exploration.

# PRACTICAL INFORMATION FOR SHANNON

**TOURIST OFFICES.** The main tourist office for the Shannon area is at **Limerick City** in The Granary (built 1774 and worth a visit), Michael St. (tel. 061–317522). There are other offices at **Adare,** tel. 061–86255 (open June to Aug.); **Cliffs of Moher,** tel. 065–81171 (open May to Sept.); **Ennis,** tel. 065–28366 (open May to Sept.); **Kilkee,** tel. 065–56112 (open June to Aug.); **Lisdoonvarna,** tel. 065–74062 (open July to Sept.); **Lough Gur,** tel. 061–85186 (open May to Sept.); **Shannon Airport,** tel. 061–61664/04 (open year-round).

## HOTELS AND RESTAURANTS

**Adare** (Co. Limerick). *Dunraven Arms* (M), tel. 061–86209. 44 rooms with bath. Comfortable, with hunting associations—four packs hold meets in the neighborhood. Good restaurant. AE, DC, MC, V.

**Restaurant.** *The Mustard Seed* (E), tel. 061–86451. Old-world village house with original Irish kitchen. AE, DC, MC, V.

**Ballyvaughan** (Co. Clare). *Gregan's Castle* (E), tel. 065–77005. 16 rooms, most with bath. Updated castle in the Burren country, overlooking Galway Bay and mountains and close to the Ailwee Caves. AE, DC, MC, V.

**Restaurant.** *Claire's* (M), tel. 065–77029. Small and intimate. AE, DC, MC, V.

**Bunratty** (Co. Clare). *Fitzpatrick's Shannon Shamrock* (E), tel. 061–361177. 100 rooms, all with bath. Attractive ranch-style hotel, very well run, in the grounds of the 15th-century Bunratty Castle. Indoor heated pool. Convenient for Shannon Airport. AE, DC, MC, V.

**Restaurants.** *Bunratty Castle,* tel. 061–61788, and *Knappogue Castle,* at Quin, a few miles away (tel. 061–61788), are the locations for medieval banquets and entertainments. A great night out, but do book first. AE, DC, MC, V. *Durty Nelly's,* just across the bridge from Bunratty Castle. A popular spot for a drink, a laugh and maybe a song. *MacCloskey's* (E), Bunratty House Mews, just behind Bunratty Castle (tel. 061–364082). Specializes in table d'hôte dinners. AE, DC, MC, V.

**Ennis** (Co. Clare). *Old Ground* (E), tel. 065–28127. 60 rooms with bath. A gracious old building, carefully updated and extended. AE, DC, MC, V. *Auburn Lodge* (M), on the Galway road (tel. 065–21247). 40 rooms with bath. Friendly; family-owned and managed. AE, DC, MC, V. *West County Inn* (M), tel. 065–28421. 110 rooms with bath. On fringe of Ennis. AE, DC, MC, V.

**Restaurants.** *Brogan's* (M), 24 O'Connell St. (tel. 065–29859). In the center of town with a cheerful fire. AE, DC, MC, V. *The Cloister* (M), Abbey St. (tel. 065–29521). Old-world bar, and restaurant with patio garden. AE, DC, MC, V.

**Fanore** (Co. Clare). *Admiral's Rest* (I), tel. 065–76105. 10 rooms, 3 with bath. On Burren coast road. Angling, caving, scuba and wildlife tours arranged by proprietor, John Macnamara. Good restaurant (I), open May–Oct. MC, V.

**Kilkee** (Co. Clare). *Whelan's Thomond* (M), tel. 065–56025. 23 rooms, 8 with bath. *Halpins's* (I), tel. 065–56032. 11 rooms, some with bath.

**Restaurant.** *Manuel's Seafood* (M), Corbally (tel. 065–56211). Small but good. Manuel catches the fish and his wife cooks it. There's a choice of 10 main seafood courses, but if you're not a fish eater, there are other dishes. AE, DC, MC, V.

**Killaloe** (Co. Clare). *Lakeside* (M), tel. 061–76122. 32 rooms with bath. Recently upgraded with new dining room and a lounge looking out over Lough Derg, the beginning of the navigable Shannon waterway to the north. AE, DC, MC, V.

**Lahinch** (Co. Clare). *Aberdeen Arms* (M), tel. 065–81100. 48 rooms, all with bath. Good hotel with a long-standing reputation. Also an excellent place to eat. AE, DC, MC. *Atlantic* (I), tel. 065–81049. 15 rooms, most with bath. Restaurant with home-cooked food. *Sancta Maria* (I), tel. 065–81041. 18 rooms, 12 with bath.

**Limerick** (Co. Limerick). *Jury's Hotel* (E), Ennis Rd. (tel. 061–55266). 96 rooms, all with bath. Three minutes' walk from city center. Bar, café, restaurant. AE, DC, MC, V. *Limerick Inn* (E), Ennis Rd. (tel. 061–51544). 153 rooms, all with bath. Located half-way between Killarney and Connemara, beside the Shannon. AE, DC, MC, V. *Limerick Ryan* (E), Ennis Rd. (tel. 061–53922). 184 rooms, all with bath. On the road to Shannon Airport. AE, DC, MC, V. *Cruise's Royal* (M), tel. 061–44977. 73 rooms, all with bath. On the main street.

*New Greenhills* (M), tel. 061–53033. 55 rooms, all with bath. Excellent gourmet restaurant. AE, DC, MC, V. *Woodfield House* (M), Ennis Rd. (tel. 061–53023). 25 rooms, most with bath. Retains old-world atmosphere. AE, DC, MC, V. *Royal George* (I), tel. 061–44566. 58 rooms with bath. On main street. AE, DC, MC, V.

**Restaurants.** *Copper Room* (E), Jury's Hotel (tel. 061–55266). Award-winning classical French cuisine. AE, DC, MC, V. *The Granary Tavern* (M), Charlotte Quay (tel. 061–47266). In an updated 18th-century granary. A good lively spot featuring Irish music. AE, DC, MC. *Olde Tom Restaurant and Bar* (I), 19 Thomas St. (tel. 061–45961). Irish food with Irish music and dancing. City center. MC, V. *Peter's Cell* (I), downstairs at the *Belltable Arts Center.* Good for snacks and hot lunches.

**Lisdoonvarna** (Co. Clare). *Carrigan's* (I), tel. 065–74036. 12 rooms, most with bath. *Hydro* (I), tel. 065–74027. 70 rooms with bath. *Imperial* (I), tel. 065–74015. 53 rooms, most with bath. *Keane's* (I), tel. 065–74011. 12 rooms, 7 with bath. Mary Keane is an authority on the geologically interesting Burren region, to which Lisdoonvarna is a gateway. *Sheedy's Spa View* (I), tel. 065–74026. 11 rooms with bath. Friendly and family-run with open, turf fires. Tennis.

**Restaurant.** *Bruach na Haille* (M), Roadford, Doolin (tel. 065–74120). Pretty cottage restaurant outside town near the Cliffs of Moher. Varied and imaginative menu. V.

**Newmarket-on-Fergus** (Co. Clare). *Dromoland Castle* (L), tel. 061–71144. 73 rooms with bath. The present castle was built early in the last century and transformed into a luxury hotel about 20 years ago. Excellent sports facilities on 350 acres of land. AE, DC, MC, V. *Clare Inn* (E), tel. 061–71161. 106 rooms, all with bath. Located on the same estate, with a fine view across the river Fergus. Also has the same sports facilities. AE, DC, MC, V.

**Shannon Airport** (Co. Clare). *Shannon International* (M), tel. 061–61122. 118 rooms, all with bath. Good restaurant. AE, DC, MC, V.

### Youth Hostels

**Doolin,** Doolin Hostels, Doolin/Roadford, near Lisdoonvarna (tel. 065–74006). **Limerick,** 1 Pery Sq., Co. Limerick (tel. 061–314672). **Liscannor,** Village Hostel (tel. 065–81385). **Mountshannon,** Co. Clare (tel. 0619–27209).

**HOW TO GET AROUND.** In Limerick, C.I.E. operates buses with a flat fare system of about 60 pence for any distance within the city limits. Outside the city, fares vary.

Bicycles can be hired at the *Bike Shop,* O'Connell Ave., Limerick City (tel. 061–315900), and also at *Limerick Sports Store,* 10 William St., Limerick City (tel. 061–45647).

Exploration on horseback can be arranged with *The Willy Daly Riding Center,* Ballingaddy, Ennistymon, Co. Clare (tel. 065–71385). They also offer residential riding holidays.

**TOURS AND EXCURSIONS.** There are a number of tours based on Shannon Airport operated by Shannon Castle Tours and the Gray Line, going to the Cliffs of Moher, Cork City and the Blarney Stone, Galway City and Connemara. Tours are also arranged to include an "Irish Night" in Bunratty Folk Park, or medieval banquets at Bunratty or Knappogue Castle. There are also longer tours run by the Gray Line based on Shannon.

There's a Clare Postbus which carries passengers as well as mail from Ennis to outlying spots as far as Lisdoonvarna on the County Clare coast. The bus serves a number of interesting villages, including Lahinch and Liscannor on the way out and Kilfenora and Corofin on the return journey. Check locally for times. Minimum fare is around 50 pence, and for the round trip about IR£3. This is a great way to meet the people and see the Clare countryside. Only one trip on Saturday, none on Sunday.

## PLACES TO VISIT

**Ballyvaughan** (Co. Clare). **Ailwee Cave.** Guided tours into the underworld of Burren—1,120 yards can be traveled in a cave formed millions of years ago. Entry by the Ailwee Cave Visitor Center in the hillside. Open mid-Mar. to end-Sept., Sat. 10–5, Sun. 2–5; 1 Oct. to mid-Mar., Sat., Sun. and public holidays 10–3.

**Bunratty** (Co. Clare). **Bunratty Castle and Folk Park.** Castle was the stronghold of the Princes of Thomond and is the most complete and authentic medieval castle in Ireland, now restored to give an idea of 15th- and 16th-century life. Castle has good collection of art, furniture and tapestries. The Folk Park in the grounds of the castle has farm buildings and craft shops restored and furnished to show 19th-century Irish life. Medieval banquets are served here. Open daily 9.30–5. From 1 June to 15 Sept., Folk Park is open until 7 P.M. Medieval banquets twice nightly at 5.45 and 8.45 (tel. 061–61788).

**Kilfenora** (Co. Clare). **Burren Display Center.** Audio-visual presentation includes a model landscape explaining the karst limestone terrain of the Burren and its fauna. Don't miss the interesting ruins of the tiny Kilfenora Cathedral and the stone crosses behind the center. Open mid-Mar. to 31 Oct., daily 10–5.45; 1 May to 31 Aug. closes at 6.45.

**Limerick City** (Co. Limerick). **Belltable Arts Center,** 69 O'Connell St. (tel. 061–319866). Theater and regular art exhibitions. Open Mon. to Sat. 10–9.

**Good Shepherd Convent,** Clare St. For Limerick lace. Open Mon. to Sat. 9–6.

**King John's Castle.** Built in the 13th century and still in a reasonable state. Irish entertainment on summer evenings (tel. 061–47522).

**Limerick Municipal Art Gallery,** Pery Sq. (tel. 061–314668). Open Mon. to Fri. 10–1 and 2.30–8, Sat. 10–1.

**St. Mary's Cathedral.** Built in the 12th century. Has *son et lumière* presentations of Limerick history (tel. 061–46238).

**Moher** (Co. Clare). **Cliffs of Moher,** near Liscannor. Cliffs rise vertically 700 ft. out of the Atlantic. Best view from O'Brien's Tower. The Visitor Center provides interesting exhibitions. Center is open 1 Mar. to 28 Oct., Mon. to Fri. 10–6, Sun. 12–6.

**Plassey** (Co. Limerick). **National Gallery of Self-Portraits.** On the campus of the National Institute of Higher Education, Limerick. Growing collection of self-portraits.

**Castletroy** (Co. Limerick). **Hunt Collection,** National Institute of Higher Education, Plassey (tel. 061–333644). Collection of 1,000 Irish and European treasures (archeology, painting, sculpture). Well worth seeing.

**Corbally** (Co. Clare). **Coosheen Folk Museum,** near Kilkee (tel. Kilkee 112). Displays historic domestic artifacts.

**Corofin** (Co. Clare). **Clare Heritage Center.** Helps visitors to understand rural life a century ago. Offers help in tracing ancestors from Clare. Open 17 Mar. to 31 Oct., daily 10–6. Other times by appointment.

**Currahchase** (Co. Limerick). **Currahchase Forest Park.** Located 13 miles from Limerick on route N69. The house, now derelict, was the home of the poet Aubrey de Vere (1814–1902). Signposted nature trails on 568 acres.

**Ennis** (Co. Clare). **Ennis Friary.** Franciscan friary founded in 13th century by the king of Thomond. Striking stone carvings. Open mid-June to mid-Sept., daily 10–6. Rest of the year, key with caretaker.

**Glin** (Co. Limerick). **Glin Castle,** Glin. Georgian-Gothic castle noted for neo-Classical plasterwork and collection of 18th-century Irish paintings and furniture. Castle open during May, daily 10–12 and 2–4 and to groups by appointment (tel. 068–54173).

**Quin** (Co. Clare). **Craggaunowen Project.** Full-scale replica of bronze-age lake dwelling, containing replicas of furniture, tools and utensils. Also has a replica of the boat in which St. Brendan made his voyages in the 6th century. This replica was sailed to America in 1976–7. Located about six miles east of Quin. Open Apr., May, Sept. and Oct., daily 10–5; 1 June to 31 Aug., daily 10–6.

**Knappogue Castle.** Built in 1467 as the home of the Macnamara Clan. Original Norman structure has later additions. Medieval banquets are held here in carefully restored setting. Open 1 Apr. to 31 Oct., daily 9.30–5.30. Banquets twice nightly 1 May to 31 Oct., 5.45 and 8.45 (tel. 061–61788).

**Quin Abbey.** Franciscan foundation of the 15th century, built with stones from an old castle on the site. Cloisters are the best-preserved of their type in Ireland.

**Rathkeale** (Co. Limerick). **Castle Matrix.** Built in 1440; has authentic furnishings, objets d'art. First potatoes in Ireland grown here. Castle and grounds open 1 June to 1 Sept., Sat. to Tues. 1–5. Other times by arrangement (tel. 069–64284).

**Scariff** (Co. Clare). **Tuamgraney Church.** Said to be the oldest church in Ireland still in use. Part built in 10th century, part built 200 years later.

# THE WARMTH OF THE WEST

## *Where the Next Parish Is America*

North of County Clare is the ancient province of Connacht, the area generally known as the west of Ireland. It is the most westerly seaboard in Europe and has always been something of a place apart, where the old ways die hard. It is a land of romantic, empty landscapes, and rugged, craggy coastlines. Its isolation goes a long way toward explaining the survival of Gaelic here. Indeed, the area boasts a genuinely bi-lingual culture, and the daily inter-action of English and Irish gives a freshness to the way of life, continuing to produce a unique cultural mix.

The people of the west are proud and hospitable: when they say *"Cead Mile Fáilte,"* they really do mean that you are a thousand times welcome. But like many other parts of Ireland, the west has known its sorrows and hardships, and the "Hungry Forties" saw vast numbers of emigrants leave in search of a new and brighter future, with many a shipload of families sailing from Galway for America and Canada.

Electricity has long since come to the homes of the west, but in some more rural areas the traditional turf, or peat, fire is still maintained. It is very much a symbol of family continuity and hospitality, and in a traditional home is never allowed to go out. The thin line of blue smoke rising from the chimney of a hillside cottage is a welcoming sign, and you can be sure that as soon as you cross the threshold you will be offered "a drop of tea" from the pot brewing on the hob.

The west is an area of strong contrasts, from the rustic simplicity of life on the Aran Islands to the sophisticated pleasures of a modern seaside resort like Salthill. You can still find many people eking out a living on the family "farm"—10 or 12 acres providing little more than a subsistence level of income. At the same time other parts of the region have marched confidently into the high-tech era, with a good many modern industries establishing themselves, the result of a successful Government campaign to bring new prosperity to a traditionally poor area of Ireland. Nonetheless, the region remains predominantly agricultural.

Eastern, inland Galway is extremely fertile, but to the north of the county the land becomes rocky and barren. Fishing continues to be a major industry, with both deep-sea trawlers and many smaller craft fishing the teeming waters of the Atlantic. At the same time, the traditional craft industries of weaving and knitting remain of economic importance in the area.

Beyond Galway City, between Lough Corrib and the Atlantic, lies Connemara, a land of great beauty and loneliness, where you will discover that mountains really can look blue. The water in the bog streams is every shade from pale tan to a dark translucent brown, and white limestone punctuates the landscape. Not surprisingly, the beauty of the area has attracted many of Ireland's finest painters, among them Sean Keating (1889–1977), Maurice McGonigal (1900–79) and Jack B. Yeats (1871–1957). The preservation of an older way of life attracted many writers to the area in the early part of this century including John Millington Synge (1871–1909), who drew the inspiration for his play *Riders to the Sea* from the Aran Islands. Later, John Ford's marvellously evocative film, *The Quiet Man* (1952), starring John Wayne and Maureen O'Hara, was made here.

## Galway City

Galway City, by some way the largest city of the west, is an ancient town, well-established even before the Anglo-Normans arrived in the 13th century. It was founded by a Celtic king whose daughter, Galvia—the ancient Irish name for the city—drowned in Lough Corrib. To commemorate her, the king established a camp on the spot. The Normans transformed Galway when they arrived, rebuilding the city walls and turning the little town into a flourishing port. Among these early settlers were the "14 Tribes of Galway:" the families of Athy, Blake, Bodkin, Browne, D'Arcy, Deane, ffont (or Fant), French, Joyce, Kirwan, Lynch, Martin, Morris, and Skerret. Their coats of arms can still be found in many places in the city and their names are still among the most common in Galway. However, the Normans never quite came to terms with the hostile and war-like Irish, who raided Galway persistently. An inscription over the West Gate still bears the heartfelt legend, "From the fury of the O'Flahertys good Lord protect us." The persistent fighting and raiding of the Irish here were, many years later, to lead Oliver Cromwell, no friend of the Irish it must be said, to claim that Galway and Hell were the only suitable places for the Irish.

Interestingly, over the centuries the town developed important trading links with Spain and France: Spanish Parade and Spanish Arch are among the city's relics of the period. In 1484 Galway's prosperity and importance were underlined further when King Richard III granted the city a royal charter, an event celebrated in fine style in 1984, the 500th anniversary of the charter.

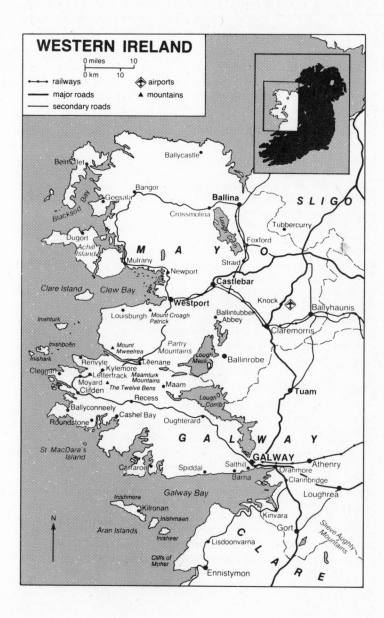

## Exploring Galway City

The city is compact and easily explored on foot, using Eyre Square, with its Great Southern Hotel, as a base. In 1963, following the visit of President Kennedy to Galway, the square was renamed Kennedy Square, but has since reverted to its original name. The square was named after the Eyre family who built it. In 1709 they also donated a five-foot silver mace to the city. The mace and a 17th-century ceremonial sword were subsequently given to Mayor Edmund Blake, in lieu of money owed to him. Ninety years later, his daughter sold the heirlooms to an art dealer and, in turn, they were bought by American newspaper tycoon William Randolph Hearst for $14,000. Just before his death in 1951, he gave instructions that the regalia, then at his ranch home in California, should be given to Galway. Nine years later they were duly handed back to the city.

In one corner of the square there is a statue of a little old man with a battered hat. He is Padraic O'Conaire (1882–1923), a Galway-born story-teller of great renown. In 1984 another monument was added to O'Conaire's corner: a steel fountain representing the sails of a traditional Galway Bay sailing craft, a Galway Hooker.

The road to the left of the square leads on past Lynch's Castle (today a bank), an interesting 16th-century tower house. The design is unusual for Ireland and it still bears the arms of King Henry VII of England and the Lynch family, famous among the old tribes of Galway. A member of the Lynch family may have added the word "lynch" to the language when he hanged his son, the executioner having refused to perform the duty, for murdering a Spanish guest in his house. The gruesome event is commemorated by a marble stone set in a wall by a walled-up door, near the Collegiate Church of St. Nicholas, which recalls "the stern and unbending justice of Chief Magistrate of this city, James Lynch FitzStephen, elected Mayor 1493, who condemned and executed his own guilty son, Walter, on this spot."

The neighboring church in Lombard Street, officially the Collegiate Church of St. Nicholas of Myra, dates back to 1320, although it has many later additions. Its interior is unusual because the aisles are wider than the nave. Underlining Galway's Spanish connection, it is believed that Christopher Columbus prayed here before sailing westwards in the *Santa Maria*. The story does not suggest that it was on his history-making journey of 1492, but it is probable that he visited the port at some earlier time. There is evidence in the records of Columbus' journey that his crew included a man from Galway.

In nearby Chapel Lane is the Druid Theater. It started as a pub theater with only 110 seats, and has recently moved to new premises in a converted warehouse seating 350. Its standards of presentation and performance are outstanding. Productions appear regularly in Dublin and at the Edinburgh Festival, and some have transferred successfully to London's West End.

The new Cathedral of Our Lady Assumed into Heaven and St. Nicholas is built on the site of the old Galway jail. It is of cut limestone, with Connemara marble flooring, and was officially dedicated in August 1965 by the late Cardinal Cushing of Boston. It combines classical and traditional Irish designs and impressively dominates the Galway skyline.

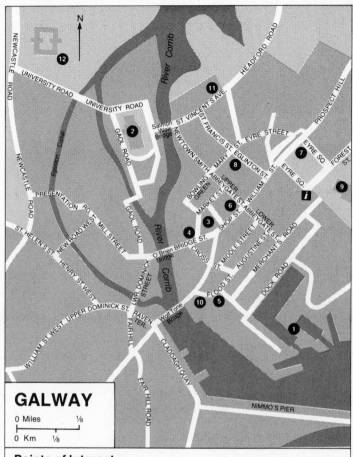

**GALWAY**

0 Miles     ⅛

0 Km     ⅛

### Points of Interest

1   Aran Passenger Terminal
2   Cathedral
3   Church of St. Nicholas
4   Galway Market
5   Galway City Museum
6   Lynch's Castle
7   Padraic O'Conaire statue

8   Post Office
9   Rail and bus station
10   Spanish Arch
11   Town Hall
12   University College

**𝒊**   Tourist Office

Beside the Cathedral is the Salmon Wier Bridge which provides one of Galway's most interesting sights. In season shoals of salmon lie in the clear water beneath the bridge before making their way upstream to the spawning grounds of Lough Corrib. The weir can be fished for a fee.

On the west bank of the Corrib estuary is the Claddagh, said to be the oldest fishing village in Ireland. It retained its Irish identity outside the walls of the Anglo-Norman city for many years. Today it is no longer Irish-speaking, nor dependent on fishing, and the traditional thatched cottages have long since been replaced by more conventional housing, but the Claddagh has nevertheless retained many of its old traditions. Among them is the famous Claddagh ring, apparently medieval in origin. The ring depicts a heart and two hands clasped in friendship and, until marriage, is worn with the point of the heart facing the fingertip. Once married, the ring is then reversed. It is still made by Galway goldsmiths, though in many families the ring is handed down from mother to daughter.

Another marvelous old tradition is the Blessing of the Fleet, which takes place every year before the opening of the herring season in mid-August. The fishing fleet, decorated with flags, moves slowly down Galway Bay with the leading ship carrying a priest from the Dominican Priory in Claddagh. At an appointed place the fleet stops, the sails are lowered and the Blessing of the Fleet and the Sea takes place. At around the same time of year there is a race across the bay from Kinvara to the Connemara coast between a large number of turf-carrying Galway Hookers. Hookers are no longer used to transport turf, but the race is still held in the old style.

Galway's Race Week in late-July and early-August is one of the most popular events on the Irish horse-racing calendar, with side-shows and funfairs providing plenty of added amusement. The bar at the Galway race track is reputed to be the longest bar in Britain or Ireland, measuring 210 feet. Ballybrit, as the race track is called, gained a new significance for many people in 1979 when it was used as the site for the Young People's Mass which was celebrated by Pope John Paul II during his historic visit to Galway. It was the first visit by the present Pope, as Pope, to any country outside his native Poland. His stark Papal message to the youth of the world—"I love you!"—was delivered here and relayed internationally by television. A simple memorial stands on the actual site in Ballybrit where the Papal Mass was celebrated.

A little further west along the coast is the bustling seaside resort of Salthill, which offers a variety of amenities for holiday-makers, including an 18-hole golf course. Salthill Promenade is the traditional place to go and watch the sunset over Galway Bay: "To sit and watch the moon rise over Claddagh, and see the sun go down on Galway Bay" in the words of the city's most famous song.

## The Aran Islands

The three Aran Islands lie 30 miles out to sea from Galway, and can be reached by ferry from Galway City and Rossaveale, or by air from Oranmore Airport near Galway. The sturdy fisherfolk of the Aran Islands have preserved some of their traditional ways, and a visit to the islands will be a memorable experience.

The islands—Inishmore (the largest), Inishmaan and Inisheer—are rugged and barren. The islanders have made soil from sand and seaweed over the years, eking out a living from a few acres of such land and the surrounding sea. Some of the fishermen still use *currachs*—traditional boats made of thin strips of wood, or laths, covered with tarred canvas.

About two-thirds of the islands' population of 1,500 live on Inishmore, whose main town is Kilronan. Irish is the native language of the islanders, though English is also widely spoken. Perhaps the most famous export of the islands today are hand-knitted Aran sweaters, with intricate designs and symbols, and made of white wool (*bainín* in Irish—pronounce it "bawneen"). They have been worn here for generations, only lately becoming fashionable. The origin of their intricate designs gives some idea of the sort of hardships endured by islanders through the ages: a body lost at sea could be identified by the pattern on its sweater, as each district of each island had its own special pattern. Often indeed this was the only means of identification.

Until quite recently, the women of Aran wore thick red woolen skirts to keep out the Atlantic winds, and the men dressed in homespun tweeds with *pampooties,* a hide shoe without a heel suitable for walking on rocks, and a wide woven belt called a *crios.* Nowadays only a few old men wear traditional dress. But the people of Aran are still proud of their identity as an Irish-speaking community and of the simple island way of life. The visitor will find a quite different atmosphere from the mainland. There is virtually no traffic on the two smaller islands, and recreation consists of an evening stroll, a chat with the neighbors and, in some cases, a visit to the pub.

The islands, like the Burren, are of limestone Karst, and share the same unusual flora and abundant bird life. The islands are explored by walking along narrow paths between high stone walls. There is good, safe bathing from the rocks and beaches, and there can be few places as unspoilt and uncrowded in which to enjoy the outdoor life. There are also some remarkable archeological remains, including the great fort of Dun Aengus, perched on the edge of a 300-foot cliff.

## South of Galway City

Gort, the main market town of south Galway, is situated just north of the border with County Clare in a natural gap between the Slieve Aughtry mountains and the Burren. Its hinterland is rich in historical and natural curiosities.

The 7th-century king Guaire, who lived in Gort and gave his name to the splendid castle of Dún Guaire on Galway Bay (now a center for nightly medieval banquets and Anglo-Irish literary entertainment), in a less martial mood gave one of his relations the site for a cathedral about three miles southwest of Gort at Kilmacduagh. It was replaced in the 15th century by a new cathedral, which can still be seen. Don't worry about your eyesight if you have the impression that the neighboring Round Tower is leaning like Italy's Tower of Pisa. It is about two feet out of perpendicular.

Gort has many literary associations with the so-called Irish Renaissance, which took place in the late-19th and early-20th centuries when a group of predominantly Anglo-Irish intellectuals re-discovered native Irish culture.

The poet William Butler Yeats (1865–1939) was among their number, and lived near Gort at Thoor Ballylee during the latter part of his life.

Thoor Ballylee—or Ballylee Castle, to give it its official name—was one of 32 Norman towers built here by the de Burgo family. Yeats bought it for the princely sum of £35, the price including two cottages and a walled garden.

He came across the tower during a visit to Lady Augusta Gregory at her home at Coole House, Gort. Lady Augusta, a formidable figure by any reckoning, played a prominent part in the Celtic revival and was for long an important patroness of Yeats himself. Sadly her house has now been pulled down, and a few ruined walls and some stables are all that are left today. But the estate has been preserved and has beautiful forest walks and gardens that can be enjoyed. The highlight of Coole for literary-minded visitors is Lady Gregory's famous autograph tree. It was Lady Gregory's wish that her many famous guests should carve their names or initials on a particular tree. There they remain, some a bit distorted by age and the weather: George Bernard Shaw, Sean O'Casey, George Moore, John Masefield, Augustus John, Oliver St. John Gogarty, the art collector Hugh Lane, and Douglas Hyde, the first president of Ireland, among many others.

The coast of south Galway is famed for its oyster beds. The road from Gort to Oranmore passes through Clarinbridge, the village which hosts Galway's annual Oyster Festival in September. The late Paddy Burke, of Paddy Burke's Oyster Tavern, founded the festival to draw attention to the superlative product of the village's oyster beds, which have justly become world famous. A glass of Guinness is the traditional accompaniment to oysters in this part of the world.

### West to Connemara

Romantic and evocative Connemara is the name of the western part of County Galway between Lough Corrib and the Atlantic, dominated by the rocky Twelve Bens mountain range. It is a sparsely populated region of superb scenic grandeur, with dramatic changes of color and mood. The ever-changing combinations of sea, sky, mountain and lake have inspired many famous painters and writers over the years. A large part of the area is Irish-speaking and much of the rich linguistic, musical and folkloric heritage has been maintained.

Connemara is also famous for its fishing. Lough Corrib provides the largest free fishing waters in Europe, and salmon, pike and perch abound in the waters of this island-studded lake.

Many people who have never seen Connemara have heard of Connemara ponies. This sturdy little breed is seen at its best at the Connemara Pony Show which is held each August in Clifden. The famous Connemara Pony Stud Farm at Adrahan in Galway was bought in 1983 by an American, Mrs. Kieran Breedan.

### Exploring Connemara

There are two routes into Connemara from Galway City, of which the most scenic is that along the coast. Be warned, however, that not all road signs are in English, so it is as well to take along a good map.

We explore the coastal road first. Barna, to the west of Galway City, marks the beginning of the Connemara Gaeltacht, the Irish-speaking re-

gion. Smallholdings and fields enclosed by stone walls indicate the continuing importance of home-steading for many of the community.

The local preference for building thoughtlessly-sited, flamboyant modern bungalows has been much criticized by conservationists, who claim
that such architecture is totally inappropriate and is ruining an area of
great scenic beauty. The coast road will give you plenty of opportunities
to make up your own mind about this particular aspect of modern Ireland.

Spiddal, the next village along the coast, has a good sheltered beach.
Spiddal, or An Spidéal to give it its Irish name, has one of the country's
oldest Irish summer colleges, founded in 1909. It attracts hundreds of students between June and August, and organizes musical and cultural events
throughout the year.

The road continues west past rocky headlands and bays, skirting a number of small characteristic villages, to Carna, an important lobster fishing
center. A little off the coast from Carna is MacDara's Island, or Oileán
MacDara. It is the most famous of the many small and mostly uninhabited
islands on this stretch of coast as it is home to a small ruined church and,
more importantly, the grave of St. MacDara. He is greatly honored by
the people of the region and a three-day festival is held around his saint's
day in July. In the past fishermen used to dip their sails three times as
they sailed by the "holy island."

Just up the coast from Carna is Cashel, a good angling center. Its name
is derived from the circular stone fort here, remains of which lie on the
slope of a mountain just outside the northeast side of the village. Cashel,
and the next two villages along the coast, Roundstone and Ballyconneely,
are quiet holiday resorts. Towering above Roundstone is Errisberg mountain, with excellent views from its summit of the lake-dotted countryside
to the north and magnificent seascapes in other directions. Mannin Bay,
near Ballyconneely, has a beautiful coral strand and other good beaches
for swimming.

## Taking the Straight Road

The main road from Galway City into Connemara—the N59—is rather
less interesting until it reaches Oughterard, an important angling center
on Lough Corrib. Boats can be hired for excursions to the many wooded
islands studding the lake. It is an excellent center for exploring the beauty
spots of the Twelve Bens, the Maamturk and Cloosh mountains.

The road to the west from Oughterard runs beside a string of small lakes
between the two mountain ranges mentioned above to Maam Cross, traditionally the site of a big monthly cattle fair, which still survives to some
extent. The next village on the road, Recess, is beautifully situated beside
Lough Glendalough and beneath Lissoughter Mountain. This is the
mountain from which the famous green Connemara marble is quarried.
From Recess to Clifden the road runs under the shadow of the Twelve
Bens, easily identifiable by their conical tops, and follows the shore of
Lough Ballinahinch.

Near Recess, on the southern shore of Lough Ballinahinch, there is a
castle which was once the home of the remarkable Richard Martin
(1754–1834), a duelist of renown, known in his youth as Hairtrigger Dick.
He became known in later years as Humanity Dick because of his interest
in the welfare of animals; indeed he was one of the founders of the Royal
Society for the Prevention of Cruelty to Animals.

Clifden is the principal town of Connemara, and has an almost Alpine setting, nestling on the edge of the Atlantic with a spectacular mountain backdrop. Two beautiful churches dominate the town when viewed from a distance. The Protestant church, built in 1820, is a fine elegant structure. The Catholic church, built in 1830, stands on the site of the ancient *clochán* from which the town takes its name. Clifden is a popular base for visitors touring the western part of Connemara.

Letterfrack, nine miles north of Clifden, is a charming village in beautiful surroundings, founded by the Quakers, or the Society of Friends, in the last century as one of a series of missions along the Connemara coast. This area is now part of the Connemara National Park. Short graveled walks have been laid out, one of which, from Letterfrack to the top of Diamond Hill, gives superb views of mountain, sea and lake.

Kylemore, just a little way up the road, is an enchanting valley with three lovely lakes well stocked with salmon and sea trout. The wooded mountains rise almost perpendicularly from the lake shore, and on the lower slopes is the magnificent many-turreted castle built by Mitchell Henry, M.P. between 1864 and 1868. This fairy-tale like castle is now a convent of the Benedictine nuns of Ypres. Displayed in the great hall is a flag captured by the Irish Brigade in the French Royal Army at the Battle of Fontenoy (1745). Visitors are welcome to the restaurant, pottery showrooms and the beautiful grounds.

The fishing village of Cleggan, seven miles northwest of Clifden on the coast road, is the gateway to Inishbofin, Inishturk and Inishark, three small islands containing much of interest to antiquarians and naturalists. St. Colman established a monastery on Inishbofin in the 7th century. The island was captured from the O'Flahertys by the O'Malleys in the late-14th century. Later, Grace O'Malley (Gráinne Uí Mháille, c. 1530–c.1600) is said to have based her fleet in Inishbofin. She was a brave and independent woman, described by the poet Sidney as "a most famous sea captain," and by other contemporaries as a pirate. It is said that when she visited Queen Elizabeth in London she spoke to her as one queen to another. In 1586 Sir Richard Bingham accused her of plundering the Aran Islands, and prepared a gallows to execute her. She was released on a pledge from her son-in-law, Richard Burke, and later pardoned by Queen Elizabeth. Inishbofin surrendered to the Cromwellians in 1652 and remained a garrison post until 1700. It was used by the Cromwellians as a sort of concentration camp for monks and priests.

Killary Harbor, on the road to the northwest, is in fact not a harbor at all, but an eight-mile long fjord-like inlet from the Atlantic. It was at one time a British naval base, and was large enough to shelter the whole fleet. Mweelrea, on its northern shore in County Mayo, rises straight out of the sea to a height of 2,500 feet.

Just at the head of Killary Harbor is Leenane, dominated by the Devil's Mother, a 2,000-foot high mountain about which many legends have been told. The mountainous country between Leenane and Lough Mask still bears the name Joyce Country after a tribe which settled in the district six centuries ago. It is a wild and lonely region, but as one travels east to Clonbur the scenery becomes gentler and more wooded. Clonbur itself lies on the neck of land which separates Lough Corrib from Lough Mask. Rivers flow beneath, linking the two loughs. At one spot on the isthmus, known as the Pigeon Hole, these underground linking streams can be seen.

Lough Mask stretches 10 miles northwards, and is rich in trout, perch and pike. As on Lough Corrib, the fishing is free.

It was near Ballinrobe on the eastern shore of Lough Mask that a new word was added to the English language in the last century. Lough Mask House was the home of Captain Charles Boycott, the land agent for Lord Earne. He was ostracized by the tenants during the agrarian troubles of the 1880s because he imported labor from elsewhere for the harvest. The pressure of non-cooperation became so severe that he lived under police protection for a time, and was eventually forced to leave Ireland. The action of the tenants became known as a "boycott" and the word found its way into the dictionaries.

## Cong

Across the border from Clonbur and into County Mayo lies the pretty village of Cong. It is on the shores of Lough Corrib and only a few miles south of Lough Mask. There are several stone canal locks around Cong, but no canal. There is a simple explanation for this: 19th-century engineers thought that it would be an easy task to link the two loughs by canal. However, when the water was allowed to flow into the canal, it disappeared into the porous limestone.

The dominant feature of Cong is Ashford Castle, now a deluxe hotel, where President Reagan stayed during his visit to Ireland in June 1984. The story of Ashford Castle goes back to the Norman de Burgo family who arrived in the area in 1228. They built a castle at Cong and held it until the troops of Elizabeth I seized it from them. The property was allowed to become run down until, in the 19th century, it was purchased by the Guinness brewing family. Sir Benjamin Lee Guinness then rebuilt the castle, creating a magnificent building with castellated towers on the site of the old castle and laying out new and extensive gardens and parklands. The coat of arms of a member of the Guinness family, Lord Ardilaun, is still on the west side of the castle. It was then sold in 1939 to a famous family of Irish hoteliers, the Huggards, of Waterville in County Kerry, who developed Ashford Castle as a hotel. It was subsequently sold to John A. Mulcahy, an Irish-American who also owns another hotel in Waterville.

Close by the hotel are the ruins of Cong Abbey, originally built in the 12th century. The last Abbot died in 1829, after which the foundation declined and fell into ruins. The main entrance to the abbey ruins is a doorway from the village of Cong, a fine piece of Gothic design. The remains of the abbey confirm records which speak of the large numbers of scholars and students who attended the abbey—3,000 at one time. There is a domestic note down by the river, where the monks had their refectory and kitchen. The nearby fishing house was designed over the river with a fish trap beneath the floor in which the fish were caught and held until needed for the kitchen. In the south wall of the refectory is the hatch through which food was passed to strangers who called at the abbey.

The abbey's great days were ended with its suppression in 1542 and the expulsion of the monks. Its treasures were taken by the invading forces and although some were given to Trinity College, Dublin, many of them were lost. One of the treasures that has happily survived is the *Cross of Cong* which was made of oak, plated with copper and embellished with gold filigree work in Celtic designs. It was made at Roscommon, in the northwest of Connacht, in 1123 and subsequently taken to Cong, where it disappeared. It was only re-discovered early in the last century, in a chest in a house in the village. The *Cross of Cong* is now a major possession in the collection of the National Museum in Dublin.

The land stretching to the east of Cong towards Tuam was the scene of great battles 3,000 years ago and there are a number of megalithic tombs in the area. There is a "Giant's Grave" just off the main road a mile west of Cong; it is a tomb built of stones with an average thickness of eight inches. The lid of the tomb is a single stone measuring six feet by five.

At Headford, about half-way along the road back into Galway from Cong, there are some remains of a 14th-century Franciscan friary.

### Ballintubber Abbey

Westward in County Mayo is one of the most historic of all Irish abbeys, Ballintubber, a few miles south of Castlebar. It is unique because it is the only royal abbey in Ireland or Britain that has been in continuous use for over 750 years. The abbey was founded near the site of a church which had been established by St. Patrick about 441. Patrick's visit is commemorated in the place name in Irish, which means "Homestead of the Well of Patrick."

Ballintubber was suppressed like all other religious establishments by Henry VIII, but although the monks lost all their possessions, they continued to live and worship here. After the Catholic Emancipation Act (1829) was passed by the British parliament, work was started on the restoration of the abbey. Father Thomas A. Egan renewed the drive for restoration during the early '60s and by 1966, when the 750th anniversary of the abbey was celebrated, he achieved success, not only ensuring the continued life of the abbey but contributing to the knowledge and understanding of monastic life centuries ago. More than 1,000 stones were unearthed during the excavations, revealing the fact that there were two cloisters, one of the 13th century and one of two centuries later; both have been restored.

Twenty miles to the west is the famous pilgrimage mountain of Croagh Patrick, 2,500 feet high and the scene of the oldest pilgrimage in the western world, held on the last Sunday of July every year. The pilgrim road which passed the abbey was called Tochar Phadraigh, Patrick's Causeway; excavations have shown that there was a guesthouse for pilgrims built over a stream and there are signs of burned stones which were heated and thrown into the water to heat it for the weary pilgrims. The pilgrimage owes its origins to the fact that St. Patrick is believed to have spent 40 days fasting on the summit in 441. Even today many pilgrims follow the ancient tradition of walking up the mountain in their bare feet. The focal point of the pilgrimage is a Mass said at the very summit of the mountain at dawn.

### Bay of Many Islands

Westport is a fine, mainly 18th-century town overlooking Clew Bay, studded with almost 400 islands. It is dominated by Westport House, seat of the Marquess of Sligo, and it is believed that his 18th-century forebear employed an architect to design the town to his taste. There is a beautifully proportioned 18th-century bridge over the canalized river. The main feature of the town is the Octagon which has, as its name implies, eight sides of equal length, three of which are broken by street entries. There is a tree-lined mall and some splendid Georgian houses, one of which has a unique five-bay window. The elegantly designed warehousing by the quays is a reminder of the town's past importance as a port. Nowadays it is an excellent center for deep-sea angling.

Westport House is built over the ruins of an older house, and the dungeons still remain. It was originally designed by Richard Cassells but completed by the English architect James Wyatt in the late-18th century. The house may be visited any afternoon between April and October, and contains a collection of paintings, Waterford glass, old Irish silver and historical mementoes of the 1798 rebellion. The extensive grounds associated with the house have become a well-stocked zoo-park.

A road from Westport follows the north shore of Clew Bay through great hedges of fuchsia around Mulrany; there is a fine view here from Lookout Hill across the bay to the towering church-topped peak of Croagh Patrick on the southern shore.

## Achill Island

Achill Island, the largest island off the Irish coast, is linked to the mainland by a bridge, yet retains a distinctive character of its own. It is the destination chosen by many Irish people for vacations, and comes to life in the summer months, though its miles of sandy beaches never seem crowded. Most of the land is bog and mountain and unsuitable for cultivation.

The Atlantic Drive around the island is a noteworthy scenic tour, but much of the island is best explored on foot. There is plenty of marine wildlife to observe along its cliffs. Basking sharks (they are harmless to man) shoal in these waters from April to July. In days gone by fishermen used to net them along the shore of Keem Bay, spearing the shark from a *currach* then towing them away in a net to have the oil extracted.

Near Dugort, beside the island's highest mountain, Slievemore (2,204 feet), is a strange deserted village known locally as The Settlement. It is the remains of a mission established by the Reverend Edward Nangle in 1830 in an attempt to get the inhabitants to convert to the Protestant religion. He founded a school and an orphanage and even had his own printing press on which he produced a newspaper. The scheme was as enthusiastically supported by donations from London as any mission to convert the heathen, and was highly praised by English visitors, including the historian Thomas Carlyle. However, when the local Catholic archbishop launched a vigorous campaign to bring the children back to Catholicism, Nangle's mission soon foundered, and all that remain are ruined buildings and scattered graveyards.

## Apparitions and Airports

Among County Mayo's most famous sites is the Shrine of Our Lady of Knock, located in the southeast of the county a few miles north of Claremorris. On 21 August, 1879 local people saw an apparition of the Blessed Virgin Mary, St. Joseph and St. John on the wall of the parish church. Archbishop John McHale (the same man who dealt so firmly with Achill Island's Protestant missionaries) held a Commission of Enquiry which accepted that the apparition was genuine. Knock has been recognized as a Marian shrine ever since, and was visited by Pope John Paul II in 1979. A huge church, capable of holding 20,000 people, was opened in 1976. Each county of Ireland contributed one of the 32 pillars in the circular ambulatory. Local people are intensely proud of the new church. But the building has also been widely criticized as being ugly in the extreme.

Knock has attracted a deal of controversy, too, over the building of the new Connacht regional airport just outside the town. Government spending on the project was the subject of much debate, with many arguing that the area did not need an airport. Cardinal Monsignor Horan, the controversial cleric behind the project, inaugurated the airport in 1986 when two planeloads of pilgrims took off for Rome.

Heading north through County Mayo there are two further places of interest. The first is at Straide, on the N58 northeast of Castlebar. It is the site of the Michael Davitt Museum, opened in 1984. Michael Davitt (1846–1906) helped to found the Land League, a crucial early step in the fight for independence, when he returned to Ireland after seven years' transportation. He had bitter memories of his father's eviction in 1851 when he was five years old. His commitment to the Land League was largely responsible for Irish farmers winning independence from absentee landlords.

Finally, there is Ballina, on the river Moy in the north of Mayo, an excellent angling center. But Ballina also has a unique place in Irish history as the first town to be captured by French troops during the insurrection of 1798. 1,100 soldiers under General Joseph Humbert landed nearby in Killala Bay to come to the aid of Irish rebels in their fight against the English. The superior numbers and weaponry of the English crushed the rebels with a vengeance. Thomas Flanagan's prize-winning novel, *The Year of the French,* gives a vivid account of life in Mayo in 1798.

## PRACTICAL INFORMATION FOR THE WEST

**TOURIST OFFICES.** The main tourist office for the West is in **Galway City,** Victoria Palace, near Eyre Square (tel. 091–63081). It's open year-round. There are other offices at **Achill Sound,** tel. 098–43249 (open June to Aug.); **Ballina,** tel. 096–22422 (open July to Aug.); **Ballinasloe,** tel. 0905–42131 (open July to Aug.); **Castlebar,** tel. 094–21207 (open July to Aug.); **Clifden,** tel. 095–21163 (open June to Aug.); **Knock,** tel. 094–88193 (open June to Sept.); **Louisburgh,** tel. 098–66036 (open July to Aug.); **Salthill,** tel. 091–63081 (open June to Aug.); **Tuam,** tel. 093–24463 (open July to Aug.); **Westport,** tel. 098–25711 (open year-round).

### HOTELS AND RESTAURANTS

**Achill Island** (Co. Mayo). *Achill Head* (I), Keel (tel. 098–43108). 23 rooms. *Ostan Gob A'Choire* (Achill Sound Hotel) (I), tel. 098–45245. 36 rooms, all with bath. *Wave Crest* (I), Dooagh (tel. 098–43115). 15 rooms,

1 with bath. Pleasant and inexpensive guesthouses include *Clew Bay,* Dooagh (tel. 098–43119), and *Gray's,* Dugort (tel. 098–43244).

**Restaurant.** *The Booley House* (M), Keel (tel. 098–43147). Candle-lit cottage restaurant with good reputation.

**Aran Islands** (Co. Galway). *Hotel Inishere* (I), Lurgan, Inishere (tel. 099–75020). 10 rooms, 1 with bath. *Kilmurvey House* (I), Kilronan, Inishmore (tel. 099–61218). 8 rooms. *Mrs. A. Faherty* (I), Creigmore, Inishmaan (tel. 099–73012). 5 rooms. One of the many B & B accommodations on the islands.

**Restaurant.** *Dun Aonghusa* (M), Kilronan, Inishmore (tel. 099–61104). Unique setting; seafood. AE, MC, V.

**Ballina** (Co. Mayo). *Beleek Castle* (E), tel. 096–22061. 16 rooms with bath. Set in forest by a salmon-fishing river. Has restaurant, bar, nightclub, medieval hall, display of armor. Golf, fishing. AE, V. *Downhill Hotel* (E), tel. 096–21033. 54 rooms, 53 with bath. Cheerful place by the salmon-fishing river Moy. Heated indoor pool, health center with squash courts, sauna, sunbed and Jacuzzi. Three 18-hole golf courses, fishing. AE, DC, MC, V. *Mount Falcon Castle* (E), tel. 096–21172. 11 rooms, 10 with bath. Elegant country mansion in fine parkland. Fishing, pony trekking. AE, DC, MC, V. *Bartra House* (I), tel. 096–22200. 30 rooms, 15 with bath or shower. AE, DC, MC, V.

**Restaurants.** *Downhill Hotel* (M), tel. 096–21033. Excellent cuisine. AE, DC, MC, V. *Swiss Barn* (M), Foxford Rd. (tel. 096–21117). Family-run with continental food. Booking recommended. AE, MC, V. *Cafe Royal* (I), Garden St. (tel. 096–21961). Good home cooking by owner-cook. V.

**Ballinasloe** (Co. Galway). *Hayden's* (M), Dunloe St. (tel. 0905–42347). 56 rooms, 44 with bath. Excellent reputation. AE, DC, MC, V.

**Ballyconneely** (Co. Galway). *Erriseask House* (I), tel. 095–23553. 11 rooms, 7 with bath. Country-house hotel; private beach, pony riding. AE, DC, MC, V.

**Ballynahinch** (Co. Galway). *Ballynahinch Castle* (E), tel. 095–31006. 28 rooms, all with bath. At the foot of the Twelve Pins mountains, overlooking the Owenmore river. Comfort and good fishing. AE, DC, MC, V.

**Carraroe** (Co. Galway). *Hotel Carraroe* (M), tel. 091–95116. 20 rooms, all with bath. 10 self-catering cottages in the hotel grounds. In the heart of Connemara. AE, MC, V.

**Restaurant.** *An Ciseog* (M), tel. 091–95222. Owner-run. Seafood and steaks.

**Cashel Bay** (Co. Galway). *Cashel House* (E), tel. 095–31001. 29 rooms, 27 with bath. Secluded and quiet, overlooking a pleasant bay, with own harbor and small private beach. Lovely garden with interesting shrubs from Tibet. The restaurant (M) is highly regarded for its country food. AE, DC, MC, V. *Zetland* (E), tel. 095–31111. 19 rooms with bath. With some of the best sea trout and salmon fishing in the country. AE, DC, MC, V.

**Castlebar** (Co. Mayo). *Breaffy House* (M), tel. 094–22033. 40 rooms, all with bath. Stone-built mansion in parkland; good reputation. AE, DC, MC, V.

**Clarinbridge** (Co. Galway). **Restaurants.** *Moran's of the Weir* (M), tel. 091–86113. Seafood pub lunches on the shores of Galway Bay, near Kilcolgan. *Paddy Burke's Oyster Bar* (M) is, of course, famous for its oysters; also bar food and a pleasant spot for dinner. *Rafter's* (M), Kilcolgan. Also a great spot to enjoy the fruits of the Galway oyster beds.

**Claremorris** (Co. Mayo). *D'Alton Inn* (I), tel. 094–71604. 10 rooms with bath. Well-appointed accommodations above a busy bar and restaurant (I) on the main road west from Knock Airport (9 miles).

**Cleggan** (Co. Galway). **Restaurant.** *The Harbour* (M), tel. 095–44605. Serves the day's catch of this pretty fishing village.

**Clifden** (Co. Galway). *Abbeyglen Castle* (E), tel. 095–21201. 40 rooms, all with bath. Heated pool, tennis. AE, DC, MC, V. *Clifden Bay* (M), tel. 095–21167. 30 rooms, all with bath. On the square in the middle of the village. AE, DC, MC, V. *Rock Glen Country House* (M), tel. 095–21035. 30 rooms, all with bath. Converted hunting lodge, dating from 1815, one mile from town. AE, DC, MC, V. *Dun Aengus* (I), tel. 095–21069. 6 rooms with bath. A newly built bed and breakfast, well recommended.
**Restaurant.** *Shades* (M), tel. 095–21215. Excellent nouvelle cuisine in an intimate setting.

**Cong** (Co. Mayo). *Ashford Castle* (L), tel. 092–46003. 82 rooms, all with bath. On the edge of Lough Corrib. Based in a former castle. Superb restaurant and service, plus a 9-hole golf course. President Reagan stayed here on his Irish visit in 1984. One of Ireland's top hotels. AE, DC, MC, V.

**Furbo** (Co. Galway). *Connemara Coast* (E), tel. 091–92108. 53 rooms with bath. Eight miles from the city overlooking Galway Bay. Newly opened in 1988; outdoor pool. AE, DC, MC, V.

**Galway City** (Co. Galway). *Great Southern* (E), Eyre Sq. (tel. 091–64041). 120 rooms, all with bath. In the heart of Galway City. Rooftop heated pool, sauna, health complex. *Fagin's* is a popular late-night spot. AE, DC, MC, V. *Corrib Great Southern* (E), Dublin Rd. (tel. 091–55281). 110 rooms with bath. Good views of Galway Bay and hills of Clare. Indoor heated pool, saunas. AE, DC, MC, V. *Galway Ryan* (E), Dublin Rd. (tel. 091–53181). 96 rooms, all with bath. AE, DC, MC, V.
*Ardilaun House* (M), Taylors Hill (tel. 091–21433). 95 rooms, all with bath. In pleasant grounds midway between Galway City and Salthill, Galway's seaside suburb. AE, DC, MC, V. *Anno Santo* (M), tel. 091–22110. 14 rooms, most with bath. AE, DC, MC, V. *Flannery's* (M), tel. 091–55111. 98 rooms with bath. AE, DC, MC, V. *Imperial* (M), tel. 091–63033. 50 rooms, most with bath. AE, DC, MC, V. *Salthill* (M), tel. 091–22115. 47 rooms with bath. AE, DC, MC, V. *Skeffington Arms* (I), tel. 091–63173. 21 rooms, most with bath. DC, MC, V.

Among the inexpensive guesthouses in Galway City and Salthill are: *Adare,* Father Griffin Pl. (tel. 091–62638); *Glendawn House,* Upper Salthill (tel. 091–22872); *Osterley Lodge,* Salthill (tel. 091–23794); *Rio,* Lower Salthill (tel. 091–23580). 30 rooms, some with bath.

**Restaurants.** *Oyster Room* (E), Great Southern Hotel, Eyre Sq. (tel. 091–64041). As well as this new restaurant, there's another pleasant restaurant (M) on the ground floor and a sophisticated rooftop grill room (E) where you can enjoy your meal and watch the sun go down on Galway Bay. AE, DC, MC, V. *Conlon & Son* (I) tel. 091–62268, Eglinton St. (opposite main G.P.O.). Superior fish and chips, local shellfish and seafood chowder. Open till late. *Fat Freddie's* (I) tel. 091–67279, The Halls, Quay St. Lively spot for freshly-made pizza. *Tigh Noctan's* (I) tel. 091–66172, corner of High St. and Cross St. Long-established bohemian pub popular among Irish-speakers. Outstanding buffet lunches; excellent upstairs restaurant (M) which is open evenings in summer.

**Geesala** (Co. Mayo). *Ostan Synge* (M), tel. 097–86801. 32 rooms, all with bath. Built in 1982 in a beautiful location beloved by the playwright John Millington Synge, hence the hotel's name. Views of moorland and ocean. AE.

**Kinvara** (Co. Galway). **Restaurant.** *Dun Guaire Castle,* tel. 091–37108. Third of the Shannon castles. From 15 May–30 Sept., features medieval banquets and entertainment. On the southern shore of Galway Bay. For reservations tel. 061–61788.

**Knock** (Co. Mayo). *Belmont* (I), tel. 094–88122. 27 rooms with bath. *Knock International* (I), tel. 094–88281. 10 rooms with bath. AE, MC, V. Both convenient to Knock International Airport.

**Kylemore** (Co. Galway). *Kylemore Pass Hotel* (I), tel. 095–41141. 10 rooms with bath. A beautiful location on one of the Twelve Pins mountains overlooking Kylemore Lake. Good touring base. AE, DC, MC, V.

**Letterfrack** (Co. Galway). *Rosleague Manor* (E), tel. 095–41101. 15 rooms with bath. A Georgian mansion overlooking Ballinakill Bay. Restaurant is (M). AE, DC, MC, V.
**Restaurant.** *Doon* (I). Lunch only. Unique one-man operation two miles west of town.

**Louisburgh** (Co. Mayo). *The Old Head* (M), tel. 098–66021. 12 rooms with bath. AE, DC. *Killadoon Beach* (I), tel. 098–68605. 10 rooms, 5 with bath.

**Maam** (Co. Galway). *Leckavrea View* (I), tel. 092–48040. 6 rooms, 4 with bath. Noted farmhouse accommodations on the shore of Lough Corrib. Free fishing; boat hire.

**Moyard** (Co. Galway). *Crocnaraw* (M), tel. 095–41068. 8 rooms, 6 with bath. Another good Connemara spot. Guesthouse that boasts a good restaurant.

**Moycullen** (Co. Galway). **Restaurants.** *Drimcong House* (M), tel. 091–85115. Located in 300-year-old lakeland house, eight miles from Galway City. Award-winning owner-chef. Well worth a detour. AE, DC, MC, V.

**Mulrany** (Co. Mayo). *Mulrany Bay* (M), tel. 098–36222. 43 rooms, most with bath. Outdoor pool, tennis. AE, DC, MC, V. *Avondale House* (I), tel. 098–36105. 8 rooms.

**Newport** (Co. Mayo). *Newport House* (M), tel. 098–41222. 20 rooms, all with bath. Historic house in gardens and park by the river Newport. Freshwater fishing and sea fishing on Clew Bay. AE, DC, MC, V.

**Oughterard** (Co. Galway). *Connemara Gateway Hotel* (E), tel. 091–82328. 62 rooms, all with bath. Outdoor heated pool, tennis courts. Welcoming and concerned for visitors AE, DC, MC, V. *Sweeney's Oughterard House* (E), tel. 091–82207. 20 rooms with bath. Early-Georgian country house beside river. Irish and French cuisine. DC, MC, V. *Currarevagh House* (M), tel. 091–82313. Top-rated country-house guesthouse in extensive private woodlands beside Lough Corrib. Excellent for fishing (own boats), also tennis court. *The Boat Inn* (I), tel. 091–82196. 6 rooms, 3 with bath. *Egan's Lake* (I), tel. 091–82275. 22 rooms with bath. In the village; home cooking.

**Renvyle** (Co. Galway). *Renvyle House* (E), tel. 095–43444. 40 rooms with bath. A spot for comfort and enjoyment in pleasant company. Sauna/solarium, outdoor pool, tennis, golf. DC, MC, V.

**Rosscahill** (Co. Galway). *Knockferry Lodge* (I), tel. 091–80122. 10 rooms with bath. On the shores of Loch Corrib, half an hour from Galway. Popular with anglers; full board available. AE, DC, MC, V. *Ross Lake House* (I), Rosscahill (tel. 091–80109). 12 rooms with bath. Landscaped gardens, sauna, tennis. MC, V.

**Spiddal** (Co. Galway). *Teach Osta na Pairce* (Park Lodge Hotel). (M), tel. 091–83159. 25 rooms with bath; 7 self-catering cottages. Panoramic views of Galway Bay.

**Westport** (Co. Mayo). *Hotel Westport* (E), The Demesne (tel. 098–25122). 49 rooms, all with bath. In own parkland five minutes from town. AE, DC, MC, V. *Westport Ryan* (E), Louisburgh Rd. (tel. 098–25811). 56 rooms, all with bath. In wooded grounds beside lake. AE, DC, MC, V. *Castlecourt* (I), Castlebar St. (tel. 098–25920). 40 rooms with bath or shower. AE, MC, V. *Clew Bay* (I), tel. 098–25438. 27 rooms with bath. DC, MC, V.

**Restaurants.** *Ardmore* (M), The Quay (tel. 098–25994). Restaurant–cocktail bar, overlooking Clew Bay. AE, MC, V. *Asgard* (M), The Quay (tel. 098–25319). Pub with award-winning food in both bar and first-floor restaurant. AE. *Quay Cottage* (M), The Harbour (tel. 098–26412). Small with unique atmosphere. Shellfish specialties.

## Youth Hostels

**Bru na n'Oige,** Indreabhan, Tully, Co. Galway (tel. 091–93154). **Cong Holiday Hostel,** Lisloughrey, Quay Rd., Cong, Co. Mayo (tel. 092–46089). **Currane,** Achill Sound, Westport, Co. Mayo (tel. 098–45280). **Doorus House,** Kinvara, Co. Galway (tel. 091–37173). **Galway Tourist Hostel,** Gentian Ville, Gentian Hill, Knocknacarra, Salthill, Co. Galway (tel. 091–25176). **Killary Harbor,** Rosroe, Renvyle, Co. Galway (tel. 095–43417). **Pollatomish,** Ballina, Co. Mayo. **The Twelve Bens,** Ben Lettery, Ballinafad, Co. Galway (tel. 095–34636). **Treanlaur Lodge,** Lough Feagh, Newport, Co. Mayo (tel. 098–41358).

**TOURS AND EXCURSIONS.** C.I.E. operate day tours of Connemara out of Galway City. You can get details of departures at the Galway Railway Station, off Eyre St., or the Tourist Information office.

Lough Corrib can be cruised either from Galway City, where *Frank Dolan* is based at Wood Quay, tel. 091–654841, or from Cong at *Corrib Cruises,* tel. 092–46029. *The Galway Sailing Center,* for sailing and windsurfing tuition, is based at Renvyle Harbor, tel. 091–63522. And for the more adventurous, Michael Clarke of *Western Ocean Yacht Charters,* 5 New Docks, Galway City (tel. 091–65589) operates skippered charters in Galway Bay and along the Atlantic coast of Connemara.

*The Little Killary Adventure Center,* at Salbruck, near Renvyle, Co. Galway (tel. 095–43411), provides adventure for the young and the not-so-young. For trout fishing at its best, contact *Western Pride,* Creagh, Lough Mask, Ballinrobe, Co. Mayo (tel. 094–71671).

Bicycles can be hired at *Salthill Rentals,* Galway City, Co. Galway (tel. 091–22085); *John Mannion,* Railway View, Clifden, Co. Galway (tel. 095–21160). In Co. Mayo at *Kilbane Stores,* Achill Sound (tel. 098–45245); *Casey's,* Market Sq., Castlebar (tel. 094–22347); *J.P. Breheny & Sons,* Castlebar St., Westport (tel. 098–25020).

Rita Higgins (tel. 091–61476) runs walking tours of Galway City.

## PLACES TO VISIT

**Aran Islands** (Co. Galway). **Dun Aengus.** Prehistoric stone fort perched on a cliff edge on Inishmore, 200 ft. above the sea.

**Banagher** (Co. Galway) **Clonfert Cathedral.** Fine detailed Hiberno-Romanesque doorway in church founded by St. Brendan in 563 (present church is 12th century). Off the Ballinsloe–Birr road, five miles from Banagher.

**Museum Arainn,** Kilronan, Inishmore. Has historic material relating to the Aran Islands. There's also a museum on another of the islands, Inishmaan, with exhibits on folklife and the playwright J.M. Synge.

**Castlebar** (Co. Mayo) **Ballintubber Abbey.** Founded in 1216 for the Augustinians by the king of Connacht, it has been in continuous use for 766 years. Restored church with 15th-century cloister. Seven miles south of Castlebar on the Ballinrobe road.

**Belcarra Folk Museum.** Covers the Great Famine of the 1840s.

**Claremorris** (Co. Mayo). **Knock Shrine.** Site of a reported apparition of the Virgin Mary, witnessed on 21 August 1879. Pope John Paul II raised the church to the status of a basilica during his visit in 1979. The Knock Folk Museum here (tel. 094–88100) has religious, archeological and historical displays.

**Cong** (Co. Mayo). **Cong Abbey,** near Ashford Castle Hotel. An Augustinian friary built about 1200 by the kings of Connacht.

**Connemara** (Co. Galway). **Kylemore Abbey,** Connemara. Lovely 19th-century building in beautiful setting. Home of Benedictine nuns and also a boarding school. Grounds and part of the abbey open 1 May to 30 Oct., daily 10–6. Admission free. The associated pottery is open year-round.
**Connemara National Park,** south of the Leenane–Clifden road (N59). Ireland's second national park; covers about 5,000 acres. Signposted nature trails offering views of sea, mountain and lake. Visitor Center at Letterfrack is housed in converted farm buildings and has good collection of farm furniture and an audio-visual presentation. Park open all year. Visitor Center open Easter to 30 Sept., daily 10–1 and 2–6.

**Foxford** (Co. Mayo). **Foxford Mills,** Foxford. The craft center and woolen mills here make an interesting tour.

**Galway City** (Co. Galway). **Galway City Museum,** Spanish Arch. Charts the history of Galway City, and the folklife of Co. Galway.
**St. Nicholas's Church,** Lombard St. Founded in 1320. Columbus is reputed to have prayed here before his voyage of discovery.

**Gort** (Co. Galway). **Thoor Ballylee.** 16th-century tower house, restored. Was the summer home of the poet-playwright William Butler Yeats in the 1920s. Has some rare first editions of his work and other Yeatsiana. Four miles from Gort off the Gort–Loughrea road. Open 1 May to 30 Sept., daily 10–6.
**Kilmacduagh.** Remains of monastery founded by St. Colman in the 7th century. Has collection of churches and well-preserved round tower, leaning about two ft. out of perpendicular. Three miles from Gort off the Corofin road.

**Headford** (Co. Galway). **Ross Errilly.** The best-preserved of the Franciscan friaries in Ireland; most of buildings date from 15th century. Two miles from Headford on the Galway–Castlebar road.

**Kinvara** (Co. Galway). **Dun Guaire.** 16th-century castle on the shores of Galway Bay. Medieval-style banquets are held here in season. Castle open 1 Apr. to 30 Sept., daily 10–5. Banquets held 15 May to 30 Sept., twice an evening at 5.45 and 8.45; tel. 091–37108. Reservations also on 061–61788.

**Letterfrack** (Co. Galway). **Connemara Handcrafts.** One of the best of many craft shops in this area, stocking a wide variety of handmade Irish products. Open seven days a week.

**Lough Derg** (Co. Galway). **Portumna Forest Park,** on the shores of Lough Derg. A wildlife sanctuary with hides for bird-watching.

**Moycullen** (Co. Galway). **Connemara Marble Factory.** Famous marble quarry nearby; here you can see the marble polished and worked.

**Oughterard** (Co. Galway). **Aughnanure Castle.** A riverside castle near Lough Corrib. Stronghold of the "ferocious O'Flahertys" in the 16th century. Open mid-June to mid-Sept., daily 10–6. Rest of year, key with caretaker.

**St. Macdara's Island** (Co. Galway). **Monastery.** Off the Galway coast near Carna. Monastery founded in 6th century by St. MacDara. Has restored church and remains of some early-Christian decorated stone slabs.

**Tuam** (Co. Galway). **Mill Museum,** Shop St. (tel. 093–24463). Features a waterwheel operating a corn mill.

**Westport** (Co. Mayo). **Westport House,** Westport (tel. 098–25430). The stately home of the Marquis of Sligo is the dominant feature of the Westport Estate, which has become a remarkable playground for young and old. There is also a children's zoo and a holiday center. A number of farm and estate buildings have been converted into holiday homes for visitors. Open 1 June to 31 Aug., Mon. to Fri. 11.30–6, Sat. and Sun. 2–6; 17 May to 31 May and 1 Sept. to 13 Sept., daily 2–5.

# SLIGO AND THE NORTHWEST

### Yeats Country and the Donegal Highlands

This chapter covers the four counties of Sligo, Roscommon, Leitrim and Donegal. The area they encompass is both one of the loveliest and the most varied in Ireland. It is also one of the most remote, and indeed large parts of western Donegal, away in the northwest tip of Ireland, are still Irish-speaking, a fact tourists will quickly realize when they discover that practically all the signposts are in Irish! Take along a good map.

The coastal regions of Sligo and Donegal are rugged and wild, punctuated by numerous rocky bays and islands. Heading north into Donegal the landscape is also famed for its apparent ability to change color and character as fast-moving clouds speed across the sky, deep gloomy greys and tans giving way to vibrant shades of purple, blue and green. It is often said that the texture and subtle colors of the region's most famous product—Donegal tweeds—owe much to this delightful and infinitely varied, ever changing landscape.

County Sligo is noted for its seaside resorts, the famous golf course at Rosse's Point and its links with Ireland's most famous 20th century poet, William Butler Yeats (1865–1939) who is buried just north of Sligo town, at Drumcliffe, "under bare Ben Bulben's head." It is easy to see why the remarkable beauty of County Sligo influenced and inspired the poet.

Inland lie the gentler fertile lands of County Roscommon and the profusion of lakes and waterways of County Leitrim, one of the most attractive and appealing coarse angling centers in Ireland. The region's remoteness and isolation have all helped ensure the survival of numerous archeological remains, indeed practically every stage of early Irish history and civilization is represented here. Tory Island, off the Donegal Coast, for example, has been inhabited since prehistoric times. Similarly, there is the unique ancient earth and stone fort of Grianán of Aileach in Donegal, just inside the border with Northern Ireland and commanding fine views of the surrounding countryside.

There is a good network of roads throughout the region and little commercial traffic, a factor which adds greatly to the pleasures of exploring this wild and spectacular land.

## Sligo Town

In so pronounced a rural area, it is no surprise that the principal town of the northwest should be the little town of Sligo, lying on the coast and straddling the river Garavogue, with lovely Lough Gill just behind it. Despite its small scale, however, it has always enjoyed considerable strategic significance, controlling much of the trade between the northwest and the rest of the country. The original little settlement was plundered by the Vikings in the 9th century, but grew to importance in the mid-13th century when the Anglo-Norman Maurice FitzGerald made it his base for an intended invasion of Donegal. The castle he built here has long since disappeared, chiefly as a result of repeated assaults by the O'Donnells, the principal clan of the northwest.

FitzGerald also built an abbey for the Dominicans here. In 1414 it was destroyed by fire and rebuilt, only to be reduced to ruins again during the sack of Sligo by Cromwell's men in 1641. Nonetheless, its ruins are well preserved and can be seen in Abbey Street—some of the carving is very beautiful. At St. John's Church on John Street there is a memorial in the north transept to Susan Mary Yeats, mother of the poet W. B. Yeats and his painter brother, Jack B. Yeats.

There is an important collection of paintings by Jack B. Yeats to be seen in the Sligo Museum on Stephen Street. He was sent to live in Sligo with his grandparents at the age of eight, and his boyhood there gave him a lifelong delight in country scenes, traveling people, circuses and seafarers, as well as contributing to his unusual and vigorous use of color. A number of paintings with Yeats family associations were given to the Sligo Museum by a New York stockbroker, James A. Healy, whose own mother was an emigrant to America in 1884.

## Yeats Country

The region has been immortalized by the poetry of W. B. Yeats and it is a unique experience to pick up a book of his poems and seek out the places that inspired him. Take a boat from Sligo up to river Garavogue into Lough Gill and see *The Lake Isle of Inishfree* and the many other islands of this delightful lake. The circular road around the lake shore passes Aghamore and Dooney Rock, commemorated by Yeats in *The Fiddler of Dooney*.

The churchyard at Drumcliffe where Yeats is buried is a short distance to the north of Sligo. In fact, he died in the south of France in 1939, but his body was brought back to Ireland after the War for a state funeral in 1948, and was interred, as he requested, under a limestone slab "quarried near the spot." On the stone is inscribed the epitaph he wrote for himself, which ends with the lines "Cast a cold eye/On life, on Death,/Horseman, pass by." The poet and his works are discussed by scholars at the Yeats International Summer School which is held every August in Sligo.

Lissadell House, a substantial mansion, dating from 1830, on the north shore of Drumcliffe Bay, figured prominently in the writings of Yeats, and he stayed there many times. It was the home of the Gore-Booth family (members of whom still live there) and Yeats often mentions both Eva Gore-Booth (1870–1926) the poet, and her sister Constance Gore-Booth, later Countess Markievicz (1884–1927) in his verse. "The light of evening, Lissadell,/Great windows open to the south;/Two girls in silk kimonos,/Both beautiful, one a gazelle . . . " Countess Markievicz took part in the 1916 Easter Rising. She was subsequently sentenced to death, only to be reprieved. Two years later she became the first woman elected to the British House of Commons, though she never took her seat. Her niece, Aideen, lives in the house today, and it's open to the public. Though somewhat shabby due to dwindling family fortunes and a lack of government support, it is well worth a visit.

On the edge of the Lissadell Estate on the road to Carney there is a wildlife Bird Reserve, known locally as "the goose field." In winter it is the home of Ireland's largest colony of Barnacle geese, which migrate here from Greenland. But many other species of wildfowl can be seen, and a timber hide has been constructed at the edge of the wood. Large numbers of the common seal also frequent Drumcliffe Bay, and can often be seen basking on the offshore sandbank.

As in so many places along the rocky Irish coast, around which the doomed Spanish Armada was swept in 1588 by terrible gales after their disastrous attempt to invade England, at least one Spanish vessel was shipwrecked here. She was discovered at Streadagh Point, to the north of Drumcliffe Bay in 1985. The ship, believed to be the *Juliana,* is in a remarkably good state of preservation.

### Books, Waterfalls and Graves

What was probably the first copyright action in history took place near Drumcliffe, at Cuildrevne, between the followers of two monks. St. Columba had borrowed a psalter from St. Finian, but before returning it, Columba made a copy. St. Finian claimed both book and copy and the dispute was submitted to High King Diarmuid who ruled, in a Solomon-like judgment: "To every cow its calf, and to every book its copy." Since there was no court of appeal, Columba's followers went to war with those of Finian, and in the Battle of the Books (A.D. 561) many men were killed. In subsequent anguish Columba sailed away from the north coast to the Scottish island of Iona.

The Drumcliffe area also boasts a remarkable natural phenomenon at Glencar Lough, about four miles east of Drumcliffe itself. It's a waterfall, known as Struth-in-Aghaidh-an-Aird, Stream against the Height. The waterfall has an unbroken drop of 50 feet but gets its name from the fact that when the wind blows from the south, the water is blown up into the air and gives the appearance of a waterfall that is going both up and down.

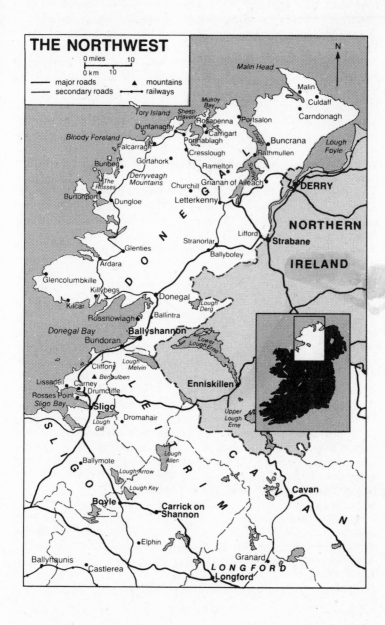

## THE NORTHWEST

0 miles 10
0 km 10

— major roads ▲ mountains
— secondary roads --- railways

N

Malin Head

Malin
Culdaff
Carndonagh

Mulroy Bay
Tory Island
Sheep Haven
Rosapenna
Portsalon
Dunfanaghy
Carrigart
Porthablagh
Buncrana
Bloody Foreland
Falcarragh
Cresslough
Rathmullen
Lough Foyle
Gortahork
Ramelton
Bunbeg
Derryveagh Mountains
Churchill
Grianan of Aileach
The Rosses
Burtonport
Dungloe
Letterkenny
DERRY

D O N E G A L

NORTHERN

Stranorlar
Lifford
Glenties
Ballybofey
Strabane
Ardara
IRELAND

Glencolumbkille
Killybegs
Donegal
Lough Derg
Kilcar
Ballintra
Rossnowlagh
Donegal Bay
Bundoran
Ballyshannon
Lower Lough Erne

Cliffony
Lough Melvin
Lissadell
▲ Benbulben
Enniskillen
Carney
Drumcliffe
Rosses Point
Sligo Bay
Sligo
Dromahair
Lough Gill
Upper Lough Erne

S L I G O
Ballymote
Lough Allen
L E I T R I M
C A V A N
Lough Arrow
Lough Key
Boyle
Cavan
Carrick on Shannon
Elphin
Ballyhaunis
Granard
Castlerea
LONGFORD
Longford

Sligo and Donegal are rich in prehistoric monuments, evidence of a large and active population dating back as far as 4,000 years ago. At Carrowmore, a low hill about three miles southwest of Sligo Town, there is one of the largest concentrations of megalithic tombs in Europe. There were at least 65 tombs in the immediate area, all of the passage-grave type; many were obviously raided during the centuries since they were used. From them has come a collection of passage-grave pottery of the Neolithic period (the late Stone Age, between 2500 and 2000 B.C.), food vessels, stone balls, bone pins and charred human bones. Beside Carrowmore is the mountain of Knocknarea (1,078 ft.) which is not difficult to climb. Here is an unopened cairn, reputedly Queen Maeve's grave, or Miscaun Maedbh in Irish. Maeve was queen of Connacht almost 2,000 years ago and her grave, 200 feet in diameter and 80 feet high, makes her status and grandeur clear.

Perhaps the best Neolithic cairn in the region, if not in the whole of Ireland, is at Creevykeel off the Sligo–Bundoran road, the N15. It's well signposted and easy to find. The basic feature, believed to have been used in the burial ceremonials, is an enclosed rectangular court, giving access to a gallery. Neolithic pottery, stone arrow heads and polished stone axeheads were among the finds here.

## South of Sligo

Ballymote, about nine miles down the N4 from Sligo, was of considerable importance in the 14th century as can easily be seen from the size of the ruined but impressive castle. The ruins cover a considerable area and are flanked by six towers. During the Cromwellian wars in the mid-17th century Ballymote Castle held out for nine years before falling to the forces of General Henry Ireton, Cromwell's chief officer in Ireland. Also of interest here, and close by the castle, are the remains of a Franciscan Friary, famed chiefly as being where the *Book of Ballymote* was compiled in 1391. This manuscript is of very considerable importance as it gives the key to the Ogham alphabet, an ancient form of Gaelic vaguely based on the Roman alphabet, and otherwise found only on standing stones dating from the 4th and 5th centuries A.D. The manuscript is now in the library of the Royal Irish Academy in Dublin.

About two miles southwest of Ballymote just off the N17, is Temple Lodge. This Georgian mansion has been lived in since 1665 by the Perceval family, and was redesigned in 1864. It overlooks Temple Lake and the ruins of a castle built by the Knights Templar in 1200 A.D.

The south of County Sligo is renowned among lovers of Irish traditional music. Michael Colman, one of the most famous of Ireland's traditional fiddle players—whose virtuoso playing was happily preserved in the early years of this century on some American recordings—was born at Killavil near Tubbercurry. Indeed, the whole area boasts a distinctive style of fiddle and flute playing, and the musicians are often joined by step-dancers. The larger bars of Tubbercurry and Gurteen play host to a significant number of traditional musicians.

## Roscommon

Roscommon, the principal town of County Roscommon, is situated in the middle of rich pasture lands, noted for the quality of their cattle and sheep. Like Sligo Town, Roscommon was the site of an important Norman castle, built toward the end of the 13th century. It was almost immediately captured by the Irish and destroyed, only to be rebuilt a few years later. Thereafter its history was one of almost continuous siege and struggle, culminating in its surrender in 1652 to the Cromwellians. Today, its ivy-clad ruins, a substantial tower at each corner, stand impressively on a hillside to the north of the town.

Boyle, 20 miles to the north, is the other important town in the county. It lies at the foot of the Curlew mountains between Lough Gara and Lough Key. Lough Key is one of the most beautiful lakes in Ireland, measuring about six miles across and studded with enticing wooded islands. It was once part of the Rockingham Estate, but when Rockingham House was sadly burned down in 1957 it was incorporated into a forest park.

Lough Gara is a good trout lake. But it has also proved to be extremely rich in archeological material. A large number of little fortified islands have been excavated and many implements and artifacts, including 31 dug-out boats, have been found here. Beside the river on the north side of the town of Boyle are the ruins of a Cistercian Abbey. It was founded in the 12th century and took 60 years to complete.

Midway between Boyle and Roscommon is the town of Castlerea, prettily situated in woodland on the banks of the river Suck. It was the birthplace of Sir William Wilde (1845–1876), surgeon and antiquary, and father of the celebrated wit and dramatist, Oscar Wilde. Just west of the town is Clonalis House, a 19th-century mansion built on the site of the ancestral home of the clan O'Conor. The O'Conors gave 11 high kings to Ireland, and 24 kings to Connacht. Indeed, the last high king of Ireland, who abdicated after the Anglo-Norman invasion of 1169, was of the O'Conor clan. A more recent member of the family, Charles O'Conor, was the first Catholic candidate to contest an American presidential election. He was defeated by Ulysses Grant in 1872. Clonalis House is open to the public and contains an interesting collection of historical mementoes.

## Music Makers

Music lovers will be intrigued by one priceless item in the collection at Clonalis House: Carolan's harp. Turlough Carolan (1670–1738), harpist and composer, lost his sight from smallpox at the age of 14. Having demonstrated his budding musical talent, his friends and patrons, the MacDermott-Rosses, apprenticed him to a harper. At the age of 21 they then provided him with a horse, a servant and a small sum of money, and sent him out to earn his living as an itinerant harper. In return for the hospitality of both rich and poor, he would compose songs and airs, dedicating them to his patrons. After his marriage he lived at a house at Mahill in County Leitrim, and often visited the O'Conors at Clonalis to entertain them, as he did most of the old Irish noble families of Ulster and Connaught. Fortunately for posterity, many of his airs and arrangements were written down and preserved by one Edward Bunting. While his work shows traces of some Italian influences, Italian music having flourished in Dublin at that time, it also has a unique charm and appeal. His influence has persisted and many of the compositions featured on recordings by Irish traditional musicians like the Chieftains, Planxty and Da Danaan, are based on compositions by Carolan. *Carolan's Cottage, Planxty Mac-Guire, The Lamentation of Owen O'Neil* and *Carolan's Concerto* are among his best-known pieces. He lived in the village of Keadue for the last years of his life and is buried nearby in the ancient cemetery of Kilronan on the shores of Lough Meelagh.

Roscommon's other famous musician is something of a contrast: Percy French (1854–1920) made his name as a touring singer and entertainer in the music halls of England and America. He was born at Clooneyquin near Elphin, mid-way between Boyle and Roscommon, and qualified as a civil engineer at Trinity College, Dublin in 1881. While employed as a Surveyor of Drains he started writing songs to make a little extra money. *Abdullah Bull Bul Ameer* and *The Mountains of Mourne* were among his earliest successes. Once he had turned professional he worked mainly outside Ireland, and was especially adept at capturing the emigrant's longing for home. Songs such as *Come Back, Paddy Reilly* and *The Emigrant's Letter* have brought tears to the eyes for generations. His humorous work has proved equally enduring, particularly songs like *Slattery's Mounted Fut, Phil the Fluter's Ball,* and his account of a journey on the West Clare Railway *Are Ye Right There, Michael?* A revival of his work, devised by James N. Healy and featuring the brilliant young soprano, Jacinta Mulcahy, had a successful tour of the United States in 1985. There are also recordings of the work of Percy French available, sung by the tenor, Brendan O'Dowda, who has done much to revive the public's interest in French's songs.

The little town of Elphin itself is not without interest. It has been the seat of a bishopric for over 1,500 years, indeed it was St. Patrick who founded the first religious establishment here. The churchyard of the cathedral contains the graves of the Goldsmiths and the Frenchs, ancestors of the poet and playwright Oliver Goldsmith (1728–1774) and Percy French. It is said that many scenes described in *The Deserted Village,* Goldsmith's finest poem, were based on events, people and places that he saw around Elphin where he spent his boyhood.

### Leitrim

County Leitrim has an international reputation for coarse fishing, and attracts angling enthusiasts from all over the world. It is known as "Lovely Leitrim" because of the beauty of its many lakes and waterways. It has no major industrial center, and is populated mainly by rural farming people who are proud of their reputation for friendliness and hospitality. The county is divided in two by Lough Allen, the first of the many lakes through which the river Shannon runs. The capital of Leitrim is the little town of Carrick-on-Shannon. A flotilla of river cruisers and pleasure craft are available for hire here to enable visitors to explore the many waterways.

## South Donegal

The southernmost town of Donegal is Bundoran, located on the south-western shore of Donegal Bay. It's one of Ireland's major holiday resorts, and has excellent sandy beaches, as well as a disproportionately long main street running parallel to the sea. There is a championship golf course at Aughrus Head just above the town. Between the cliffs of Aughrus Head and Tullan Strand are the Fairy Bridges, strange rock formations caused by the action of the sea on the rocks. Lough Melvin, two and a half miles inland from Bundoran, provides excellent fishing for trout and char.

The road north from Bundoran—the N15—is bordered by sandhills and leads to the town of Ballyshannon, which winds up a steep hill above the river Erne. Where the Erne flows into Donegal from Northern Ireland, four miles from Ballyshannon, is the village of Belleek, which has long been famous for its lustruous pottery. Visitors can watch the craftsmen at work on the figurines and weave-effect pottery which has had a great revival in popularity in recent years. Old Belleek is an expensive collector's item, but modern Belleek is reasonably priced and very likely to appreciate in value over the years.

## St. Patrick's Purgatory

Lough Derg is signposted from the village of Ballintra, four and a half miles from Ballyshannon. This lonely lake, surrounded by heather-clad hills, is famous chiefly for the pilgrimage of St. Patrick's Purgatory. St. Patrick, the story runs, spent 40 days of prayer and fasting on an island in Lough Derg, in the process expelling evil spirits which had infested its cave. The fame of the island, known by then as Patrick's Island, grew rapidly. By the Middle Ages it had become almost as famous a place of pilgrimage as St. James of Compostela in Spain. However, the pilgrimage had a somewhat troubled existence and Pope Sixtus ordered an enquiry in 1479. Eighteen years later Pope Alexander IV ordered that the "Purgatory" be destroyed. Nonetheless the pilgrimages continued, with the result that the buildings on the island were not finally destroyed until 1632 when the local Protestant bishop personally witnessed the demolition work. It was probably during the "Penal" years, when Catholicism in Ireland was suppressed, that the pilgrimage moved to its present site on Station Island, half a mile from the shore.

Today the island is again a place of pilgrimage, the pilgrimage season lasting from June 1 to August 15, during which time the island is closed to all but pilgrims. The pilgrimage itself is excessively rigorous, and takes three full days. There are two modern churches on the island, and pilgrims are accommodated in hospices. The pilgrim must go without sleep for the first 24 hours, and have no more than one meager meal of dry bread and black tea per day. The penitential exercises include the recitation of certain prayers and circuits of the basilica and the "Penitential Beds," remains of stone cells belonging to early Christian monks. A vigil is held in the basilica during the first night. In spite of—or because of—the tough regime, an average of 23,000 pilgrims visit the island each year.

## Donegal Town

Donegal Town, at the head of Donegal Bay, was an early Viking settlement. The name is a corruption of the Irish Dun na Gall, Fort of the Foreigners. It remained important until the early-17th century, as the seat of the princes of Tir Chonaill, the O'Donnells. Donegal Castle was the residence of Hugh Roe O'Donnell, the last chief of Tir Chonaill. It is now an imposing ruin, and is open to visitors. It was rebuilt in the early-16th century by Hugh O'Donnell, who was responsible also for the remarkably large tower. The adjoining Jacobean manor house was added by Sir Basil Brooke who was granted the castle in 1607 by James I.

A quarter of a mile south of the town, on the banks of the river Eske, are the ruins of a 15th-century Franciscan friary. It was captured by the English in 1601 but then largely destroyed in an explosion. However, portions of the north and east cloister have survived, as has a decorated east window. The friary enjoys a special place in Irish history as it was here that the *Annals of the Four Masters* were compiled. Following the destruction of the friary, a number of monks remained here writing the *Annals,* the story of Ireland's saints and people. The task was completed in 1636. The four friars who worked on the *Annals* are commemorated by a 25-foot-high obelisk in the center of Donegal.

Donegal is of course famous chiefly for its tweed, and the place to see it being made is Magee's, a firm which began as a draper's shop 120 years ago and now caters for an international clientele. There is also a cluster of smaller craft units in the town which were introduced in 1984 as part of a Government sponsored project to ensure the continuance of small-scale tweed production.

## The Northwest Coast

The coast road to the west from Donegal, the N56, leads to Killybegs, an important fishing village with a fine natural harbor, today gaining a reputation as a center for watersports. The arrival of the fishing fleet and the unloading of the catches is a sight well worth seeing. The small boats are escorted into the harbor by flocks of swooping seagulls, who swarm around the pier as the fish are unloaded. Besides being a major center for the Irish fishing industry, many trawlers from foreign ports tie up here, and it is not unusual to hear Spanish and Breton spoken in village streets.

Donegal hand-tufted carpets are manufactured in Killybegs, and the factory is open to visitors. Examples of this much sought after product can be found as far afield as the White House and the Vatican, and, a little nearer to home, Dublin Castle.

Kilcar, a picturesque village eight miles west of Killybegs, is a center of the Donegal tweed industry. The nearby villages of Glenties, Ardara, and many other places in the district, abound in small outlets offering unique handwoven tweeds, and hard-wearing hand-knitted sweaters. It is fascinating to spend a while watching the tweed materialize on the hand-loom, and to appreciate the time and skill that goes into its making. This is also a particularly beautiful stretch of coast with fine cliff scenery at Tormore Head and Ballagh Pass, with the typical blues and purples and deep greens of the Donegal landscape all around.

A short distance west of Killybegs on the coast lies Glencolumbkille, the valley where St. Colmcille is said to have destroyed the last demons, which somehow evaded St. Patrick, by driving them into the sea. He founded a monastery here, the most conspicuous remains of which are standing pillars decorated with crosses and geometric designs. There are 15 pillars, and on St. Colmcille's Day (June 15), there is a three-mile pilgrimage around them known as The Stations of the Cross. Even the non-devout will find this worth following, as it takes in many of the sites of antique interest in the valley. The pilgrimage is known in Irish as *an tures,* the journey.

## The Rosses

About 20 miles to the north of the "tweed villages" lies a remarkable district on the coast known as The Rosses, 60,000 acres of rocky, boulder-strewn land intersected by streams and numerous small lakes. Dungloe, a small fishing port with several offshore islands in view, is known locally as the Capital of the Rosses. This is an Irish-speaking area, and in spite of the poor soil most of its residents still manage to make their living from the land. This is largely due to the efforts of one Paddy Gallagher (1873–1964) who left school at ten years old and worked as a hired hand on farms in Scotland and England. He eventually saved enough money to buy a farm in his native Donegal, and used the knowledge he had accumulated on his travels to introduce new farming methods into the area. He became known as "Paddy the Cope." In spite of considerable opposition, his "cope" flourished and expanded its activities to include the export of Donegal tweeds and hand-knits to England and the United States. He is still remembered locally with gratitude and affection.

Burtonport, five miles from Dungloe, claims to land more salmon and lobster than any other fishing port in Ireland. It is also the departure point for trips to Aranmore Island, the largest of the islands off the coast of The Rosses. It is a populous island, and from the evidence obtained at a promontory fort on the south of the island it seems that it has been inhabited for many thousands of years. It has some striking cliff scenery and some interesting caves to explore. Rainbow trout can be fished in Lough Shure on Aranmore.

The road running inland from Burtonport to Gweedore, just four miles away, crosses spectacularly wild country of great beauty. The area around Gweedore is renowned for game fishing in the Gweedore, Crolly and Clady rivers. It is difficult to decide just which part of Donegal provides the greatest spectacle of scenic beauty, but there is another wonderful stretch between Gweedore and Mount Errigal where the road runs beside Lough Nacing and Lough Dunlewy into the Derryveagh mountains. Errigal, Donegal's highest mountain, has a white quartzite cone from which, on a clear day, you can see both the mountains of Scotland and the peaks of Connemara.

## Bloody Foreland and Tory Island

West of Errigal, beyond the villages of Dunlawy and Bunbeg is the headland known as Bloody Foreland. For once the name does not recall the carnage of some long ago battle, but was given to the place because of the play of light which, particularly at sunset, gives a reddish hue to the rocks.

North of Bloody Foreland, nine miles from the mainland, is Tory Island. It is not an easy place to reach by boat, and before the introduction of a helicopter service was often cut off from the mainland for weeks on end. But you can also reach Tory in good weather by taking a boat from Maheraroarty Pier, just outside Gortahork. The major feature of the cliffs of Tory is a round tower, built of pink granite, which, while partially ruined on one side, still retains part of its conical cap. Tory Island has been inhabited since prehistoric times, when an elaborate fort was built at the east end of the island. It is known as Dun Shaloir, or Balor's Fort. Balor was the Celtic god of darkness, and had one eye in the middle of his forehead. Tory also has a set of "cursing stones" which may be turned against an enemy on whom evil is wished. The story goes that when the British gunboat *Wasp* attempted to land troops and police on Tory in 1884 to collect rates from the islanders, the stones were turned against it. The *Wasp* sank with loss of life.

In spite of these morbid stories, visitors will be assured of a warm welcome from the hardy Tory islanders. Some, however, have an unusual sideline. Some years ago the renowned artist, Derek Hill, was painting on the island. One of the islanders watching remarked that he could do better than Mr. Hill. Derek Hill took up the challenge, and from a casual remark a whole new style of painting was born. The islanders produce work which experts call "naive," but which has a strong appeal and was well received at its first overseas exhibition in Paris in 1984. Their work is stark and simple and depicts the scenery of the island and the daily life of the people.

Falcarragh and Gortahork, on the mainland near Tory, are at the center of a predominantly Irish-speaking district, and there is an important Irish college, Colaiste Uladh, in the area, which attracts many students during the summer months. Both villages are good bases for climbing the nearby Muckish Mountain. Gortahork is also the place from which to plan a journey to the smaller offshore islands, Inishbeg, Inishbofin and Inishdhooey.

Creeslough (pronounce it "Kreesh-la") at the head of Sheep Haven Bay, is on the opposite side of Muckish Mountain, which dominates this part of Donegal. Nearby is Doe Castle which was occupied by MacSweeneys from about 1440 until 1890. They came to Ireland from Scotland as "gallowglasses" (a corruption of the Irish *gall-oglach,* meaning foreign warrior) at the invitation of the O'Donnell chieftain, who wished to use them as professional soldiers to fight for his causes. The castle is on an impressive site protected by the sea on three sides and by a deep moat on the fourth. There is a four-story keep, with other buildings of various dates sprawling out from it. The castle is surrounded by a lawn, and the lawn in its turn is enclosed by another curtain wall punctuated by towers, beyond which is the sea. Doe Castle is open to the public throughout the year.

At the tip of Sheep Haven Bay is Horn Head, a cliff which rises straight out of the sea to a height of over 600 feet. There are many unusual sea birds around Horn Head, and the views it affords make it a memorable place to visit. Inland the mountain ranges containing Muckish and Errigal are spread out before you, while the great Atlantic Ocean on the opposite side is broken by numerous islands and headlands.

## The Shores of Lough Swilly

The next sizeable peninsula on the Donegal coast lies to the north of Sheep Haven and is bounded by the long inlet of Mulroy Bay and Broad Water in the west and Lough Swilly in the east. The peninsula can be explored by following the Fanad Peninsula Scenic Tour, a 45-mile circuit. Sandy beaches, lakes, streams and heather-clad hills make it a splendid drive.

Rathmullan makes a useful base for exploring Mulroy Bay and the western shores of Lough Swilly. It is a quiet village with many historic associations, the most famous of which is the kidnapping of "Red" Hugh O'Donnell. He was tricked into boarding an English naval ship, which was camouflaged as a merchant vessel, by an invitation to sample wines, a sound ploy given his nationality. The ship took him to Dublin Castle where he remained a prisoner for four years, before he managed to escape. Rathmullan harbor was one of the main anchorages of the Royal Navy during World War I. There is an old fort near the pier which is the remains of one of six Martello towers—fortified towers—which were built on either side of Lough Swilly to protect the area from invasion by Napoleon's armies.

Ramelton, a small town on the road to Letterkenny, is something of an architectural surprise, as it was designed and laid out in the 17th century for the English settlers. Its castle has been carefully restored and is open to the public as an exhibition center.

Letterkenny is the chief town of Donegal, and is situated near the head of Lough Swilly. The town is dominated by St. Eunan's Cathedral, built between 1890 and 1900. Ten miles west of Letterkenny, near the shore of Gartan Lough, is the little village of Churchill. Gartan was the birthplace of St. Colmcille, the 6th-century saint who is so closely connected with Donegal's history.

Derek Hill the artist and stage designer who inspired the Tory islanders to form their own school of painting, donated his Regency home at Gartan Lough, and his extensive art collection, to the Irish state in 1980. The house is decorated and furnished in the pre-Raphaelite manner, and the collection includes works by Braque, Corot, Dégas, Picasso, Renoir and Jack B. Yeats. The land surrounding Derek Hill's house has been incorporated into Glenveagh National Park which extends for 24,000 acres into the Derryveagh mountains. Lough Beagh is at the heart of the park, a long narrow lake running along a gorge for some five miles. The mountains rise sharply from the edge of the lake, streams and waterfalls tumbling down them. This richly-wooded park is one of the splendors of Donegal, and contrasts with the barren rugged coastal lands. A castle was built here in the 19th century, and provides the first of a series of links between Glenveagh and America. It was built by John George Adair who bought the land in 1857 and married the daughter of an old American family, Cornelia Wadsworth, whose father had been a general in the Union Army during the Civil War. Adair died in 1885 leaving the property to his wife. She continued to improve the surrounding land, and acquired local fame as a "lady bountiful." After her death it was sold to Professor Kingsley Porter of Harvard. In 1933, three years after buying Glenveagh, he was drowned while visiting Inishbofin island. His widow then sold the property to Henry P. McIlhenny, whose grandfather had emigrated from nearby Carrigart. After further improvements, Mr. McIlhenny generously donated Glenveagh to the nation. Formal French and Italian gardens have since been added, and blend in pleasingly with the beautiful natural surroundings. Glenveagh also has in its grounds one of only two herds of red deer in Ireland. From Letterkenny, Glenveagh is reached by the road marked L27, from the west (Falcarragh) the route is L82 through the Muckish Gap.

### Inishowen Peninsula and Grianán of Aileach

Inishowen stretches out between Lough Foyle and Lough Swilly to Malin Head, Ireland's most northerly mainland point. There is a road right to the tip, which is best approached by taking the western road from Letterkenny through Buncrana. To get some idea of the wonderful scenery to come on the circuit round the peninsula, stop off at Grianán of Aileach, signposted beyond Newton Cunningham.

Grianán of Aileach is an ancient circular stone fort built on the summit of Grianán mountain and commanding fine views over the surrounding countryside, including both Lough Swilly and Lough Foyle. The enclosure is 77 feet in diameter and its terraced walls rise to a height of 17 feet. It is believed to have been built 4,000 years ago and was at one time the residence of the kings of Ulster, the O'Neills. The fort was restored in 1870. The town below to the east is Derry, in Northern Ireland, and the Grianán is a popular outing with its residents. It is also a fitting place to stand and view the old kingdom of Ulster and take a last look at Donegal.

For a different, and some might say more characteristically Irish view, drive up the western side of Lough Foyle. At a suitably scenic spot turn to face south over the Lough. This is one of those rare places on the globe where looking south you get a view of the north, Northern Ireland that is. Similarly, if you look north you get a view of the south, the Republic of Ireland. It could only happen in Ireland.

# PRACTICAL INFORMATION FOR
# THE NORTHWEST

**TOURIST OFFICES.** The main tourist office for the Northwest is in **Sligo,** Temple St. (tel. 071–61201). There are other offices at **Boyle,** tel. 079–62145 (open June–Aug.); **Bundoran,** tel. 072–41350 (open June to Aug.); **Carrick-on-Shannon,** tel. 078–20170 (open June to Sept.); **Donegal,** tel. 073–21148 (open June to Aug.); **Dungloe,** tel. 075–21297 (open June to Aug.); **Letterkenny,** tel. 074–21160 (open year-round); **Roscommon,** tel. 0903–6356 (open June to Aug.).

## HOTELS AND RESTAURANTS

**Ardara** (Co. Donegal). *Nesbitt Arms* (I), tel. 075–41103. 27 rooms, some with bath. Well recommended. AE, MC.

**Restaurant.** *Woodhill House* (M), tel. 075–41112. Well-run by owner-chef. Great views. AE, MC, V.

**Arranmore Island** (Co. Donegal). *The Glen* (I), tel. 075–21505. 10 rooms. For an island holiday with a difference. Rock-bottom rates; like many other hotels in the northwest, it's seasonal, open Apr. to Oct. only.

**Ballybofey** (Co. Donegal). *Jackson's* (I), tel. 074–31021. 39 rooms, all with bath. The sort of place travelers detour to visit. DC, MC, V. *Kees* (I), tel. 074–31018. 26 rooms with bath. Located in neighboring Stranorlar. Family-run with a good restaurant. AE, DC, MC, V.

**Ballymote** (Co. Sligo). *Temple House* (M), tel. 071–83329. 6 rooms, 3 with bath. Bed and breakfast accommodations in 90-room mansion set in 1,000 acres: lots of woodland walks and organic farm. Full board available.

**Ballyshannon** (Co. Donegal). *Dorrian's Imperial* (M), tel. 072–51147. 26 rooms, all with bath. DC, MC. *Creevy Pier* (I), tel. 072–51236. 10 rooms with bath. Good seafood restaurant.

**Boyle** (Co. Roscommon). *Royal* (M), tel. 079–62016. 16 rooms with bath. Good location for lake fishing. AE, DC, MC, V.
**Restaurant.** *Lakeshore* (I), Lough Key Forest Park (tel. 079–62214). Self-service in daytime; bistro with waitress-service in evening. Interesting and varied menu; a lively spot popular with the locals.

**Bunbeg** (Co. Donegal). *Gweedore* (M), tel. 075–31177. 40 rooms with bath. In Donegal highlands; seaviews; V. *Seaview* (I), tel. 075–31159. 28 rooms with bath. Good restaurant (M). V.

**Bundoran** (Co. Donegal). *Great Northern* (M), tel. 072–41204. 96 rooms, all with bath. In the middle of a golf course. AE, DC, MC, V. *Holyrood* (I), tel. 072–42132. 61 rooms, all with bath. AE, DC, MC, V.

**Carrick-On-Shannon** (Co. Leitrim). *Aisleigh House* (I), tel. 078–20313. 7 rooms, 6 with bath. Well-recommended bed and breakfast. MC, V. *The Bush* (I), tel. 078–20014. 20 rooms with bath. Owner is an expert on river Shannon cruising—he was doing it long before it became popular. AE, MC, V.

**Carrigart** (Co. Donegal). *Carrigart Holiday* (M), tel. 074–55114. 48 rooms, most with bath. On shores of Mulroy and Sheephaven bays. Heated indoor pool, sauna, solarium, squash, tennis, golf. Family-operated.

**Creeslough** (Co. Donegal). *Creeslough Holiday Cottages,* tel. 074–38101. Has several self-catering cottages for rent at around IR£220 a week.

**Cruit Island** (Co. Donegal). *Donegal Thatched Cottages* have eight traditional cottages with modern conveniences available in West Donegal at around IR£220 a week. Contact Conor and Mary Ward, Rosses Point, Sligo (tel. 071–77197).

**Donegal Town** (Co. Donegal). *Abbey* (M), tel. 073–21014. 43 rooms, all with bath. AE, DC, MC, V. *Hyland Central* (M), tel. 073–21027. 62 rooms, all with bath. AE, DC, MC, V.

**Dromahair** (Co. Leitrim). *Drumlease Glebe House* (E), tel. 071–64141. 8 rooms with bath. Georgian country house, with trout and salmon fishing in its own grounds. Gourmet restaurant for residents only.

**Dunfanaghy** (Co. Donegal). *Arnold's* (I), tel. 074–36208. 36 rooms, 26 with bath. Overlooking Sheephaven Bay. AE, DC, MC, V. *Carrig Rua* (I), tel. 074–36133. 22 rooms, all with bath. AE, V.

**Dungloe** (Co. Donegal). *Ostan na Rosann* (I), tel. 075–21088. 48 rooms with bath. Overlooking Dungloe Bay. Indoor heated pool. AE, DC, V.

**Gortahork** (Co. Donegal). *McFadden's* (I), tel. 074–35267. 20 rooms, some with bath. One of the best-known hotels in the country; cheerful hospitality. AE, DC, MC, V.

**Letterkenny** (Co. Donegal). *Mount Errigal* (M), tel. 074–22700. 56 rooms, all with bath. Good food. AE, DC, MC, V.

**Moville** (Co. Donegal). *Redcastle Hotel and Country Club* (M), Redcastle (tel. 077–82073). 29 rooms, all with bath. On wooded estate on the Innishowen Peninsula. Facilities include 9-hole golf course. AE, DC, MC, V. *McNamara's* (I), tel. 077–82010. 15 rooms, 11 with bath. Family hotel with good food. DC, MC, V.

**Rathmullan** (Co. Donegal). *Fort Royal* (M), tel. 074–58100. 18 rooms, some with bath. Beside Lough Swilly in garden and woodland. Private beach, golf, squash, tennis, sailing. DC, MC, V. *Rathmullan House* (M), tel. 074–58188. 19 rooms, most with bath. Also on Lough Swilly, outstanding hotel with lovely gardens. AE, DC, MC, V.
**Restaurant.** *Water's Edge* (M), tel. 074–58182. Seafood a specialty, on the shores of Lough Swilly. Reservations advised. DC, MC, V.

**Riverstown** (Co. Sligo). *Coopershill* (M), tel. 071–65108. 6 rooms with bath. Exceptional country-house hospitality in a Georgian mansion, just off the main Dublin–Sligo road.

**Rosapenna** (Co. Donegal). *Rosapenna Golf* (M), tel. 074–55301. 40 rooms, all with bath. Close to one of the finest golf courses in the country. AE, DC, MC, V.

**Rosses Point** (Co. Sligo). *Ballincar House* (M), Rosses Point Rd. (tel. 071–45361). 20 rooms with bath. Converted country house in own gardens. Excellent food. Squash, tennis, sauna-solarium. AE, DC, MC, V. *Yeats Country Ryan* (M), tel. 071–77211. Beside the championship golf course at the seaside; tennis. AE, DC, MC, V.

**Rossnowlagh** (Co. Donegal). *Sand House* (M), tel. 072–51777. 40 rooms, most with bath. Overlooking the beach, great for surfing. Food is excellent. AE, DC, MC.

**Sligo Town** (Co. Sligo). *Sligo Park* (M), Pearse Rd. (tel. 071–60291). 60 rooms, all with bath. AE, DC, MC, V. *Southern* (I), tel. 071–62101. 50 rooms with bath. AE, DC, MC, V.

**Restaurant.** *Knockmuldowney* (E), Culleenamore (tel. 071–68122). A fine country-house restaurant just outside town on Ballisodare Bay, near Strandhill. AE, DC, MC, V. *Bonne Chere* (M), 45 High St. (tel. 071–2014). Family-style. AE, MC, V. *Gulliver's* (I), Gratten St. (tel. 071–42030). Pizzeria. AE, DC, MC, V.

## Youth Hostels

**Arranmore Island,** Burtonport, Letterkenny, Co. Donegal. **Ball Hill,** Donegal Town, Co. Donegal (tel. 073–21174). **Bundoran,** Bayview Ave., Homefield (tel. 072–41288). **Crohy Head,** Dungloe, Co. Donegal (tel. 075–21330). **Errigal,** Dunlewy, Gweedore, Letterkenny, Co. Donegal (tel. 075–31180). **Tory Island,** Co. Donegal (open Jul. and Aug. only). **Tra-na-Rosann,** Downings, Co. Donegal (tel. 074–55374).

**TOURS AND EXCURSIONS.** Bus tours into Donegal highlands are operated from Sligo Town (the railway station) by C.I.E. In Donegal the *Londonderry and Lough Swilly Railway Company* has long since ceased to run a railway, but it does run useful bus services from Buncrana, tel. 077–61340, and Letterkenny, tel. 074–22863.

Cruises on Lough Gill depart from the riverside landing stage at Doorly Park Gates, at the eastern end of Sligo Town. A cruise takes about 1¼ hours and provides a commentary on the places mentioned in the poems of W.B. Yeats. Contact Jerry Sweeney, *Lough Gill Cruises* (tel. 071–62540). The fare is about IR£4.

Bicycles can be hired from *Gerry Conway,* Wine St., Sligo Town (tel. 071–61240); *C.J. Doherty,* Main St., Donegal Town (tel. 073–21119).

## PLACES TO VISIT

**Boyle** (Co. Roscommon). **Boyle Abbey.** A Cistercian abbey built in the 12th and 13th centuries. Of considerable architectural interest. Open mid June to mid Sept., daily 10–6. Rest of year, key with caretaker.

**Buncrana** (Co. Donegal). **Grianán of Aileach.** A massive circular stone fort of the early Christian era, very well preserved. Eight miles south of Buncrana off the Buncrana–Letterkenny road.

**Castlerea** (Co. Roscommon). **Clonalis House.** 19th-century mansion with a fine collection of antique furniture and portraits, plus the harp of the famous Turlough O'Carolan and the Coronation Stone of the Kings of Connacht. Open May to June, Sat. and Sun. 2–5.30; Jul. to 8 Sept., daily 11–1 and 2–5.30.

**Churchill** (Co. Donegal). **Glebe Gallery,** (tel. Churchill 71). Contains the fine Derek Hill art collection. Churchill is on the Letterkenny–Gweedore road.

**Cliffony** (Co. Sligo). **Creevykeel Court Cairn.** One of the best examples of this type of megalithic tomb; dates back to about 3000 B.C. Located close to the Sligo–Bundoran road, near Cliffony.

**Creeslough** (Co. Donegal). **Doe Castle.** 16th-century castle built by MacSweeney na d'Tuath, surrounded by sea and a moat cut through the rock. Two miles from Creeslough off the Creeslough–Carrigart road. Freely accessible.

**Donegal** (Co. Donegal). **Donegal Castle.** 16th-century tower and adjoining 17th-century manor house, once the home of Hugh Roe O'Donnell, a chieftain of great renown. Freely accessible to the public.

**Dromahair** (Co. Leitrim). **Creevelea Friary,** Dromahair. Build in 1508; has some interesting carvings depicting St. Francis on the pillars of the cloister. Established just before the suppression of the monasteries by King Henry VIII.

**Drumcliffe** (Co. Sligo). **Drumcliffe Churchyard.** Burial place of the poet William Butler Yeats, at his specific request. There is a fine High Cross in the neighborhood with interesting carvings.

**Rossnowlagh** (Co. Donegal). **Donegal Museum,** Franciscan Friary, Rossnowlagh (tel. 072–65342). Folklife, archeology, militaria, numismatics.

**Sheephaven Bay** (Co. Donegal). **Ards Forest Park.** On shore of Sheephaven Bay. Variety of flora and fauna over 1,188 acres, including nature trail with interesting geological features. Two miles north of Creeslough on N56. Open all year, 9–9.

**Sligo** (Co. Sligo). **Hawk's Well Theater,** Temple St. (tel. 071–61526). A lively center staging interesting productions.
**Lisadell House.** Former home of Constance Gore-Booth, who took part in the 1916 Rising and was later the first woman elected to the British House of Commons. Of some architectural interest, the house is still the home of the Gore-Booth family. Open 1 May to 30 Sept., Mon. to Sat. 2–5.15. Last tour at 4.30.
**Sligo County Museum,** Stephen St. (tel. 071–2212). Covers the folklife of the area, rare printed books and memorabilia of the painter J.B. Yeats.

# NORTHERN IRELAND

# FACTS AT YOUR FINGERTIPS

## *Planning Your Trip*

*For general vacation information—Travel Agents and Tours, Passports, Health and Insurance, Hints for Handicapped Travelers, Student and Youth Travel, Irish Time, etc., see* Facts at Your Fingertips *on page 1.*

**NATIONAL TOURIST OFFICE.** Though to some extent within the British Tourist Authority umbrella, the Northern Ireland Tourist Board has its own offices overseas. These are the primary sources of information for all tourists hoping to visit the Province. Where there is no N.I.T.B. office, however, the British Tourist Authority can usually supply information.

Addresses of the N.I.T.B. overseas are:

**In the U.S.:** 40 West 57th St., Third Floor, New York, NY 10019 (212–765–5144).

**In the U.K.:** Ulster Office, 11 Berkeley St., London W.1 (01–493 0601); 38 High St., Sutton Coldfield, B72 1UP (021–354 1431).

B.T.A. offices overseas are:

**In the U.S.:** 2580 Cumberland Parkway, Suite 470, Atlanta, GA 30339 (404–432–9635); 875 North Michigan Ave., Chicago IL 60611 (312–787–0490); 2305 Cedar Springs Rd., Suite 210, Dallas, TX 75201 (214–720–4040); World Trade Center, Suite 450, 350 Figueroa St., Los Angeles, CA 90071 (213–628–3525).

**In Canada:** 94 Cumberland St., Suite 600, Toronto, Ont. M5R 3N3 (416–925–6326).

Within Northern Ireland, the N.I.T.B. is located at River House, 48 High St., Belfast BT1 2DS (0232–246609).

**SEASONAL EVENTS. January** Royal Ulster Agricultural Society Show, Balmoral, Belfast. **February** Ulster Harp National (steeplechase), Downpatrick. **March** St. Patrick's Day celebrations, Downpatrick. **April** Belfast Civic Festival and Lord Mayor's Show. **May** Ballyclare Horse Fair; Belfast City Marathon; Royal Ulster Agricultural Show, Balmoral; Ulster Classic angling festival, Lough Erne. **June** Black Bush Causeway Coast Amateur Golf Tournament. **July** International Rose Trials, Belfast; 300th Anniversary of the Battle of the Boyne (processions and many other events on and around July 12), Belfast and other centers. **August** Ancient Order of Hibernians Processions; Oul Lammas Fair, Ballycastle. **September** Belfast Folk Festival. **November** Queen's University International Arts Festival, Belfast.

**National Holidays 1990.** January 1; March 17 (St. Patrick's Day); April 13 (Good Friday); April 16 (Easter Monday); May 1 (May Day Bank Holiday); May 28 (Spring Bank Holiday); July 12 (Orangemen's Day); August 27 (August Bank Holiday); December 25–26 (Christmas Day and Boxing Day).

**COSTS IN NORTHERN IRELAND.** Northern Ireland is generally inexpensive, both in comparison to the rest of the U.K. and the Republic of Ireland. This disparity is neatly highlighted by the floods of cars that pour over the border from the Republic as the Irish stock up in Northern Ireland's supermarkets every week. In addition, the strong dollar helps make Northern Ireland even more affordable. But with exchange rates so unpredictable this currently favorable situation can easily change, so keep an eagle eye on the rate both while planning your trip and during it.

**Currency.** The unit of currency in Northern Ireland is the pound sterling, divided into 100 pence. There are notes of £50, £20, £10, and £5, and coins of £1, 50p, 20p, 10p and 1p. Irish currency may sometimes be accepted, as may dollars.

At the time of writing (spring 1989), the pound stood at around $1.70 and IR£1.23.

## Getting to Northern Ireland

**FROM NORTH AMERICA BY AIR.** Air links between the U.S. and Canada and Northern Ireland are patchy. There are no direct scheduled flights, though there are some charter flights in the summer. For details, check with your travel agent. Otherwise, fly to Shannon, Dublin, London or Manchester and pick up a connecting flight to Belfast.

**FROM THE U.K. BY AIR.** The British Airways Super Shuttle from London (Heathrow) makes flying to Belfast simple. This is a walk-on service with no reservations necessary. If the plane is full, British Airways claim that they will lay on an extra plane, if necessary just for one passenger. But with seven flights every day, this is a rare occurrence. Flying time is just over one hour, and the full round-trip fare about £139, but only £85 if booked at least 14 days in advance. The British Midland service is also excellent.

Dan Air have three flights every day to Belfast from London (Gatwick). Belfast International also operate direct flights from Exeter, Bristol, Cardiff, Birmingham, East Midlands, Liverpool, Leeds, Teeside and Manchester.

**FROM THE U.K. BY TRAIN.** Belfast can be reached by several routes. The shortest sea crossing, around two and a half hours, is from Stranraer in southern Scotland to Larne, a few miles north of Belfast. This route is operated by Sealink British Ferries (Stranraer, tel. 0776–2262). There's a connecting boat train from London (Euston) to Stranraer. The morning train will get you to Belfast by late evening, while the overnight service gets you there by lunch the following day. There are first- and standard-class sleepers on this overnight train, as well as ordinary standard-class carriages. These through trains may be replaced by a bus service from Carlisle in the near future. Alternatively, Belfast Ferries (tel. 051–922 6234) operate a regular ferry service between Liverpool and Belfast, the crossing taking around eight hours. On this route, the early morning train from London (Euston) will get you to Belfast just after 8 P.M. There's a special bus service between Liverpool's Lime Street Station and the ferry terminal.

Finally, you can also cross over to Dublin from either Liverpool or Holyhead and get the train up to Belfast. For details of these routes, see *Getting to Ireland—From the U.K. By Train* on page 15.

**FROM THE U.K. BY BUS.** There are both daytime and overnight bus services to Belfast from London (Victoria Coach Station) operated by Supabus (marketed by International Express). These services all go via Stranraer and Larne. Total journey time is around 14 hours. The daytime service leaving London at 8.30 A.M. reaches Belfast 10.30 P.M. The round-trip fare is about £55. For more details, see *Getting to Ireland—From the U.K. By Bus* on page 15.

**FROM THE U.K. BY CAR.** The Stanraer/Cairnryan–Larne and Liverpool–Belfast ferry routes both take cars. There's little to choose between them in terms of journey time, however, as the shorter drive to Liverpool from London, say, is canceled out by the longer ferry crossing, whereas the longer drive to Stranraer/Cairnryan is canceled out by the shorter sea crossing. The advantages of traveling via southern Scotland are the shortness of the crossing (two hours), and the frequency of the service, with up to 14 crossings daily in summer. The Cairnryan–Larne route is operated by P.&O. European Ferries (tel. 05812–276). Fares of the Stranraer/Cairnryan–Larne run are now virtually identical at around £170. For Liverpool–Belfast allow around £180 round trip excluding cabin accommodations.

Alternatively, it may be easier to sail to Dublin from Holyhead or Liverpool, or even to Rosslare in southern Ireland from Fishguard and drive up to Ulster. For details, see *Getting to Ireland—From the U.K. By Car* on page 16.

**CUSTOMS ON ARRIVAL.** There are two levels of duty-free allowance for people entering the U.K.; one, for goods bought outside the E.E.C. or for goods bought in a duty-free shop within the E.E.C.; two, for goods bought in an E.E.C. country but not in a duty-free shop.

In the first category you may import duty free: 200 cigarettes or 100 cigarillos or 50 cigars or 250 grammes of tobacco (*Note* if you live outside Europe, these allowances are doubled); plus one liter of alcoholic drinks over 22% vol. (38.8% proof) or two liters of alcoholic drinks not over 22% vol. or fortified or sparkling wine; plus two liters of still table wine; plus 50 grammes of perfume; plus nine fluid ounces of toilet water; plus other goods to the value of £28.

In the second category you may import duty free: 300 cigarettes or 150 cigarillos or 75 cigars or 400 grammes of tobacco; plus 1½ liters of alcoholic drinks over 22% vol. (38.8% proof) or three liters of alcoholic drinks not over 22% vol. or fortified or sparkling wine; plus five liters of still table wine; plus 75 grammes of perfume; plus 13 fluid ounces of toilet water; plus other goods to the value of £163 (*Note* though it is not classified as an alcoholic drink by E.E.C. countries for Customs' purposes and is thus considered part of the "other goods" allowance, you may not import more than 50 liters of beer.)

In addition, no animals or pets of any kind may be brought into the U.K. The penalties for doing so are severe and are strictly enforced; there are *no* exceptions. Similarly, fresh meats, plants and vegetables, controlled drugs and firearms and ammunition may not be brought into the U.K. There are no restrictions on the import or export of British and foreign currencies.

## Staying in Northern Ireland

**CHANGING MONEY.** Bank opening hours are 9.30–12.30 and 1.30–3 Monday to Friday. All banks are closed on Saturdays. You should be able to change money at any of the larger central banks, but there is also a bureau de change at Belfast's Aldergrove airport. This is open from 9–12.15 and 1.15–3 and 6–8 Monday to Friday, and 10–12 Saturdays and Sundays.

Most of the larger hotels can also change traveler's checks, but the rate of exchange will not be as favorable as at a bank.

**HOTELS.** Standards in Northern Ireland are much the same as in the Republic of Ireland (see *Staying in Ireland*). The Northern Ireland Tourist Board publishes an annually revised listing of all hotels in the Province *(Northern Ireland—All the Places to Stay)*. Room numbers, prices, months open and facilities are all listed.

We have divided all the hotels in our listings into four categories: Deluxe (L), Expensive (E), Moderate (M), and Inexpensive (I). These grades are determined solely by price.

Two people in a double room can expect to pay:

| | |
|---|---|
| Deluxe (L) | £90 and up |
| Expensive (E) | £60 to £90 |
| Moderate (M) | £35 to £60 |
| Inexpensive (I) | under £35 |

**CAMPING.** There are over 100 camp sites in Northern Ireland. The Northern Ireland Tourist Board's *Camping and Caravan Parks* (20p) booklet gives details of all sites, with information on facilities and prices. It's best to book ahead during July and August. You may also be able to camp away from the official sites. Ulster farmers are usually obliging about short stays, but ask first.

The Northern Ireland Forest Service allows campers to stay in most of the Province's forest parks. Permits are required. For further information and a useful leaflet called *Touring in the Trees,* contact the *Forest Service,* Dept. of Agriculture, Dundonald House, Upper Newtownards Rd., Belfast (tel. 0231–650111).

**YOUTH HOSTELS.** The Youth Hostels Association of Northern Ireland (YHANI), at 56 Bradbury Pl., Belfast (tel. 0232–324733), can supply information on all nine hostels in Ulster. Their *YHANI Handbook* also gives full information on rambling and walking tours throughout the year. You must be a member of the Youth Hostels Association in your own country to use any of Northern Ireland's hostels, except the one in Belfast. Book ahead for all hostels in July and August.

**BED & BREAKFAST AND FARMHOUSES.** Northern Ireland has a wide range of this type of accommodation. You will find many addresses listed in the *All the Places to Stay* booklet (£1.95). The Northern Ireland Tourist Board also issues a booklet devoted entirely to these types of accommodations called *Farm and Country Holidays* (50p). Rates vary from place to place, but you can expect to pay from around £8 to £12 per person per night. In the fishing centers there are also special accommodations for anglers in private houses. For details it is best to contact the local Tourist Office.

**RESTAURANTS.** Though Northern Ireland can hardly claim to be a gastronomic wonderland, there are a number of pleasant restaurants throughout the Province. These are mainly concentrated in the middle and lower price ranges, which means that you can generally expect to be able to eat out here for a good deal less than in most other places in Europe. For a comprehensive list of restaurants throughout Northern Ireland, see the Belfast Tourist Office's booklet, *Where to Eat* (£1.25).

We have divided the restaurants in our listings into three grades: Expensive (E), Moderate (M), and Inexpensive (I). These grades are determined solely by price.

Approximate prices per person excluding drinks:

| | |
|---|---|
| Expensive (E) | £18 and up |
| Moderate (M) | £12 to £18 |
| Inexpensive (I) | under £12 |

**TIPPING.** As in the rest of Great Britain, tipping is not as widespread as in the rest of Europe, and certainly not as much as it is in the U.S. In restaurants, check the bill to see if service is included. If it isn't, tip about 10% if you're satisfied with the service you've received. Taxi drivers don't normally expect tips, but again, tip about 10% of the fare if you think it appropriate.

**OPENING TIMES.** Shops in Belfast are open 9–5.30, Monday to Friday, with a late night on Thursday, usually 9 P.M. Elsewhere, shops close at lunch once a week, usually Wednesday or Thursday. This varies from region to region, so it's best to check locally. Most smaller shops also close for an hour or so at lunch.

Post offices are open 9–5.30 Monday to Friday, and 9–1 on Saturdays. Some also close for an hour at lunch.

Pubs in Northern Ireland are open from 11.30–11, Monday to Saturday, and 12.30–2.30 and 7–10 on Sundays. Sunday opening is, however, at the publican's discretion.

**MAIL.** Airmail rates to the U.S. and Canada are 32p for letters and postcards (not over 10 grams). To the rest of the U.K. and the Republic of Ireland, rates are 19p for first-class letters, and 14p for second class. These rates may well increase before or during 1990. Letter boxes are red.

**PLACES OF INTEREST.** Northern Ireland has a host of historic houses and castles open to the public. There is also a wide variety of museums, nature reserves and folk parks. You will find the best of these described in the texts on Belfast and the Rest of Northern Ireland. A list of details such as opening hours, main attractions and admission fees can be found in the *Places of Interest* sections at the end of these chapters. For a fully comprehensive list of all the historic houses, castles and gardens open to the public you should buy a copy of the annual magazine *Historic Houses, Castles and Gardens* which covers the whole of Great Britain and Ireland (cost around £2).

**SPORTS. Fishing.** Northern Ireland is a great place for anglers. With a long coastline (466 miles), part of it in the Atlantic Ocean and the other in the Irish Sea, it has a number of well-equipped boats available and boatmen who know the right places. Porbeagle shark and conger off Rathlin Island. Strangford Lough is the place for big skate and tope. Even in Belfast Lough there's plenty of cod within easy reach of the city.

If you're after game fish—salmon and trout—you'll need a permit (around £7) for 15 days for great sport in the rivers of the Glens of Antrim, the River Bush (*Department of Agriculture Fisheries Branch,* 2–4 Queen St., Belfast, for permission), the River Bann (*Bann Fisheries,* Coleraine), and the River Foyle (*Foyle Fisheries Commission,* Londonderry).

The waters of the province have an abundance of coarse fish—pike, roach and bream. A general coarse fishing permit (around £4) is needed, plus the local owner's permission. In the Foyle Fisheries Commission area (roach fishing is particularly good here) you don't need a rod license. In areas controlled by the Department of Agriculture you will need a permit (50p). Shops all over the country sell the license.

**Golf.** There are eight golf courses within Belfast's city boundary and about 60 more throughout the province, including the international championship courses at Royal Portrush and Royal County Down, the latter considered by many to be one of the finest courses in the world outside America. Visitors are welcome.

**Horse Riding and Pony Trekking.** Popular sports throughout the whole area, particularly in the forest parks and the Glens of Antrim. *Greenacres Riding Center* in Co. Down has a western-style ranchhouse for guests. Top center for advanced horse riders is the *Ashbrooke School* at Colebrooke, a 1,200-acre estate in County Fermanagh. Several Northern Ireland hunts, such as the *County Down Staghounds* (they do not kill the stag), welcome visitors and will provide a mount if you have an introduction to the Master. The Northern Ireland Tourist Board can arrange this.

**Sailing.** This is another popular sport in Northern Ireland with Strangford Lough one of the most favored centers; another is at Ballyholme Bay, Bangor. Inland, on Lough Erne the *Lakeland Sailing School* at Kesh, Co. Fermanagh, provides instruction for the novice and craft for the experienced.

**Walking.** This is a great recreation in Northern Ireland and the 450-mile long Ulster Way, part of a scenic footpath that encircles Ireland, takes the walker through spectacular coastal scenery. There are 23 caravan sites in forest parks located 30 miles apart to provide for an easy day's staging—all are in pleasantly secluded situations. Admission to the parks themselves is usually free.

## *Getting Around Northern Ireland*

**BY TRAIN.** The state-owned Northern Ireland Railways have three main rail routes, all operating out of Belfast's Central Station (tel. 0232–230310). These are north to Londonderry, via Ballymena and Coleraine; east to Bangor along the shores of Belfast Lough; and south to Dublin and the Republic of Ireland.

Other than on the Dublin line, all trains are one class only with fares about the same as in the Republic. There is also a seven-day Runabout ticket giving unlimited travel for £21.

**BY BUS.** All services are operated by the state-owned Ulsterbus company. Services are generally good, with particularly useful links between those towns not served by train. In addition, there is a Runabout ticket costing about £16 for seven days' unlimited travel. Ulsterbus also operate a wide range of bus tours. For details, see "Tours and Excursions" in *Practical Information for Belfast.*

**BY CAR.** The road network in Northern Ireland is good and, outside Belfast, uncrowded. Indeed, it is claimed that there are only 21 cars per mile of road compared with 66 in the rest of Britain.

If you drive up to Northern Ireland from the Republic, use the approved roads only; for details of these, see *Getting Around Ireland—By Car* on page 29.

Be careful to note parking signs in towns and cities. In some town centers there are Control Zones, always marked by a yellow sign. Don't park near these or you'll be fined.

**BY BIKE.** Cycling is popular in Northern Ireland and a bike is great for exploring. It costs about £3.50 a day to hire one, or £17 for a week; if you want to ride tandem, a bicycle made for two is about £7 a day. Centers at the *Cycle Shop,* 8 Railway St., Lisburn; *P. McNulty & Son,* 24–26 Belmore St., Enniskillen; and *W. Nutt,* 20 Circular Rd., Coleraine.

**BY INLAND WATERWAY.** Inland cruising on the Erne Waterway—300 square miles of lakes and rivers—is one of Ulster's big attractions. Upper and Lower Lough Erne are surrounded by some of Ireland's finest scenery, studded with over 100 islands, few of them inhabited, and offering plenty of room for those who want to get away from it all, and good company at loughside hostelries when you feel gregarious. The Erne Charter Boat Association maintains high standards among its members. A sample mid-season charge for a 4-berth cruiser is around £300. Contact *Erne Charter Boat Association,* Tourist Office, Enniskillen, Co. Fermanagh.

If you want to view the spectacular landscape from afloat without effort there are cruises on Lough Erne on Sundays (more frequent in July and August) and on Lough Neagh, Easter-September. The Lough Erne trip is the more interesting; about £2.50 for a two-hour cruise. Contact *Lough Erne Tours* (tel. 0365–22882) for details.

# NORTHERN IRELAND

*An Introduction*

by
**PAUL STRATHERN**

Northern Ireland, with a population of one and a half million, occupies the Six Counties of Ulster, the northeastern corner of Ireland. Unlike the rest of Ireland, this territory remains part of the United Kingdom. Legend has it that well over a millennium ago a marauding chieftain caught sight of the shores of Northern Ireland from the deck of his boat, whereupon he offered this green fertile land to whichever of his two sons could first lay hand on it. Immediately the two rival sons began rowing furiously for the shore in their separate boats. One began to draw ahead. But such was the grim determination of the other that upon seeing his brother reaching the breakers he drew his sword, cut off his own hand, and threw it ahead of him over the breakers onto the beach. Thus he was the first of the two brothers to lay hand on the new land, and became its ruler. To this day the arms of Northern Ireland feature this same severed bloody limb: the celebrated "Red Hand of Ulster."

Northern Ireland has had a long and often violent history and its legacy is evident today in certain areas of the country. Motorists will encounter random spot checks and roadblocks in the border area, manned by heavily armed soldiers. Security is necessarily strict in the centers of Belfast and

Armagh and wherever there has recently been tension. Visitors must expect hand-luggage to be searched and perhaps a body-frisk. Police stations near the border are reinforced with concrete and barbed wire and may look alarming, but such trouble spots are localized and confined to specific stretches of the border. Elsewhere there is little or no reminder of such problems, and the determined traveler will find that Northern Ireland offers genuinely warm hospitality and some of the most unspoilt scenery you can ever hope to find. Here you can see the beautiful granite Mountains of Mourne, a "Giant's Causeway" of extraordinary volcanic rock whose huge formations rise to over 600 feet, and the largest lake in the United Kingdom, Lough Neagh. Ancient castles and superb old country mansions are numerous on the ground—and each has its own tale to tell. There are also over 200 miles of coastline and a host of rivers and island-strewn lakes which provide some of the finest fishing you'll find anywhere.

## Ulster's Famous Sons

Ulster is only the size of Massachusetts, or half the size of Wales, yet the descendents of Ulstermen have exercised a disproportionate influence on the affairs of the world. Many of the original "Scotch-Irish" who emigrated to Northern Ireland in the 17th century eventually re-emigrated to the New World, where they became pioneers in the frontier territories of the United States and Canada. In the process U.S. history soon began to feature many celebrated names of Ulster stock. It was an Ulsterman, Charles Thomson, who wrote out the Declaration of Independence in his office while holding the post of Secretary to the Continental Congress; and this Declaration was first printed by another Ulsterman, John Dunlap, who learnt his trade in Strabane in County Londonderry. In all there have been no less than ten U.S. presidents descended from Ulster stock. Among the best-known of these is President Andrew Jackson, who held office between 1829–37, and whose parents hailed from Boneybefore, near Carrickfergus. The family of General Ulysses S. Grant, who commanded the Union forces in the Civil War and was President from 1869–77, originally came from County Tyrone. President Woodrow Wilson was also descended from an Ulster family. The family of the first President of the Republic of Texas, General Sam Houston, emigrated from Ballynure in County Antrim early in the 18th century. Likewise, Davy Crockett's parents came from Derry, and General "Stonewall" Jackson's grandfather came from County Armagh. Other famous American Ulstermen include the writer Edgar Allen Poe, whose grandfather was a Derry man; the millionaire financier Thomas Mellon, who left Ulster at the age of five in 1918; and Paul Getty. Meanwhile, across the border in Canada, the great Eaton Store was founded by an Ulsterman. Indeed there was a time when Toronto was known as "the Belfast of Canada."

During the 19th century over four and a half million Irishmen made the fateful journey across the Atlantic to seek their fortune in the New World, and it is estimated that over one in six of these was from Ulster. Northern Ireland is proud of these transatlantic associations, and many of the original homesteads of these pioneer families are preserved. Likewise, there are also commemorative plaques where the appropriate buildings themselves have disappeared. You can pick up a fascinating illustrated map of the Ulster American Heritage Trail from the Tourist Office in Belfast.

## A Long Divided History

Ulster's past is an integral part of the history of the rest of Ireland. Indeed, the patron Saint of Ireland, St. Patrick, established himself here in Armagh and his traditional burial place is at Downpatrick in County Down. To this day, the seat of the Roman Catholic Bishop of Ireland remains "across the border" in Armagh. At the same time, Northern Ireland's past has also been closely linked with its neighbor across the 12-mile stretch of sea to the northeast: Scotland. In A.D. 503 St. Columba set sail from Ulster to establish his monastery on the Scottish island of Iona. And it was from here that he took Christianity to the Scottish mainland. Centuries later, the traffic was to turn the other way, with dire results. After the English forced the "Flight of the Earls" in 1607, the estates of the Irish earls, which totaled some 750,000 acres, remained unoccupied. Much of this land was in Ulster and King James I of England (and VI of Scotland) encouraged large numbers of Presbyterian Scots to cross from the lowlands of Scotland to take over these estates. These immigrants had a different character, different culture, and more significantly, a different religion from the indigenous Irish Catholics in Ulster. The Scots also depended upon the English army for their safety and owed their allegiance to the kings of England (who at this time were descended from the kings of Scotland). The two separate peoples lived a life apart, while occupying the same territory, having little close contact with each other, and living in an atmosphere of mutual suspicion. Thus the seeds of future strife were sown.

The following century was a time of great upheaval throughout Britain, with religion playing a central part in the struggle for power. These upheavals spread with divisive and disastrous consequences to Northern Ireland, exacerbating an already difficult situation. Any simplification of Ulster's divided history only aggravates this problem, yet suffice it to be said that the vicious battles and civil wars of these past centuries remain very much in the minds of the inhabitants to this day. For the Protestants (descendant community of the original Scottish settlers) their "National Day" is the Twelfth of July, when the Orangemen march in their somber best suits, bowler hats and bright orange sashes, behind their ornate banners, and sturdy drummers beat out a rousing roll. These processions, with fife and drum and blaring brass, celebrate the Battle of the Boyne (1690) when the troops of the Protestant King William (of Orange) defeated those who fought to protect the right of the Roman Catholic King James II to the throne of England. Needless to say, the Catholics take no part in these celebrations, preferring to celebrate their own historic victories on other days.

In 1921 Ireland gained her independence from Great Britain. However, the Protestant majority in Northern Ireland decided that they wished to remain part of Great Britain. The Catholic minority in Northern Ireland have meanwhile always retained a deep loyalty to their co-religionists in the Irish Republic—and thus the difficulty remains. There have been many attempts to solve this problem, but none as yet has proved acceptable to the extremists on both sides. The latest initiative involves an injection of $250 million over five years from the American government to create jobs and housing.

## The Present Situation

When Northern Ireland decided to remain part of the United Kingdom in 1921 it was given its own parliament at Stormont, just outside Belfast. This parliament had responsibility for virtually all services, with the exception of general taxation, external relations and foreign trade, which remained the responsibility of the British parliament in London. However in 1972, following the resurgence of community strife in the late '60s, the Stormont parliament was suspended and direct rule from London instigated, with a Secretary of State for Northern Ireland administering the affairs of the Province through the Northern Ireland Office. Though attempts have been made since to establish a local executive, whose power would be shared between the Protestant and Catholic communities, these have so far failed. Even so, efforts to establish some kind of independent Parliament for Northern Ireland continue, with ever-closer cooperation between the British administration in London and the Irish administration in Dublin (who naturally have a special interest in the Catholic minority in Northern Ireland). So far, however, these efforts have come to little, largely owing to the opposition of extremist opinion on both sides of the political and religious divide. Catholic and Protestant children continue to go to different schools; the two communities worship in their different churches; and both stoutly maintain their separate cultural identities and traditions. Even on the simplest level the division is difficult to overcome. For the Protestants, the Lord's Day is sacred, to be observed with due solemnity. Whereas the Catholics, like their brethren in the south, and the Catholics of Europe, would prefer after visiting church for Mass to spend their Sundays in more lively form, with soccer matches and other entertainments. On the other hand, for the Catholics divorce and birth control—tolerated by Protestant traditions—are both anathema.

Contrary to the uninformed opinions of many outsiders, Northern Ireland's problems are not simple, or easily disentangled, and indeed can finally only be resolved in an atmosphere of reconciliation and mutual good will between the two communities, both of whom have suffered far more than their fair share. Fortunately, there are more and more people in Ulster who have the will to see this come about. The best thing you can take to Northern Ireland is an open mind.

## Economy and Traditions

Northern Ireland suffered badly from the world recession of the early '80s and its accompanying blight of unemployment. Indeed, in some areas unemployment is still as high as 25%, causing many to cross over to mainland Britain in search of work. But there is still industry in Northern Ireland, and a large untapped source of hard-working skilled labor. The products of the ship-yards of Belfast were once renowned throughout the seven seas. More recently, they have built some of the world's largest supertankers. As world trade begins to pick up, so orders are beginning to be placed here once more.

Another well-known Northern Ireland firm is Short and Harland, the aircraft manufacturers, whose plant is also in Belfast. Belfast is also the center of the linen industry, which was originally encouraged by Huguenot weavers who fled from religious persecution in France in the 17th century. The products of this industry—such as superb tablecloths and napkins—make ideal high-quality gifts or mementoes of your trip. However, Northern Ireland remains, as ever, largely a rural community. It is among the villages and market towns of the Province that you will find the more typical way of life. Here life goes on as it has done for centuries, and you will discover a hospitality and friendliness which is justly renowned. It is in these parts of Ulster that many ancient traditions and customs persist which have long since lapsed in more frequently-visited parts of Ireland. During the summer each of the Six Counties hold their ancient *Fleadh Cheoils*—festivals of traditional music and dancing. These begin in May and feature a series of competitions for the great All-Ireland finals, which take place in August across the border in the Republic. At these gatherings you can watch rousing examples of fiddle-playing, tin whistling and traditional dancing. Afterwards you can mix with the competitors over a pint in the local bars. But be warned: these occasions are no staid, artificially maintained traditions. The celebrations and spontaneous music-making go on long into the night: a thirsty business for all concerned! In the summer and early-fall there are also traditional harvest fairs. If you're here in early-August be sure not to miss the Lughnasa Medieval Fair in Carrickfergus, County Antrim, at the fine old Norman castle, where ancient stalls are set up and all kinds of medieval entertainments are staged. Also in early-August is the Oul Lammas Fair, held on the shores of Lough Neagh, near Cookstown, County Tyrone. This attracts visitors from all over Ulster and has dozens of stalls selling all kinds of antiques and traditional confectionery.

## Arts and Sports

Ulster's greatest claim to fame in the arts of this century is its poets. The well-known poet of the '30s and '40s, Louis MacNiece, was an Ulsterman. Many claim that the finest poet writing today in the English language (on either side of the Atlantic) is Seamus Heaney, who is also an Ulsterman. But he is by no means alone in the present flowering of Ulster's poets, which includes Derek Mahon, John Montague and Michael Longley, all of whom rank with the very best of their contemporaries throughout the English-speaking world.

In music, Sir Hamilton Harty (1874–1941), who was born at Hillsborough, County Down, and Carl Hardbeck (1869–1945) have both contributed greatly to the development of Irish music in the 20th century.

In the sporting field, Ulstermen have long excelled. George Best, who achieved fame and notoriety playing for Manchester United, is considered by many to have been among the greatest footballers of all time. But unquestionably the brightest star in the Ulster sporting firmament today is Barry MacGuigan, who in May 1985 won the World Featherweight boxing title. His status extends beyond the confines of the boxing ring, however, for he has united all Irishmen in passionate support for him. Intelligent and articulate, MacGuigan recognizes, and more than lives up to, his demanding role as Ireland's leading sporting ambassador. Sport also unites the Irish when it comes to Rugby, with the Irish team drawn from both sides of the border, and also contributing members to the British Lions, whose other players come from England, Scotland and Wales. Ulster teams also take part in the All-Ireland Championships for Hurling and Gaelic Football. If you fancy watching a fast and furious game which you've never seen before, try going to one of these fixtures. The rules are easy to pick up, and the games themselves are highly competitive and entertaining, attracting strong partisan support. One of the best teams in Northern Ireland is that which represents County Down. And in true Irish fashion their supporters wear colored rosettes bearing the slogan "Up Down!" Another less well-known but highly traditional Northern Irish game is a local version of bowls, known in the Province as "bullets." This is because the original bowls used for this game were cannon balls. The game takes place in winding country lanes, and the competitors attempt to reach the end of the two-mile course with as few throws as possible. This may sound simple, but go along to the All-Ireland Championships which are held outside Armagh City on the first weekend in August and you'll see that it's all much more skillful than it sounds. The game attracts a highly colorful crowd, who indulge in heavy betting on the various competitors, the greatest of whom are celebrated as heroes in traditional ballads. This ancient game is now only played in Armagh, and in County Cork (in the Republic), and is the last surviving remnant of a game which was first played before the discovery of America.

# BELFAST

## *Victorian Boomtown*

Belfast was originally a fort guarding a ford across the river Farset, from which the city takes its name. For centuries it was little more than a village, but with the advent of the Industrial Revolution it began a period of rapid expansion. With the establishment of such industries as ropemaking, linen, tobacco, and shipbuilding the city began to prosper—to such an extent that during Victorian times its population doubled in size every ten years. Today it has nearly 400,000 inhabitants.

The city itself has as fine a setting as you'll find anywhere in Britain. Ringed with high hills, its main river the Lagan runs out into the wide blue waters of Belfast Lough, which itself runs 12 miles out to the open sea. To this day, Belfast retains strong maritime connections. The shipyards which once built the ill-fated *Titanic* still contain the world's largest dry dock; and from the foot of the Albert Memorial Clock Tower you can see the massive cranes of the shipyards at the end of High Street.

Even today the city remains a largely Victorian creation, though its most impressive building, the City Hall, in Donegall Square, in fact dates from Edwardian times (being completed in 1906). The building itself was designed by Sir Brumwell Thomas and is reminiscent of an American State capitol, apart from the large statue of Queen Victoria which stands outside. Queen Victoria herself visited Belfast in 1849, leaving behind her an indelible mark on the city. Dozens of streets, the harbor's deep water channel, a hospital, the university, and a park are all named after her.

## A Heritage in Stone

The whole of the center of Belfast is now a pedestrians-only precinct, though there are plenty of buses if you don't fancy walking. Just outside this area to the south is Queens University. The main college building, which dates from 1849, was designed in Tudor style by Charles Lanyon, who based his plans on Magdalen College, Oxford. Charles Lanyon played a leading role in Belfast's Victorian expansion and designed many fine buildings throughout the city. The area around the university has several pleasant Victorian terraces and in this district you'll find a host of good little pubs, shops, restaurants and theaters. This is one of the best areas for strolling around.

However, a word of warning: Owing to the present situation, Belfast is not a city for strolling about at random. Certain areas, such as the Falls Road and the Shankhill Road (both in west Belfast) are best avoided. This said, there are many other areas which are ideal for walking and taking in the sights, but be prepared for airport-style security checks when entering certain hotels, museums and shops. Many of the city's larger buildings are decorated with ornate carvings of gods, mythological characters, royal figures, and even Indians and Chinamen. Right by the Tourist Office are several old bank buildings worthy of interest. Almost next door you'll see the yellow-and-red facade and copper domes of the Bank of Ireland, which was designed by William Bath in 1897. In nearby Waring Street you'll find the Ulster Bank which was built in 1860. Step inside and you'll see that the interior is designed like a Venetian palace. Look out too for the Northern Bank, on the same street, which was designed as a market house in 1769. To the north of here in Donegall Street you come to St. Anne's Cathedral, which was started in 1899 and is still in the process of completion. This building is constructed in the "Irish Romanesque" style, and contains the tomb of Lord Carson, who played a leading role in the partition of Ulster from the rest of Ireland in 1921.

Where else but in Ireland would the National Trust take over a pub? In Great Victoria Street, near the Opera House, you will find the ornate pillared front of the Crown Liquor Saloon. The interior is a superb example of rich Victorian decor, dating from 1885. (They pull a good pint here too!)

## Museums and Gardens

To the south of the city center beside Queens University you'll find the Botanic Gardens with its superb 19th-century glass-domed Palm House. Also in these gardens is the Ulster Museum. This contains many fascinating exhibits, especially in the Natural History collection, not least the famous Coelacanth, a pre-historic fish thought to have been long extinct, that was caught in deep waters off Madagascar in 1973. There is also a skeleton of the extinct Great Irish Deer and a Giant Japanese Spider Crab. Be sure not to miss the nearby *Girona Treasure,* which contains relics from one of the ships of the Spanish Armada which was wrecked off the Irish coast in 1588. The Art Collection here features several works by great modern artists, including Pissaro, Sickert, Dubuffet and Henry Moore. The watercolor and drawings section contains some superb Fuselis.

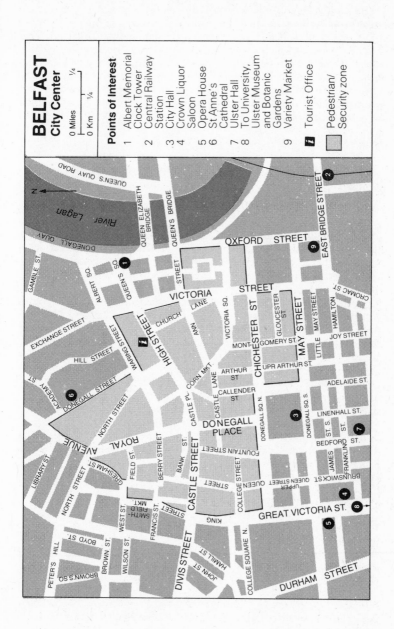

**BELFAST**
**City Center**

0 Miles ¼
0 Km ¼

N

**Points of Interest**

1 Albert Memorial
  Clock Tower
2 Central Railway
  Station
3 City Hall
4 Crown Liquor
  Saloon
5 Opera House
6 St Anne's
  Cathedral
7 Ulster Hall
8 To University,
  Ulster Museum
  and Botanic
  Gardens
9 Variety Market

ℹ️ Tourist Office

Pedestrian/
Security zone

There is an excellent view of the shipyards from the Albert Clock Tower at the end of High Street. For security reasons it is not possible to gain free access to the port itself, but arrangements can be made for guided tours. (Enquire at the Tourist Center.) Be sure not to miss the Sinclair Seamen's Church which is just off Donegall Quay. This contains fascinating maritime memorabilia which highlight the city's strong nautical connections. The Belfast Zoo is north of the city center in Bellevue Park on the Antrim Road. Here, in 13 green acres on the slopes of Cave Hill, you can see a collection of animals which includes lions, monkeys and a pack of home-bred wolves.

## PRACTICAL INFORMATION FOR BELFAST

**GETTING TO TOWN FROM THE AIRPORT.** From Belfast's Aldergrove airport, 15 miles away from the city center, there is a regular bus service into the city's Great Victoria St. bus station. Belfast's Harbor airport, which handles a small number of flights from the U.K., is four miles from the city center. From here there are regular train services into Belfast's Central Station.

**TOURIST OFFICES.** The main tourist office for Belfast is the *Tourist Information Center,* River House, 48 High St. (tel. 0232–246609). It is open Mon. to Fri. 9–5.15, Easter to Sept. Sat. 9–2. They can supply information on all aspects of the city, and can also help make reservations in hotels, guesthouses, and the like.

**Telephone Code.** The area code for Belfast is 0232.

**HOTELS.** Belfast has an adequate range of hotels and guesthouses, though by American standards there is little choice in the upper price range. The booklet *Where to Stay* (£1.95), available from the tourist office at 52 High St. and bookshops, gives a fully comprehensive listing. For an explanation of hotel price gradings, see *Facts at Your Fingertips* on page 265.

### Deluxe

**Culloden Hotel,** 42 Bangor Rd., Hollywood (tel. 02317–5223). 76 rooms, all with bath, including 4 special family suites. Fishing and shooting facilities available. To the northeast of the city. AE, DC, MC, V.

**Europa Hotel** (formerly Belfast Europa), Great Victoria St. (tel. 0232–327000). 200 rooms, all with bath. 12-story modern block in center of city with wide range of amenities, including nightclub. AE, DC, MC, V.

### Expensive

**Conway,** Dunmurry (tel. 0232–612101). 78 rooms, all with bath. Golfing arrangements. On outskirts of town. AE, DC, MC.

**Drumkeen,** Upper Galwally (tel. 0232–491321). 28 rooms, all with bath. Good restaurant and pleasant grounds. Reduced terms for children. AE, DC, MC, V.

**Stormont,** 587 Upper Newtownards Rd. (tel. 0232–658621). 67 rooms, all with bath. Facilities include evening entertainment. AE, DC, MC.

**Wellington Park Hotel,** 21 Malone Rd. (tel. 0232–381111). 50 rooms, all with bath. Evening entertainment. Shooting, fishing, sailing arranged. AE, DC, MC, V.

## *Moderate*

**Ambassador Hotel,** 462 Antrim Rd. (tel. 0232–781016). 21 rooms, all with bath. Evening entertainment, and facilities for children. AE, DC, MC.

**Beechlawn Hotel,** Dunmurry Lane (tel. 0232–612974). 10 rooms, 8 with bath. In pleasant grounds on outskirts of city. AE, DC, MC.

**Hotel Greenan Lodge,** Blacks Rd. (tel. 0232–301234). 13 rooms, all with bath. Pleasant restaurant; facilities for children. AE, DC, MC, V.

**La Mon House Hotel,** 41 Gransha Rd. (tel. 0232–448631). 30 rooms, all with bath. Southeast of city at Castlereagh. Wide range of facilities, including indoor pool and arrangements for shooting and horseriding. AE, DC, MC, V.

**Park Avenue Hotel,** Holywood Rd. (tel. 0232–656271). 40 rooms with bath. Pleasant grounds; golf and fishing by arrangement.

## *Inexpensive*

**Belmont Court Hotel,** 45 Park Ave. (tel. 0232–659724). 11 rooms without private bath. Facilities for children.

**Parador Hotel,** 473 Ormeau Rd. (tel. 0232–491883). 14 rooms, 10 with bath. Golfing arrangements.

**York Hotel,** 59 Botanic Ave. (tel. 0232–329304). 18 rooms, 15 with bath. Facilities for children.

## Guesthouses

**Botanic Lodge,** 87 Botanic Ave. (tel. 0232–327682). 14 rooms, 1 with bath.

**Camera House,** 44 Wellington Park (tel. 0232–660026). 11 rooms, 7 with bath.

**Eglantine,** 21 Eglantine Ave. (tel. 0232–667585). 6 rooms.

**Rossmore,** 37 Rossmore Ave. (tel. 0232–643924)

**Somerton,** 22 Lansdowne Rd. (tel. 0232–370717). 8 rooms.

## Camping

**Belvoir Forest Touring Caravan Site.** A Forest Service site, just off the A504 and central to both Belfast and the Lagan valley, south of the city.

**Jordanstown Lough Shore Park,** Shore Rd., Newtownabbey (tel. 0232–868751). Run by the Newtownabbey Borough Council. Maximum stay two nights.

## Youth Hostels

**Belfast Youth Hostel** (tel. 0232–647865). On the A24, the Saintfield Rd., just south of the city. Take bus 83 from Donegall Sq.

The Youth Hostel Assoc. headquarters are at 56 Bradbury Pl., Belfast 7 (tel. 0232–324733).

**RESTAURANTS.** Belfast does not have a wide range of haute cuisine. However, things are beginning to change here. There are a number of pleasant, moderately-priced restaurants. At lunchtime you will find that the pubs provide a good place for an inexpensive meal in relaxing surroundings. For an explanation of restaurant price gradings, see *Facts at Your Fingertips* on page 265.

### Expensive

**La Belle Epoque,** 103 Great Victoria St. (tel. 0232–223244). First-class French fare.

**Oscar's,** 34 Bedford St. (tel. 0232–247757). Award-winning French-style cooking; seafood specials.

**Restaurant 44,** 44 Bedford St. (tel. 0232–244844). Game in season and classic fish dishes.

### Moderate

**Ashoka,** 363 Lisburn Rd. (tel. 0232–660362). Award-winning Indian restaurant; Tandoori and Biryani specialties. Highly recommended. Open till 11.30 P.M.

**La Mon House,** 41 Gransha Rd. (tel. 023123–631). Excellent hotel restaurant southeast of city at Castlereagh. Try their Baked Ulster Ham in Guinness. Also has good buffet lunch and Sunday carvery. AE, DC, MC, V.

**Saints and Scholars,** 3 University St. (tel. 0232–225137). Bistro menu with vegetarian and seafood dishes, and coq au vin.

**The Strand,** 12 Strandmills Rd. (tel. 0232–682266). Acclaimed by many food writers; try the baked aubergine or chilli con carne.

**Thompson's,** 47 Arthur St. (tel. 0232–323762). Tender local steaks, and some fine seafood dishes. Last evening orders 9 P.M.

### Inexpensive

**Capers,** 63 Great Victoria St. (tel. 0232–247643). Offers Caribbean pizza, lasagne and Knickerbocker glories.

**Chez Delbart,** 10 Bradbury Pl. (tel. 0232–238020). Good standard continental fare. Excellent pepper steaks. Bring your own wine.

**Lacey's,** 50 Dublin Rd. (tel. 0232–249269). Informal place serving pasta, fish, chicken and steak.

**Malone House,** Barnett Park (tel. 0232–681246). Restaurant in restored 19th-century house serving inexpensive lunchtime quiches and lasagnes.

**Truffles,** 3a Donegall Sq. West (tel. 0232–247153). Popular central lunch spot. Imaginative dishes at reasonable prices. Evening meals as well on Fri. and Sat.

**Zomorode,** 157 Stanmills Rd. (tel. 0232–664557). Salad bar, pasta and chilli; Mongolian specialties in the evening.

**Pubs.** The best pubs to try are the **Crown Bar,** opposite the Europa Hotel, whose decor is so prized that it is preserved by the National Trust; just nearby is **Robinson's** which has excellent old-fashioned mahogany and brass decor and serves traditional oysters and Guinness. There's also good pub grub at the **Linenhall Bar,** 9 Clarence St., behind the B.B.C., with jazz (Sat. afternoon).

There are several good musical pubs which offer traditional Irish music in a relaxed setting. Try **Madden's** in Smithfield (most nights); the **Errigle**

**Inn,** Ormeau St. (Mon. and Thur.); the **City Folk Club,** Parador Hotel, Ormeau Rd. (Sun.), and the **Rotterdam,** Pilot St. (most nights).

**HOW TO GET AROUND.** Much of the center of Belfast is a pedestrians-only area, but it is easy to get around Belfast (including the central area) by bus. Most of the bus routes start from the city center at City Hall in Donegall Square. Buses from the south of the square go south, and from the west of the square go north and east. Routes 69 and 71 go to Queens University, the Ulster Museum and the Botanic Gardens, and routes 2 to 6 go to the Zoo.

The Central Railway Station is in East Bridge St., and this has trains running to all destinations except Larne Harbor. The boat train to Larne Harbor runs from York Road Station.

Taxis can be found at ranks around the city; the most central is at City Hall. Empty taxis do not cruise the streets, so check the Yellow Pages and book one by phone. A number of taxis don't have meters, so settle the fare before you set off. You may be asked to share a cab if there is a long line.

**TOURS AND EXCURSIONS. City Tours.** Ulsterbus, located at the Great Victoria St. bus station, have a city tour covering all the main sights in Belfast. The Belfast Civic Trail is a do-it-yourself walking tour of the city, starting in Shaftesbury Sq. A free, illustrated guide giving architectural and historical information to accompany the walk is available from the Information Office in the City Hall or from the Tourist Information Center, 48 High St.

**Excursions.** Ulsterbus runs full- and half-day tours to the Glens of Antrim, the Antrim coast and the Giant's Causeway, Fermanagh Lakeland, the Mountains of Mourne, the Ards Peninsula and Armagh. Tours runs from late-July to the end of August and leave Belfast daily from the Great Victoria St. bus station. For details of all Ulsterbus tours, call 0232–320011.

**PLACES TO VISIT. Botanic Gardens.** South of city center. Ulster Museum and 130-year old Palm House with its carved glass and wrought iron. Open Mon. to Fri. 10–4.50, Sat. 1–4.50, Sun. 2–4.50.

**Carrickfergus Castle,** eight miles northeast of city at Carrickfergus, Co. Antrim, on northern shore of Belfast Lough. 12th-century Norman stronghold, with fine set of 19th-century cannon, on rocky promontory. Also has military museum. Open Apr. to Sept., daily 10–6, Sun. 2–6; Oct. to Mar., daily 10–4.

**City Hall,** Donegall Square. Edwardian edifice in city center designed by Sir Brumwell Thomas. Tours Wed. 10.30 by appointment (tel. 0232–320202; ext. 227).

**Giant's Ring,** off Ballyleeson Rd. close to Lagan towpath, south of city. Large Neolithic earthwork with impressive central dolmen.

**Hillsborough Fort,** at Hillsborough, seven miles outside southern outskirts of city. Castle with 19th-century mansion and impressive 18th-century Gothic gatehouse. Open Apr. to Sept., Tues. to Sat. 10–7, Sun. 2–7; Oct. to Mar., Tues. to Sat. 10–4, Sun. 2–4.

**Port of Belfast.** Tours of port and maritime installations must be prearranged through Senior Administration Officer, Belfast Harbor Commissioners, Harbor Office, Corporation Sq.

**Queens University,** University Rd. South of city center. Pleasant neo-Tudor campus designed by Charles Lanyon in 19th century.

**St. Anne's Cathedral,** Lower Donegall St. Started in 1899 in Irish Romanesque style. Contains tomb of Lord Carson.

**Sinclair Seamen's Church,** Corporation Sq. Dating from 19th century, designed by Charles Lanyon. Interior contains large range of fascinating maritime relics. Tel. 0232–232081 for details of visiting arrangements.

**Ulster Folk and Transport Museum,** seven miles from the city center on Bangor road. An open-air museum set in the extensive grounds of Cultra Manor provides a unique introduction to Ulster's heritage. Open Apr. to Sept., Mon. to Sat. 11–6, Sun. 2–6; Oct. to Mar., Mon. to Sat. 11–5, Sun. 2–5.

**Ulster Museum,** in Botanic Gardens, south of city center. Relics dating from prehistoric times to present day, including Armada treasure. Also has good art gallery. Open 10–5, Sat. 1–5, Sun. 2–5.

**Belfast Zoo,** Bellevue Park, Antrim Rd. North of city center. All kinds of wild animals housed on 13-acre site. Special home-bred wolf pack. Open Apr. to Sept., daily 10–5; Oct. to Mar. daily 10–4.30.

**MUSIC, MOVIES AND THEATER. Music.** The **Grand Opera House,** Great Victoria St. (tel. 0232–241919), has been restored to its late-Victorian glory and is well worth a visit for everything from pantomime to opera. The **Harberton Theater,** Harberton Park, Balmoral (tel. 0232–661302), is home to the Ulster Operatic Society, and presents concerts and musicals. The Ulster Orchestra performs at the **Ulster Hall,** Linenhall St. (tel. 0232–241917), which is also a major venue for other musical events from rock concerts to organ recitals (the hall boasts a splendid Victorian organ). The **Grosvenor Hall,** Glengall St. (tel. 0232–241917), presents country and western music and folk and gospel concerts. For concerts and recitals organized by the university or the Students Union, **Whitla Hall,** Queens University (tel. 0232–245133) is the place.

A cultural high spot in Belfast is provided by the Queens University Arts Festival, which takes places every year in November. A full program of dramatic and musical entertainment is offered, centered on the Whitla Hall. For details, see the local press or contact the Tourist Office.

**Movies.** Belfast's movie theaters are the **ABC Film Center** and the **New Vic Cinema,** both on Great Victoria St., and the **Curzon,** Ormeau Rd., which boasts three screens. Check the local press for details of what's playing. For more arty movies, try the **Queens Film Theater,** University Sq. Mews; it's open during semesters only.

**Theaters.** The **Arts Theater,** Botanic Ave. (tel. 0232–224936) specializes in popular productions, and musicals from time to time, while the **Lyric Theater,** Ridgeway St. (tel. 0232–660081) presents dramatic works from Ireland's rich literary heritage, as well as new Irish plays and international works. The **Group Theater,** Bedford St. (tel. 0232–229685) is the home of Belfast's local dramatic societies.

**SHOPPING.** Belfast boasts a pleasant pedestrianized central shopping area, with shops open Monday through Saturday. Fine Irish linens, hand-made woolens, pottery and glassware are only a few of the many excellent traditional Irish goods available. Be prepared for fairly tough security measures, both entering the central area and in many shops. Though cars are excluded from the shopping areas, there are good bus services from all parts of the city to the center.

The southern part of the city around Botanic Avenue and the university is good for both gift shopping and second-hand books. Look out especially for the **Variety Market** in May St., the nearest thing to a flea market in the city. It's open Tuesday and Friday mornings and is at its best around 7.30A.M.

**USEFUL ADDRESSES. Airlines.** *Aer Lingus,* 46 Castle St. (tel. 0232–245151). *British Airways,* Fountain Center (tel. 0232–240522).

**Car Hire.** *Avis,* 69 Great Victoria St. (tel. 0232–240404). *Budget Rent-a-Car,* 511 Lisburn Rd. (tel. 0232–682439). *Godfrey Davis Europcar,* 32 Linenhall St. (tel. 0232–233773). All also have desks at Aldergrove airport.

**Consulates.** *U.S. Consulate,* Queens House, Queen St. *Canadian Consulate,* Canada House, North St.

**Emergencies.** For police, fire or ambulance, call 999.

**Travel Agents.** *American Express,* Hamilton Travel, 23 Waring St. (tel. 0232–230321). *Thomas Cook,* 11 Donegall Pl.

# AROUND THE SIX COUNTIES

## *The Rest of Northern Ireland*

A visit to the Ulster Folk and Transport Museum, seven miles from Belfast on the Bangor road, provides a glimpse into the region's past. The Folk Museum is set in some 70 acres around Cultra Manor, encircled by a larger park and recreation area. Historic buildings have been reconstructed in the form of an extended village and furnished in authentic period style; visitors can explore the interiors. There's an 18th-century thatched weaver's cottage, a 19th-century hill farm and a Victorian terrace of industrial workers' houses, as well as an indoor gallery of domestic and agricultural artifacts. The Transport Museum has a miniature railway and all kinds of vehicles from a Victorian Brougham to a World War II Spitfire.

Moving on down the coast towards the Mountains of Mourne, you come to a string of resort towns. The first and largest of these is Bangor, a pleasant spot with a host of rocky coves and walks along the coast. This was once one of the most important early-Christian centers in Ireland, and ruins of the original abbey (first established in the 6th century) now form part of the 19th-century Church of Ireland Abbey Church.

The coastal road now continues south along the green shoreline of the Ards Peninsula. At the end of the peninsula there is a car ferry which takes you across the neck of Strangford Lough to the mainland.

There are many associations with St. Patrick hereabouts; he is reputed to have established Ireland's first Christian church at Saul, in A.D.432. A tiny replica of the church marks the spot. Also at Saul, a large statue of

St. Patrick overlooks Strangford Lough. Struell Wells, about a mile to the east of Downpatrick, have an ancient reputation for curative properties predating St. Patrick, who is believed to have blessed them. Two of the stone bathhouses have been restored. The saint's "traditional" (but unlikely) burial place is marked by a large granite stone in the grounds of Down Cathedral, Downpatrick.

Two places in the county are noted for their literary associations: Captain Thomas Mayne Reid (1818–83) was born at Banbridge and emigrated to America where, after fighting in the Mexican War, he began to write his first Western novel; and at nearby Emdale, Patrick Brontë, father of the novelists Charlotte, Emily and Anne, was born and taught at the local school before going to Cambridge and later to Haworth Parsonage.

There are impressive forest parks at Tullymore and Castlewellan (the latter with an important arboretum). These have cafés and exhibition halls, and if you feel like staying overnight, there are well-serviced caravan parks. If gardens are your interest don't miss the National Trust's Rowallane Gardens, near Killyleagh, which is full of exotic plants from places as far apart as Tibet and New Zealand.

The south of the county is occupied by the spectacular Mountains of Mourne whose peaks sweep down 2,000 feet to the sea; though the highest peak here, Slieve Donard, reaches nearly 3,000 feet. This countryside is criss-crossed with a number of excellent walks which take you over the granite mountains past several hidden lakes. On your walks you'll see deposits of Mourne Diamonds—semi-precious quartz crystals, which can be severed from the rocks with little difficulty.

Straddling the border between County Down and County Armagh is the market town of Newry, one of the earliest cities in all Ireland. The picturesque canal here is the oldest in Britain, and is now the venue of the Ulster coarse fishing championships. On market days large numbers of shoppers cross the border from the Republic (just four miles down the road) to take advantage of the less highly taxed goods on sale here, giving the town a lively festive air.

## County Armagh

East of Newry you are in County Armagh, the smallest of the Six Counties, which lies along the border with the Republic. Visiting the border area for tourist purposes is not recommended during the present situation, as this rural area has been the scene of several notorious incidents. However, in Armagh Town itself there is much to see. This city has been a major ecclesiastical center for over 1,500 years. St. Patrick himself established a church here, and to this day the city remains the seat of the Catholic Bishop of All Ireland. The city now has two cathedrals, both dedicated to St. Patrick. The Gothic Catholic Cathedral on a hilltop to the north of town is an impressive limestone construction with twin towers, and is reached by a fine flight of steps. The interior includes much ornate design by Continental artists, and there is a 39-bell carillon. The Church of Ireland Cathedral is on a hilltop to the south of town. It has a number of curious carved heads around the exterior and a plaque marking the reputed grave of Brian Boru, the High King of Ireland who defeated the Danes at the Battle of Clontarf in the 11th century. In 1973 a copy of *Gulliver's Travels* by Dean Swift (first published in 1723), with annotations in the author's own hand, was discovered in the cathedral library. The irascible Dean's comments are well worth reading.

However, the principal attraction in Armagh is the Planetarium and Hall of Astronomy. It contains a wealth of fascinating astronomical exhibits, and incorporates the original Observatory, founded in 1789.

Ten miles northeast of Armagh Town you come to Portadown, which is the center of Northern Ireland's apple orchards and horticultural industry. The town is part of the Craigavon New Town Development, an ambitious urban scheme which was intended to unite the two religious communities in a modern project involving widescale socio-economic development. The aim was to create eventually a city of 110,000 inhabitants. But owing to the continuing troubles the scheme was largely abandoned in 1978, and the funds allocated for it were diverted to the rebuilding of inner Belfast.

By contrast, you can visit a more successful social scheme at Bessbrook, just outside Newry. This was founded in 1846 by the Quaker manufacturer, John Grubb Richardson, as a model linen town. It has a fine mill of granite stone and cottages and a community center—but its founder decreed that it should have no pub. (A fact which goes a long way to explaining why the tiny hamlet of Camlough, just a mile down the road, has no less than six pubs!)

## Antrim: Land of the Giant

The northeast corner of Northern Ireland is occupied by County Antrim. Torr Head on the extreme northeasterly tip of the county is separated from Scotland by just 12 miles of sea, and in times gone by the immigrant Scottish inhabitants around here used to row across this stretch of water on Sundays to worship in the churches of their homeland. Antrim is one of the five counties which border on Lough Neagh, Northern Ireland's "inland sea" whose 153 square miles make it the largest lake in the British Isles. This has been a famous fishing region for over 5,000 years and its waters are rich in salmon, eels and freshwater herring, or pollan.

The best way to see Antrim is to head north from Belfast along the A2. This attractive coastal route leads you along the northern edge of Belfast Lough and then across to Larne, which is the terminal port for the car ferries from the Scottish mainland and has two excellent golf courses. As you head north from here along the coast you enter the land of the glens— the nine valleys of the northeast. The most beautiful of these is at Glenariffe. Some of the other names recall battles of long ago: Glenarm (Glen of the Weapon); Glencoy (Glen of the Sword); Glencorb (Glen of the Slaughtered); and Glendun (Glen of the Fort). It was in a cave on Rathlin, an island off the adjacent coast, that the Scottish king, Robert the Bruce (1274–1329), took refuge and watched a spider spinning its web with a patience that inspired him to try and try again for the victory over the English which he eventually achieved at Bannockburn in Scotland in 1314. In more recent times Guglielmo Marconi (1874–1937) established his first island to shore wireless telegraph station in 1898 on Rathlin, linking it with Ballycastle on the mainland; a plaque commemorates this pioneer feat. Ballycastle is famous for its Oul Lammas Fair, held on the last Tuesday in August, a survival of the ancient Irish festival of Lughnasa, an initial stage of harvest festival celebrations. Sheep are the main business of

the fair today; though they also sell tradition̄a
low (pronounced "yella") Man which is made

Nearby at Carrick-a-Rede there is a famous
walk across the narrow passage to the island,
sea boils 80 feet below. (The bridge is only ope⸗

Five miles down the coast road from her⸗
Causeway with its 38,000 regular shaped ba⸗
of lava of an ancient volcano. This fascinating
11-mile walk if you're going to see it all—was ⸗
of the famed Irish giant, Finn McCool; it is a⸗
McCool who with one mighty sweep scooped out the hole which is now
Lough Neagh and dumped it in the Irish Sea to form the Isle of Man.

Dunluce Castle is a dramatic ruin clinging to the edge of a cliff above
a great cave. It was the stronghold of the Irish MacDonnells, chiefs of
Antrim, and was abandoned when the kitchen (and the cooks) fell into
the sea during a storm.

Inland from here is the little town of Bushmills, home of what is claimed
as the world's oldest whiskey, with a visitors center and guided tours of
the distillery if you book in advance. (Enquire at Tourist Office in Belfast.)

Shane's Castle, a short distance from here, has ancient cannons pointing
out over the lough, and a narrow-gauge railway with steam locomotives
to take you through the estate's nature reserve. Farther north on the road
west from Ballymena (A42) is Gracehill, with its 18th-century Moravian
houses and church; the Moravian community now consists of only 100
people.

## County Londonderry

County Londonderry occupies the northwestern corner of Northern
Ireland, and has the province's second largest city, Derry. Outside the city
the countryside is mainly rugged and mountainous, with many long winding glens and some fine remote scenery. The beaches to the north are
washed by the Atlantic breakers, and to the south of the county the Sperrin
Mountains rise to well over 2,000 feet.

The city of Derry (and the county) was originally named Derry, from
the Irish *Doire,* meaning Oak Wood. The prefix "London" was added
when merchants in London sent "planters" to the area in the 17th century.
However, in 1984 the City Council formally changed their name back to
Derry, though you'll still hear both names used.

Derry is a hill town situated above the River Foyle. In 1689 its walls
were unsuccessfully besieged by the army of James II. During that time
over 30,000 people are said to have taken refuge in the city and nearly
a quarter of them died of starvation before the city was finally relieved.
To this day, you can see Roaring Meg, the largest cannon of the period,
which played a leading role in the siege, in the southwest corner of the
walls.

In the 17th and 18th centuries large numbers of Derrymen fled to the
New World to escape the privations of the period. Both Davy Crockett
and Daniel Boone are descended from these early emigrants.

The best way to see the city is to take a walk around the walls, whose
20-foot-wide ramparts still enclose the inner city. Most of the walls remain
much as they have done for centuries, though the four gates have been

the walls there are also several steep, ancient, winding

as two cathedrals. The Anglican St. Columb's Cathedral was 1633 and is a fine example of the simple Gothic style known as ter's Gothic," with its handsome Georgian tower and spire. Inside re is a memorial window to the siege of 1689. The Catholic Cathedral of St. Eugene's, with its granite spire, is in the Flamboyant Gothic style and was designed in the 19th century by J.J.McCarthy. Also not to be missed is Magee University College, situated in the suburbs to the north. This is now affiliated with the New University of Ulster. It has an attractive neo-Gothic facade, and inside you can see some of the artifacts salvaged from a Spanish Armada ship, *La Trinidad Valencera,* which was wrecked in Glengivney Bay, County Donegal, in the fall of 1588, another of the doomed ships of the Spanish Armada. The impressive Guildhall, which has relics of the siege, was partly destroyed in the disturbances of 1972, but reopened five years later. It has since suffered minor damage again, but it is well worth seeing.

Inland to the southeast of Derry you come to the Sperrin Mountains. This desolate area once contained Stone Age settlements, and you can still see ancient stone circles and monoliths outside Strabane. Behind these mountains at Gorteade, near Maghera, is the birthplace of Charles Thomson (1729–1824), Secretary of the Continental Congress, who originally wrote up the Declaration of Independence. A plaque marks the site of his birthplace.

## Land of Lakes and Moors

County Fermanagh is Ulster's "Lake District." As the river Erne flows towards the sea it passes through two large loughs, Upper Lough Erne and Lower Lough Erne. The world record for coarse fishing was achieved on these lakes, so this is the place to bring your rod. You can also hire boats at many lakeside centers—including Kesh, Enniskillen and Carrybridge. Indeed, this is one of the finest spots in Europe for a safe inland boating holiday, with miles of navigable water and over 150 leafy islands to explore. Be sure to visit Devenish Island on Lower Lough Erne. This was once a thriving Celtic monastic center, but now only the ruins remain. There are a vast number of them scattered among the windswept ferns, giving the place a curiously poignant air. (In summer there is a ferry across to the island from Enniskillen.) Also of interest on Lower Lough Erne is the long, narrow Boa Island, joined to the mainland by a bridge at both ends. The island contains the Caldreagh Cemetery, one of the most ancient in Britain, with two stone carvings which date from the 1st century A.D.

Also worth a visit is the marina at Castle Archdale Forest and Country Park. The original castle here was burned down in the 17th century, and when its successor was built in 1776 "sacred stones" from an old abbey were used, bringing down a curse on the occupiers. Of course, there's many a story like that around Ulster. One of the best claims is that Noah's grandson landed in his own personal ark on the slopes of Slieve Beagh mountain near Lisnaskea by Upper Lough Erne.

There are few other areas in the whole of Ireland which can offer such a diversity of sport in such an attractive location as County Fermanagh. Hunting, shooting, fishing, sailing, walking—you name it. And at Lough

Navar Forest there's the start of the Ulster Way, a walking route that encircles the whole of Northern Ireland. There is also a wildlife reserve beside Castle Caldwell; and at Marble Arch you can explore spectacular caves and potholes in the limestone rock.

At the border village of Belleek you come to the famed Belleek Pottery, just inside the Republic. This is a good place for souvenirs; and since there are still lacemakers in some of the villages of Fermanagh, it is well worth seeking out the products of their craft too.

In the market town of Lisnaskea on the A34 road from Enniskillen to Clones there's a strange museum incorporated in a bar. Look for the sign that reads "Cassidy Old Corner House Bar and Folk Museum;" the collection here includes many early domestic utensils and equipment of bygone days.

Enniskillen, Fermanagh's principal town, is on an island in the river Erne between the two loughs. The town contains a fine 15th-century castle and the round-towered Water Gate, which dates from the 17th century. The main winding street of the town contains several fine Georgian and Victorian buildings, while one and a half miles southeast of the town is Castlecoole, claimed by the locals to be Ireland's most picturesque country mansion. West of the town is Portora School, which was established in 1608 by King James I, and whose grounds contain the ruins of Portora Castle, also dating from the 17th century. In the 19th century the poet and dramatist Oscar Wilde was educated here, and earlier in this century its pupils included Samuel Beckett, who went on to achieve fame as Ireland's latest Nobel Laureate for Literature.

## County Tyrone

County Tyrone is the largest of the six counties and is dominated by the moorlands of the Sperrin Mountains, which spill over from County Londonderry. Running along the south of the county close to the border with the Republic is the Clogher Valley, a picturesque stretch of unspoilt countryside. Here at Dergina, near Ballygawley, you can see the cottage which was once the home of Hannah Simpson, mother of Ulysses S. Grant, who was President of the U.S. from 1869 to 1877.

The Clougher Valley contains several ancient monuments, the most interesting of which are the Neolithic remains at Knockmarry and Sess Kilgreen. The ancient graves here have large stones decorated with intricate prehistoric designs which echo similar designs that have been found as far afield as Brittany and northern Spain. Another superb ancient monument is to be found on the shores of Lough Neagh, which forms the eastern boundary of the county. Here you can see the 18-foot Ardboe Cross, the best example of an old High Cross to be found in Northern Ireland, which has several sculpted scenes depicting incidents from the Bible.

Ten miles inland is Cookstown, whose wide, mile-long main street is like an elegant promenade. It was laid out by a planter called Cook in the early 17th century. Four miles west, the Wellbrook Beetling Mill has been restored to demonstrate the final process in linen making: "beetling." The cloth is hammered by "beetles" to give it an even finish. Linen making was a boom industry in Ulster between the 18th and 20th centuries, and there are many reminders of its past importance in the province.

Twenty-seven miles west of Cookstown you come to Omagh, the county town of Tyrone. Here the museum of the Royal Inniskilling Fusiliers features many historic relics of this famous regiment. Four miles north of Omagh at Camp Hill stands the old white-washed cottage which is the ancestral home of Andrew Mellon, the American millionaire. The cottage is now a museum and centerpiece of the Ulster American Folk Park. This has been designed to present a Tyrone village of two centuries ago and also an American log-built settlement of the same period, depicting the role played by Ulstermen in America's history. The latest addition to the folk park is the reconstructed thatched cottage which was the boyhood home of Archbishop John Hughes, founder of New York's St. Patrick's Cathedral. He emigrated to the U.S. at about the same time as Mellon.

County Tyrone is also famous for its crystal glass, which is available at shops throughout the county and makes an excellent souvenir of your trip to Ulster.

# PRACTICAL INFORMATION FOR
# THE REST OF NORTHERN IRELAND

**TOURIST OFFICES.** Among the principal regional tourist offices, all of which can help with finding accommodations, are: **Armagh,** 40 English St., tel. 0861–527808 (open year-round); **Ballymena,** 2 Ballymoney Rd., tel. 0266–46043 (open year-round); **Bangor,** 43 Quay St., tel. 0247–454069 (open year-round); **Carrickfergus,** Castle Green, tel. 09603–63604 (open June to Aug.); **Derry,** Foyle St., tel. 0504–269501 (open year-round); **Enniskillen,** Lakeland Visitor Center, Shore Rd., tel. 0365–23110/25050 (open year-round); **Larne,** Council Offices, Victoria Rd., tel. 0574–72313 (open year round); **Newry,** Arts Center, Bank Parade, tel. 0693–66232 (open year-round); **Portrush,** Town Hall, tel. 0265–823333 (open Apr. to Sept.); **Strabane,** Lifford Rd., tel. 0504–883735 (open June to Sept.).

## HOTELS AND RESTAURANTS

**Annalong** (Co. Down). **Restaurants.***Glassdrumman House* (E), tel. 03967–68585. Guesthouse with two restaurants: *Memories* (E) and *The Kitchen Garden* (M) serve excellent cuisine based on fresh local produce. Reservations essential. Also 8 rooms with bath.

**Armagh** (Co. Armagh). *Drumsill House* (M), tel. 0861–522009. 12 rooms, all with bath. Much character. AE, DC, MC, V. *Charlemont Arms* (I), tel. 0861–522028. 14 rooms, 9 with bath. In center of town.

**Ballycastle** (Co. Antrim). *Antrim Arms* (I), tel. 02657–62284. 17 rooms.

**Ballygally** (Co. Antrim). *Ballygally Castle* (M), tel. 0574–83212. 30 rooms, all with bath. Rural location, and good restaurant. AE, DC, MC, V.

**Ballymena** (Co. Antrim). *Adair Arms* (M), tel. 0266–653674. 36 rooms, all with bath. AE, DC, MC, V.

**Banbridge** (Co. Down). **Restaurants.** *Banville House* (M), Lurgan Rd. *Half-Way House* (M), Half-Way Rd. Convenient halt mid-way between Belfast and the border with the Republic.

**Bangor** (Co. Down). *O'Hara's Royal* (M), tel. 0247–271866. 32 rooms, all with bath. Good seafood restaurant. *The Sands* (M), tel. 0247–270696. 12 rooms with bath. Fishing and golf. *Tedworth* (M), tel. 0247–463928. 13 rooms with bath. *Winston* (M), tel. 0247–454575. 46 rooms, half with bath.
**Restaurant.** *Skandia* (M), 99 Main St. (tel. 0247–461529).

**Bushmills** (Co. Antrim). **Restaurant.** *Auberge de Seneirl* (E), tel. 02657–41536. Outstanding French cuisine. Reservations essential.

**Carrickfergus** (Co. Antrim). *Dobbin's Inn* (M), tel. 09603–51905. 13 rooms, all with bath. AE, DC, MC, V.

**Coleraine** (Co. Londonderry). *Bohill Auto Inn* (M), tel. 0265–44406. 15 rooms, all with bath. AE, DC, MC. V. *The Lodge* (M), tel. 0265–4848. 20 rooms, all with bath. AE, DC, MC, V.
**Restaurants.** *MacDuff's* (M), Killeague Rd. (tel. 0265–86433). Specialties include fish and herb pâté. Reservations recommended. *Salmon Leap* (M), Castleroe Rd. Recommended buffet lunches feature game and smoked fish.

**Crawfordsburn** (Co. Down). *Old Inn* (E), tel. 0247–853255. 32 rooms, all with bath. Pleasant old hotel with beautiful garden.

**Cushendall** (Co. Antrim). *Thornlea* (I), tel. 02667–71223. 14 rooms, 9 with bath. Friendly hotel with better-than-average restaurant in the heart of the Glens of Antrim.

**Derry** (Co. Londonderry). *Everglades* (E), tel. 0504–46722. 40 rooms, all with bath. Pool, facilities for children. AE, DC, MC, V. *White Horse Inn* (I), tel 0504–860606. 44 rooms, all with bath. Good restaurant. AE, DC, MC, V. *Clarence House* (I), tel. 0504–265342. 7 rooms.

**Downpatrick** (Co. Down). *Abbey Lodge* (M), tel. 0396–614511. 22 rooms, all with bath. A modern building, next to the remains of Inch Abbey.

**Dunadry** (Co. Antrim). *Dunadry Inn* (E), tel. 08494–32474. 64 rooms, all with bath. Converted and atmospheric old mill. Good restaurant; fishing. Highly recommended. AE, DC, MC, V.

**Enniskillen** (Co. Fermanagh). *Killyhevlin* (E), tel. 0365–23481. 22 rooms, most with bath. AE, DC, MC, V. *Fort Lodge* (M), tel. 0365–23275. 12 rooms with bath. *Manor House* (M), tel. 03656–21561. 14 rooms, some with bath. Well recommended. AE, DC, MC, V.

**Giant's Causeway** (Co. Antrim). *Causeway* (M), tel. 02657–31226. 16 rooms with bath.

**Kilkeel** (Co. Down). *Cranfield House* (I), tel. 06937–62327. 12 rooms, 4 with bath. Good restaurant. AE, DC, MC, V.

**Larne** (Co.Antrim). *Magheramorne House* (M), tel. 0574–79444. 23 rooms, all with bath. Handsome mansion in fine grounds, four miles south of Larne. With excellent inexpensive restaurant, *The Kiln.*

**Limavady** (Co. Londonderry). *Gorteen House* (M), tel. 05047–63333. 32 rooms with bath, Fishing, boating and golf by arrangement. MC, V.

**Newcastle** (Co. Down). *Burrendale* (E), tel. 03967–22599. 30 rooms, all with bath. Good seafood restaurant. AE, DC, MC, V. *Slieve Donard* (E), tel. 03967–23681. 120 rooms, all with bath. One of the North's top spots. AE, DC, MC, V. *Enniskeen* (M), tel. 03967–22392. 12 rooms, 10 with bath. AE, DC, MC, V.

**Newtownabbey** (Co. Antrim). *Chimney Corner Hotel* (E), tel. 02313–44925. 64 rooms, all with bath. AE, DC, MC, V. *Glenavna House* (M), tel. 0232–864461. 16 rooms, all with bath. AE, DC, MC, V.

**Omagh** (Co. Tyrone). *Royal Arms Hotel* (M), tel. 0662–3262. 21 rooms, 19 with bath. Fishing, golf and horseback riding by arrangement.

**Portadown** (Co. Armagh). *Carngrove* (M), tel. 0762–339222. 35 rooms, all with bath. Modern building. MC, V.

**Portaferry** (Co. Down). *Portaferry* (M), tel. 02477–28231. 5 rooms with bath. AE, DC, MC, V.

**Portrush** (Co. Antrim). *Northern Counties* (M), tel. 0265–823755. 88 rooms, some with bath. Indoor pool. AE, DC, MC, V. *West Bay View* (I), tel. 0265–823375. 39 rooms, some with bath.
**Restaurants.** *Eglington Inn* (M), tel. 0265–822371. For fine local dishes. *Harbor Inn* (M), tel. 0265–825047. Good fresh seafood; folk music and ballads.

**Portstewart** (Co. Londonderry). *Edgewater* (M), tel. 026583–3314. 29 rooms, all with bath. Fabulous views of the bay. MC. *Windsor* (I), tel. 026583–2523. 30 rooms, 9 with bath.
**Restaurant.** *Galvey Lodge* (M), Station Rd. (tel. 026583–2218). Game in season, and lobster.

**Saintfield** (Co. Down). **Restaurant.** *The Barn* (M), tel. 0238–510396. Imaginative dishes; worth a detour. Reservations essential.

**Seaforde** (Co. Down). **Restaurant.** *Seaforde Inn* (M), tel. 039687–232. Cold buffet and steaks.

**Strabane** (Co. Tyrone). *Fir Trees Lodge* (M), tel. 0504–382382. 26 rooms with bath. Modern building. AE, DC, MC, V.

## PLACES TO VISIT

**Armagh** (Co. Armagh). **Armagh County Museum,** The Mall East. 19th-century schoolhouse with wide range of exhibits charting local history; plus Victorian doll collection. Open Mon. to Sat. 10–1, 2–5.

**Astronomy Center.** Planetarium and astronomical exhibit. Shows daily in July and August, and every Saturday at 3 rest of year. Open Mon. to Sat. 2–4.45.

**Sovereign's House.** Military museum of the Royal Irish Fusiliers, one of the finest regiments in the British Army. Open Mon. to Fri. 10–12, 2–4.30.

**Coleraine** (Co. Londonderry). **Hezlett House.** Thatched cottage dating from 1690 of unusual construction. Now furnished as it might have been in Victorian times. At the Lifford intersection, four miles west of Coleraine. Open Apr. to end-Sept. daily 2–6, closed Fri.

**Cullybackey** (Co. Antrim). **Arthur House.** One-time home of President Chester A. Beatty's grandfather. Open Apr. to Sept., Mon. to Sat. 2–5.

**Derry** (Co. Londonderry). **Foyle Valley Railway Museum,** near east end of Craigavon bridge. Relics and exhibits of old narrow-gauge railways. Open Mon. to Sat. 10–5.

**Enniskillen** (Co. Fermanagh). **Florence Court** and **Castle Coole.** Two fine 18th-century houses in extensive landscaped grounds to the southeast and southwest of the town. Grounds open all year. Florence Court (house) open Apr. to Sept., daily 12–6. Castle Coole (house) open Jul. and Aug., daily 12–6; Apr., May and Sept., Sat. and Sun. 12–6.

**Marble Arch Caves.** A fascinating underworld of lakes, rivers and waterfalls. 13 miles west of Fermanagh. Conducted tours include underground boat trip; they last one and a half hours. Open Easter to Oct., daily from 11. Best to book on tel. 036582–8855.

**Lough Neagh** (Co. Antrim). **Shane's Castle Railway and Nature Reserve.** Narrow-gauge steam railway leads through the reserve itself. Open most days 12–6, but check by calling 08494–63380.

**Maghera** (Co. Londonderry). **Middle House Museum,** Upperlands. Private textile museum owned by the Clark family. All equipment is original and locally made. Call 0648–42214 to arrange a guided tour.

**Moneymore** (Co. Londonderry). **Springhill.** Small but handsome 17th-century manor house with magnificent oak staircase; also houses costume museum. Jun. to Aug., Wed. to Mon. 2–6, closed Tues.; Apr., May and Sept., Sat. and Sun. only.

**Newtownards** (Co. Down). **Mount Steward House and Gardens.** 18th-century mansion with associations with Lord Castlereagh. Gardens contain rare trees and shrubs from around the world and 18th-century replica of an Athenian temple. House open mid-Mar. to Oct., weekends and some weekdays. Tel. 024774–387 for details.

**Omagh** (Co. Tyrone). Ulster-American Folk Park. Tells the story of the people of Ulster in the New World. Ancient Irish village, American log cabin settlement and many other facinating Ulster-American exhibits. Open May to end-Aug., Mon. to Sat. 11–6.30, Sun 11.30–7; Sept. to end-Apr. daily 11–4.30. Closed Sat. and Sun. and public holidays mid-Oct. to mid-Mar.

**Saintfield** (Co. Down). **Rowallane Garden.** Fine display of rare plants and shrubs; particularly beautiful in spring and fall. Open Apr. and July to end-Oct., Mon. to Fri. 9–6, Sat. and Sun. 2–6; May and June, Mon. to Fri. 9–9, Sat. and Sun. 2–6; Nov. to end-Mar., Mon. to Fri. 9–4.30, closed Sat. and Sun.

**Strabane** (Co. Tyrone). **Gray's Printing Press,** Main St. It was here that John Dunlap, printer of America's Declaration of Independence, learned his trade. Open Apr. to end-Sept. daily 2–6, closed Thurs., Sun. and public holidays.

**Wilson House,** Dergalt. Home of President Woodrow Wilson's grandfather who emigrated in about 1807. About two miles from Strabane. Open daily 2–6. Call at farm to gain entrance.

**Strangford** (Co. Down). **Castle Ward.** 18th-century mansion built in part neo-Classical and part neo-Gothic manner in lovely grounds. Open Apr., May and Sept., Sat. and Sun. 2–6; Jun. to Aug., Wed. to Mon. 2–6, closed Tues. Grounds open all year.

# INDEX

# Index

Please note: The index for Northern Ireland follows the index for the Republic of Ireland.

### General Information

## Geographical

## NORTHERN IRELAND

### General Information

### Geographical